CW00545798

STUDIES IN WELSH HISTORY

Series editors

RALPH A. GRIFFITHS   CHRIS WILLIAMS
ERYN M. WHITE

23

THE WOMEN'S SUFFRAGE MOVEMENT
IN WALES, 1866–1928

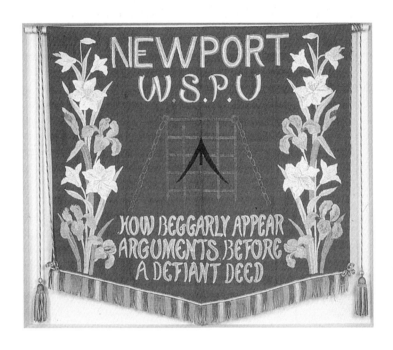

Banner of the Newport WSPU, from the collection
of Newport Museum and Art Gallery.

THE WOMEN'S SUFFRAGE MOVEMENT IN WALES, 1866–1928

by

RYLAND WALLACE

*Published on behalf of the
University of Wales*

CARDIFF
UNIVERSITY OF WALES PRESS
2009

www.uwp.co.uk

British Library Cataloguing-in-Publication Data.
A catalogue record for this book is available from the British Library.

ISBN 978-0-7083-2173-7

Printed in Great Britain by CPI Antony Rowe, Chippenham, Wilts.

SERIES EDITORS' FOREWORD

Since the foundation of the series in 1977, the study of Wales's history has attracted growing attention among historians internationally and continues to enjoy a vigorous popularity. Not only are approaches, both traditional and new, to the study of history in general being successfully applied in a Welsh context, but Wales's historical experience is increasingly appreciated by writers on British, European and world history. These advances have been especially marked in the university institutions in Wales itself.

In order to make more widely available the conclusions of original research, much of it of limited accessibility in postgraduate dissertations and theses, in 1977 the History and Law Committee of the Board of Celtic Studies inaugurated this series of monographs, *Studies in Welsh History*. It was anticipated that many of the volumes would originate in research conducted in the University of Wales or under the auspices of the Board of Celtic Studies, and so it proved. Although the Board of Celtic Studies no longer exists, the University of Wales continues to sponsor the series. It seeks to publish significant contributions made by researchers in Wales and elsewhere. Its primary aim is to serve historical scholarship and to encourage the study of Welsh history.

CONTENTS

SERIES EDITORS' FOREWORD   v

PREFACE   ix

LIST OF ABBREVIATIONS   xi

Introduction   1

I   The Victorian Women's Suffrage Campaign   10

II The Women's Social and Political Union,
1903–1914   52

III The Women's Freedom League, 1907–1914   101

IV The National Union of Women's Suffrage Societies,
1897–1914   131

V   The Opposition to Women's Suffrage   184

VI The Impact of the First World War   219

VII The Campaign for Equal Suffrage, 1918–1928   251

Epilogue   287

BIBLIOGRAPHY   296

INDEX   321

PREFACE

The origins of this study lie in my earlier book, *'Organise! Organise! Organise!' A Study of Reform Agitations in Wales, 1840–1886*, which was published by the University of Wales Press in 1991. This included a chapter on 'Women's rights', which focused on the early women's suffrage movement and the contagious diseases campaign. Further research into women's suffrage in late nineteenth and early twentieth-century Wales beckoned as a natural development. It continued the theme of extra-parliamentary agitation and, moreover, the subject was one which had scarcely been touched by historians of Wales.

I embarked on the research with the notion, based at that time on no substantial body of evidence, that the suffrage movement made little impression on Wales and that what I should uncover would be minimal. I could not have been more wrong, and the subsequent enterprise has proved to be one of unforeseen scale and scope. To begin with, I dived into the early issues of *The Suffragette* newspaper of 1912. Turning the pages of the bulky volume in the Bodleian Library, Oxford, I was immediately startled by the weekly reports of activity all over the country. As I continued my investigations into the movement's archives, I found avenues opening in many directions and numerous potential lines of enquiry presented themselves. A major study proved inescapable.

This book has been a long time in the making. Full-time teaching and summers dominated by cricket have led to lengthy periods of neglect. At the same time, the sheer wealth of primary source material surviving in libraries and record offices around the country has made research into the theme labour intensive and time consuming. Information for the study of women's suffrage in Wales is abundant but invariably lies tucked away in scattered archives and in a variety of newspapers and periodicals.

My researches have left me indebted to the librarians and archivists at the various institutions listed in the bibliography. I am grateful to the staff at my local public libraries in

Abergavenny and Brecon for patiently dealing with my many requests for inter library loan material; my daughter, Laura, did likewise while at university. I thank my sister, Diana, for conveniently living in north London and providing me with food and shelter on my countless visits to libraries and other institutions over the years. I thank Sue Baylik and Graham Strange for similar hospitality.

Professor Geraint H. Jenkins, director of the Centre for Advanced Welsh and Celtic Studies in Aberystwyth, carefully read a draft of the first chapter and offered valuable advice. I am also grateful to the editors of the Studies in Welsh History series, Emeritus Professor Ralph A. Griffiths, Professor Chris Williams and Dr Eryn White, for their thorough reading and comments on the original manuscript. The errors and short-comings that remain are, of course, my own responsibility.

I am particularly indebted to Professor Ralph Griffiths for his considerable support and encouragement to this work; certainly, before contacting him, my attempts at gaining publishers' interest had proved fruitless. I also thank those members of staff at the University of Wales Press – especially Sarah Lewis, Elin Lewis, Siân Chapman and Bethan James – who so efficiently and considerately guided the volume through the various stages of publication. Teleri Williams proved a splendid copy-editor. Rachael Anderton (Newport Museum and Art Gallery) and Katrina Coopey (Cardiff Central Library) were very helpful in my pursuit of illustrations.

Finally, I gratefully acknowledge the financial support of £870 towards research costs awarded to me by the British Academy.

ABBREVIATIONS

NEWSPAPERS AND PERIODICALS

ASR	Anti-Suffrage Review	SWDN	South Wales Daily News
CC	The Common Cause	SWDP	South Wales Daily Post
CDH	Carnarvon and Denbigh Herald	SWWP	South Wales Weekly Post
		VW	Votes for Women
CN	Cambrian News	WF	Women's Franchise
CT	Cardiff Times	WM	Western Mail
ER	Englishwoman's Review	WSJ	Women's Suffrage Journal
NWC	North Wales Chronicle		

ORGANIZATIONS

BWSWS	Bristol and West of England Society for Women's Suffrage
BWTA	British Women's Temperance Association
CCNSWS	Central Committee of the National Society for Women's Suffrage
CDWSS	Cardiff and District Women's Suffrage Society
CLWS	Church League for Women's Suffrage
CNSWS	Central National Society for Women's Suffrage
CSU	Cymric Suffrage Union
CUWFA	Conservative and Unionist Women's Franchise Association
CWSS	Catholic Women's Suffrage Society
EFF	Election Fighting Fund
ELFS	East London Federation of Suffragettes
EPRCC	Equal Political Rights Campaign Committee
FCL	Free Church League for Women's Suffrage
FCSU	Forward Cymric Suffrage Union
ILP	Independent Labour Party
IWSPU	Independent Women's Social and Political Union
NFWT	National Federation of Women Teachers
NLOWS	National League for Opposing Woman Suffrage

NSWS	National Society for Women's Suffrage
NUSEC	National Union of Societies for Equal Citizenship
NUT	National Union of Teachers
NUWSS	National Union of Women's Suffrage Societies
NUWT	National Union of Women Teachers
NWF	West Lancashire, West Cheshire and North Wales Federation (of the NUWSS)
SJC	Standing Joint Committee of Industrial Women's Organisations
SPG	Six Point Group
SWF	South Wales and Monmouthshire Federation (of the NUWSS)
SWSPU	Suffragettes of the Women's Social and Political Union
WCA	Women Citizens' Association
WCG	Women's Co-operative Guild
WFL	Women's Freedom League
WILPF	Women's International League for Peace and Freedom
WLA	Women's Liberal Association
WLF	Women's Liberal Federation
WLL	Women's Labour League
WNASL	Women's National Anti-Suffrage League
WSF	Women's/Workers' Suffrage Federation
WSPU	Women's Social and Political Union
WSS	Women's Suffrage Society
WUWLA	Welsh Union of Women's Liberal Associations

OTHERS

BLPES	British Library of Political and Economic Science
HO	Home Office Papers
MEPO	Metropolitan Police Papers
NA	National Archives
NLW	National Library of Wales
ODNB	*Oxford Dictionary of National Biography*
Parl. Deb.	*Parliamentary Debates*
SFC	Suffragette Fellowship Collection
WL	Women's Library

INTRODUCTION

Wales was part of the women's suffrage agitation from its beginnings in the mid 1860s until the achievement of equal voting rights in 1928. All of the major suffrage societies formed during this period made headway in Wales, establishing branch associations and committees. Countless column inches in the Welsh press were devoted to the thousands of meetings held in Wales, to debates on the merits or otherwise of the demand and to the reporting of parliamentary and agitational developments. The leading activists of the day travelled to various parts of the country in a bid to invigorate the cause, none more often than the most celebrated personality, Emmeline Pankhurst. While a number of Welsh women stand out as notable figures in the national suffrage organizations that had their headquarters in England, the following pages record the names of many hugely committed but unsung individuals on whom local impact was dependent. Wales was, moreover, the scene of some of the most serious and dramatic campaigning incidents outside London, in particular the widely publicized clashes between demonstrators and assailants at the National Eisteddfod in Wrexham in September 1912 and again at Llanystumdwy a few weeks later. Of importance, too, was the fact that key ministers in the pre-war Liberal governments had close connections with Wales. At the very heart of British political life was, of course, David Lloyd George, from 1905 to 1922 successively president of the Board of Trade, chancellor of the Exchequer, minister of munitions and prime minister. In addition, the home secretary between 1911 and 1915, and therefore to the fore in formulating government policy towards suffragette militancy, was the North Monmouthshire MP, Reginald McKenna, while the Anglesey member, Ellis Griffith, was his under-secretary from 1912 to 1915. Over the period as a whole, some of Westminster's most committed anti-suffragists sat for Welsh constituencies – from the Pembrokeshire member, J. H. Scourfield, in the 1870s to the Cardiff MP, Ivor Guest, and

J. D. Rees, MP for Montgomery Boroughs, both strong
supporters of the National League for Opposing Woman
Suffrage (NLOWS) in the immediate pre-war years. At the
same time, Wales had some staunchly suffragist MPs, men who
were prepared to speak out for the cause, such as Swansea's
Sir Alfred Mond, Pembrokeshire's Walter Roch and Merthyr
Boroughs's Keir Hardie, the last also proving a resolute apolo-
gist for suffragette militancy.

This study is grounded in primary research of extensive
archival material. While few of the records of the many individual local suffrage societies established in Wales have
survived, those of the central bodies which spearheaded and
coordinated the campaign across Britain are comprehensive:
these comprise minute books, reports, correspondence and
other material. Individuals have also left papers and recollections which cast light on the agitation in Wales. Especially
valuable are the movement's various newspapers and periodicals, for buried in the pages of the *Women's Suffrage Journal,
The Common Cause, Votes for Women, The Vote, The Suffragette,* the
Woman's Leader and many more is a mine of information on all
manner of provincial activity. Moreover, for Wales and elsewhere in Britain, these decades were the golden age of the
local newspaper, a time before national dailies began reaching
an extensive readership and benefiting from low publication
costs and the spread of literacy. 'The growth of journalism,
and of vernacular journalism in particular, in the Principality
has of late years been little short of phenomenal', observed
one informed commentator in 1889.[1] Every sizeable town and
district in late Victorian and Edwardian Wales had not just
one but several newspapers, which provided an enormous
political education through coverage of local, national and
parliamentary affairs, editorial comment across the spectrum
and lively letter columns. 'The vast mass [of reading matter]
which poured from the scores of red-hot presses up and down
the country', writes Ieuan Gwynedd Jones (who first encouraged and nurtured my interest in historical research and
writing), thus represents an immense source, lying 'in the
National Library [of Wales] awakening feelings of awe in the

---

[1]   J. E. Vincent, *Letters from Wales* (London, 1889), 118.

researcher'.[2] In its early years the women's suffrage issue frequently attracted press attention out of novelty and curiosity; in the decade prior to the First World War it did so through the intensity of its agitation. At the same time, suffragists assiduously courted publicity, requested the attendance of reporters at meetings and also forwarded their own information to them. Accordingly, local newspapers often contain full accounts of activities, including lengthy verbatim speeches and details of annual general meetings and annual reports.

For the sixty years or so covered by this book, I have been drawn into tracking an array of suffrage societies and related organizations and into the pursuit of scores of activists whose dedication, energy and determination, in the face of hostility, indifference and repeated setbacks, are remarkable. Nevertheless, I remain aware of the need for further work – including detailed studies on specific areas of Wales and on such themes as the advance of women professionally, in local government, in party organizations, their links with other movements and their opposition to the war.

The fact that the women's suffrage movement has been the subject of extensive research and writing in recent decades bears witness to the importance of the theme in understanding the society of late Victorian and Edwardian Britain. Much has now been published on the nature, characteristics and policies of the major campaigning organizations, on prominent personalities and on a variety of particular themes, while a diversity of approaches has also generated new perspectives and interpretations. The flood of books and articles during the past twenty years or so has produced a transformation in the historiography of the movement. In the first place, there has been a shift away from concentration on the Pankhurst family and the militant campaign conducted through the Women's Social and Political Union (WSPU), which so dominated historical interpretations during much of the twentieth century. The studies undertaken, in particular, by Leslie Hume, Sandra Holton, David Rubinstein and Jo Vellacott, have provided an appreciation of the major role

---

[2] Ieuan Gwynedd Jones, *Explorations and Explanations: Essays in the Social History of Victorian Wales* (Llandysul, 1981), 295.

played by the non-militant and law-abiding National Union of Women's Suffrage Societies (NUWSS). Research has also demonstrated the significant progress made towards franchise reform by campaigners in a range of organizations during the Victorian era, before the creation of either the WSPU or the NUWSS. I have drawn on the detailed narratives of those historians named above and others, including Martin Pugh, Andrew Rosen and (particularly for the anti-suffragist movement) Brian Harrison, to guide me through this study. At the same time, I have been anxious to cover the entire lifetime of the movement, up to its successful conclusion in 1928, rather than cease in 1914 or 1918 as the vast majority of authors have tended to do, and in this regard the work of Cheryl Law, Johanna Alberti and Harold Smith has proved especially helpful.

The recent reinterpretation and reappraisal of the British suffrage movement have entailed a move away from the aims, policies and activities of the national leaderships of the main organizations in London towards recognition of the importance of other parts of the country. Studies of English cities and regions have been undertaken, serving to demonstrate the significance of the political realities of the local and regional context, and detailed work has been carried out on Scotland and Ireland. Such analyses reveal a much more complex and diverse movement than had hitherto been recognized. 'An understanding of grass-roots activism', observes June Hannam, 'does not just add interesting details to an existing national picture, it also transforms our view of the nature and meaning of suffragism for the participants.'[3]

Wales has lagged behind in all of these historiographical developments. Introducing their contribution to the pioneering collection of essays published in 1991 as *Our Mothers' Land: Chapters in Welsh Women's History, 1830–1939*, Kay Cook and Neil Evans wrote thus:

> Traditionally the women's suffrage movement has been the one part of women's history that has not been hidden from historians. Yet in Wales

[3] June Hannam, '"I had not been to London": women's suffrage – a view from the regions', in June Purvis and Sandra Stanley Holton (eds), *Votes for Women* (London, 2000), 242.

women have not even been given this consolation prize. The participation of Welsh women in the movement has been overlooked and disregarded, though recently attempts have been made to redress the balance. We need a thorough study of the impact of women's suffrage activity in Wales. This chapter is not that, but is simply a preliminary exploration based on evidence gathered more widely than has been done hitherto.[4]

Prior to this essay, only a small body of work on the subject had been published. Caernarfonshire had received most attention through Peter Ellis Jones's survey of the movement in the county and also two accounts of the dramatic events at Llanystumdwy in 1912, when suffragette hecklers who interrupted the opening of the village institute by David Lloyd George were violently attacked. In addition, Ursula Masson had undertaken a brief study of activity in Swansea, while other writers had focused on Carmarthen and Llanelli. *Our Mothers' Land* also contained some discussion of the links with temperance, by Ceridwen Lloyd-Morgan, while its editor, Angela John, touched on early Welsh support for the suffrage movement. My own examination of the early decades of the women's suffrage campaign in Wales also appeared in 1991.[5]

In recent decades, there has been an upsurge of interest in the history of women in Wales and this has brought fruitful research on the suffrage campaign. Ursula Masson has added to her work on Swansea and has explored the links between suffrage and party politics, in particular.[6] Angela John's studies

[4] Kay Cook and Neil Evans, '"The petty antics of the bell-ringing boisterous band"? The women's suffrage movement in Wales, 1890–1918', in Angela V. John (ed.), *Our Mothers' Land: Chapters in Welsh Women's History, 1830–1939* (Cardiff, 1991), 159.

[5] Peter Ellis Jones, 'The women's suffrage movement in Caernarfonshire', *Transactions of the Caernarfonshire Historical Society*, 48 (1987); Dylan Morris, '"Merched y screch a'r twrw": yr WSPU yn Llanystumdwy, 1912', ibid., 46 (1975); Ann Holt, 'The battle of Llanystumdwy', *New Society* (18 September 1987); Ursula Masson, 'The Swansea suffragettes', in Luana Dee and Katell Keineg (eds), *Women in Wales: A Documentary Reader*, vol. 1 (Cardiff, 1987); Vernon Jones, 'A champion of women's rights', *Carmarthenshire Historian*, XX (1985); Catherine Thomas, 'Suffragettes in Llanelli', in *Amrywiaeth Llanelli Miscellany*, no. 4 (Llanelli, 1989); Ceridwen Lloyd-Morgan, 'From temperance to suffrage', and Angela V. John (ed.), 'Beyond paternalism: the ironmaster's wife in the industrial community', in *Our Mothers' Land*, 56–7, 152–5; Ryland Wallace, *'Organise! Organise! Organise!' A Study of Reform Agitations in Wales, 1840–1886* (Cardiff, 1991), ch. XI.

[6] Ursula Masson, 'Votes for women – the campaign in Swansea', *Minerva:*

of the movement have concentrated largely on the importance of national identity, the contribution of Welsh women in London and on the nature and extent of male support, while J. Graham Jones has examined relations between the suffragettes and Lloyd George and other politicians.[7] Deirdre Beddoe has given some attention to the franchise struggle in her wide-ranging history of women in twentieth-century Wales, while a few other authors have published articles on different aspects of the agitation.[8] Recent developments have extended to the publication of primary source material relating to women's suffrage in Wales, most notably in *Project Grace*, in John Gibson's *Emancipation of Women*, in the minutes of the Aberdare Women's Liberal Association and in an anthology of Welsh women's political writings, each of which contains highly informative introductions by the editors.[9] Moreover,

---

Transactions of the Royal Institution of South Wales, 1 (1993); eadem, 'Divided loyalties: women's suffrage and party politics in south Wales, 1912–15, *Llafur: Journal of Welsh Labour History*, 7, 3/4 (1998–9); eadem, '"Political conditions in Wales are quite different . . .": party politics and votes for women in Wales, 1912–15', *Women's History Review*, 9, 2 (2000); eadem, '"Hand in hand with the women, forward we will go": Welsh nationalism and feminism in the 1890s', ibid., 12, 3 (2003); eadem (ed.), *'Women's Rights and Womanly Duties': The Aberdare Women's Liberal Association, 1891–1910* (Cardiff, 2005); eadem, 'Women versus "the people": language, nation and citizenship, 1906–11', in T. Robin Chapman (ed.), *The Idiom of Dissent: Protest and Propaganda in Wales* (Llandysul, 2006).

[7] Angela V. John, '"Run like blazes": the suffragettes and Welshness', *Llafur: Journal of Welsh Labour History*, 6, 3 (1994); eadem, '"A draft of fresh air": women's suffrage, the Welsh and London', *Transactions of the Honourable Society of Cymmrodorion*, new ser., I (1994); eadem, *'Chwarae Teg': Welsh Men's Support for Women's Suffrage* (Aberystwyth, 1998); eadem, 'Margaret Wynne Nevinson: Gender and national identity in the early twentieth century', in R. R. Davies and Geraint H. Jenkins (eds), *From Medieval to Modern Wales: Historical Essays in Honour of Kenneth O. Morgan and Ralph A. Griffiths* (Cardiff, 2004), ch. 14; J. Graham Jones, 'Crawshay-Williams, Churchill and the suffragettes: a note', *National Library of Wales Journal*, XXX, 4 (1998); idem, 'Lloyd George and the suffragettes at Llanystumdwy', *Journal of Liberal Democrat History*, 34/35 (2002); idem, 'Lloyd George and the suffragettes', *National Library of Wales Journal*, XXXIII, 1 (2003).

[8] Deirdre Beddoe, *Out of the Shadows: A History of Women in Twentieth Century Wales* (Cardiff, 2000), 42–6, 72, 100–2; David Pugh, 'The suffragette campaign in Newtown during the general elections of 1910', *The Newtonian*, 7 (2001); Kirsti Bohata, '"For Wales, see England?" Suffrage and the new woman in Wales', *Women's History Review*, 11, 4 (2002).

[9] Pamela Michael, Annie Williams and Neil Evans, *Project Grace* (Bangor, 1994); John Gibson, *The Emancipation of Women* (Aberystwyth, 1891; repr. with introduction by W. Gareth Evans, Llandysul, 1992); Masson, *'Women's Rights and Womanly Duties'*; Jane Aaron and Ursula Masson (eds), *The Very Salt of Life: Welsh Women's Political Writings from Chartism to Suffrage* (Dinas Powys, 2007). See also, Graham Martin,

discussion of suffrage activity in Wales is now to be found in several books on the movement in Britain as a whole and biographical information on leading Welsh suffragists is available in a number of recent texts.[10]

Thus, in the past two decades or so a substantial number of valuable insights have been offered on aspects of the women's suffrage movement in Wales, sufficient in body to constitute a historiography. Yet the need for a comprehensive account of the entire campaign, highlighted by Kay Cook and Neil Evans in 1991, has still not been met. This task is clearly long overdue in terms of both women's and mainstream Welsh history for, while nonconformist and national causes and increasingly powerful labour issues dominated the political and social landscape of late nineteenth- and early twentieth-century Wales, the women's suffrage agitation also made a significant impression. The principal objective of the present study is therefore to fill a major lacuna in the historiography of modern Wales. At the same time, in investigating the nature and realities of the campaign at local and regional levels, I have sought to add substantially to our knowledge and understanding of the British women's suffrage movement as a whole.

The structure of this book is broadly chronological, though for the Edwardian period, when the campaign was at its most intense, the chapters centre on key organizations in distinct but parallel strands. Chapter I examines the Victorian suffrage movement, from the mid 1860s until the reunification of a hitherto often fragmented campaign under the umbrella of the NUWSS in 1897. Albeit intermittently, both north and south Wales were drawn into the agitation from the early stages through petitioning, meetings, press coverage and local committees and societies. Regional centres at Bristol and

'The culture of the women's suffrage movement: the evidence of the McKenzie letters', *Llafur: Journal of Welsh Labour History*, 7, 3/4 (1998–9).

[10] Elizabeth Crawford, *The Women's Suffrage Movement: A Reference Guide, 1866–1928* (1999); eadem, *The Women's Suffrage Movement in Britain and Ireland: A Regional Survey* (2006); June Hannam, Mitzi Auchterlonie and Katherine Holden, *International Encyclopedia of Women's Suffrage* (Santa Barbara, California, 2000); Hilda Kean, *Deeds Not Words: The Lives of Suffragette Teachers* (London, 1990); H. C. G. Matthew and Brian Harrison (eds), *Oxford Dictionary of National Biography* (Oxford, 2004).

Manchester instigated much of the early activity, but there were always female and male enthusiasts in Wales itself. The almost annual parliamentary debates on the issue afforded opportunities for suffragists to press their case publicly, while the widening role of women in late nineteenth-century society – through educational developments, career opportunities, local government participation and involvement in political parties – opened up new lines of argument and agitation.

A dramatic new era beckoned in 1903 with the foundation of the WSPU, the vehicle by which Emmeline Pankhurst, her eldest daughter, Christabel, and their 'suffragette' supporters sought to galvanize what they perceived to be the inadequate efforts of suffragists during the previous four decades. Chapter II concentrates on this, the most famous of the host of women's suffrage societies operating in Britain in the years immediately before the First World War. It examines the militancy of an illegal and violent character for which the WSPU became notorious, and gives equal attention to its often over- looked yet highly significant propaganda and educational role in the campaign. Normally attributed to a *Daily Mail* article of January 1906, the term 'suffragette' thereafter came into common usage to distinguish, in the words of the *Western Mail*, 'the less orderly demonstrators – the shriekers, the raiders and the martyrs' from the peaceable, law-abiding campaigners in the NUWSS and other 'constitutional' soci- eties.[11] As we shall see, the compartmentalizing of activists raises problems, and there was a frequent tendency among the press and public of the time (as is the case today) to use the term 'suffragette' loosely, indiscriminately and inaccur- ately. In this book, it specifically denotes members of the two main militant organizations, the WSPU and its principal offshoot, the Women's Freedom League (WFL), while the term 'suffragist' denotes any supporter of the women's suffrage movement.

Over the years, the WSPU suffered several internal crises, the first of which, in 1907, marked the birth of the WFL. Chapter III deals with this major body, which sought to create

---

[11] *Daily Mail*, 10 January 1906; *Western Mail* (*WM*), 15 June 1908. The word 'suffragette' had, in fact, been used in the Victorian period. See, for example, *Women's Gazette*, 14 September 1889.

its own militant identity and which had a notable impact in parts of Wales. By the outbreak of war in 1914, membership of the WFL and the WSPU was vastly outnumbered by that of the NUWSS, which had become the focus of a very large non-militant movement. Over the previous few years, an array of new organizations, mostly grounded in religious, party and professional identities, had sprung to life; the *Suffrage Annual and Women's Who's Who*, published in 1913, catalogued forty-four separate societies working for women's suffrage, while the 'Suffrage Directory' in the journal *Votes for Women* listed fifty-eight on the eve of the war in August 1914.[12] Chapter IV concentrates principally on the NUWSS but also encompasses other constitutional bodies that made an impression on Wales. Parliamentary initiatives are interwoven into the narrative at this point.

There was, of course, entrenched opposition to the cause both inside and outside parliament, and chapter V analyses the arguments presented by anti-suffragists over the period and the organization of their resistance, fitful in the decades before 1908 but concerted thereafter, particularly through the National League for Opposing Woman Suffrage (NLOWS). Chapter VI covers the First World War years, the varied responses of individuals and suffrage societies to the crisis, the survival of the campaign in spite of the difficulties and the eventual achievement of partial women's enfranchisement some ten months before the end of the conflict.

Far from being the close of a protracted struggle, the 1918 Act signalled the opening of a new decade-long campaign, which showed clear continuities with both the Edwardian era and the war years. Chapter VII focuses on this last phase of the movement when, in a somewhat fragmentary fashion, a proliferation of women's societies addressed a wide range of issues yet nevertheless forged sufficient unity on the question of equal suffrage to maintain persistent pressure on politicians and eventually to emerge triumphant in July 1928.

---

[12] A. J. R. (ed.), *The Suffrage Annual and Women's Who's Who* (London, 1913); *Votes for Women* (*VW*), 7 August 1914.

I

THE VICTORIAN WOMEN'S SUFFRAGE CAMPAIGN

> Do you feel the spirit of the Great Crusade, a Great Adventure stirring within you? Do you realise you are a New Force in the New World which is destined to rise, clean, sweet and white on the ruins of the Old Order now expiring amidst blood, savagery, lust, disease and famine?

These rousing sentiments, expressed in 1918, some months before the end of the First World War, were those of Alice Abadam, the daughter of a radical Carmarthenshire squire and one of the suffrage movement's most prolific public speakers in the early twentieth century. Like other activists hailing the advent of women's suffrage, she both reflected upon the culmination of a marathon struggle and euphorically anticipated the dawn of a glowing future: *'O Femina gloriosa! Procede, prospere et regna'*.[1]

A continuously organized women's suffrage campaign in Britain had spanned almost all of the sixty-two-year-old Miss Abadam's life. Though the issue had been periodically raised and promoted for a number of decades, through publications, petitions and female political associations, the agitation essentially dates from the mid 1860s, as part of a broad-ranging and disparate women's movement which embraced demands for legal rights, especially over property ownership and custody of children, repeal of the Contagious Diseases Acts, higher education for women, female emigration and employment opportunities. In time, the parliamentary vote emerged as the principal objective. Specifically, the suffrage campaign was launched with the landmark Ladies' Petition of 1866, inspired by the Kensington Society, one of a number of groups of middle-class women which gathered in London at this time. The network of friends, relations and contacts of Kensington members led to the circulation of petition sheets

---

[1] Alice Abadam, *The Feminist Vote: Enfranchised or Emancipated?* (1918), 1, 4. The full text of the pamphlet is reprinted in Aaron and Masson (eds), *Very Salt of Life*, 288–94.

around the country and the collection of 1,499 signatures in just a few weeks. It was subsequently presented to the House of Commons in June 1866 by the radical MP for Westminster, John Stuart Mill, who supplemented this the following May with his historic amendment proposing the substitution of the word 'person' for 'man' during the debates on the Conservative government's Reform Bill.

Wales had but minor participation in these developments. The 1866 petition contained twenty-six signatures with Welsh addresses.[2] In the short, two-hour parliamentary debate instigated by Mill's 1867 amendment, in which only seven other speakers participated, there were no contributions from Welsh representatives, who then voted by ten to two against the inclusion of women in an overall defeat of 196 votes to 73.[3] The reaction of the press in Wales was largely muted; some newspapers carried no reference whatsoever, while several used the same column as *The Times*, referring to a House of Commons discussion which was 'more jocular than serious', and few offered editorial comment. The *Brecon County Times*, reporting 'a good deal of merriment' in the division lobby, patronizingly urged 'ladies who desire to have a vote' not to despair, for they had found 'a most respectable' number of 'warm admirers', while the *North Wales Chronicle* extended the light-hearted tone to welcome future women's suffrage propositions so that 'a pleasant interlude may be afforded the house when bored to death by politics and polemics'. The *Cardiff Times* was particularly frivolous, calling for 'some industrious statistician' to analyse the division list 'so that we may judge what are the female influences brought to bear on the seventy-three ... how many have "expectations" from rich maiden aunts anxious for a vote, and how much do they calculate on these "expectations" being raised by their late adhesion to Mr. Mill'. More serious coverage was provided by the *Brecon Reporter* and the *Carmarthen Journal*, though the latter, while

---

[2]   *To the Honourable the Commons of the United Kingdom of Great Britain and Ireland, in Parliament Assembled*, Helen Blackburn Collection, Girton College, Cambridge. [Copy in WL] The signatures included three from Merthyr, eight from Denbigh and ten from the Swansea area.

[3]   *Parl. Deb.*, 3rd ser., 187, cols 817–45, 20 May 1867. The two in favour were G. C. Morgan (Conservative, Breconshire) and C. R. M. Talbot (Liberal, Glamorgan).

expressing 'the general sympathy of the sterner sex', propounded the most entrenched of anti-suffragist arguments in
a forceful reminder to women: 'They must not forget that
their destiny in this world is marriage, that their chief function
is maternity, and their sphere lies in the domestic and the
social circle. Why try to alter that destiny? It must surely be
happy enough in itself?' Notably supportive of a 'very harm-
less and reasonable motion' and scathing of Mill's derisive
parliamentary opponents was the *Hereford Times*, a newspaper
penetrating well into south-east Wales at this time.[4]

The enthusiasm generated by the petition and amendment
led to the setting up of women's suffrage societies in Manchester, London, Edinburgh and Dublin, which, in November
1867, came together in a loose federation under the umbrella
of the National Society for Women's Suffrage (NSWS); newly
formed organizations in Bristol and Birmingham affiliated
during 1868. A vital unifying role in a largely provincially based
and often fractious movement was played by the *Women's
Suffrage Journal* under its founder and editor from 1870 to 1890,
Lydia Becker, secretary of the Manchester Society for Women's
Suffrage. A second journal was the more wide-ranging
Englishwoman's Review, which ran from 1866 to 1910.

In the early years of their campaign, Victorian suffragists
placed great store on the traditional method of petitioning in
order to illustrate that the demand extended well beyond a
discontented minority. Over seventy petitions calling for
women's suffrage emanated from Wales in the period 1869–
74; generated either by the initiative of enthusiastic local
canvassers or the result of a public meeting, they varied
considerably in size from several hundred signatures (as in the
cases of Denbigh, Monmouthshire, Merthyr Tydfil, Pembroke
and Pontypool) to scarcely a dozen in some instances.[5] Many
of the local petitions expressed support for the almost annual
women's suffrage bills presented to the House of Commons

[4] *Brecon County Times*, 25 May 1867; *North Wales Chronicle* (*NWC*), 25 May 1867;
Cardiff Times (*CT*), 25 May 1867; *Brecon Reporter*, 25 May 1867; *Carmarthen Journal*,
25 May 1867; *Hereford Times*, 25 May 1867.
[5] *Englishwoman's Review* (*ER*), April, July 1867, January 1869, July 1871, July
1872; Manchester National Society for Women's Suffrage, *Annual Reports*, 1870–4.
For details on the early petitions from Wales, see Crawford, *A Regional Survey*, 211.

by backbench MPs during the 1870s. While private members' bills had but an outside chance of becoming law, they nevertheless served a useful role in keeping the issue before the public in an age when the local press gave extensive space to parliamentary debate and comment.

The more conspicuous face of the campaign was first introduced to Wales by two participants in the fledgling London feminist movement of the 1850s and 1860s, Rose Mary Crawshay and Viscountess Amberley, both of whom sought to promote the cause in their localities. The former, a native of Berkshire, came to Merthyr Tydfil in 1846 as the eighteen-year-old wife of Robert Thompson Crawshay, head of the great Cyfarthfa ironworks, while the latter moved to a 'quiet nook in Wales', a country home overlooking the Wye valley between Monmouth and Chepstow, in 1870, and there she lived until her premature death in 1874.

Well known as a local philanthropist, prominent in the alleviation of distress and in promoting education among the Cyfarthfa workforce, for many years Rose Crawshay confined her feminist activities to London, where she spent a good deal of time and was a member of both the Society for Promoting the Employment of Women and the London National Society for Women's Suffrage (though she was not a signatory of the 1866 'Ladies' Petition'). Her advocacy of women's suffrage in Merthyr in the early 1870s therefore came as something of a surprise locally. She it was who organized the first public meeting on women's suffrage ever held in Wales, at the Temperance Hall, Merthyr Tydfil, on 3 June 1870. Taking the chair herself, she was also one of the principal speakers, along with one of her London suffragist friends, the Finsbury Nonconformist minister, Revd Moncure Conway. Steering clear of the controversial issue of whether the suffrage should be limited to property-holding spinsters and widows or include married women, she argued her case with assurance and a touch of humour.[6] In subsequent years she continued to advocate the cause at meetings in Merthyr and further afield,

---

[6] *Merthyr Telegraph*, 11 June 1870; *Cardiff and Merthyr Guardian*, 11 June 1870; *Merthyr Express*, 11 June 1870; *Y Fellten*, 10 Mehefin 1870; *ER*, July 1870; *Women's Suffrage Journal* (*WSJ*), 1 July 1870.

as well as in the press, and she also served as a vice-president of the Bristol and West of England Society for Women's Suffrage (BWSWS). But her views and interests were too varied for women's suffrage to be the sole focus of her energies, and as a result Merthyr never became a centre of the movement. She had considerable literary and intellectual pursuits, held advanced views on cremation, euthanasia, corporal punishment in schools and domestic service for gentlewomen ('lady-helps'), and, in 1871, she was the first woman to be elected to a school board in Wales; uniquely, she sat simultaneously on two, Merthyr and Vaynor.[7]

Among the many and varied visitors to Cyfarthfa Castle was Kate Amberley, wife of a radical MP and the daughter-in-law of the former prime minister, Lord John (Earl) Russell. A signatory of the 1866 women's suffrage petition and present in the Ladies' Gallery of the House of Commons to hear John Stuart Mill (with whom she and her husband developed a close friendship) put his amendment in May 1867, she had been a committed activist from the movement's earliest days. She delivered her first suffrage lecture at Stroud in May 1870, her name and social position guaranteeing both the publicity and ridicule which was so often the lot of advocates of the cause.[8] On moving from Gloucestershire to east Monmouthshire a few months later, she sought to implant the campaign there, too, in far from promising conditions. In January 1871 she spoke for an hour to a meeting of 'nine women & one man' at the village of Treleck, while on the next occasion 'no one came except Mrs Williams from the school'.[9] Never-

---

[7] Angela V. John, 'Crawshay, Rose (1828–1907)', *ODNB*; *Woman's Herald*, 19 March 1892. Obituaries in *Merthyr Express*, 8 June 1907; *Brecon County Times*, 7 June 1907; *Merthyr Guardian*, 8 June 1907; *WM*, 4 June 1907.

[8] 'I sympathise with you heart and soul. It *is* painful to be abused and laughed at', consoled fellow activist and friend Helen Taylor (John Stuart Mill's step-daughter). Bertrand and Patricia Russell (eds), *The Amberley Papers: Bertrand Russell's Family Background*, vol. 2 (2nd edn, London, 1966), 345. For Viscountess Amberley, see ibid., esp. 36–7, 329–38; Theodore Martin, *Queen Victoria as I Knew Her* (London, 1908), 69; Crawford, *Women's Suffrage Movement*, 9–10; O. Banks, *The Biographical Dictionary of British Feminists, Vol. 1: 1800–1930* (Brighton, 1985), 3–4; Ann P. Robson, 'Russell, Katharine Louisa, Viscountess Amberley (1842–1874)', *ODNB*; R. Fulford, *Votes for Women* (London, 1957), 53, 60, 74–5; *ER*, July 1870; obituary in *WSJ*, 1 August 1874.

[9] Russell, *Amberley Papers*, 391.

theless, she did manage to establish a local committee (the first in Wales), though this seems to have done little more than gather two petitions (in 1871 and 1872), amidst some local anxieties. 'A charming Miss Prosser came to see me about the W's Suffrage Comte', Lady Amberley recorded in her journal for 28 January 1871, '& said she wished to join it but wd it prevent their voting for the Duke [of Beaufort] as they must do that & so must everyone about here; she said she cd get no signatures if it wd be against the Duke as there was great terror of being turned out.'[10] Indeed, a personal overture in this direction to one of the duke's sons, a Monmouthshire MP, brought a sharp response: 'I tried to get Lord Henry [Somerset] on the committee, but he only snubbed me very much, wondering how I could dream that any of HIS FAMILY could sanction such a thing; that the word Women's Suffrage was revolting to him, and that he really thought I must be chaffing.'[11]

Viscountess Amberley became the first president of the BWSWS in 1868 and it was this organization, along with the Manchester National Society for Women's Suffrage, which was largely responsible for much of the early campaigning in Wales. They sponsored lecture tours, arranged public meetings, disseminated literature and stimulated local groups. The support of 'gentlemen of influence' was seen as central to local success. Accordingly, religious leaders, councillors and professional men, such as solicitors and academics, were approached to chair meetings and act as supporting speakers. The female lecturers were sometimes accompanied on their visits by male supporters from within Wales, most notably John Griffith ('*Y Gohebydd*'), *Baner ac Amserau Cymru*'s influential correspondent. In northern and western regions, local

---

[10]   Ibid., 392. See also *Star of Gwent*, 18 February 1871; *County Observer*, 18 February 1871; *WSJ*, 1 March 1871; *ER*, April, July 1871. Though adopting the name 'Monmouthshire Committee', it actually comprised six women living within a few miles of Lady Amberley's home.

[11]   Ray Strachey, *The Cause: A Short History of the Women's Movement in Great Britain* (London, 1928), 122. Enduring 'disagreeables for the sake of one's opinions' was frequently a depressing experience. 'I shall be so glad to see you', wrote Lady Amberley to Helen Taylor in February 1871, 'for I have been thrown into such low spirits by being very much laughed at at Gladstone's party the other night, as my poor little committee somehow found its way into the London papers.' Ibid., 121–2.

speakers commonly gave translations of addresses and made their own contributions in Welsh, 'knowing that this was most acceptable to the people who have clung so tenaciously to their own strange but musical tongue'.[12] The normally well-attended public meetings doubtless reflected people's curiosity in the sheer novelty of hearing women speak in public. Referring to a tour of south Wales in November 1872, Lilias Ashworth of the Bristol society recalled that 'audiences always came expecting to see curious masculine objects walking on to the platform, and when we appeared, with our quiet black dresses, the whole expression of the faces of the audience would instantly change'.[13]

Although substantial numbers of local women attended the early suffrage meetings in Wales, they rarely played a prominent role in the proceedings; men predominated among the speakers. Among the exceptions were Rose Crawshay and Gertrude Jenner, sister of the squire of Wenvoe castle, both of whom chaired and addressed meetings. Elsewhere, women were prepared to play an active, if less public, role. Of the twelve 'corresponding secretaries' of the BWSWS in Wales during the years 1873–8, five were women; Lady Amberley's 'Monmouthshire' committee of 1871 comprised her husband and seven women, while the Cardiff committee established two years later included five men and five women.[14] Although female activists gathered signatures for petitions and undertook other tasks, public speaking was altogether more daunting and demanded a considerable degree of moral courage. This was a field in which they were wholly inexperienced, and where, as the veteran campaigner Elizabeth Mitchell of Llanfrechfa later recalled, it was widely considered 'an outrageous thing for a woman to make a speech', and they were open to the sneers of audiences and the press.[15] The *Western Mail* ridiculed an early Cardiff meeting thus:

[12]   See *Carnarvon and Denbigh Herald* (*CDH*), 31 January 1871; *Baner ac Amserau Cymru*, 4 Chwefror 1874; *Cambrian News* (*CN*), 6 February, 3 April 1874; *Aberystwyth Observer*, 7 February 1874; *WSJ*, 2 March, 3 May 1874. For John Griffith, see *Dictionary of Welsh Biography* (Cardiff, 1959), 294–5.

[13]   Helen Blackburn, *Women's Suffrage: A Record of the Women's Suffrage in the British Isles* (1902), 110.

[14]   *WSJ*, 1 March 1871, 1 February 1873.

[15]   Mrs (Elizabeth) Mitchell, *Women's Place in Politics* (1903), 5.

The audience was numerous, but, judging from the air of curiosity which showed itself on the faces of a large number of those who entered the room, a considerable portion came in anticipation of a little fun rather than in genuine sympathy with the objects of that novel association of widows and old maids, which has earned for itself the sobriquet of the 'shrieking sisterhood'. . . . These included half a dozen men – who sat in the back seats and had the bad taste to laugh at everything that was said – and three or four young ladies, who, as prospective wives, could hardly be supposed to have taken any serious interest in the proceedings. Exclusive of the visitors from Bristol, the *savante* of Wenvoe [Gertrude Jenner] was the only representative of the classes concerned in the agitation, and she, on being elected to the chair, said more about the [Irish] Land League than the pertinent question of women's rights and wrongs![16]

Gertrude Jenner (1835–1904) was the most active campaigner in south Wales in the 1870s and 1880s. She sat on the general council of the BWSWS from 1873 to 1888; she was secretary of the Cardiff committee and organized meetings in Cardiff and elsewhere, some of which she either chaired or addressed. In appearance and character, she fitted the parodied early suffragist of satirical magazines like *Punch* almost perfectly – the bespectacled, middle-class, middle-aged spinster, eccentric and indomitable. Year after year, for almost four decades, she carried on litigation in a vain attempt to recover what she believed to be her right to portions of her father's Wenvoe estate, conducting her own case, even as far as the High Court of Justice, and leaving herself penniless in her later years. In what she called her 'public work', she was the lifelong champion of the 'poor and downtrodden', endlessly seeking financial support for the charitable institutions of Cardiff and for the families of the victims of local mining disasters and noted, above all, for her apparently successful battles to petition for the lives of young women across south Wales sentenced to death for infanticide; she and her tin collecting box were a common sight at the entrance to Cardiff market. No doubt it was her commitment

[16] *WM*, 10 March 1881. In contrast, for highly complimentary press comment, see *Pontypool Free Press*, 23 November 1872; *Star of Gwent*, 23 November 1872; *Haverfordwest and Milford Haven Telegraph*, 27 November 1872; *South Wales Daily News* (*SWDN*), 10 March 1881.

to philanthropy, humanitarianism and justice that fired her women's suffrage involvement. Women, she told a Cardiff meeting in 1881, 'were all too often the victims of tyranny and oppression and they were simply anxious to secure any protection they could'.[17]

In Cardiff, Gertrude Jenner was one of a nucleus of suffragists, both male and female, principally Nonconformist ministers and professional men and their wives, whose presence mirrored the nature of prominent support in other parts of Wales at this time. A number of those who came forward to declare their support inevitably already had links with radical and progressive causes – including Revd Dr Thomas Thomas, the Pontypool Baptist minister and college principal, the extraordinary Dr William Price of Treforest, a speaker at the first suffragist meeting in Cardiff, other former Chartist stalwarts, notably J. W. Manning in Cardiff and J. W. James in Merthyr, and enlightened industrialists like the Darby brothers (W. H. and C. E.) of Brymbo and the Cory brothers (John and Richard) of Cardiff.[18]

With the exception of the aristocratic Lady Amberley, early female activists in Wales were of middle-class background. Often they were strongly evangelical and the wives of male suffragists. Lord and Lady Amberley were the most striking marriage partners prominent in the cause, but there were certainly others. In Cardiff, there was Mr and Mrs Richard Cory, and several Nonconformist ministers – Revds Alfred Tilly, Joseph Waite and Henry Chester – and their wives. In Swansea, the Unitarian Revd Edward Higginson and his wife, Emily, were conspicuous advocates; in Merthyr there was C. H. James, a lawyer, a leading Unitarian and an energetic public figure, and his wife Sarah; while in Tenby, Henry Goward, a private school headmaster, and his wife were energetic supporters.

Dissenting voices at early women's suffrage meetings in Wales were rare and there was generally little of the calculated

[17]   *SWDN*, 26 February 1881. Obituaries (and sketched portraits) in *WM*, 18 April 1904; *South Wales Echo*, 18 April 1904; *CT*, 23 April 1904; *Weekly Mail*, 23 April 1904; *Barry Dock News*, 22 April 1904; *Penarth Observer*, 23 April 1904.
[18]   *CT*, 23 November 1872; *SWDN*, 21 November 1872; *WSJ*, 1 December 1872. For the involvement of these figures in Victorian reform movements, see Wallace, *'Organise!'*, passim.

disruption that emerged in later years. The moderate tone adopted by deputations contributed to this. Time and again speakers insisted that their demand was limited to duly qualified widows and spinsters rather than married women (thereby enfranchising only about one-seventh of householders), and also that they were not seeking to elect female MPs. Clearly, local male support was often given only on these bases. In reality, however, the movement was far from united on this and other issues throughout the Victorian period and beyond.

An important source of division in the 1870s and 1880s was the relationship with the Ladies' National Association for the Repeal of the Contagious Diseases Acts, the 'great crusade' of the charismatic Josephine Butler. Motivated by concern at the high incidence of venereal disease among the armed forces, the Contagious Diseases Acts (of 1864, 1866 and 1869) empowered policemen to require women suspected of being prostitutes to submit to a medical examination and subsequent treatment. While some welcomed the legislation on public health grounds, others saw it as an unjust infringement of women's civil liberties and a national protest movement kept up a vigorous agitation for almost seventeen years until repeal in 1886. Suffragists generally opposed the Acts but many feared discrediting their own movement by identification with a campaign dealing with matters of prostitution, venereal disease and intimate medical examination, subjects of 'a decidedly immoral and indecent character'.[19] Nevertheless, in Wales, as elsewhere, there were clear links in personnel between the two movements. The suffrage speaker and organizer, Jessie Craigen, addressed meetings in south Wales on behalf of the repeal campaign in 1880–2, while local dual activists included Gertrude Jenner in Cardiff, Emily Higginson in Swansea and Sarah James in Merthyr, as well as several male suffragists (including C. H. James, Richard Cory and the Revds Alfred Tilly, Joseph Waite and Edward Higginson).[20] There was certainly as much repeal as suffrage activity in Wales during the 1870s and 1880s and the contagious

---

[19]   *Cambrian*, 7 February 1873.
[20]   *SWDN*, 2 September 1880; *CT*, 4 September 1880; *Aberdare Times*, 7 January 1882; *National League Journal*, 2 January 1882. Sarah James, who normally used the title 'Mrs C. H. James' following her marriage in 1842, was a signatory of the 1866

diseases agitation evidently played a significant role in bringing women in various parts of Wales into the political arena. In March 1879, under the headline 'A Women's Conference about Women in Cardiff', the *Cardiff Times* reported 'a novelty ... the first public meeting here to which ladies alone were invited'. Further meetings followed, with activists also establishing local bodies to organize fund-raising, the distribution of literature, the raising of petitions and other activities.[21]

Similarly, of course, a key task of the Bristol, Manchester and other provincial suffrage societies was 'to form committees in every town ... for the purpose of directing attention to the subject, and affording information and aid to all friends of the cause'. The Bristol society sought to establish an organizational framework across the west of England and south Wales region. The names of 'corresponding secretaries' listed in its annual reports for the 1870s presumably equate to local committees or societies and by 1878 there were twenty-five of these, including seven in Wales – at Llanelli, Monmouth, Neath, Newport, Pembroke, Swansea and Tenby – to which the Bristol office could direct pamphlets and other literature, some of which were translated into the Welsh language. Earlier in the decade, corresponding secretaries had also been listed for Haverfordwest, Pembroke Dock and Pontypool. A committee existed in Cardiff too, affiliated directly to the NSWS.[22]

Links between headquarters and the outlying areas were also cemented by the appointment of vice-presidents and council members. Those committees and societies formed in

'Ladies' Petition', a friend and ally of Rose Mary Crawshay, and a subscriber to the Ladies' National Association for many years. While invariably present at local suffrage and repeal meetings, she herself never spoke in public, though her husband often did.

[21]   *CT*, 29 March 1879; *SWDN*, 25 March 1879; *WM*, 25 March 1879; Ladies' National Association, *Annual Report*, 1879, 9–10; *Star of Gwent*, 28 March 1879; *CT*, 24 December 1881; *National League Journal*, 2 January 1882; Ladies' National Association, *Annual Reports*, 1881, 24, and 1882, 9–10. For the contagious diseases campaign in Wales, see Wallace, *'Organise!'*, 170–83.

[22]   *WSJ*, 1 February 1873. One of the Bristol society's first propaganda initiatives was to issue and circulate 1,000 copies of Lady Amberley's Stroud lecture, originally published as 'The claims of women' in the *Fortnightly Review*, XI (1871), 95–110, BWSWS, *Annual Report*, 1871, 4.

Wales at this time were almost certainly small; meetings and activities were intermittent and touring speakers often provided much needed stimulus. In the early 1870s Wales provided three vice-presidents – Rose Crawshay (who remained so for the next thirty years), the countess of Mar, of Hilston Park, near Monmouth, and Major Alexander Rolls of Monmouth. The town also provided four of the eight council members from Wales at this time, a reflection no doubt of the influence of the society's president, Lady Amberley, who lived a few miles away. (The other four members were from Cardiff, Haverford-west, Neath and Swansea.)[23]

Women's suffrage bills and resolutions provided an impetus and a focus for local activity by inspiring speaking tours, petitioning and the formation of committees. The only year during the 1870s when a parliamentary debate was not held on a bill was 1874, though all were defeated in a division apart from that of 1875, which was 'talked out'. In the nine debates of the decade, only two of Wales's MPs participated, J. H. Scourfield (Pembrokeshire) and George Osborne Morgan (Denbighshire), both on the opposition side. The former, a vehement anti-suffragist, spoke against the first four bills and, as a result, his constituency was a particular target for early campaigners in Wales.

The suffragist campaign of the 1870s culminated in a series of major demonstrations in nine principal cities in England and Scotland during 1880–2. The first, held in Manchester in February 1880, set the tone and pattern for others. Chaired and addressed entirely by women, the hundred or so men present were confined to the galleries, while the thousands of women, of all classes and occupations, proved too numerous to be accommodated. Similarly, thousands gathered in Bristol later in the year, again to hear exclusively women speakers, among whom was Gertrude Jenner.[24] Women-dominated meetings now became more evident at a local level too; a

[23]   BWSWS, *Annual Reports*, 1872, 10, and 1873, 2. The durability of local organ-ization is difficult to gauge, though occasional references indicate a greater degree of permanence than is otherwise indicated. See, for example, *Tenby Observer*, 8 September 1881.
[24]   *WSJ*, 1 December 1880; *The Times*, 8 November 1880; *Daily Bristol Times and Mirror*, 5 November 1880; *Western Daily Press*, 5 November 1880.

Cardiff meeting in February 1881, for example, was chaired by Gertrude Jenner and addressed solely by women.[25]

During the early 1880s prominent English-based activists continued to carry out speaking engagements in Wales. A familiar figure was Jessie Craigen who, though something of a maverick in suffrage circles, was a particularly powerful and effective speaker whose appeal to working-class audiences was a valuable asset to an essentially middle-class movement. 'Working men are especially invited', ran the notices for her open-air meetings in Cardiff in August 1880.[26] Seeking to reach out to working women, the Bristol society recruited the services of Jeanette Wilkinson, secretary of the Upholstresses' Union in London, to lecture on its behalf. During the winter of 1884–5 she addressed several meetings in south Wales, evidently with some impact; in December 1884 the Aberdare, Merthyr and Dowlais District Miners' Association pronounced in favour of extending the franchise to women and instructed its agent 'to do all that he can to get up meetings for Miss Jeanette G. Wilkinson to advocate her claims on behalf of women's suffrage'.[27]

The campaign of the early 1880s was invigorated by optimism that a third parliamentary reform bill, widely anticipated from the new Liberal government, would be amenable to a successful women's suffrage motion. When the bill appeared in 1884, however, the prime minister, William Gladstone, gave the amendment, moved by William Woodall, Liberal MP for Stoke-on-Trent, his 'strongest opposition', arguing that women's suffrage would give the House of Lords an opportunity to reject the whole measure. In the subsequent division, suffragists calculated that 104 'known friends' voted against and ensured women's exclusion by a margin of 271 to 135. Many activists were left incensed. 'Gladstone has been our

[25]   SWDN, 26 February. 1881; WSJ, 1 April 1881. See also, ibid., 2 June 1884; Montgomeryshire Express, 2 April 1884.
[26]   SWDN, 31 August 1880. For Jessie Craigen, see Sandra Stanley Holton, 'Silk dresses and lavender kid gloves: the wayward career of Jessie Craigen', Women's History Review, 5, 1 (1996), 129–50; eadem, 'Craigen, Jessie Hannah (1834/5–1899)', ODNB.
[27]   WSJ, 1 January, 2 February, 2 March 1885; ER, 15 January, 14 February 1885; Merthyr Telegraph, 20 December 1884; June Hannam, 'Wilkinson, Jeanette Gaury (1841–1886)', ODNB.

ruin ... the evil genius of our sex and of our country ... our arch-enemy', thundered the feminist writer and activist, Frances Power Cobbe.[28] Even more galling, the Act added some two million working-class men to the electorate. Frances Power Cobbe was one of many who highlighted a situation whereby 'a rabble of illiterates' was deemed fit for the franchise, but educated women not. This 'ludicrous injustice' she later vividly exposed in relation to the Dolgellau neighbourhood where she spent the last twenty years of her life (1884–1904):

> There is in the village in question a man universally known therein as 'The Idiot'; a poor slouching, squinting fellow, who yet rents a house and can do rough field work, though he can scarcely speak intelligibly. *He* has a vote, of course. The owner of his house and of half the parish, who holds also the advowson of the living, is a lady who has travelled widely, understands three or four languages, and studies the political news of Europe daily in the columns of the *Times*. That lady, equally, of course, has *no* vote, and no power whatever to keep the representation of her county out of the hands of the demagogues naturally admired by the Idiot and his compeers.[29]

Although in this period Welsh newspapers and periodicals often expressed broad support for the principle of women's suffrage, Woodall's 1884 amendment aroused mixed reactions. The Tory *Western Mail*, in an analysis of the voting of Wales's MPs in the division, condemned the betrayal of a 'righteous' demand by 'cowardly, weak-kneed Liberals' in the face of leadership pressure. The Liberal press generally accepted Gladstone's stand and emphasized party loyalty. Some, like the *South Wales Daily News*, went further, berating campaigners for their untimeliness, endangering the whole franchise bill and also damaging their own case by their 'saucy

[28]   Frances Power Cobbe to Lydia Becker, 5 August, 26 November [1884], Women's Suffrage Collection, Manchester Central Library, M50/1/2/50–1. For Frances Power Cobbe, see Barbara Caine, 'Cobbe, Frances Power (1822–1904)', *ODNB*. For Gladstone's influence on the voting, see the explanation of C. H. James, the Merthyr suffragist and local MP from 1880 to 1888. *Merthyr Express*, 20 December 1884.
[29]   Frances Power Cobbe, *Life of Frances Power Cobbe by Herself*, vol. 2 (1894), 211. See also *CN*, 14 March 1890: 'It is almost incredible that women ... are still compelled to struggle for privileges which, by legal right, belong to the most ignorant and degraded of men.'

vindictiveness'. The glaring exception was the Aberystwyth-published *Cambrian News*, which, under the direction of the irrepressibly outspoken Lancastrian, John Gibson, adopted a typically uncompromising position: 'A Reform Bill that refuses the franchise to qualified women is a hollow sham, and ought to be repudiated by every man who calls himself a Liberal.'[30]

Parliamentary developments in the years following the 1884 setback were dispiriting for suffragists. At various times, parliamentary friends of the cause introduced motions and bills, but with little or no progress made. An exception was Sir Albert Rollit's bill of April 1892, which generated a high-level debate before being defeated by only twenty-three votes (175 to 152), an encouraging result in the face of determined and organized opposition. Figuring prominently in the latter was Samuel Smith, Liberal MP for Flintshire, whose speech moving the rejection of the bill was the only contribution from Wales's representatives.[31] The next debate and division, five years later, afforded further evidence of the advance of suffragism when Ferdinand Faithfull Begg's bill achieved a comfortable majority of seventy-one (230 votes to 159) in February 1897. Again, there was a solitary speech from the ranks of Wales's MPs, this time by the anti-suffragist Liberal leader in the House of Commons, Sir William Harcourt (West Monmouthshire). Though subsequently blocked at committee stage – 'talked out' as opponents tactically prolonged earlier debates – the victorious division arguably signified a major breakthrough, presaging a series of suffragist parliamentary successes after 1904.[32]

Most of the bills placed before Parliament sought the vote for women on the same terms as men, a comprehensive-sounding but actually limited demand which also served to gloss over the perennial and often bitter divisions between radicals and moderates. Since the right to vote was related to property qualifications and, under the law of coverture, wives could not hold real property independently of their husbands,

[30]   *WM*, 14 June 1884; *SWDN*, 14 June 1884; *CN*, 28 March 1884. Of Wales's 33 MPs (29 Liberals and 4 Conservatives), 5 Liberals and 2 Conservatives supported Woodall, 18 Liberals voted against; 8 were absent for the division.

[31]   *Parl. Deb.*, 4th ser., 3, cols. 1471–84, 27 April 1892.

[32]   Ibid., 45, cols 1225–9, 3 February 1897.

in effect married women were excluded by such bills, though they did not expressly say so. To many suffragists, confining their demand to single women and widows seemed to have the merits of conforming to the property-holding basis of citizenship of the time and also of allaying fears of a female majority in the electorate. From the dawn of the campaign, however, more radical suffragists, particularly in the Manchester society, objected to this stance on the grounds of both principle and tactics. 'A slur on marriage', regretted the Monmouth activist, Mary Maclaverty. 'We cannot exclude them [married women] without making ourselves and our cause ridiculous', protested another activist. 'How sadly we have been weakened by the timidity of our friends both in and out of Parliament'.[33]

Tension and conflict between radical and moderate suffragists were pronounced at the time of the 1884 Reform Bill, and by the end of the decade the fragile unity of the NSWS had collapsed, a major rift occurring in December 1888. The precise nature of the suffrage demand remained an issue, but the actual split came as a consequence of the emergence of women's party political organizations during the 1880s. A majority of the central committee of the NSWS agreed to the affiliation of these, but a rival faction, led by Lydia Becker and Millicent Fawcett who feared a takeover of a traditionally non-party movement by women's Liberal associations, adamantly refused. (Habitations of the Conservatives' Primrose League were forbidden affiliation by their constitutions.) The minority, adhering to the old rules, now set up a separate organization at new premises but, confusingly, retained the name of Central Committee of the National Society for Women's Suffrage (CCNSWS). The majority, accepting political affiliation, established themselves as the Central National Society for Women's Suffrage (CNSWS), and quickly emerged as much the more powerful body, with sixty-eight affiliated societies by 1893, the bulk of which were women's Liberal associations (WLAs).[34]

---

[33] *CN*, 31 May 1895; Ursula Bright to Henry Fawcett, 8 February 1884, quoted in Linda Riley, 'The opposition to women's suffrage, 1867–1918' (B.Litt. thesis, University of Oxford, 1977), 172.

[34] More conveniently, contemporaries often referred to the two societies by the

The two bodies cooperated significantly in the mid 1890s in arousing support for a mass petition in favour of women's suffrage, 'An Appeal from Women of all Parties and all Classes', organized after the defeat of Rollit's bill in 1892. Some 257,000 signatures were eventually collected, the largest parliamentary petition since the heyday of Chartism half a century earlier. The strongest support for the 'Special Appeal' in Wales came from Cardiff (which contributed over 2,000 signatures), Carmarthen Boroughs and Brecknock (both over 1,500). The initiative invigorated activists, generated a host of meetings around the country and the circulation of literature, and ultimately paved the way for reunion of the movement.[35]

Of the two splinter organizations, only the CNSWS had any impact in Wales where affiliations were all WLAs, the number increasing from one (Newport and South Monmouthshire) in 1890 to nine in 1893, and to eleven in 1895.[36] The society disseminated literature and supplied speakers to associations and, thereby, some forty or fifty women's suffrage meetings were held in Wales in these years. Several leading figures were also instrumental in forging strong links between the suffrage cause and the emerging women's Liberal organizations in Wales. One was Leonora Philipps (wife of the Pembrokeshire landowner and Liberal MP, J. Wynford Philipps), who served on the executive of the CNSWS, then on that of the National Union of Women's Suffrage Societies (NUWSS), and was closely involved in the growth and organization of WLAs in the 1890s. She addressed meetings throughout Wales on the suffrage and other political and national issues related to Welsh Liberalism, and also contributed to journals such as *Young Wales* and the *Welsh Review*. Though not a native of Wales, marriage led her to become a lifelong champion of its culture and heritage.[37] Other frequent CNSWS speakers in

---

addresses of their headquarters – the CCNSWS as the 'Great College Street Society' and the CNSWS as the 'Parliament Street Society'.

[35]   David Rubinstein, *Before the Suffragettes: Women's Emancipaton in the 1890s* (Brighton, 1986), 147–9; CNSWS, Annual Report, 1894, 4; *The Times*, 13 July 1894; Crawford, *Women's Suffrage Movement*, 648–9.

[36]   Bangor, Cardiff, Flint, Merthyr and District, Milford Haven, Narbeth, Newport and South Monmouth, Newtown, Pembroke Dock, Rhyl and Swansea. CNSWS, Annual Reports, 1890–5.

[37]   For further details of her work at this time, see *Woman's Herald*, 20 February

Wales were the Chepstow-born temperance, social and moral reformer, Laura Ormiston Chant, and Eva McLaren, treasurer and organizer of the Women's Liberal Federation (WLF) and a member of a whole clan of suffrage activists.[38] Finally, a CNSWS executive member from 1895 was Sybil Thomas, wife of the great south Wales coal magnate and MP for Merthyr Boroughs, D. A. Thomas. Taking to the women's suffrage platform in the early 1890s, she was to be a stalwart of the cause over the next four decades.[39]

The CCNSWS remained committed to a franchise demand which excluded married women, while the CNSWS, which was divided on the matter, supported bills confined to single women and widows and those seeking equal rights, but would not go as far as promoting legislation expressly including married women. As a result, radicals chose to reject the compromise of past decades and broke away to form a third suffrage society, the Women's Franchise League, the first to press explicitly the claims of married as well as single and widowed women.[40] Formed in 1889 and active for most of the next decade, it had firm Welsh connections from the outset.

1892; NLW, MS 21971B, *Letters of Well Known Women* [to Leonora Philipps]; Masson, 'Hand in hand', 365–6; Aaron and Masson, *Very Salt of Life*, 172–9, 198–205; Linda Walker, 'Philipps, Leonora, Lady St David's (1862–1915)', *ODNB*. She was elected to the first NUWSS executive in 1897 and remained active in women's Liberalism in the early years of the twentieth century but withdrew from political campaigning during the course of the decade. She subsequently gained a reputation as a political hostess, busied herself in philanthropic and social work in London and, as a 'lady bountiful', in Pembrokeshire. Obituaries (as Lady St David's) in *SWDN*, 31 March 1915; *WM*, 31 March 1915; *Haverfordwest and Milford Haven Telegraph*, 31 March, 7 April 1915; *Pembrokeshire Times*, 1 April 1915; *County Echo*, 1 April 1915; *Pembroke Dock and Pembroke Gazette*, 2 April 1915. J. Wynford Philipps (1860–1938): Liberal Member for Mid-Lanark, 1888–94, and for Pembrokeshire, 1898–1908; created baron St David's in 1908 and viscount in 1918.

[38] For Laura Ormiston Chant, see Crawford, *Women's Suffrage Movement*, 105. For Eva McLaren, see ibid., 397–9, and Linda Walker, 'McLaren, Eva Maria (1852/3–1921)', *ODNB*. The latter's husband, the Liberal MP Walter McLaren, also addressed women's suffrage meetings in Wales, while her sister-in-law, Laura McLaren (subsequently Baroness Aberconway), residing at Bodnant, Denbighshire, was another lifelong suffrage campaigner. See Elizabeth Crawford, 'McLaren, Laura Elizabeth, Lady Aberconway (1854–1933)', *ODNB*.

[39] For an appreciation of 'Mrs David Thomas' as a women's suffrage speaker at this time, see *Weekly Star*, 13 August 1892. See also Deirdre Beddoe, 'Sybil Margaret, Viscountess Rhondda (1857–1941)', *ODNB*.

[40] For the league, see Sandra Stanley Holton, *Suffrage Days: Stories from the*

Its first council, established at the inaugural meeting in late July, included two members from Aberystwyth, John Gibson and Elizabeth James, while a week later, Thomas Ellis, MP for Merioneth, was one of three Liberal MPs who sponsored its Women's Electoral Disabilities Bill in the House of Commons. The Aberystwyth connection proved a durable one and the town was the venue for the league's sixth annual conference, in May 1895, when Elizabeth James (now a member of the executive committee) took the chair, and Gibson delivered a typically forceful address. Other prominent speakers were Mary Maclaverty of Monmouth and the author 'Gwyneth Vaughan' (Annie Harriet Hughes) of Caernarfon.[41] The league paid particular attention to north and mid Wales prior to the 1892 general election, two of its representatives visiting twenty towns across the region in June.[42]

Women's Suffrage Movement (London, 1996), 76–86, 100–2; eadem, 'Now you see it, now you don't: the Women's Franchise League and its place in contending narratives of the women's suffrage movement', in Maroula Joannou and June Purvis (eds), *The Women's Suffrage Movement: New Feminist Perspectives* (Manchester, 1998). The league itself was soon suffering internal tensions over personal relationships, Elizabeth Wolstenholme Elmy resigning as secretary within the year and founding a breakaway organization, the Women's Emancipation Union in 1891. Having similar objectives to the league, though with differences of emphasis, the union did a good deal of 'educational work', especially through distribution of literature, in an eight-year existence but did not build up a large membership or broad network of branches. Its Welsh connections were confined to a few individuals, Nora Philipps being a subscriber and addressing the final meeting in July 1899, Dr Frances Hoggan contributing a paper to a conference in March 1893 and Agnes Pochin (active, along with her husband, in the Manchester campaign from the outset and from 1874 owners and residents of the Bodnant estate in the Conwy valley, Denbighshire) a council member. Women's Emancipation Union, *Annual Report* (Congleton, 1894), 42; ibid. (1899), 50. See also Holton, *Suffrage Days*, 82–8, 102–5; Crawford, *Women's Suffrage Movement*, 557–9, 713–15.

[41] *CN*, 31 May 1895. Elizabeth James was the wife of John James, a major businessman and prominent public figure in the town. See W. J. Lewis, *Born on a Perilous Rock: Aberystwyth Past and Present* (Aberystwyth, 1980), 243–4. She remained a determined suffragist for the rest of her life. *The Vote*, 15, 22 September 1916. The league's *Annual Reports* consistently listed Dr Frances Hoggan as a 'corresponding vice-president' and Elizabeth James, John Gibson and Agnes Pochin as vice-presidents, and recorded a local branch in Cardiff in 1894–5. Nora Philipps was among the speakers at a major conference of the league at the home of Richard and Emmeline Pankhurst in London in December 1891.

[42] Reportedly, they were 'everywhere well received, especially by the Nonconformist ministers, who appeared to be cordially in favour of the wife's vote'. Women's Franchise League, *Annual Report*, 1892–3, 1. For a list of the towns visited and the support received from WLAs, see ibid., 15–17. The tour may well have originated in the league's response to the outspoken opposition to women's suffrage

Aberystwyth was chosen to host the annual meeting in 1895 (the first time it had been held outside London) because the league had, in the words of one of its founders, Alice Scratcherd of Leeds, 'very good friends' there. In particular, 'they had a wonderful friend in the *Cambrian News* ... a beacon of light to all reformers ... and they could not be too grateful to the Editor for the justice with which he treated women'.[43] The annual report two years later gave official stamp to the same commendation:

> Your committee desire publicly to acknowledge their great indebtedness to Mr John Gibson of Aberystwith [sic], a vice-president of the League, and one of the best workers for justice towards women which we have ever had. As editor of the *Cambrian News*, he continually and fearlessly advocates equality of civil rights for women, and continuously stirs women themselves to that courageous action which alone can bring the desired equality.[44]

John Gibson directed the *Cambrian News*, first as editor and then owner-editor, for over forty years, from 1873 until his death in 1915, turning it into a crusading newspaper exerting an influence far beyond its locality. His advocacy of women's rights in the most wide-ranging of senses was passionate, unqualified and unstinting. Hard-hitting editorials regularly berated women for their lack of passion and enthusiasm, for confining themselves to politely worded requests for justice and for the 'academic, drawing-room' nature of their campaign. The parliamentary franchise had to be 'wrested from men' and, to achieve this, women had to 'fall back upon force ... the only argument that has weight with Governments'. He urged them to adopt tactics designed to cause 'uproar' and compel politicians to concede their demands – widespread tax resistance, rousing working-class women and opposing anti-suffragist candidates at elections. At the same time, male attitudes were fiercely denounced: Welsh constituency MPs, including 'mongrel Liberals' such as Samuel Smith and William Harcourt who spoke out against women's suffrage bills, were particular targets for his

from the Flintshire MP, Samuel Smith, his constituency being visited by representatives in 1890 and a leaflet published. WFL, *Annual Report*, 1889–90, 6, 19.
43   *CN*, 31 May 1895.
44   *Woman's Signal*, 27 May 1897.

wrath.[45] Gibson's own advanced views, which were very much in tune with the Women's Franchise League's objects, were also in 1891 published in a seventy-page book entitled *The Emancipation of Women*.[46] No newspaper editor in Britain adopted a more consistently forthright stance on the whole issue of women's rights at this time than did John Gibson, and this gave the *Cambrian News* a nationwide celebrity status among campaigners.

While moderate suffragists were at pains to reassure meetings of the limited nature of their demands, radicals trumpeted their concept of full citizenship. Thus, at the Aberystwyth conference, Women's Franchise League speakers alluded to equal political, legal and property rights, equal educational opportunities and equal access to civil and ecclesiastical positions for all women. It was the formulation and promotion of this bold, expansive suffragism, rather than the degree of agitation it stimulated, which gave the Women's Franchise League its significance. At most, it appears to have attracted only a few hundred members and a small number of branches but it certainly had its supporters in Wales, the 1895 conference inferring a network of contacts in Wales and with England, while John Gibson's *Cambrian News* gave women's radicalism an impassioned, articulate voice.[47]

For much of the 1880s and 1890s women's suffrage activity had not, in fact, been principally generated by the two central societies nor by the Women's Franchise League. A new and vigorous flank to the campaign had opened up following the emergence of party political organizations, especially Liberal ones, in the wake of the Corrupt Practices Act of 1883, which prohibited the employment of paid election agents and obliged political parties to rely on volunteer workers. The Conservative Party established the Primrose League in 1883, which had a million members by 1891, about half of whom

[45]   *CN*, 25 April, 28 March, 25 April, 6, 20 June 1884; 14 March, 30 May 1890, 29 April 1892; 24 November 1893, 13 March 1898. Smith was bluntly told to 'clear out of Wales, where advocates of the enslavement of women are not required'. Ibid., 1 May 1891. See also ibid., 1 April 1892.

[46]   Gibson, *Emancipation of Women*.

[47]   *CN*, 31 May 1895. The Women's Franchise League disappears from the records in the late 1890s.

were women.[48] From the outset, the Primrose League deliberately avoided the women's suffrage question, recognizing its
contentious, divisive nature, and thus never sought to pressurize the party into taking up the issue. Nonetheless, plenty
of Conservative men and women were ardent supporters of
the cause and party conferences periodically discussed the
issue. The National Union of Conservative and Constitutional
Associations first adopted a women's suffrage resolution in
1887, and reaffirmed this stance in later years, with regional
gatherings following suit; for example, the Welsh division of
this body did so in Swansea in 1888.[49] A number of the
Victorian suffragist leaders were Conservatives; so too were
many local activists. A stalwart for almost half a century in
Monmouthshire, for example, was Elizabeth Harcourt
Mitchell of Llanfrechfa Grange, near Caerleon, dame president of a Primrose League habitation, a staunch Church-
woman and local government representative. In Monmouth
itself, support for women's suffrage largely centred on the
leadership of the town's Primrose League habitation, which
included John Allan Rolls and his wife (from 1892, Baron and
Lady Llangattock) and their circle of family and friends.[50]
    While Primrose League rules prevented it from becoming
a women's suffrage pressure group, the Liberal position
was always very different. Indeed, it was radical suffragists,
disenchanted with the progress of the NSWS and seeking an
alternative strategy to advance the cause, who lay behind the

---

[48]   By the end of the century, some 169 Primrose League habitations (probably
amounting to more than 35,000 members) had been founded in Wales. See Martin
Pugh, *The Tories and the People, 1880–1935* (Oxford, 1985), 249–51.
[49]   *ER*, 15 March 1888. See Lori Maguire, 'The Conservative Party and women's
suffrage', and Philippe Vervaecke, 'The Primrose League and Women's Suffrage',
in Myriam Boussahba-Bravard (ed.), *Suffrage Outside Suffragism: Women's Vote in
Britain, 1880–1914* (Basingstoke, 2007), 52–76, 180–205 respectively.
[50]   Founded in 1884, the Rolls (Monmouth) habitation had '82 Knights and
Dames and 955 Associates making a total of 1037 members' by 1891. John Rolls
served as Conservative MP for Monmouth Boroughs from 1880 to 1885, voting in
favour of William Woodall's women's suffrage amendment to the 1884 Reform Bill.
Glynis McIntyre, 'An investigation into the development of women's suffrage in
Monmouth town, 1871–1913: with particular reference to the identity and influence of the leading women activists' (BA dissertation, University of Wales College,
Newport, 1993), 4, 15, 26–28, 38–40. (John Rolls and Elizabeth Mitchell were
brother and sister.)

formation of the first women's Liberal associations, initially in Bristol and then elsewhere. In 1887 the forty or so existing local bodies came together in the Women's Liberal Federation (WLF), which by 1895 had 82,000 members in 448 branches. Within a few years of its inception, the issue of whether women's suffrage should be one of the objectives of the new organization became a major source of contention, with two distinct factions emerging – 'progressives' (who wished to include it in the programme) and 'moderates' (who were generally in favour of the demand but unwilling to make it an official aim for fear of turning the federation into little more than a women's suffrage society). Following victory for the former in a somewhat acrimonious executive election in 1892, some 10,000 members and fifty to sixty branches split away to establish the Women's National Liberal Federation, while 'progressives' pressed for adoption of the 'test question policy' – that is, refusal by local associations to work for parliamentary candidates who did not declare themselves in favour of women's suffrage – and founded a pressure group, the Union of Practical Suffragists, to work towards this end. Appearing to have firmly committed the WLF to this stance in 1903, the union was dissolved.[51]

Wales was very much part of these developments. Its first Women's Liberal Association (WLA) was established in Denbigh in 1883 (making it one of the earliest in Britain), followed by Bala in 1887, while in the south, 'Newport and South Monmouthshire' was founded in January 1888 and was the first to affiliate to the WLF, immediately aligning itself with the 'progressives'. By 1891 Wales had twelve WLAs, five of which were affiliated to the WLF.[52] The early months of 1892 witnessed a transformation of this situation as 'progressives'

[51]   Eva McLaren, *The History of the Women's Suffrage Movement in the Women's Liberal Federation* (1903); Martin Pugh, *The March of the Women: A Revisionist Analysis of the Campaign for Women's Suffrage, 1866–1914* (Oxford, 2000), 132–6; Linda Walker, 'Gender, suffrage and party: Liberal women's organisations, 1880–1914', in Boussahba-Bravard (ed.), *Suffrage Outside Suffragism*, 77–102. For the Union of Practical Suffragists, see Hester Leeds, *Origin and Growth of the Union* (Union of Practical Suffragists, leaflet XII, 1898); *Woman's Signal*, 27 May 1897; Holton, *Suffrage Days*, 105–8, 164–5; Crawford, *Women's Suffrage Movement*, 694–5.
[52]   WLF, *Annual Reports*, 1889, 21; *Annual Report*, 1890, 22; 1891, 7; WUWLA, *Annual Report*, 1894, appendix.

determinedly set about winning a majority on the WLF executive. Eva McLaren and Nora Philipps energetically undertook
the organizing of a network of WLA branches in north and
south Wales respectively, with the result that when the Welsh
Union of Women's Liberal Associations (WUWLA) was inaugurated in March it had twenty-nine affiliates; a year later, this
had increased to thirty-seven (all but three of which were affiliated to the WLF) and by the beginning of 1895 to forty-seven,
embracing almost 9,000 members.[53] Nora Philipps was elected
president of the new body, Eva McLaren secretary, and Sybil
Thomas (who took over as president in 1895) filled one of the
executive positions; all three were prominent WLF 'progressives' and successfully stood as candidates for this 'party' in the
1892 executive election.[54] Such 'progressives' put the franchise at the very heart of their political philosophy.

   While broadly committing itself to the promotion of Liberal
Party organization, principles and policies, the WUWLA naturally showed particular concern for those issues which
preoccupied late nineteenth-century Welsh Liberals – disestablishment of the Anglican Church, temperance and land
reform, education and home rule. But women's suffrage was
always central to its agenda, one of its original objects being
'to strenuously support all measures of just legislation for
women, including their Parliamentary enfranchisement and
to work for the incorporation of this important measure of
reform into the programme of the Liberal Party'.[55] The Welsh
Union thus adopted women's suffrage as an official objective
before the WLF committed itself and the issue often figured
prominently at its executive and annual meetings; 'We *will*
have the vote' ran the large inscription above the platform at

[53]   WUWLA, *Annual Report*, 1894, 3–4, appendix; *CN*, 1 April 1892; *Woman's
Herald*, 7 May 1892; *Cambrian*, 17 March 1893; *Young Wales*, January, February 1895,
March 1896. Between 1891 and 1892, the total number of WLF affiliates increased
from 177 to 367. WLF, *Annual Report*, 1892, 7. For the growth of women's Liberal
organizations in Wales, see also Masson, *Women's Rights*, 13–16, 58–62.
[54]   *Woman's Herald*, 9, 16 April 1892. Another executive member with strong
Welsh connections and again firmly in the 'progressive' camp – she also sat on the
executive of the WUWLA – was Katherine Price Hughes, a social worker at the
pioneering West London Mission and wife of the outstanding Methodist orator,
organizer, journalist and reformer, Hugh Price Hughes.
[55]   *Woman's Herald*, 9 April 1892.

the annual conference held in Newtown in 1896.[56] Women's
suffrage was also prominent in the deliberations and activities
of individual WLAs in Wales, the vast majority making it a
principle of their organizations. Some affiliated to the CNSWS
and many collected signatures for petitions; in April 1892,
nineteen put their names to a memorial urging MPs to
support Rollit's bill.[57]

Welsh associations gave emphatic support to the campaign
by 'progressives' to make women's suffrage explicitly part of
the WLF programme – as many as eighty-seven delegates from
Wales voted with the 'progressives' at the 1892 annual meeting,
in the wake of which there were allegations that 'Welsh delegates were swamping the Federation' through malpractice.[58]
Wales was to remain prominent in the suffragist wing of the
WLF throughout the decade, Nora Philipps, Eva McLaren
and Sybil Thomas serving on the executive and becoming
members of its suffrage subcommittee at its inception in 1899.
At the 1903 annual meeting delegates from Cardiff (easily
Wales's largest WLA with 1,083 members in ten wards in
1901) pressed impatiently for a suffrage resolution.[59] Indeed,
some Welsh activists had long advocated an uncompromising
line. At the Welsh Union's 1896 annual meeting, the Aberystwyth WLA unsuccessfully moved the 'test policy' resolution:
'That this Council is of opinion that the time has arrived when
members of Women's Liberal Associations should not work
for any candidate who is opposed to the enfranchisement of
all duly qualified women.' Radicals were very much to the fore
in Aberystwyth, which was an outpost of the Women's
Franchise League and the home of John Gibson and his ally
Elizabeth James, stalwart of both the league and the local
WLA.[60]

---

[56]   *Young Wales*, May 1896. See also ibid., February 1897.
[57]   *Woman's Herald*, 23 April 1892. For a detailed discussion of the involvement of
Liberal women in Wales in the suffrage campaign, especially at Aberdare, see
Masson, *Women's Rights*, 16–31.
[58]   Masson, 'Hand in hand', 369, citing WLF Annual Council minutes, 1892,
13–14; *Woman's Herald*, 7, 21 May 1892.
[59]   WLF, *Annual Report*, 1903, 3.
[60]   *CN*, 3 Apr. 1896. See also NLW, MS 19865C, minute book of the Aberystwyth
Women's Liberal Association (1894–8), committee meetings, 25 March 1895,
3 October 1898. At the inauguration of the Aberystwyth WLA in January 1892, Eva
McLaren paid tribute to Gibson as 'the staunch friend of women [who] had been

The Newtown meeting also portrayed the other end of the spectrum, arousing in particular the wrath of the anti-suffragist Emily Morgan, wife of the Denbighshire MP, George Osborne Morgan. Objecting strongly to the fact that 'the Welsh Women's Liberal Union has pushed women's suffrage to the front', she argued that 'it would sow dissension among our ranks' for there were 'many ardent Liberal workers indifferent, doubtful or opposed to that measure'. Moreover, it was the Conservative Party, she insisted, which would benefit from women's suffrage; 'what right', she wrote, 'has a party organisation to call itself Liberal if it makes a Conservative measure one of its objects, let alone a test question at elections?'[61] Earlier, as president of the newly formed Rhosllannerchrugog WLA in 1892, she had failed to dissuade the organization from making women's suffrage one of its objects and had also been an unsuccessful candidate for the 'anti-progressive party' in the WLF executive election of the same year.[62] The majority of Welsh Liberal women were somewhere in the middle, torn between suffragism and party loyalty, and often giving precedence to the latter. A good example was Evelyn Pelham, president of the Newport WLA and, in the words of the *South Wales Daily News*,

> one of those enlightened workers for Liberalism, who, while strongly desiring the women to have the Parliamentary franchise, is content to allow this question to take its proper place in practical politics, in order that she may work the more thoroughly in the interests of Liberalism generally.[63]

Such patience or, worse, outright anti-suffragism left 'progressives' deeply frustrated. 'There is something pathetic as well as

---

for years educating the town in the matter of women's suffrage'. *CN*, 22 January 1892. A few months later Gibson himself, looking forward to the foundational conference of the WUWLA, was urging it to 'pronounce strongly in favour of enfranchisement of women', proudly asserting that 'nobody need mince their words at Aberystwyth where justice for women has long been a popular cry and a prominent article of the Liberal creed'. Ibid., 1 April 1892.

[61] *CN*, 20 March 1896.

[62] *Woman's Herald*, 2, 16 April 1892.

[63] *SWDN*, 6 October 1891. See also *Woman's Herald*, 3, 17 October 1891. Evelyn Pelham became an executive member of the CNSWS in 1893 and was later active in the Newport branch of the NUWSS. Ibid., 15 June 1893; A. J. R., *Suffrage Annual*, 332. See also Masson, *Women's Rights*, 81, n. 301.

ludicrous', wrote Nora Philipps, 'in the sight of women ... who undertake the arduous and difficult work of organisation and public speaking and who yet disclaim even the desire for the best instrument of political action, the vote itself'.[64]

Suffragists were always in the ascendant in the councils of the Welsh Union and were intent on seizing every opportunity to advance their claims. Thus, when a vigorous campaign for cultural nationalism under the banner of Cymru Fydd ('Young Wales') developed into a political campaign for Welsh home rule in the mid 1890s, they ensured that their voice was heard. Forceful representation at the founding conference of the ill-fated 'Welsh National Federation', which sought to unite the North and South Wales Liberal Federations and the Cymru Fydd League, in Aberystwyth in April 1895, ensured that women's suffrage was included among the objects, while another clause of the constitution gave the WUWLA representation on the executive of the new body.[65]

The precise number of WLAs in operation in Wales at any one time is difficult to establish. The WUWLA appears to have fallen away from a peak of fifty-seven affiliates in 1896 until it disappears from the records after 1907. WLF *Annual Reports* show that the number of affiliations from Wales declined from forty-one in 1896 to fifteen in 1901 and to five in 1907.[66] Nevertheless, women's Liberal organizations certainly represented an alternative means of progress during much of the 1890s at least, and helped keep the women's suffrage flag flying at a time of controversy and division within the mainstream movement.

Progressives in the WLF were also active in the temperance movement and sought to generate support for women's suffrage through this avenue. Moreover, successive presidents of the main British temperance organization, the British

---

[64]   *Welsh Review*, February 1892, 355. See also *Women's Gazette*, 15 June 1891. At the same time, her *Appeal to Women*, a version of which was later translated into Welsh, sought to rouse women to political action. WUWLA, *Annual Report*, 1896, 8.

[65]   WUWLA, *Annual Reports*, 1895, 11, 33–4; 1896, 13–15; *Summary of Federation News*, May 1895; *Baner ac Amserau Cymru*, 24 Ebrill 1895. See also Masson, 'Hand in hand', 357–85.

[66]   WUWLA, *Annual Report*, 1896, 18–23; WLF, *Annual Reports*, 1901, 6; 1907. The surviving WLAs in 1907 were in Cardiff, Merthyr Tydfil, Newport, Swansea and Whitchurch.

Women's Temperance Association (BWTA) – Margaret Bright Lucas, Lady Isabella Somerset and Rosalind Howard, countess of Carlisle – were committed suffragists.[67] Indeed, Lady Somerset's strategy of integrating the association in the suffrage campaign and other elements of the women's movement, as in the United States, resulted in a clash with those who believed that it should be a single-issue organization, the latter breaking away to form the Women's Total Abstinence Union following the 1893 annual meeting. 'We must not omit to mention the splendid help given to the cause by the British Women's Temperance Association and by the dauntless spirit of Lady Henry Somerset', recorded one CNSWS *Annual Report*.[68] To a large extent, women temperance campaigners in Wales operated independently of England, establishing Undeb Dirwestol Merched Gogledd Cymru (the North Wales Women's Temperance Union) in 1892 (with 106 branches and almost 12,000 members by 1896) and Undeb Dirwestol Merched y De (the South Wales Women's Temperance Union) in 1901 (with ten branches by the end of the year and 140 by 1916). Neither body made women's suffrage part of its programme, but the issue was certainly discussed at annual meetings and individual temperance workers publicly voiced support.[69] Though jealously guarding their autonomy, both Welsh unions affiliated to the BWTA, and thus to a degree were influenced by events at the centre. There were also BWTA branches in Wales, some of which certainly responded to the leadership's commitment to women's suffrage.[70]

[67]   Margaret Bright Lucas (the sister of John and Jacob Bright) toured north and mid Wales speaking on behalf of the Manchester National Society in 1874. For the BWTA under these three presidents, see Margaret Barrow, 'Teetotal feminists: temperance leadership and the campaign for women's suffrage', in Claire Eustance, Joan Ryan and Laura Ugolini (eds), *A Suffrage Reader: Charting Directions in British Suffrage History* (London, 2000), 69–89.

[68]   CNSWS, *Annual Report*, 1892, 29. Lady Isabella Somerset had Welsh connections as the wife of the second son of the duke of Beaufort and for a time sat on the executive of the WUWLA. Some BWTA branches affiliated to the CNSWS. For the split in the BWTA, see Lilian Lewis Shiman, 'Changes are dangerous: women and temperance in Victorian England', in Gail Malmgreen (ed.), *Religion in the Lives of English Women, 1760–1930* (London, 1986), 205–9.

[69]   See Lloyd-Morgan, 'From temperance to suffrage'.

[70]   Those at Cwmbran, Hay-on-Wye and Sennybridge, for example, devoted time to the issue in the summer of 1894. *Women's Signal Budget*, July 1894.

Among the most dynamic of BWTA activists was 'Gwyneth Vaughan', the pseudonym of Annie Harriet Hughes, who claimed to have organized as many as 243 branches in different parts of Britain. Born in Talsarnau, Merioneth, the daughter of a miller, in 1852, she worked as a milliner before marrying a local man and moving to London where her husband trained and worked as a doctor. It was on the family's return to Wales in the early 1890s that she threw herself into public life as a remarkably energetic propagandist for an array of causes, including temperance, cultural and political nationalism, Liberalism and women's suffrage. She lectured widely, was a prolific contributor to the press, worked as a newspaper editor and served as secretary of the WUWLA from 1898 to 1907. A radical on the issue of women's Liberalism and the suffrage, she was a strong supporter of the 'test question' to parliamentary candidates, serving on the executive of the Union of Practical Suffragists and addressing meetings on its behalf in south Wales in 1897. In addition, she served as a poor law guardian and district councillor in Caernarfonshire, while also establishing a literary reputation as a Welsh-language novelist.[71]

Yet another pressure organization actively supporting women's suffrage in the 1890s was the Women's Co-operative Guild (WCG). Founded in 1883 as a wing of the cooperative movement, the guild grew into a large organization; by 1889 it had some 1,800 members and 51 branches, by 1895 over 8,000 members and 196 branches, and by 1900 almost 13,000 members and 273 branches. The first WCG branch in Wales was founded in Newport in 1891 and several others followed

[71] Gwynedd Archives, Guy Hughes Papers, Section 1 – Gwyneth Vaughan Papers, XD 85/1/51, *A Record of a Quarter of a Century's work: Literary, and in the interest of Liberal politics*, written and amended by Gwyneth Vaughan herself and dated 14 April 1908. This was the basis of an appeal for financial assistance at a time when she was overwhelmed with 'great domestic afflictions' – widowhood, family ill health and destitution; she died, aged fifty-seven, in 1910. Bangor University, X/GEN.67 VAU, *A Petition addressed to the Right Hon. Henry Herbert Asquith, Prime Minister and first Lord of the Treasury, to place the Welsh writer, Gwyneth Vaughan, on the Civil List for a substantial subsidy* (n.d., *c.*1909). For Gwyneth Vaughan, see Thomas Parry, 'Gwyneth Vaughan', *Cylchgrawn Hanes a Chofnodion Sir Feirionnydd/ Journal of the Merioneth Historical and Record Society*, VIII, 3 (1979), 225–36; *Young Wales*, January 1897, August 1901; *Woman's Signal*, 27 May 1897. Obituaries in *SWDN*, 26 April 1910; *WM*, 26 April 1910; *North Wales Weekly News*, 29 April 1910.

in south Wales over the next few years, though most proved short lived.[72] The guild's principal concerns were social and economic and its congress did not formally adopt women's suffrage until 1904. Nevertheless, during the 1890s, with its long-serving general secretary, Margaret Llewelyn Davies, to the fore, it did become directly involved in the agitation, serving to increase significantly working-class involvement in the campaign, particularly in the Lancashire and Cheshire textile industries. Guildswomen petitioned heavily on the issue (most significantly contributing over 2,200 signatures, nearly one-quarter of the total membership, to the 'Appeal' launched in 1893), discussed the demand at regional conferences and in local branches and passed resolutions of support.[73]

While suffragists framed and justified their demand in various guises, there was of course much common ground in the broad lines of argument. Essentially, these were threefold: the vote was an individual right, the vote was a necessity and women had particular qualities that could enrich the body politic. These formed the core of John Stuart Mill's case when presenting his women's suffrage amendment to the second Reform Bill in 1867 and they were to reappear time and again in the campaign over the next half-century.

While mid-Victorian suffragists voiced the liberal principle of equal rights, they were also acutely conscious of conforming to the political realities of an age that stressed personal fitness for the franchise. This most obviously meant pressing the claims of those women who met the existing property qualifications and insisting on the maxim that taxation and representation went hand in hand. The Tenby resolution of

[72]   During the 1890s branches were formed at Newport, Cardiff, Swansea, Cross Keys, Risca, Abertillery, Pembroke Dock and Ton Pentre. WCG, *Annual Reports*; Helen Thomas, "'A democracy of working women': the Women's Co-operative Guild in south Wales, 1891–1939' (MA thesis, University of Glamorgan, 2006), 30–1, 66.

[73]   WCG, *Annual Report*, 1894, 76–7; Gillian Scott, *Feminism and the Politics of Working Women: The Women's Co-operative Guild, 1880s to the Second World War* (London, 1998), 102–3; Catherine Webb, *The Woman with the Basket: A History of the Women's Co-operative Guild, 1883–1927* (Manchester, 1927), 96–9; Jill Liddington and Jill Norris, *One Hand Tied Behind Us: The Rise of the Women's Suffrage Movement* (London, 1978), 141; Rubinstein, *Before the Suffragettes*, 148–50; *Co-operative News*, 7 July 1894, 27 March, 13 July 1897.

September 1881, 'that in the opinion of this meeting the franchise attached by law to the occupation or ownership of property liable to imperial and local taxation should be exercised by women in the election of members of Parliament', typically and neatly encapsulated a fundamental contention.[74] 'The reason for giving political power to women', explained an exasperated John Gibson in the *Cambrian News*, 'is that they have to obey law as men obey it; that they are taxed as men are taxed; and that they are qualified as men are qualified'.[75] The Swansea *Cambrian* was similarly vigorous, insisting from the early days of the movement that the admission of females to the franchise was a right:

> A woman rules us. Women are freeholders, copyholders and *lords* of the manor! They are as much subjects of the law as men. If they possess property they are as much pecuniary supporters of the Government as men. Their property is as much taxed, as if they were men. They have as much interest as men, and perhaps more, in the prosperity of the country. In morals they are more exemplary. In economy they are more prudent, and with the welfare of the nation they are more bound up than men. Why should they be excluded from equal privileges, when circumstances render their positions similar?[76]

For reasons of expediency, many activists confined the demand to spinsters and widows in the belief that this would increase the prospects of success. More radical elements, however, asserted motherhood and domesticity as entitlement to citizenship rights. 'Was the office of life-giver not as useful to the State as that of the life-taker, and did it not equally merit recognition?' asked the Monmouth suffragist, Mary Maclaverty, thereby proffering a retort to the physical-force argument that the vote should be restricted to men because only they could be called upon to fight for their country.[77]

The suffragists' insistence that the franchise was a necessity ran counter to the Victorian notion of 'virtual representation', that women's interests were safely entrusted to husbands,

---

[74]   *Tenby Observer*, 8 September 1881.
[75]   *CN*, 28 March 1890.
[76]   *Cambrian*, 25 September 1868. See also the letter from 'An Unprotected Female', ibid., 29 April 1859.
[77]   *CN*, 31 May 1895.

fathers and brothers. Mill and others after him strongly argued that women needed the vote to protect and advance their interests, particularly in law, education and employment. 'Go where you will, to France, Germany, Italy, nay even to Russia and Turkey', declared the Welsh suffragist, Frances Hoggan, 'and you will find, in many important particulars, some recognition of maternal rights which puts to shame our marriage laws, or our laws relating to inheritance and to the care and custody of children.'[78] The assertion by one Cardiff suffragist that 'if women had had votes they would never have been disgraced by the present Contagious Diseases Acts' was a common sentiment.[79] Equally passionately, Elizabeth Mitchell urged women's habitations of the Primrose League to give greater attention to the suffrage as 'the only one remedy . . . to remove the disabilities under which we labour', especially with regard to the exclusion of women from certain employments.[80]

By the end of the century, following legislation on a number of women's rights issues, anti-suffragists like Samuel Smith were asserting that, while parliament might have been culpable in the past, the main injustices had now been removed, a view which left campaigners unimpressed. One of John Gibson's scathing attacks on Smith ran thus:

> That any Member of Parliament, and especially a Welsh Member of Parliament, should be so utterly ignorant is incredible. What would Mr SAMUEL SMITH say if wives could get a divorce from their husbands for adultery, while husbands had to prove cruelty as well as adultery against their wives before they could get a divorce? What would he say if he were taxed as heavily as anybody else, and was not allowed even to vote for the election of members who spent the money? What would he say if the law decreed that he should not be a Member of Parliament, or a magistrate, or a lawyer, or a Church of England parson, or a juryman, or a Town Councillor, or a County Councillor, or the Mayor of a town?[81]

While much disagreement surrounded women's intellectual qualities, suffragists and opponents were at one in accepting

---

[78]   Frances Hoggan, *The Position of the Mother in the Family in its Legal and Scientific Aspects* (1885), 16.
[79]   *CT*, 23 November 1872.
[80]   Mitchell, *Women's Place in Politics*, 8–12.
[81]   *CN*, 22 April 1892.

the contemporary notion of female moral superiority, though they differed, of course, on their political conclusions. In Cardiff, the veteran radical J. W. Manning maintained that women's suffrage would 'purify politics', while Rose Crawshay anticipated 'a higher standard of morality introduced into the world'.[82] Public demonstration of female attributes and capabilities was facilitated by the expansion of local government in the late nineteenth century. Moreover, women's skills, knowledge and experience in the fields of health, education, welfare and, indeed, financial management were, it was argued, invaluable as the domestic sphere increasingly merged with national government, especially with the development of significant state social reform in Edwardian Britain. 'The aim of Liberal women to-day', insisted the principal speaker at the WUWLA annual conference in Newport in 1897, 'was to induce the Liberal Party to fall into line and take up this great reform [women's suffrage], which lay at the base of social and moral reform.'[83]

Campaigners also claimed benefits to women themselves. 'Possession of a vote will tend to ennoble women's characters', insisted Rose Crawshay.[84] To Annie Mary Dobell, first headmistress of the County School for Girls at Pontypool, enfranchisement would give 'a nobler outlook in life, a larger possibility of self-realization, and an opportunity of rendering that service to the State which it so sorely needs'.[85] Alice Abadam argued that advantages accrued to family life (in contrast to opponents' claim of domestic disharmony):

> To limit a woman's interest to her home is to make her an amateur hotel manageress whose highest achievement is the ministration of material comfort. It makes of the home a dwelling of the most uninspiring dullness. To limit her interests to her husband makes her a stupid wife and an unhelpful comrade. To limit her interests to her children makes her a foolish and idolatrous mother, and an inefficient guide and friend to them.[86]

---

[82] *SWDN*, 10 March 1881; *Cardiff and Merthyr Guardian*, 11 June 1870.
[83] *Young Wales*, February 1897.
[84] *Cardiff and Merthyr Guardian*, 11 June 1870.
[85] *Free Church Times*, June 1913.
[86] *Women and Progress*, 4 January 1907.

The case for women's suffrage was strengthened by the substantially wider role in society undertaken by women in late nineteenth- and early twentieth-century Britain. At the heart of this development lay great advances in all levels of education. In Wales, the campaign for equal educational opportunities for women ensured that the network of intermediate schools established after 1889 catered for girls as well as boys. Moreover, by the mid 1880s, women were admitted to the three Welsh university colleges – at Aberystwyth, Bangor and Cardiff – and the founding charter of the federal University of Wales in 1893 proclaimed equal status of the sexes. The training of women teachers became firmly established in the education departments of all three, and also at specific colleges in Swansea and Bangor.[87]

Education was a central tenet of the women's movement in Victorian Britain, and by the 1880s it was both a symptom and an agent of increasing emancipation. A *Cambrian News* editorial of April 1887, reflecting on a meeting of the Association for Promoting the Education of Girls in Wales at Aberystwyth, observed:

> Individual women are widening the sphere in which their sisters can move. The change during the last twenty years has been enormous. Twenty years ago a meeting like that held at the Assembly Rooms would have been impossible. We question whether in the whole of the United Kingdom twenty years ago as many women could have been found able to make speeches as stood on that platform, and spoke calmly and quietly, and without a single thought of impropriety entering anyone's mind ... Miss Dilys Davies and Mrs Verney are wise in struggling for fuller and larger opportunities of education. With completer education will come greater strength for strife in other fields.[88]

Educational progress earned women a wider share of employment opportunities. While domestic service continued to dominate the paid labour force in late Victorian and Edwardian Wales, the period brought a significant increase in those engaged in professional occupations (from about 2 per cent in 1851 to about 9 per cent in 1911). Teachers easily

---

[87]   See W. Gareth Evans, *Education and Female Emancipation: The Welsh Experience, 1847–1914* (Cardiff, 1990), especially 142–52.

[88]   *CN*, 22 April 1887.

formed the largest category, but there were growing numbers employed in nursing, local government, the post office, banks and insurance companies. Advancement was slow in the medical profession, which had been penetrated by pioneers like Elizabeth Garrett and Frances Hoggan (the first Welsh woman and the third in Britain to qualify as a medical doctor) in the 1870s and 1880s. Wales had fewer than a dozen female doctors in 1911.[89] The new educated professional class often adopted a feminist stance on political and social issues. Frances Hoggan, disparaged in the House of Commons as 'one of the leaders of the new sedition', was not only a leading campaigner for the admission of women into medicine and for female education but also an ardent supporter of marriage law reform and of women's suffrage.[90] Above all, many teachers in the new girls' secondary schools of Wales were staunch suffragists and, as the campaign intensified in the pre-war years, they often emerged as key figures in local societies. Particularly prominent were several highly respected headmistresses – Annie Dobell in Pontypool, Mary Collin in Cardiff, Mabel Vivian in Newport, Beatrice Holme in Carmarthen, Catherine Davies in Llanelli and Emily Phipps and Clara Neal in Swansea. Education, via the University College of South Wales and Monmouthshire, Cardiff, provided two other leading suffrage activists in the shape of Millicent Mackenzie, the institution's first woman professor (1904–15), and her successor, Barbara Foxley (1915–25).[91]

The opening up of local government to women presented equally significant opportunities during this period, the avail-

[89]   Evans, *Education and Female Emancipation*, 32–4; Beddoe, *Out of the Shadows*, 31–7.

[90]   *Parl. Deb.*, 3rd ser., 228, col. 1709, 26 April 1876. For Frances Hoggan, see Evans, *Education and Female Emancipation*, 100–4; Onfel Thomas, *Frances Elizabeth Hoggan, 1843–1927* (Brecon, 1970); M. A. Elston, 'Hoggan, Frances Elizabeth (1843–1927)', *ODNB*; Neil McIntyre, 'Frances Hoggan – Doctor of Medicine, Pioneer Physician, Patriot and Philanthropist', *Brycheiniog*, XXXIX (2007); Mary L. Shanley, *Feminism, Marriage and the Law in Victorian England* (Princeton, New Jersey, 1989), 17–18, 144–6.

[91]   For Millicent Mackenzie, see ch. 7. For the latter, see Deirdre Beddoe, 'Foxley, Barbara (1860–1958)', *ODNB*. Two other educationalists, women's suffrage advocates and WUWLA executive members were Miss E. A. Carpenter, first 'Lady Principal' of the University College of Wales, Aberystwyth, and Kate (most often, 'Mrs Viriamu') Jones, wife of the first principal of the University College of South Wales and Monmouthshire.

able public positions being in many ways an extension of the kind of voluntary, charitable and religious work which many Victorian women had already undertaken. In Wales four women sat on school boards during the 1870s – Rose Crawshay in both Merthyr (1871–4) and Vaynor (1871–9), Margaret Elizabeth Marsh in Llandinam (1872–7) and, in Swansea, Emma Brock (1876–9) and Emily Higginson (1879–82).[92] By the 1890s women were evidently playing a much fuller part in the triennial school board contests, though successful candidatures continued to be rare.

The first woman poor law guardian elected in Wales was Ellen Fielder, who served as a member of the Abergavenny Poor Law Union from 1878 to 1883.[93] A handful of others followed over the next decade or so, before a considerable widening of the franchise through the abolition of the property qualifications in 1894 brought a dramatic increase. By 1904, Wales had ninety-nine female guardians, Radnorshire being the only Welsh county without such representation.[94]

The Local Government Act of 1894 made women eligible for three new authorities – the parish, rural district and urban

[92] *Merthyr Telegraph*, 24 March 1871; *WSJ*, 1 April. 1871; *School Board Chronicle*, 16 March 1872, 28 February 1874, 3 May 1879; *Newtown and Welshpool Express*, 30 January 1872; *Montgomeryshire Express*, 27 January 1877; *Cambrian*, 1, 22 December 1876, 28 November, 5 December 1879; *Swansea Journal*, 2 December 1876, 29 November, 6 December 1879; *Swansea and Glamorgan Herald*, 22 November, 6 December 1876, 19 November 1879; *The Graphic*, 10 January 1874; *The Queen*, 5 March 1892; *Merthyr Express*, 8 June 1907. Rose lost her Merthyr seat in 1874 but occupied the chair of the Vaynor Board for the eight years she sat on it. In a previous work, I erroneously omitted Emma Brock from among the early members of school boards in Wales. Wallace, *'Organise!'*, 168, n. 43. She was also elected a member of the Swansea Board of Guardians in 1893 and was an executive member of the WUWLA in the 1890s. See also Masson, *Women's Rights*, 196, n. 439.

[93] Clearly a woman of some means, the 1881 census records her as a sixty-year-old widow, of Irish birth, with a housekeeper, a housemaid and a coachman. Mrs Fielder stood unsuccessfully in 1877, was then elected on five successive annual occasions, before being defeated in 1883. *Abergavenny Chronicle*, 7, 14, 21 April 1877, 30 March, 13, 20 April 1878, 31 March, 7, 14 April 1882, 30 March, 13 April 1883. The Cardiff suffragist Gertrude Jenner unsuccessfully contested two boards of guardian elections in the Cardiff area in 1882. *ER*, 15 April 1882.

[94] *List of Women Poor Law Guardians and Rural District Councillors in England and Wales, 1904* (1904), 17, 31–4. Thirty-four of Wales's fifty-three poor law unions had women guardians, though the total of ninety-nine still represented only a small proportion of the 2,037 guardians in Wales. See also *Young Wales*, May 1896, June 1901; Patricia Hollis, *Ladies Elect: Women in English Local Government, 1865–1814* (Oxford, 1987), 241; WUWLA, *Annual Report*, 1895, 6–7.

district councils. In Wales, women established an immediate and significant presence at parish level, made a modest impression in rural districts (seven by 1904) and a negligible one in the urban districts.[95] It was not until 1907 that women were granted the right to serve on borough and county councils, and in the English and Welsh local elections of November of that year twelve were duly elected. These included Gwenllian Elizabeth Morgan, who was elected to Brecon Town Council in 1907. More commonly known as 'Miss Philip Morgan' after her father, a Breconshire vicar and JP, she had long been active in local public affairs as a poor law guardian, a school board representative and a member of the County Council Education Committee, and went on to become Wales's first 'lady mayor' in 1910.[96]

By the Edwardian era a significant number of women had thus obtained local office in Wales; others, of course, had stood unsuccessfully. The pursuit of such positions often meant participation in hard-fought contests, which required a very public profile and an organized campaign involving election notices, the distribution of handbills and the canvassing of voters. By eroding the distinction between male and female spheres and enabling women to demonstrate their abilities and aptitude in public affairs, the local government experience served both to complicate and to undermine the anti-suffragist case, and made the parliamentary vote much less of a dramatic step.

Similar effects were produced by the extensive female involvement in party political organizations and parliamentary elections from the 1880s. In Wales, as elsewhere in Britain, women flocked to the habitations of the Primrose League and the branches of the WLF that sprang up in all corners of the land. While much of the activity centred on organizing social and fund-raising events such as fetes and

---

[95]   Hollis, *Ladies Elect*, 365, 372–3; Martin Pugh, *Women and the Women's Movement in Britain* (2000 edn, London), 57; Rubinstein, *Before the Suffragettes*, 169; *List of Women Poor Law Guardians and Rural District Councillors in England and Wales, 1904* (1904), 17, 31–4; Richard Heath, 'The rural revolution', *Contemporary Review*, LXVII (1895), 197–8.

[96]   Hollis, *Ladies Elect*, 333, 396–7; *Brecon County Times*, 18, 25 October, 1, 8 November 1907, 28 October, 11 November 1910. For the entry of Liberal women into local government in Wales, see Masson, *Women's Rights*, 36–44.

garden parties, for many women participation extended to canvassing voters and speaking on public platforms. By the end of the century Liberal and Conservative MPs throughout Wales were paying tribute to the key electioneering role played by 'the ladies'. Activists in both political parties, but particularly members of WLAs, were also winning seats in local government.[97] Clearly, in these sorts of ways, women were moving well beyond their traditional sphere, while their demonstration of political talents and party loyalty served to diminish fears about their parliamentary enfranchisement. In terms of the campaign itself, party activity strengthened women's conviction that they should be enfranchised. 'It is illogical to urge women to organise and work for the triumph of a political party without encouraging them to obtain the vote', ran part of the resolution proposed by Evelyn Pelham, president of the Newport WLA, at a regional women's suffrage conference convened by the Bristol WLA in 1889.[98]

Party activism and involvement in crusading organizations introduced women to public speaking, committee work, administrative responsibilities, propaganda and local politics, a development which both contributed to and bore witness to changing perceptions of women's role in society, to 'the utter change that has been brought about in . . . the collective prejudices of ordinary persons, as to what women <u>can</u> do and what women <u>ought</u> to do' – an essential prerequisite to eventual enfranchisement.[99] Newspapers and periodicals also did much to advance the female cause in the late Victorian period. The *Women's Suffrage Journal* ceased publication in 1890, shortly after the death of Lydia Becker who had been its driving force for twenty years. The *Englishwoman's Review*, however, ran from 1866 to 1910, and in the late 1880s and 1890s it was joined by several others, including the *Women's*

[97]   *The Gentlewoman*, 27 July, 3, 10 August 1895, 17 November 1900; *Primrose League Gazette*, 1 August 1895; *Summary of Federation News*, February 1895, March 1896. The much more modest Women's Liberal Unionist Association was formed in 1888; it totalled 15,700 members in sixty branches by 1895. See also Mitchell, *Women's Place in Politics*, 3–7.

[98]   *Women's Gazette*, 7 December 1889.

[99]   Florence Fenwick Miller, *An Uncommon Girlhood* (draft autobiography), Wellcome Library, 397. She addressed meetings in Wales at just nineteen years of age in 1874.

Gazette, the *Women's Penny Paper*, *Women's Herald*, *Woman's Signal* and *Shafts*. Wales was served by its own publications, both specific women's periodicals and mainstream newspapers, most notably *Baner ac Amserau Cymru* and, of course, the *Cambrian News*. Speaking at the ceremonial laying of the foundation stone for a women's hostel, Alexandra Hall, in 1895, T. Francis Roberts, principal of the University College of Wales, Aberystwyth, underlined the point:

> Before there was a hall of residence in Wales, there had been a movement for the advancement of women . . . Before there was any general organization, small magazines had been issued devoted to the advancement of women. They were the *Cymraes*, the *Ceiniogwerth*, as well as the *Brythones* . . . and any reference to the movement, especially in Aberystwyth, would be incomplete and ungrateful if it did not refer to the efforts for the advancement of women by the able newspaper published in that town. Whether they agreed or disagreed with the principles or criticism of that paper, they could not refrain from admiring the work it had done for the advancement of women.[100]

The first periodical for women in Wales, *Y Gymraes* (The Welshwoman), was essentially a response to the alleged moral failings of Welsh women as identified by the 1847 Education Report (the infamous 'Blue Books') and, during its brief independent existence (1850–1), it expounded the ideals of marriage and motherhood. Its successors, *Y Frythones* (The Female Briton) (1879–91) and a second *Y Gymraes* (1886–1934), carried the same message but also, with female editors and contributors, gave coverage to women's public role, particularly their participation in the temperance movement.[101] In the mid 1890s the cause of women in Wales was also advanced in the nationalist journal, *Young Wales*, which gave prominence to the 'progress of women' in the fields of education, local government, Liberal Party activism, the suffrage and temperance. By this time, some local newspapers

---

[100]   *CN*, 15 March 1895.
[101]   For these Welsh-language periodicals, see Sian Rhiannon Williams, 'The true "Cymraes": images of women in women's nineteenth-century Welsh periodicals', in John, *Our Mothers' Land*, 69–91. The two outstanding female journalists in Wales in advocating gender equality during this period were Sarah Jane Rees (Cranogwen), editor of *Y Frythones*, and her protegée, Ellen Hughes, columnist of *Y Gymraes* for thirty years. For the former, see Deirdre Beddoe, 'Rees, Sarah Jane [Cranogwen] (1839–1916), *ODNB*. For examples of their writings, see Aaron and Masson, *Very Salt of Life*, 69, 74–5, 91–108, 142–58.

had introduced separate women's columns, which, in due course, became more wide ranging and moved on from fashion and domestic themes to addressing questions of female emancipation. By the Edwardian period, newspapers such as the *Western Mail*, the *North Wales Chronicle*, the *North Wales Observer* and the *Holyhead Chronicle* carried regular 'suffrage news'.

Edwardian suffragettes, justifying the case for militancy, looked back disparagingly to the state of the campaign in the late nineteenth century. The 2nd Viscountess Rhondda, who, as Margaret Mackworth, was one of Wales's foremost militants, wrote thus:

> After 1884, when the third Reform Bill passed without including votes for women among its provisions, something like a lethargy of despair seemed to settle on a great number of the British suffragists, and the movement died down for sixteen or seventeen years. It was still in a slough of despond in 1900.[102]

To Rachel Barrett, an even more prominent Welsh activist, 'between 1884 and about 1905 and 1906, there was little heard of the movement at all'.[103] Certainly there were serious divisions within organized suffragism during this period, and a sharp decline in the annual income of the various societies reflected the difficulties. At the same time, the advancement of the cause through new and indirect channels – most notably through party organizations, local government and the temperance and cooperative movements – testified to the variety and complexity of the women's suffrage movement in the 1890s. There was also significant parliamentary progress, the voting on Faithfull Begg's bill of 1897 indicating a majority in support of the general principle of women's enfranchisement. Wales, as we have seen, shared in these experiences and, at successive elections in 1892, 1895 and 1900, returned clear suffragist majorities; of a total of thirty-four MPs, sixteen voted in favour of the 1897 bill and only three against.[104]

---

[102] Viscountess Rhondda, 'The political awakening of women', in *These Eventful Years: The Twentieth Century in the Making, II* (Encyclopaedia Britannica, 1924), 559.

[103] *Free Press of Monmouthshire*, 23 February 1912.

[104] *Parl. Deb.*, 4th ser., 45, cols 1235–6, 3 February 1897.

The women's suffrage cause had thus come a long way during the thirty years since the pioneering amendment of John Stuart Mill in 1867. But translating the sympathy and broad endorsement of MPs into precise legislation involved overcoming an array of practical problems, not least that of party calculations. 'There can be no doubt that the battle against exclusion is won', wrote John Gibson in 1893, 'and the question now is only one of parliamentary expediency inside the House of Commons and pertinacity by women outside.' [105] The political obstacles, however, were to prove far more intractable than he could have envisaged, particularly given the development of the kind of fervent mass women's movement he had long been advocating.

The latter slowly emerged from the healing of the divisions that had dogged the movement from the late 1880s. Following the cooperation which had occurred over the 'Special Appeal' petition and other activities in the mid 1890s, the two main branches, the CNSWS and the CCNSWS, moved closer together and in October 1897 the National Union of Women's Suffrage Societies (NUWSS) was formally constituted, bringing into federation some seventeen regional and local associations in order 'to promote joint action in Parliament and in the country'. Seeking to heal the divisions of the past, its sole aim stipulated attainment of the parliamentary franchise for women (which prevented inclusion of both the Women's Franchise League and the Women's Emancipation Union in the NUWSS, for each had objects wider than the vote, and were unwilling to abandon them), while it was also agreed that member societies were to be strictly neutral with regard to political parties.[106]

---

[105]   *CN*, 24 November 1893.

[106]   *Young Wales*, 1896, 294; *Calendar for 1898, with Women's Suffrage Directory* (Bristol and London, 1897), 25–33; *Woman's Signal*, 5 November 1896, 7 January 1897; *ER*, 15 January 1898; Leslie Parker Hume, *The National Union of Women's Suffrage Societies, 1897–1914* (New York, 1982), 4–6; Holton, *Suffrage Days*, 100. Another factor paving the way for reunification of the movement was the highly significant amendment to the Local Government Act of 1894, which made married women eligible to vote in all local elections in which single women and widows could do so. The divisive issue of coverture in relation to the suffrage debate was now effectively dead.

In time, this development was to prove of major significance. Initially, however, it did not represent a new departure, being no more than a loose federation in which the member societies acted independently. Moreover, tactics and strategy continued as before, with reliance on petitions, public meetings, letters to MPs, cooperation with parliamentary supporters and private member bills, in much the same way as the NSWS and earlier Victorian pressure groups like the Anti-Corn Law League and the Liberation Society had operated. At the turn of the century women's suffrage remained on the sidelines. New methods of agitation and pressure were required to compel the attention of politicians and the public, and indeed these were to be adopted during the course of the next decade. Above all, it was the militants of the Women's Social and Political Union (WSPU) who, from 1905, were to propel the entire movement into a totally new era.

II

THE WOMEN'S SOCIAL AND POLITICAL UNION, 1903–1914

The Women's Social and Political Union (WSPU) was founded by Mrs Emmeline Pankhurst at a small gathering of local women members of the Independent Labour Party (ILP) at her Manchester home in October 1903. For two years it remained a rather obscure body on the fringes of northern Labour politics, whereupon it burst into the national spotlight and for the next decade its increasing militancy awakened public consciousness, generated enormous publicity – out of all proportion to membership and support – and made 'votes for women' for the first time a central issue in British politics.

Throughout its existence the WSPU was under the domination of the Pankhurst family, principally Emmeline and Christabel, widow and eldest daughter respectively of Dr Richard Pankhurst, a radical Manchester barrister who, along with his wife, was active in a number of causes including the women's suffrage movement and, latterly, the fledgling ILP. It was increased impatience with Labour's commitment to women's suffrage in the years following Dr Pankhurst's death in 1898 which convinced Emmeline and Christabel of the need for 'a women's parallel to the ILP, though with primary emphasis on the vote'.[1] 'Mrs Pankhurst, and a few other women in earnest are starting a new crusade this year to force the Labour Party to work for women', observed one commentator. 'They feel that in the past women have been too apologetic for their existence, and too submissive.'[2] The adopted motto of 'Deeds Not Words' was a statement of vigorous intent and also, of course, implied criticism of the existing forty-year-old movement. Local branches offered variations of the motto. Thus, the splendid Newport banner –

---

[1] E. Sylvia Pankhurst, *The Suffragette Movement: An Intimate Account of Persons and Ideals* (London, 1988 edn), 168.
[2] *Clarion*, 1 January 1904.

green, embroidered with purple iris, white lilies (the three colours of the organization), a prisoner's arrow and prison bars – carried the inscription 'How Beggarly Appear Arguments Before a Defiant Deed'.

In aim, the WSPU was no different from the large number of other women's suffrage organizations which came into existence in the pre-war years – 'to secure for women the parliamentary vote as it is or may be granted to men'. What distinguished it was its high profile style and its increasingly militant method of campaigning, characteristics that earned members the notorious label 'suffragettes'. 'Put in a nutshell', wrote Margaret Mackworth,

> the policy of the new militant organization differed from that of the older body, the National Union of Women's Suffrage Societies, in that instead of asking gently for help, accepting the crumbs offered ... it *demanded* a Government measure, and made it clear from the start that it intended to bring what pressure might be necessary to bear upon the Government to accede to its demand.[3]

WSPU militancy began with an impromptu protest meeting outside Parliament following the talking out of the Women's Enfranchisement Bill in May 1905. More famously, Christabel Pankhurst and Annie Kenney, a twenty-six-year-old northern 'factory girl' and a devotee of the former, interrupted a major Liberal Party meeting in Manchester the following October and were subsequently charged with disorderly behaviour and obstruction and, in Christabel's case, of assault. Refusing to pay fines, they were sentenced to several days in prison and, precisely as planned, made headline news.[4] These were the first two suffragette imprisonments; over a thousand others – including about twenty women from Wales, or with strong Welsh connections, and one Welsh man – were to follow during the course of the next decade.[5]

---

[3] Rhondda, 'The political awakening of women', 560.

[4] Andrew Rosen, *Rise Up, Women! The Militant Campaign of the Women's Social and Political Union, 1903–1914* (London, 1978), 49–52; June Purvis, *Emmeline Pankhurst: A Biography* (London, 2002), 72–6.

[5] Home Office files listed the names of 1,333 persons (1,224 women and 108 men) arrested between 1906 and 1914 for offences committed in support of the cause (some of whom were discharged). National Archives (NA), Home Office

Within a few weeks, Mrs Pankhurst was visiting ILP branches in south Wales and making 'Why two women went to prison for the vote' a central theme of her addresses. At both Cardiff and Barry, she explained that 'they were determined, as women, to make themselves so much of a nuisance, to do away with which, men would have to allow them the opportunities of helping to frame the country's laws – they must forget being ladylike'.[6] A short time later, again in Cardiff, Annie Kenney delivered the same message: 'They were going to agitate and continually remind MPs of women's suffrage ... and force the hand of legislators, until at last they would cry "For Heaven's sake give these women votes".'[7]

Indeed, in the recent general election of January 1906, members of the Cardiff Women's ILP branch had implemented this strategy locally by heckling the anti-suffragist Liberal candidate, Ivor Guest.[8] In Wales, as in Britain as a whole, however, the question of women's suffrage rarely appeared in election addresses or emerged in the contests, though Mrs Pankhurst and Annie Kenney were active at Merthyr in support of Keir Hardie, a staunch ally of both the cause and the WSPU. 'Mr Hardie was always very kind to us in those early stormy days, when we were looked upon either as mad or as outcasts' recalled Annie Kenney in her autobiography. 'He sheltered us when no other public person would have dared.'[9]

More WSPU representatives came to Wales later in the year seeking to generate support through speaking engagements and other propaganda work. As elsewhere in these years, ILP branches often supplied the public platforms and it was their female members who tended to be the early WSPU activists in

Papers (HO) 45/24665, suffragettes: amnesty of August 1914, index of names of persons arrested, 1906–1914.
    [6] *CT*, 11 November 1905; *Barry Dock News*, 17 November 1905; *Labour Leader*, 3, 17 November 1905; Purvis, *Emmeline Pankhurst*, 77.
    [7] *CT*, 27 January 1906.
    [8] *WM*, 2 January 1906; *Labour Leader*, 12 January 1906.
    [9] Annie Kenney, *Memories of a Militant* (1924), 48. For WSPU participation in the Merthyr election, see ibid., 55–6; Antonia Raeburn, *The Militant Suffragettes* (London, 1972), 11; *Merthyr Express*, 20, 27 January 1906; *Aberdare Leader*, 20, 27 January 1906; *Labour Leader*, 26 January 1906; *CT*, 27 January 1906. Local Labour women and suffrage activists also worked for Hardie's return. *Labour Leader*, 27 April 1906.

south Wales.[10] Indeed, for much of the first four years of its existence, the WSPU aimed to arouse enthusiasm for women's suffrage within the labour movement. Certainly it became an intensely debated issue, but the Labour Party's continuing preference for adult suffrage, over removal of the sex discrimination in the existing property-based franchise, brought increasingly strained relations and, eventually, in the autumn of 1907 a split between the two, with Mrs Pankhurst and Christabel resigning from the ILP.

It was in support of an anticipated Labour candidature in the Mid Glamorgan by-election of October 1906 that the WSPU made its most dramatic early impact in Wales. This was occasioned by the sitting Liberal member, Samuel Evans, seeking re-election following acceptance of a minor government office, as was then the legal requirement. Evans was actively opposed by leading suffragettes on this occasion for two reasons: first, he represented a Liberal government, which was refusing to grant women the right to vote and, secondly, because of his recent personal conduct on the issue. The latter related to Evans's role in 'talking out' Keir Hardie's women's suffrage resolution in the House of Commons in April 1906, when his deliberately protracted speech ensured that there was no time for a division. WSPU members seated in the ladies' gallery became so incensed that they interrupted proceedings and were forcibly removed.[11]

Accordingly, when the Mid Glamorgan by-election occurred a few months later, the WSPU was determined on retribution. Even though a Labour challenge did not ultimately materialize and no contest took place, Mrs Pankhurst and others addressed meetings throughout the constituency in order to attack Evans and to publicize the movement. The most lively events occurred in Maesteg where WSPU organizer, Mary Gawthorpe, an ILP activist from Leeds, brought chaos to two of Evans's meetings, local newspapers giving detailed coverage under the headlines of 'Uproarious Scenes', 'Pandemonium',

[10] By October 1905 the South Wales ILP Federation had 34 branches, two of which were women's branches – at Cardiff and Swansea. *CT*, 4 October 1905. Elsewhere, women formed a significant minority in some localities, and sometimes formed separate sections.

[11] *Parl. Deb.*, 4th ser., 155, cols 1582–4, 1586, 25 April 1906.

'Suffragette Vengeance', 'Member Prevented from Speaking' and 'Police Intervention'.[12]

The impact of the WSPU in south Wales was further increased by the considerable publicity given to the first suffragettes from the region to serve terms of imprisonment for the cause in late 1906 and early 1907. As yet, north, central and west Wales remained untouched. During this same period, national organizers – Mary Gawthorpe, Adela Pankhurst (the youngest of the daughters) and others – continued to spend time in the south-east, aiming to generate broad sympathy, attract committed individuals and establish branch associations in order to give a permanence to local agitation. The *First Annual Report* of the WSPU, published in late February 1907 and recording a total increase from just three branches to fifty-eight over the year, listed two in Wales – at Cardiff and at Ton-du. The latter was evidently set up in the wake of the Mid Glamorgan by-election, along with another at nearby Maesteg; though Maesteg claimed as many as sixty members in March 1907, neither appears to have proved enduring.[13] The Cardiff branch, on the other hand, certainly did, operating continuously from its formation in 1906 until the cessation of the WSPU campaign on the outbreak of the First World War in August 1914, though it did suffer from the serious WSPU split in the autumn of 1907. Personality clashes and the desire for internal democracy, rather than the autocratic style of leadership insisted upon by the Pankhursts, led to a number of prominent figures on the national executive breaking away to form a new society, the Women's Freedom League.

Following the split, the WSPU tightened its discipline and aimed at a more comprehensive national organization. Wales

[12]   *SWDN*, 1, 6, 9, 10 October 1906; *WM*, 24, 26, 27 September, 1, 5, 6, 11 October 1906; *Chronicle for Mid and South Glamorgan*, 28 September, 5, 12 October 1906; *Glamorgan Gazette*, 12 October 1906; *Labour Record and Review*, October 1906; Mary Gawthorpe, *Up Hill to Holloway* (Penobscot, Maine, 1962), 232–5; Emmeline Pankhurst, *My Own Story* (1914), 74; WL, Teresa Billington-Greig Papers, 397/ A6 and 398/ B7. See also below, 64–5, 134–5. For Mary Gawthorpe, see Crawford, *Women Suffrage Movement*, 242–4; Sandra Stanley Holton, 'Gawthorpe, Mary Eleanor (1881–1973)', *ODNB*; Keith Gildart and David Howell (eds), *Dictionary of Labour Biography*, XII (Basingstoke, 2005), 102–6.
[13]   WSPU, *Annual Report*, 1906–7, 3; *Glamorgan Gazette*, 22 March 1907; *South Wales Echo*, 21 March 1907.

was designated part of the west of England region under the direction of Annie Kenney, who, with volunteer workers from Bristol and Bath, gave particular attention to Cardiff and Newport in the summer of 1909; in September, two representatives, Elsie McKenzie and Gabrielle Jeffrey, were placed in temporary charge of the Cardiff and Newport districts respectively. With the expansion of the strategy of regional centres, Wales was given its own permanent organizer early in 1910, the choice being Rachel Barrett, a former Penarth teacher and now an experienced WSPU activist. Again, the bulk of her work focused on the south-east, though during the summer of 1910 she campaigned in Lloyd George's Caernarfonshire heartland and at the end of the year participated in general election activity in Denbighshire. Her transfer to the London headquarters in April 1912 brought hurried arrangements for an immediate replacement. In June 1912, Annie Williams, a former teacher and headmistress from Cornwall, who had previously served as organizer in Newcastle, Huddersfield and Halifax, took up the Welsh post, which she held until the outbreak of war.[14]

Although suffragette militancy naturally attracted the bulk of its publicity, the WSPU also had a highly significant educational and propaganda dimension. Most obviously, hundreds of public meetings were held throughout Wales, as well as many smaller private gatherings, 'at homes', where speeches were delivered by prominent national figures or by local leaders. Mrs Pankhurst toured Wales on a number of occasions and her fame usually guaranteed large audiences. Beyond the meetings organized in local halls, speakers were often to be found standing at works' entrances, dockyard gates and on street corners or using makeshift platforms in town and village squares, in all kinds of weather. Advertising was, at best, by posters and handbills, sometimes by women clad in sandwich boards, and at shorter notice by employing the local bell-ringer or by chalking pavements, a commonly used method and a cheap and effective one.

---

[14]   VW, 2 July 1910; A. J. R., *Suffrage Annual*, 396; Crawford, *Women's Suffrage Movement*, 710.

The holiday season was important for campaigning. Each August, suffragettes descended on the seaside resorts of north and west Wales, convening meetings on the beaches or promenades. Here, more eye-catching methods of advertising and propaganda were sometimes adopted – parades with parasols or umbrellas decorated with inscriptions, for example; a decorated 'votes for women boat' attracted much interest at the annual Caernarfon regatta in August 1910. Some of the Welsh holiday campaigns ventured inland too – to spa towns like Llandrindod Wells, into Snowdonia and even to the Rhondda. The latter offered, Wales organizer Annie Williams maintained, 'a unique opportunity for coming into touch with the typical Welsh collier and his surroundings' and for combining hours of strenuous suffrage work – canvassing, newspaper selling and meetings in 'crowded, growing valley towns' – with 'time for hill climbing, for enjoying the wide views of hill and dale, and for drinking in life-giving air'. Moreover, 'historic Tonypandy' could hardly 'object to militant methods!'[15]

By 1913–14 suffragettes employed more dramatic means of enlightening the public – speaking in crowded restaurants or theatres, showering theatre audiences with handbills, or interrupting church services by bursting into prayer for imprisoned comrades. A typical rendering of the latter, delivered at St Luke's Church, Newport, in March 1914, ran: 'Oh, God, we Beseech Thee, save Thy Servant, Emmeline Pankhurst, and all who are persecuted for conscience sake. Open the eyes of Thy Church, that it may protest against this torture in prison …'[16] Suffragettes frequently recited their own version of the Creed.

Use of the written word was, of course, an important propaganda method. One aim was to get as much coverage as possible in the national and provincial press through reports of activities, articles and letters. Another was wide circulation of the WSPU's own newspapers – *Votes For Women* (1907–12), *The Suffragette* (1912–15) and finally *Britannia* (1915–18).

---

[15]   *VW*, 19 August 1910; *The Suffragette*, 1, 15 August 1913.
[16]   *The Suffragette*, 13 March 1914. See also ibid., 21, 28 November, 5, 19 December 1913, 23, 30 January, 6, 20, 27 February, 6, 20 March, 3, 17 April, 22 May, 17 July 1914; *WM*, 22 December 1913, 16 January, 16 February, 6 April, 12 May, 8 June 1914.

Sympathizers were encouraged to place weekly orders but much of the selling was done in the streets or outside public gatherings. Each year, nationally, there was a week set aside for a newspaper sales drive, when local members were expected to concentrate their energies and imagination on winning readers. 'Football crowds, theatre queues, audiences going into public meetings and picture palaces, as well as the man in the street, have all been made aware of the existence of *The Suffragette* and 500 copies ordered were sold out before the end of the week', trumpeted the Cardiff WSPU branch in May 1914. Leaflets specifically directed towards Wales, some in the Welsh language, were also published by headquarters.[17]

There was also an annual 'Self-Denial Week' when members gave up some form of regular expenditure and donated the money saved to the union's national coffers (the 'war-chest'). Fund-raising was, of course, an all-year-round activity, part of which was done through membership subscriptions and donations. In Wales, Sybil Thomas and Margaret Mackworth, wife and daughter respectively of D. A. Thomas, Liberal MP and the great coal magnate, were particularly generous benefactors, the former donating £740 to WSPU funds during the years 1908–14 and the latter almost £100 in the same period.[18] There was also continuous local fund-raising through such means as jumble sales, street flower selling, garden fetes and fairs, whist drives and varied social events, while some income came simply from collections at the close of meetings. From time to time the WSPU held large fund-raising events in London – the Women's Exhibition of May 1909 and the Christmas Fair of December 1911, for example – and Welsh localities gave support to these.

Welsh contingents also participated in the big WSPU demonstrations in London, the first of which, 'Women's Sunday', took place on 21 June 1908. In south Wales, national representatives led an intensive public meeting programme, centring on Cardiff and Newport, in order to drum up support. Participants were then conveyed by special trains to

---

[17]   *The Suffragette*, 8 May 1913; WSPU, *Annual Report*, 1912, 5.
[18]   WSPU, *Annual Reports*, 1908–14. During the last financial year, 1 March 1913–28 February 1914, when the militant campaign was at its height, Sybil Thomas donated £324, the fifth largest single contribution.

Paddington, whence they marched in orderly procession to Hyde Park. Here speakers addressed the crowds from twenty platforms. Hugely impressed by the whole event, the *Western Mail* spoke of 'a demonstration unparalleled in the history of British politics', its reporter accompanying the 'Welsh Section' continuing thus:

> In a fairly long journalistic career Sunday's demonstration in London was infinitely the most impressive event, the most inspiring spectacle of which I have been a spectator. Those responsible for the organisation anticipated that about 250 suffragists and sympathisers would journey up to London from South Wales. In reality 365 persons travelled by the train, which when it left Cardiff Station at half-past nine reached from one end of the platform to the other ... When the train drew up at Paddington Station the South Walians were quickly taken into hand by processional marshals, and they formed up at the station exit. Quite befitting was it that the Cardiff contingent took the lead, and no time was lost in unfurling their pretty green banner, on which was the following Welsh motto, 'Ein Hachos yn Erbyn y Byd' ('Our Cause Against the World'). There was another green silk banner from Cardiff, which simply bore the name of the city in large letters. The Newport banner was of purple silk, and bore no inscription except the name of the town ... Dense crowds of people lined the route along which the Welsh ladies passed ... But the scene in the park! One's pen utterly fails to describe it ... In my view there was an average of 10,000 around each platform, making 200,000 in all, and that there were another quarter of a million who could not hear the speeches. Generally I found afterwards the estimated total attendance was half a million. Really, instead of twenty platforms and 80 speakers, there should have been 80 platforms and 300 speakers.[19]

Other such demonstrations took place in succeeding years, the Newport and Cardiff societies always offering the most enthusiastic support from Wales. A number of Welsh suffragettes also played a prominent part in the events themselves, acting as platform speakers on several occasions. These included Rachel Barrett, Helena Jones, a north Walian doctor of medicine, and a prominent London activist, Edith Mansell Moullin, the wife of a leading surgeon, himself a suffrage activist.[20]

---

[19]   *WM*, 22 June 1908. See also *CT*, 27 June 1908.
[20]   See *VW*, 7 May 1908, 22 July 1910.

Born Edith Thomas, of Welsh parents, the latter played an important role in rousing support for the cause among Welsh women in London from the time of the Women's Coronation Procession of June 1911. Seeking to rival the official coronation procession of George V, this was the most spectacular of the demonstrations of the pre-war years and, though the initiative came from the WSPU, all the suffragist societies, twenty-eight in total, actually participated. There were hundreds of different sections involved in this march of 40,000 women but especially striking were the Prisoners' Pageant, the Historical Pageant and the Pageant of Empire. The latter drew on all the features of national identity from around the British Empire that could be mobilized, an aspiration to which the Welsh contingent, organized by Edith Mansell Moullin, gave wholehearted support.[21] Thus, much insistence was placed on the wearing of national costume, singing Welsh-language hymns and carrying red dragons on poles. There were pleas too for a harpist, for a bard and, pushing the nationality theme to the limit, for someone to escort a Welsh goat in the procession. *Votes for Women* carried the following appeal: 'The organiser has had the offer of a real Welsh goat from the Rev. Evan [*sic*] Davies, of Llandrillo, and wants some kind friend to write immediately saying she (or he) will meet the goat at Paddington Station on the 16th, and will stable and feed it, and lead it in the Procession ... The last request is for a Welsh bard. Will some kind friend offer to wear this picturesque costume, and walk in front of the choir?' Numerical support was assured by considerable advance publicity in the suffragist press and, in London itself, by means of posters and handbills distributed throughout the Welsh chapels. The wives of several Welsh MPs, heading supporters of the different suffragist societies and members of the Cardiff Progressive Liberal Women's Union, added to the publicity success of the contingent.[22]

[21]   See Lisa Tickner, *The Spectacle of Women: Imagery of the Suffrage Campaign* (London, 1987), 122–31. For Edith Mansell Moullin, see Angela V. John, 'Moullin, Edith Ruth Mansell (1858/9–1941)', *ODNB*; eadem, 'A draft of fresh air', 85–91; eadem, '"Run like blazes"', 35–41.
[22]   *VfW*, 2, 9 June 1911; *SWDN*, 16, 19 June 1911; *South Wales Argus*, 19 June 1911. See also below, 125, 147–8.

The triumph of the enterprise inspired Edith Mansell Moullin to initiate a separate Welsh society. Launched as the Cymric Suffrage Union (CSU) in July 1911, it invited support from all shades of opinion and aimed for branches throughout Wales and among the Welsh communities of English towns and cities. From time to time, campaigns were indeed conducted in various parts of Wales, with a particular emphasis on generating interest in the Welsh-speaking areas by means of public meetings, translated literature and use of the Welsh press; as a result, some local societies were formed. There was certainly one in the Bala-Corwen district of Merioneth, the Penllyn and Edeyrnion branch, in which Revd Ivan Davies of Llandrillo was the principal activist. It was he who undertook much of the translation of pamphlets and speeches and ensured coverage of the movement in Welsh-language newspapers like *Baner ac Amserau Cymru* and *Seren Cymru*.[23] In the south, an Ogmore Vale branch was founded with Fannie Margaret Thomas, a Pontycymer elementary school headmistress, as secretary and leading light. Essentially, though, the CSU operated as a London organization, strenuously carrying out propaganda amongst the many thousands of Welsh inhabitants in the capital, canvassing concerts, lectures, chapels and places of work. The strong theme of Welshness established at the Women's Coronation Procession remained ever present; 'the whole atmosphere was thoroughly Welsh, from the stewards in their native costume to the singing of the National Anthem in Welsh', ran the report of the union's first public meeting in March 1912.[24]

The CSU was originally formed for propaganda work only. Frustration with the Liberal government's prevarication over women's suffrage, however, led to a growing feeling that 'a continuation of educational methods alone would not only be useless but a menace to the cause of Woman Suffrage' and in October 1912 the union resolved 'to oppose this or any Government which refuses the Vote to Women'. Failure to win unanimous support for this radical new departure

---

[23]   For Revd Ivan Thomas Davies, see A. J. R., *Suffrage Annual*, 219–20; John, 'A draft of fresh air', 87. See also *Seren*, 22 Mawrth, 4, 11 Mai 1912.

[24]   *The Vote*, 23 March 1912.

induced the chief advocates of that view, Edith Mansell Moullin, Mary Davies and Ellen Norbury, the union's key officials, to found a rival body, the Forward Cymric Suffrage Union (FCSU); thereafter, the original society ceased to function, while the new one carried on a lively and continuous agitation well into the war years.[25]

One of the FCSU's first public displays was in leading Welsh tributes at the funeral of the 'Epsom Downs' Martyr', Emily Davison, in June 1913. Sympathizers travelled from Wales to join London activists in making up a separate 'Welsh section' in the huge procession that followed the hearse. At the head was the union's red dragon banner carrying the society's motto, 'O Iesu, na'd gamwaith' ('O Jesus, do not allow injustice'), a wreath in the shape of a harp of red roses and evergreens bore the inscriptions 'Hiraeth' ('longing' or 'yearning') and 'Cariad mwy na hyn nid oes' ('There is no greater love than this'), and members of the party, dressed in either black or white, carried white lilies or sprays of mauve irises; they sang a number of Welsh hymns outside the church in Russell Square.[26]

During 1913 and 1914 the union and its red dragon banners and badges featured prominently in the metropolitan suffrage campaign, public meetings and processions being frequently used to denounce government policy. As the foremost Welshman in the administration, Lloyd George was the focus of much of the disillusionment. Indeed, one of the union's earliest resolutions blamed him personally for the violent public reaction to interruptions of his speeches at the National Eisteddfod in Wrexham and at Llanystumdwy in September 1912.[27] The FCSU later called for his resignation, while his repeated refusal to meet a deputation of members induced one member, Margaret Llewhellin, to protest by breaking windows in Downing Street, for which she served one month's imprisonment.[28] Attempts were also made to wake up organized religion to its 'responsibilities' by

[25]   Ibid., 19 October, 9 November 1912; *The Suffragette*, 18 October 1912.
[26]   *WM*, 16 June 1913; *CT*, 21 June 1913.
[27]   *The Suffragette*, 18 October 1912; *The Vote*, 19 October 1912.
[28]   *The Suffragette*, 28 March, 4 April 1913; *VW*, 4 April 1913; *WM*, 8 April 1913. Edith Mansell Moullin had served five days in prison in late 1911 for obstruction.

interrupting services, while leading figures defended militancy from the public platform.

During 1914 the union also worked in cooperation with the East London Federation of Suffragettes (ELFS), Sylvia Pankhurst's initiative to rouse and direct the support of working-class women. The mainspring was again Edith Mansell Moullin, who had long experience of work among the poor of south and east London, and was active in the settlement movement, the Anti-Sweating League, the Christian Socialist Union and the Christian Socialist League; 'then I gave it all up and joined the WSPU' (though she resigned in 1913).[29] In the months before the outbreak of war, she led the FCSU on a number of occasions in joint procession with the ELFS 'from the poorest parts of East London, praying for the power to get better conditions for the destitute and starving'.[30] One of the Welsh society's last pre-war public meetings aimed to pressurize the prime minister, Herbert Asquith, into receiving a suffrage deputation from working women.

By-elections and general elections offered clear opportunities to influence politicians and the WSPU campaigned in a number of Welsh constituencies over the years. In Mid Glamorgan in October 1906, its early Labour affiliations were apparent in opposition to the Liberal incumbent, Samuel Evans. In the scattered industrial communities of the Mid Glamorgan constituency, ILP officials were invariably the first point of contact for WSPU representatives and they helped to organize meetings and print and distribute handbills, while local women Labour activists spoke on suffragette platforms. Moreover, the WSPU was evidently keen to support a Labour challenge, to the extent of lobbying miners' leaders to this effect. The South Wales Miners' Federation executive, however, stuck to its decision not to put up a candidate, leaving Mrs Pankhurst 'disgusted and angry'.[31] Evans was even-

---

[29] *VW*, 22 July 1910; Museum of London, Suffragette Fellowship Collection (SFC), 57. 116/ 79, Edith Mansell Moullin to Edith How Martyn, 6 September 1935; Ann Morley with Liz Stanley, *The Life and Death of Emily Wilding Davison* (1988), 121–3.

[30] *Woman's Dreadnought*, 28 March 1914.

[31] Diary of Alice Milne, secretary, Manchester WSPU, 24 September–3 October 1906, WL, Teresa Billington-Greig Papers, 397/ A6 and 398/ B7.

tually returned unopposed, though the suffragettes could certainly claim a vigorous propaganda campaign in virgin territory.

The same can be said of the Pembrokeshire by-election of July 1908, a contest which clearly displayed the problems arising from the WSPU's policy of opposing all government candidates, whether supporters of women's suffrage or not. In a sustained campaign lasting several weeks, Mrs Pankhurst and her co-workers systematically covered every corner of the county, holding dozens of meetings in the towns, the fishing villages and in the scattered rural communities, even tackling small groups in the hayfields and at the roadside. Much of the attention was no doubt aroused by curiosity, by 'the opportunity of meeting the far-famed Suffragettes face to face'. Hostility was sometimes vehemently exhibited; Annie Kenney recalled how some antagonists 'threw dirt and grass-sods and an egg came flying and caught me on the side of the face and broke'. But generally speakers appear to have been given a reasonable hearing, with their oratory, enthusiasm and earnestness clearly impressing much of the local press. Accordingly, a good deal of valuable propaganda and educational work was carried out in an area previously untouched by the women's movement. On the other hand, a large proportion of the campaign was spent in defending a policy of opposing the ardent suffragist Liberal candidate, Walter Roch, a Cardigan solicitor who was actually a member of the Men's League for Women's Suffrage. Critics insisted that the stance was utterly illogical, 'woefully misguided', and, in allying themselves 'with the Brewers and all the reactionary forces in British politics', the WSPU was actually 'alienating the sympathy of scores of Liberals' in the constituency. Mrs Pankhurst's argument that a government defeat in 'a Welsh stronghold' would make 'Mr Asquith and his Cabinet . . . realise the insecurity of their position of blind resistance to the just demands of women' proved unpersuasive, particularly in a country where allegiance to the Liberal Party ran deep, and she had great difficulty in trying to make the electors 'understand how they could possibly advance the cause of Liberty and Reform by voting against the Liberal candidate'. For there were, of course, other election issues and a Liberal defeat could be interpreted as 'evidence that Wales was at last wavering on the question of disestablishment, hostile to temperance reform, opposed to the Education Bill and the Pembrokeshire electorate did not want its aged and outworn workers to receive decent sustenance at the hands of the State'. The eventual outcome was a comfortable Liberal victory over the Conservative contender, but with a reduced majority, of just over a thousand votes, in a higher turnout than at the previous election in 1906. Predictably, the WSPU claimed much of the credit; in reality its influence on the actual voting is impossible to assess.[32]

The WSPU's anti-government policy was strenuously put into operation in other Welsh by-elections too. In Mid Glamorgan in March 1910, Mrs Pankhurst, Emily Davison, Rachel Barrett and others campaigned against the victorious Liberal candidate, F. W. Gibbins, in a straight fight with Labour's Vernon Hartshorn, miners' agent for Maesteg district. Little impression was made on the poll but again a good deal of propaganda was carried out through the circulation of newspapers and the holding of indoor and outdoor meetings throughout the constituency; in the outlying villages, speakers who addressed audiences from a touring waggonette, decorated in the purple, white and green of the union, generated considerable interest.[33]

In January 1912, Carmarthen Boroughs was the focus of another unsuccessful WSPU effort to 'keep the Liberal out', though Llewellyn Williams was re-elected. After the poll, the union could point to a reduced Liberal majority and claim this as evidence that it was 'damaging the position of government candidates', but essentially its role was again a publicity one. Mrs Pankhurst, Annie Kenney, Rachel Barrett and other speakers addressed many meetings in Carmarthen and Llanelli, and often drew large crowds and a good deal of press

---

[32]   *Haverfordwest and Milford Haven Telegraph*, 1, 15 July 1908; *Fishguard, Goodwick and County Times*, 9 July 1908; *Cardigan and Tivyside Advertiser*, 9, 16 July 1916; *Women's Franchise* (*WF*), 9 July 1908; *VW*, 16, 23 July 1908; Gloucestershire Record Office, diary of Mary Blathwayt, 4, 5, 6, 7, 8 July 1908, and additional notes, 9, 10, 12, 13 July 1908; John, 'Chwarae Teg', 7–8. See also below, 121, 137–8.

[33]   *VW*, 29 March, 1, 8 April 1910; *Glamorgan Gazette*, 1 April 1910. See also below, 123.

comment. Two WSPU branches also came into existence in these towns shortly afterwards.[34]

Given the limited nature of WSPU resources, general election activity in Wales was largely confined to the questioning of candidates at their meetings. There were a few exceptions, as in Merthyr Tydfil in 1906 when suffragette leaders worked on behalf of Keir Hardie. In January 1910, activists held meetings in the various towns of the North Monmouthshire constituency in opposition to Reginald McKenna, while, in December, Welsh organizer Rachel Barrett spent her time campaigning in the Denbigh Boroughs constituency. Here, regular WSPU meetings in Wrexham, Ruthin and Denbigh and the widespread distribution of posters, handbills, leaflets and other literature (some in the Welsh language) brought 'votes for women' before the public. The Conservative incumbent, William Ormsby-Gore, gave support in his election address and in public speeches, while the Liberal candidate, G. Caradog Rees, evaded the issue. Accordingly, the WSPU heralded its campaign a success, Denbigh being 'held against the Liberal onslaught by 9 votes'.[35]

Full-time national speakers and organizers directed the election campaigns, local activists and sympathizers providing assistance. The WSPU attracted individual members from many parts of Wales. At best, this support was consolidated into branch associations, though Wales produced only a small number of these. Those at Cardiff, Newport, Pontypool and Barry were particularly strong, with their own offices and shops; elsewhere, in spite of claimed branches in places like Caernarfon, Carmarthen, Maesteg and Ton-du, organization achieved little permanence. Branch activity largely revolved around propaganda work and fund-raising. Stalwarts were regularly to be seen selling their *Votes For Women* or *The Suffragette* in the streets, especially on Saturday mornings and on market days, and outside theatres, conference halls and

---

[34]   *VW*, 12, 19, 26 January, 2 February 1912; *South Wales Daily Post* (*SWDP*), 13, 15, 16, 22 January 1912; *Llanelly and County Guardian*, 18, 25 January, 7 March 1912; *Llanelly Mercury*, 25 January 1912; *Carmarthen Journal*, 19, 26 January 1912; *Carmarthen Weekly Reporter*, 26 January 1912; *The Welshman*, 21 June 1912; *Cambrian*, 19, 26 January 1912. See also below, 208.
[35]   *VW*, 9, 16 December 1910; *Wrexham Advertiser*, 10 December 1910.

other public places, while newsagents and libraries were regularly pressed into giving support. The rented branch shop
naturally offered a variety of literature (for sale or on loan to
members), and also all sorts of other items too – badges,
buttons, postcards, tea, soap, cigarettes, chocolates and much
more – all carrying the 'votes for women' message and the
WSPU colours. The continual arrangement of meetings was, of
course, essential for recruiting members and attracting
support. Most often, there were the small 'at homes', usually
involving a short address, discussion, musical or recitational
entertainment and refreshment. A popular medium was the
lantern lecture, photographs of suffragette leaders and events
such as London demonstrations, arrests, trials and fund-raising
activities serving vividly to portray the militant campaign. The
larger public meetings required a good deal of organization –
hire of hall, advertising, selling of tickets, stewarding and such
like. Well-known national figures often addressed these but
there was also a role for local activists – acting as chairwomen,
proposing and seconding resolutions and giving votes of
thanks. Branch meetings sometimes offered practice both in
public speaking and in dealing with opposition. For maximum
publicity, it was important to follow up meetings and other
activities with reports to the local press. Fund-raising, taking all
manner of forms, was constantly needed to meet local
expenses and to make contributions to the central coffers.

Much, of course, depended on the commitment and zeal of
individuals, serving as branch officials or simply as isolated
supporters selling newspapers in smaller towns like
Montgomery and Llanwrtyd Wells. Indeed, some found a real
purpose in their lives for the first time. 'The militant suffrage
movement was a thrilling discovery', recalled Margaret
Mackworth, providing an escape 'from the life of unoccupied
faculties and petty futility' that apparently stretched before
her. She elaborated thus:

> One sometimes hears people who took part in the suffrage campaign
> pitied ... But for me, and for many other young women like me, mili-
> tant suffrage was the very salt of life. The knowledge of it had come like
> a draught of fresh air into our padded, stifled lives. It gave us release of
> energy, it gave us that sense of being of some use in the scheme of
> things ... It made us feel that we were part of life, not just outside

watching it. It made us feel that we had a real purpose and use apart
from having children ... It gave us hope of freedom and power and
opportunity. It gave us scope at last, and it gave us what normal healthy
use craves – adventure and excitement.[36]

Some discovered hidden abilities and characteristics. Elsie
McKenzie wrote thus to a friend in October 1909, shortly after
becoming WSPU organizer in Cardiff:

We are doing extremely well in South Wales. I spoke at a meeting in
Barry yesterday (Sat.) to a most enthusiastic audience of men and
women. They begged me to stand on my chair, so they may see my face.
I must have spoken for two hours. A resolution was passed in favour and
a vote of thanks given on my behalf. I was asked to come again. I do not
know what is happening to me. I seem to be changed into somebody
else. I never thought I could write articles, confound politics on a public
platform etc. It is all very strange to me when I do stop to think.
However, the latter is very seldom.[37]

Women's suffrage came to consume the existence of many
women and of no Welsh woman was this more true than of
Rachel Barrett, who dedicated almost a decade of her life to
the cause. Like so many activists, Rachel was from a middle-
class background, her father being a land surveyor and
engineer. Brought up in a Welsh-speaking home in Carmarthenshire, she was educated at boarding school in Stroud and
then at the University College of Wales, Aberystwyth, before
joining the teaching profession. It was while working in
Penarth that she came in contact with the WSPU as it made its
first inroads in south Wales in 1906. She joined up and in the
spring of 1907 assisted Adela Pankhurst when she came to
Cardiff as WSPU organizer. Rachel then became a regular
speaker at local meetings, much to the displeasure of her
headmistress who did not believe that women should indulge
in such public activity and who was particularly disturbed to
read in the local newspaper that her science mistress had
been drenched with flour at an open-air meeting in Cardiff
docks!
    Resigning her teaching post in 1907, Rachel briefly divided
her energies between suffrage work and study at the London

School of Economics, but by early 1908 she had accepted Christabel Pankhurst's invitation to become a full-time WSPU organizer: 'it was a definite call and I obeyed'. Based initially in Nottingham, she was also active in by-elections in various parts of the country. Indeed, so strenuously did she throw herself into the movement that within a year she had collapsed through exhaustion, needing a full year to recuperate and spending some time in a sanatorium. By late 1909, however, she was back in the fray, becoming chief organizer for Wales. For the next two and a half years she arranged innumerable meetings throughout Wales, spoke endlessly (often in Welsh), raised funds, directed and took part in protests, organized election campaigns and led deputations to MPs and ministers, most notably twice to Lloyd George in 1910. No individual worked harder than Rachel Barrett to promote the campaign in Wales. In the spring of 1912, following the police raid on WSPU headquarters in London and Christabel Pankhurst's escape to Paris, she was chosen by Annie Kenney to assist her in running the national campaign. Within a few months she was appointed assistant editor of *The Suffragette* on its launch in October 1912, and over the next two years she was one of the key figures in keeping the newspaper in print in the face of the home secretary's sustained efforts at suppression. Rachel Barrett thus reached the highest echelons of the WSPU but, with escalating militancy, it was an elevation that entailed considerable risks. When she went to France to consult with her absentee editor, she had to travel undercover and, whenever the two talked on the telephone, she recalled that she 'could always hear the click of Scotland Yard listening in'. Eventually, Rachel's position brought a conviction for conspiracy and imprisonment.[38]

Another suffragette of Welsh origins to achieve prominence in the movement was the Conwy-born Helena Jones,

[38]   SFC, 57.116/ 47, Rachel Barrett, *Draft Autobiography* (n.d.). The full text is reprinted in Aaron and Masson, *Very Salt of Life*, 298–302. Obituaries in *Women's Bulletin*, 18 September 1953; *Halstead Gazette*, 4 September 1953. Annie Kenney recalled her as 'an exceptionally clever and highly educated woman ... a devoted worker [with] tremendous admiration for Christabel. She was learned and I liked her.' Kenney, *Memories*, 179. For Rachel Barrett, see also Crawford, *Women's Suffrage Movement*, 35–6; Caroline Morrell, 'Barrett, Rachel (1874–1953)', *ODNB*. (I am indebted to Adrian Corder-Birch for the Halstead reference and for casting light on Rachel's later life.)

who, having qualified as a doctor, served as a medical officer in a number of different posts in England. An early Fabian, she became very active in the WSPU from its early years, organizing and speaking at meetings in various areas and on several occasions undertaking campaigns in north Wales. In the immediate pre-war years she appears to have sided with Emmeline and Frederick Pethick-Lawrence in their split with the Pankhursts in late 1912 and certainly worked for their Votes for Women Fellowship, which sought to maintain the circulation of the original suffragette newspaper.[39]

In Wales itself, the most striking figures were Margaret Mackworth and her mother, Sybil Thomas, daughter and wife respectively of D. A. Thomas, the great coalowner and one of the most prominent Liberals in Wales. The former joined the WSPU in the autumn of 1908, her consciousness having been aroused earlier in the year by the imprisonment of a cousin, Florence Haig, an artist based in Chelsea, and then by attendance at the 'Women's Sunday' demonstration in June. Thereafter, she threw herself passionately into the cause, 'speaking at rowdy street-corner meetings, selling papers in the gutter, walking clad in sandwich boards in processions', and writing letters and articles for the local press. She served as branch secretary at Newport, though her commitment to the cause also took her beyond the south-east Wales region to campaigning in London and other parts of England and in Scotland. The publication of an autobiography detailing her suffragette experiences, including arrest, imprisonment and a hunger strike, and her emergence after the war as one of Britain's leading feminists, has made Margaret Mackworth the best known of Welsh activists.[40] In fact, her mother was an equally significant figure in the women's suffrage movement.

[39]   *VW*, 7 May 1908, 22 July 1910, 10, 24 April 1914. Obituaries in *Daily Telegraph*, 9 September 1946; *Porth Gazette*, 14 September 1946; *Rhondda Leader*, 14 September 1946.
[40]   Rhondda, *This was My World*. Born Margaret Haig Thomas in 1883, she married a near neighbour, Humphrey Mackworth, a squire from Caerleon, in 1908, a few months before joining the WSPU. They divorced in 1923. On her father's death in July 1918 she became second Viscountess Rhondda, the first being her mother, Sybil. See Shirley M. Eoff, *Viscountess Rhondda: Egalitarian Feminist* (Columbus, Ohio, 1991); Crawford, *Women's Suffrage Movement*, 595–6; Deirdre Beddoe, 'Thomas, Margaret Haig, suo jure Viscountess Rhondda (1883–1958)', *ODNB*.

Involved from the late 1880s, Sybil Thomas was, from 1906, a firm supporter of the WSPU and its militant methods. The daughter of George Augustus Haig, a Radnorshire landowner, she was a member of a wider family with strong suffragist convictions. Three cousins, Florence, Evelyn and Cecilia Haig, daughters of a Berwickshire barrister, were all suffragettes, the first two being founders of the Scottish WSPU in Edinburgh in 1908; Evelyn was imprisoned once, Florence on three occasions, during which she also adopted the hunger strike. A sister, Janet Boyd, widow of a deputy lieutenant and high sheriff of Durham, also went to prison several times, while another sister, Charlotte Haig, was once arrested, to be discharged with a caution.[41] Sybil herself chaired and spoke at many suffrage gatherings and was involved not only with the WSPU but with the WFL, the London-based CSU (as its president) and its successor, the FCSU, and the ELFS (as its treasurer in 1914). Locally, she readily made her house and gardens at Llanwern Park available for suffragette functions, and was prepared to identify publicly with militancy; in September 1909, for example, she hosted a reception in honour of two early hunger strikers from Bristol.[42] In February 1914, in a protest against 'the outrage on humanity' perpetrated by the 'torture' of forcible feeding and the 'cruel and subversive "Cat and Mouse" Act', she was arrested for obstruction outside the House of Commons and spent the night in a police cell.[43]

---

[41]   VW, 25 November 1910; B. M. Wilmott Dobbie, *A Nest of Suffragettes in Somerset: Eagle House, Batheaston* (Bath, 1979), 66; Rhondda, *This was My World*, 161–7; Crawford, *Women's Suffrage Movement*, 256–7.

[42]   VW, 17 September 1909; *South Wales Weekly Argus*, 18 September 1909; diary of Mary Blathwayt, 11 September 1909.

[43]   Rhondda, *This was My World*, 169–70; VW, 27 February 1914; *The Suffragette*, 27 February 1914; journal of H. W. Nevinson, Bodleian Library, MS Eng. misc. e 618/2, 24 February 1914; H. W. Nevinson, *More Changes, More Chances* (1925), 334–5; Angela V. John, *War, Journalism and the Shaping of the Twentieth Century: The Life and Times of the Henry W. Nevinson* (London, 2006), 103–4. Arrested with Sybil was her niece, Katherine Haig. A copy of the petition (with 108 signatures, including that of 'Mrs D. A. Thomas') is to be found in NLW, D. A. Thomas Papers, D2. As a result of this episode, she resigned her vice-presidency and membership of the London Society for Women's Suffrage, following a formal request by the committee. WL, 2/LSW, 298/3, correspondence between the secretary (Ray Strachey) and Gladys Pott of the NLOWS, 29, 30 July, 5 August 1914.

Sybil Thomas illustrates the continuity between the constitutional suffragism of the Victorian era and the suffragette
militancy of the twentieth century. So too does Elizabeth
Mitchell of Llanfrechfa, who tenaciously promoted the cause
of votes for women from its inception in the mid 1860s until
her death in 1910, at the age of seventy-six. Like many women
of her station – she was born into the new business wealth of
the Rolls family with its mansion and estate near Monmouth,
her brother being created Baron Llangattock in 1892 – she
devoted a good deal of time to voluntary work for the church
and charitable activity in the local community, visiting and
helping the poor and the sick. In a more public role, she
served as a poor law guardian on the Pontypool board of
guardians, a parish councillor on the Llanfrechfa lower parish
council and dame president of her local Primrose League
habitation, an avenue she used to advance the women's
suffrage issue. In 1866, she had been a signatory of the Ladies'
Petition presented to Parliament by John Stuart Mill and
thereafter was an active supporter of the movement, holding
offices in various suffrage societies, speaking from the public
platform and writing letters to the press; she was a vice-
president of the London Society for Women's Suffrage when
she died in 1910. 'Whatever the merits and demerits of the
Suffragette cause', observed the vicar at her memorial service,
'long years ago she laboured for the rights of women – her
sisters – when the cause was unknown and unpopular.'[44] In
advancing age and deteriorating health, she chaired and
addressed functions of the Newport WSPU branch, though
she was at odds with the growing extremism of many activists.
'By violence and disregard for order were they not helping the
cause of Socialism and anarchy?' she asked a large gathering
at Llanwern Park in 1909. As one who had 'supported the
movement for close on half a century', she went on to protest
against its 'being degraded by being made a popular tumult'
and urged 'suffragists not to practice vulgar, or un-Christian
methods'.[45] These views were no doubt out of step with the

---

[44]   *Free Press of Monmouthshire*, 7 October 1910. Obituaries in *VW*, 30 September
1910; *Monmouthshire Weekly Post*, 24 September 1910.
[45]   *South Wales Weekly Argus*, 18 September 1909; *CT*, 18 September 1909; *VW*,
23 July, 17 September, 29 October, 5 November 1909.

general demeanour of the audience but they were accepted as the sentiments of a respected 'veteran'. At the same time, Elizabeth Mitchell's involvement in the branch is an indication of how 'broad church' the WSPU could be at a local level, at least at this time; in 1909, there was no other suffrage society in Newport.

Who were the less celebrated Welsh suffragettes? Many names, especially from Cardiff, Newport and Pontypool, appear on WSPU subscription lists over the years. A substantial number – as many as a half – were listed as unmarried, and frequently these seem to have been fairly youthful women. It was also common for mothers and daughters to be active. Young, middle-class women tended to have few domestic responsibilities and the time and money to commit themselves to the campaign. Teachers clearly formed a significant element in the Cardiff and Newport branches, sometimes holding special meetings of their own. Press reports reveal the key local activists. At Pontypool, there were Mary and Clara Butler, wife and eldest daughter respectively of the Panteg industrialist and prominent Conservative, Isaac Butler; Mary herself was president of the Panteg habitation of the Primrose League. Equally important figures, from branch formation in 1908 until the war, were their family friend and an army officer's wife, Ella Edmunds, and long-serving branch secretary, Lilian Wilton. At Newport, an obvious stalwart was Edith Pilliner, wife of a Llantarnam magistrate, while at Cardiff one of a large number of enthusiasts during the branch's eight-year existence was Edith Lester Jones, teacher and actress, and frequent speaker at meetings in the region.[46] The vast majority of those who served on committees, sold newspapers, advertised meetings and raised funds, however, are now no more than names.

There was also male backing for the WSPU campaign in Wales; in several places, individuals demonstrated their support by organizing and chairing meetings, speaking on public platforms, making donations to funds and selling newspapers. Supporters included Revd Daniel Hughes, the Pontypool Baptist minister, and several other prominent Noncon-

---

[46]   A. J. R., *Suffrage Annual*, 338.

formists, Vernon Hartshorn and George Barker, leading figures in the South Wales Miners' Federation, and Tom Williams, a stalwart of the Amalgamated Society of Railway Servants in the Rhondda. The WSPU found another 'splendid Rhondda champion' in James Grant, active locally as a socialist public speaker and propagandist. Throughout the summer of 1913 he held outdoor meetings to promote the women's cause and sold 120 copies of *The Suffragette* weekly. Arrested for obstruction while lecturing in Treorchy square in June, he refused to pay the fine imposed and, in consequence, served five days in Cardiff Gaol.[47] During 1913, branches of the Men's Political Union for Women's Enfranchisement, the counterpart of the WSPU, were formed in Cardiff (where the economist, Professor H. Stanley Jevons, was the principal figure) and Newport, though neither seems to have established an energetic existence independent of the local women's bodies.[48] A notable champion in London was the surgeon, Charles Mansell Moullin (husband of Edith), who conducted a sustained public campaign, largely through the press, against the horrors and dangers of forcible feeding. He also attended to Emily Davison during the last days of her life, following her actions at the 1913 Derby.[49]

Over the years, WSPU activists made some attempt to appeal to working-class audiences in south Wales. Speaking at works, factory and dockyard gates obviously aimed at this. From 1913, a more systematic effort focused on ILP and trade union branches, Cardiff-based organizer Annie Williams addressing a large number of meetings, of colliers and railwaymen in particular. The location was often the Rhondda valley, the target of a special three-week campaign in August 1913. With Porth as the headquarters, a party of Welsh and English suffragettes held daily meetings (some attracting several hundred people) and sold newspapers in a dozen or so towns. 'The whole series of

[47]   *The Suffragette*, 4 July, 1 August, 10 October 1913; *South Wales Worker*, 19 July, 23 October 1913.

[48]   *The Suffragette*, 23 May, 13 June, 24, 31 October 1913. D. A. Thomas and Sir Alfred Mond were listed as vice-presidents of the union in 1911. Men's Political Union for Women's Enfranchisement, *Annual Report*, 1911.

[49]   Morley with Stanley, *The Life and Death of Emily Wilding Davison*, 102–4; John, 'A draft of fresh air', 85–6.

meetings have been successful from every point of view, and cannot but succeed in producing a great effect upon public opinion', commented the *South Wales Worker*.

> Prejudice and ignorance were the two factors which militated against the Women's Movement. We rejoice to know that the campaign has somewhat helped to remove these two obstacles. Even if it only accomplished the fact of raising the women in the minds of the public it was well worth the effort of the meetings being held.[50]

It was, of course, escalating militancy that gave the WSPU notoriety. The publicity generated by the imprisonments of Christabel Pankhurst and Annie Kenney in Manchester in October 1905 convinced the leadership that sensationalism was the key to making women's suffrage a central political issue. Thus, when WSPU organizers were first dispatched to the various regions of the country, including south Wales, during 1906, one of their tasks was to seek out women willing to travel to London, participate in protests within the precincts of Parliament or in the area outside, and go to prison for the cause. In consequence, five suffragettes from south Wales were among a large number of volunteers from all parts of Britain who served sentences between December 1906 and April 1907. The first was Mary Keating Hill, the forty-year-old wife of a Cardiff insurance manager. Charged with disorderly conduct and resisting the police, following an attempt to make a speech in one of the lobbies, she was sentenced to a fine of 40s. or three weeks' imprisonment. A few days earlier, a similar conviction had resulted in a fine being paid by her brother, but such was her determination to go to prison that she took part in a second protest and spent Christmas and the New Year in Holloway Gaol, north London (the forty-second suffragette to be imprisoned).[51] 'The leading spirit of the Women's Social and Political Union in Cardiff', Mary

---

[50]   *South Wales Worker*, 30 August 1913. See also *The Suffragette*, 15, 22, 29 August, 5, 12 September 1913.

[51]   *SWDN*, 18, 20, 21, 22, 24 December 1906, 1, 4, 11, 15, January. 1907; *WM*, 18, 19, 21, 22, 24, 29 December 1906, 1, 11, 15 January 1907; *South Wales Echo*, 18, 19, 20, 21, 22 December 1906, 10 January 1907; *CT*, 22 December 1906; *Labour Record and Review*, January 1907; *VW*, 21 January, 4 February 1909; A. J. R., *Suffrage Annual*, 280–1. Her brothers, Matthew and Joseph Keating, were respectively an Irish MP and an author.

Keating Hill had already done a good deal of local public speaking for the movement and taken part in the campaign against Samuel Evans in the Mid Glamorgan by-election of October 1906. She remained active in the suffrage agitation over the next decade, though switching her allegiance to the WFL.

In February 1907 two other Cardiff activists served seven days in prison, again after refusing to pay fines for disorderly behaviour and resisting the police in another 'suffragette raid' on Westminster. They were Lilian and Ethel Gillett, a teacher and student respectively, sisters in their twenties and the daughters of an architect.[52] A month later, after similar disturbances and convictions, Jessie Arscott, a twenty-five-year-old grocer's daughter from Merthyr, and Amelia Jenkins, wife of a Maesteg insurance agent and secretary of the local WSPU branch, spent fourteen days in gaol, as did a London Welshwoman, Marie Winton Evans.[53] Such 'martyrs' were formally greeted outside Holloway by union representatives on the morning of their release, presented with a bouquet of flowers and a message of commendation from the executive and taken in procession to a London hotel for a celebratory public breakfast. On returning to Cardiff, they were similarly feted by Welsh suffragettes. The events were all given considerable publicity in the south Wales press.

'Raids' on parliament continued as a suffragette tactic, one the next year, in October 1908, turning into a particular publicity coup. Following clashes between police and demonstrators around Parliament Square, witnessed by several Cabinet ministers, Mrs Pankhurst, Christabel and another leading WSPU figure, 'General' Flora Drummond, were charged with conduct likely to lead to a breach of the peace by circulating a handbill advocating a 'rush' on the House of Commons. At the trial the three accused were ably defended

---

[52] *SWDN*, 14, 15, 21, 23 February 1907; *WM*, 14, 15 February 1907; *South Wales Echo*, 14 February 1907; *CT*, 16 February 1907; NA, MEPO 2/1016, The Suffragette Movement: disturbances and convictions, 1906–1907.

[53] *SWDN*, 22 March, 4 April 1907; *WM*, 21, 22 March, 3, 4 April 1907; *CT*, 23 March, 6 April 1907; *South Wales Echo*, 21 March 1907; *Glamorgan Gazette*, 22 March, 5 April 1907; *Chronicle for Mid and South Glamorgan*, 29 March, 5 April 1907; MEPO 2/1016. See Rosen, *Rise Up, Women!*, 81–3.

by Christabel, a qualified barrister, who subpoenaed Lloyd George and the home secretary, Herbert Gladstone, as witnesses. Although the guilty verdict led to imprisonments, the trial won a great deal of newspaper coverage, both in column inches and in photographs of the court proceedings.[54] The episode included one further element of Welsh interest. On the evening of the demonstration, Margaret Symons, Keir Hardie's secretary and the daughter of a Cowbridge architect, impulsively burst into the Commons' chamber and interrupted debate in order to protest against women's political status.[55]

A suffragette tactic widely and continuously employed from the summer of 1906 was the heckling of government ministers. Lloyd George was always a prime target, the WSPU even organizing classes where women could learn to fire appropriate sentences and phrases in Welsh at him.[56] In December 1908 it took him two hours to deliver an intended twenty-minute speech at the Albert Hall, London, and the threat of disruption was now constant, whatever the occasion. The heckling was often carefully orchestrated, as at Swansea a few months earlier. Positioning themselves in various parts of the hall, six suffragettes 'were instructed to go in rotation, nine minutes apart . . . watch the speaker and say something really apposite', the result leaving Lloyd George 'palpably annoyed to the point of anger'.[57] Militants sought ways around the inevitable precautions. In December 1909, again in Swansea, two activists were found hiding in the hall the night before

[54]   See Rosen, *Rise Up, Women!*, 110–12; Fulford, *Votes For Women*, 186–92; John Grigg, *Lloyd George: The People's Champion, 1902–11* (London, 1978), 167–9; Purvis, *Emmeline Pankhurst*, 113–17; Martin Pugh, *The Pankhursts* (London, 2001), 181–5. Both the *Daily Mirror* and *Daily Graphic* carried front-page photographs of proceedings.

[55]   See Caroline Benn, *Keir Hardie* (London, 1992), 248–9; Raeburn, *Militant Suffragettes*, 67; *CT*, 17 October 1908. She was not charged on this occasion but three years later she did serve five days in prison for obstruction. *VW*, 8 December 1911. For further information on Margaret Symons, see Benn, *Keir Hardie*, 177, 210–11, 288, 294–5; Crawford, *Women's Suffrage Movement*, 669–70.

[56]   Circular letter, 7 December 1909, quoted in Joyce Marlow, *Votes for Women: the Virago Book of Suffragettes* (London, 2000), 108–9. See also John, 'A draft of fresh air', 85.

[57]   *WM*, 2 October, 7, 8 December 1908; Clara Codd, *So Rich a Life* (London, 1951), 54–9.

one of his meetings.[58] Alternatively, noisy protests were made outside. Other ministers speaking in Wales were subjected to predetermined heckling too – Herbert Asquith by university students at Aberystwyth in late 1907, Reginald McKenna at Blaenafon in February 1909, Lewis Harcourt at Cardiff a few months later and Walter Runciman at Barry in December 1912.[59] There was spontaneous action too; while he was electioneering in Scotland in December 1910, Margaret Mackworth seized the opportunity of a slow-moving motorcar to jump upon the running-board in order to challenge the prime minister.[60]

The heckling extended to non-political gatherings. Thus, the National Eisteddfod was interrupted in 1909 in London and in 1912 in Wrexham, Asquith being in attendance on the former occasion, Lloyd George on the latter.[61] The formal procession welcoming King George V to Cardiff in June 1912 was held up by a suffragette outburst directed at home secretary and MP for North Monmouthshire, Reginald McKenna, while his ceremonial laying of the foundation stone at Caerleon Training College the following month was also disturbed; being responsible for the handling of demonstrations and the treatment of suffragette prisoners, McKenna was a detested figure.[62] The hounding of government ministers even encroached on their leisure time, neither golf course nor theatre affording refuge from militants; a Cardiff branch official recalled being thrown out of a local theatre when Lloyd George was present 'because I called out that he was the villain of the piece'.[63]

In the immediate pre-war years, WSPU heckling was consistently directed against Labour politicians too. Thus, at

[58] *VW*, 24, 31 December 1909. The two were Elsie McKenzie and Vera Wentworth, both Londoners, though the former was WSPU organizer for Cardiff at the time. See also Martin, 'Culture of the women's suffrage movement', 111–12.

[59] British Library, Arncliffe-Sennett Collection, Vol. 2, p. 15; *VW*, 11 February 1909; *SWDN*, 3 April 1909; Masson, 'Women versus "the people"', 8–10; *The Suffragette*, 13 December 1912.

[60] Rhondda, *This was My World*, 145; see also *VW*, 16 December 1910; *Time and Tide*, 6 February 1943.

[61] *VW*, 18, 25 June 1909, 13, 20 September 1912.

[62] Ibid., 5, 26 July 1912.

[63] SFC, 58.87/ 72, Lettice Floyd to Edith How Martyn, 10 May 1932.

Pontypool in late 1912, Keir Hardie was censured for helping to sustain a Liberal government 'which refuses to give justice to women and a Home Secretary who force feeds the mothers of the race'.[64] The theme of 'no peace for government supporters' was again the source of suffragette interruptions of meetings addressed by Philip Snowden and Ramsay MacDonald in Cardiff early in 1914.[65]

Heckling, together with marches on Parliament, dominated WSPU militancy until the summer of 1909, whereupon new developments emerged – window smashing in Whitehall, hunger-striking suffragette prisoners and force-feeding. Such features were essentially harbingers for the future, however, for at the end of January 1910, in response to the creation of an all-party Conciliation Committee designed to draw up a compromise women's suffrage bill, Mrs Pankhurst announced the suspension of militant tactics and the continuation of the campaign by peaceful and constitutional means only. With the exception of one week in November 1910, this truce operated until November 1911, though arguably WSPU participation in illegal resistance to the census of April 1911 amounted to militancy. South-east Wales suffragettes responded enthusiastically to the call of national and local leaders, branches making the practical arrangements for the boycott. Accordingly, at Cardiff, Newport, Barry and Pontypool, members gathered in private homes or in unoccupied premises on census night. In Cardiff, thirty or more protestors apparently spent the night in an untenanted shop in one of the suburbs, while in Newport 'a motor-car full of evaders' and decorated with placards reading 'No Vote, No Census' was driven through the town in the early hours of the morning. The census resistance was certainly effective in capturing a good deal of press attention.[66]

The militant truce held during most of 1911 while the Commons continued to debate the Conciliation Bill. Its failure in November, however, amidst WSPU accusations of

[64]   *The Suffragette*, 6 December 1912.
[65]   Ibid., 16 January, 13 March 1914.
[66]   *Morning Post*, 4 April 1911; *VW*, 7 April 1911. See also *WM*, 1, 3, 4 April 1911; *SWDN*, 3, 4 April 1911; *CT*, 8 April 1911; *Monmouthshire Weekly Post*, 8 April 1911. The initiative for the census protest came from the WFL.

government treachery, brought an eruption of anger and heralded a new and more extreme phase of suffragette militancy which lasted almost three years, until the outbreak of the First World War. Window smashing was now adopted as official policy for the first time. 'War in Whitehall', pronounced a typical headline as 223 arrests took place on 21 November 1911. The imprisoned suffragettes in November 1911 included Frances Price of Cardiff (five days) and Elizabeth (Bessie) Davies and Charlotte Rice, both of Newport (seven and five days respectively), though the last two named are rather mysterious, neither apparently being known to their local branch. Others with Welsh connections imprisoned on this occasion were Edith Mansell Moullin (five days), Margaret Symons (five days), Mildred Mansell, sister of Ivor Guest, MP for Cardiff, 1906–10 (seven days) and Janet Boyd, Sybil Thomas's sister from Radnorshire (seven days).[67] The next major outbursts of window smashing, in the West End in early March 1912, again involved thousands of pounds' worth of damage and even more arrests. The subsequent imprisonments included a number of Welsh activists, who, on their return home, were accorded celebrity status in suffragette circles, being much in demand to recount their experiences at branch meetings. Olive Fontaine, a Newport activist, served one month with hard labour for breaking a police station window during the events of March 1912. In the same episode one month's imprisonment was also imposed on Morrie Hughes, the daughter of Revd Owen Hughes of Corwen, and organizer for the Harrogate WSPU branch.[68]

Some window smashing took place in Wales itself. In one 'franchise protest' in August 1912, Katherine Gatty, a London suffragette visiting Abergavenny, put a hammer through a pane of glass of the local post office, for which she was sentenced to a month's imprisonment with hard labour.[69] The

[67] *VW*, 24 November, 1, 8, 22 December 1911; *Monmouthshire Weekly Post*, 25 November 1911; *WM*, 28 November 1911; *Evening Express*, 22, 27 November 1911; *CT*, 25 November 1911.

[68] A. J. R., *Suffrage Annual*, 242, 271; *Monmouthshire Weekly Post*, 16 March, 20 April 1912; Beddoe, *Out of the Shadows*, 42.

[69] *WM*, 22 August 1912; *SWDN*, 22 August 1912; *Abergavenny Chronicle*, 23 August 1912; *Free Press of Monmouthshire*, 23 August 1912; *South Wales Weekly Argus*, 24 August 1912; *VW*, 30 August, 20 September 1912. Prison records state that, at the time of

only other occurrence appears to have been in Cricieth in June 1914 when two English suffragettes smashed the windows of shops and businesses in the main street while Lloyd George was addressing a large meeting in another part of the town. Porthmadog magistrates sentenced each to three months' imprisonment.[70]

Damaging public and private property was now the focus of the suffragette strategy to put pressure on the government. Accordingly, late 1912 and early 1913 saw pillar-box attacks around the country. A considerable number occurred in south Wales, in Newport, Swansea, Bridgend, Porthcawl, Pembroke, Aberbargoed and, most especially, in Cardiff.[71] Most commonly, uncorked bottles containing fluid were dropped in among the letters with accompanying messages such as 'Release Mrs Pankhurst' and 'Blame Asquith for this'. Similar notes were left during the wave of telephone and telegraph wire cutting that took place in the Cardiff and Cwmbran areas in the spring and early summer of 1913.[72]

At the same time, golf courses were popular suffragette targets, though there were few such attacks in Wales. One was at Panteg, Pontypool, in February 1913, when the words 'Votes for Women' were burned into the turf with corrosive liquid and golf shoes and bags inside the clubhouse were cut.

---

her committal, Katherine Gatty was forty-two years old; her occupation was given as a journalist and her birthplace Ferozopur, India. Nominal Register, Vol. 22, 1912–13, p. 54, 21 August 1912 (HMP, Usk). For Katherine Gatty, see SFC, 60.15/ 23; Crawford, *Women's Suffrage Movement*, 241–2.

[70]   *NWC*, 5 June 1914; *CDH*, 5 June 1914; *North Wales Observer and Express*, 5 June 1914; *CN*, 5 June 1914; *Welsh Coast Pioneer*, 4 June 1914; *Manchester Guardian*, 3 June 1914; *Yr Herald Cymraeg*, 9 Mehefin 1914; *Holyhead Mail*, 12 June 1914; *The Suffragette*, 12 June 1914.

[71]   *WM*, 26 November, 21 December 1912, 2 January, 27 February, 1, 3, 6, 19 March, 7 April 1913; *The Suffragette*, 6 December 1912, 3, 10 January, 21 February 1913; *Free Press of Monmouthshire*, 3 January 1913; *Bargoed Journal*, 27 February 1913; *Monmouth Guardian*, 28 February 1913; *Porthcawl News*, 5 March 1913; *Glamorgan Gazette*, 11 April 1913.

[72]   *WM*, 7 March, 7 April, 2, 31 May 1913; *The Suffragette*, 7, 14 March, 11 April, 9 May 1913; *Free Press of Monmouthshire*, 28 February, 7 March 1913; *Daily Mirror*, 3 April 1913. Such attacks often meant difficulties for local business. For example, the cutting of telephone wires between Newport and Pontypool in early March affected 'practically all the lines to Blaenavon and adjacent industrial towns by which shipping orders from the collieries to the upper parts of Monmouthshire are transmitted to Newport. Considerable delay and inconvenience resulted.' *The Times*, 5 March 1913.

From footprints in the soil the police concluded that the perpetrators were three women.[73] The only other occurrence – and attribution for this is far from certain – was the damage to six greens at Ladyhill golf club, Newport, in the following August.[74]

In the spring of the same year, the Pontypool area saw a spate of suffragette hoaxes, including the calling out of army reservists and the sending, in unstamped letters, of halfpenny coins and women's suffrage circulars, meaning that the recipients would have to pay a fee of sixpence to the postal authorities. There was also the delivery of unordered goods to tradespeople and public men – a consignment of feathers, expensive drapery goods and, to the most unfortunate, the considerable inconvenience and annoyance of forty goats. Plenty of bomb hoaxes occurred in south Wales too, especially in Cardiff.[75]

There was nothing illusory about the bomb in February 1913, which partially wrecked the house that Lloyd George was having built near Walton Heath, Surrey. The following evening, speaking in Cardiff, Mrs Pankhurst, who had had no prior knowledge of the planned explosion, nevertheless took full responsibility for this and other acts of destruction: 'we have blown up the Chancellor of the Exchequer's house ... for all that has been done in the past, I accept responsibility. I have advised. I have incited. I have conspired ... the authorities need not look for the women who have done what they did last night.'[76] Rachel Barrett, chairing a public meeting in central London, was similarly impassioned and unapologetic in condemning the government for its 'treachery' and 'trickery' and for leaving the WSPU with no effective option other than 'active rebellion':

---

[73] *WM*, 17 February 1913; *Free Press of Monmouthshire*, 21 February 1913; *VW*, 21 February 1913.

[74] *Daily Herald*, 4 August 1913; *South Wales Argus*, 4 August 1913; *The Suffragette*, 8 August 1913; *Monmouthshire Weekly Post*, 9 August 1913; *South Wales Weekly Argus*, 9 August 1913.

[75] *Free Press of Monmouthshire*, 14, 21 March 1913; *The Suffragette*, 14, 28 March, 4 April 1913; *WM*, 3, 20 March, 24, 25, 26 April, 9, 12 May, 20 June 1913.

[76] NA, HO 45/10695/231366, head constable to assistant commissioner of police, special branch, 20 February 1913; *WM*, 20 February 1913; *SWDN*, 20 February 1913; *Morning Post*, 20 February 1913.

We have made up our minds to this, that there is to be no law, no order and no safety in this country until women get the vote. That is our position ... When we hear that there has been a fire it does not give us a shock, we say, 'thank goodness for that'. When we hear of a bomb being thrown, we say again, 'thank god for that'. We neither falter nor repent, and if we have any qualms of conscience, it is not because of the things that have been done, but because of the things we have left undone.[77]

Mrs Pankhurst's arrest in the wake of the Cardiff speech, and her subsequent sentence to three months' imprisonment for procuring and inciting women to commit violence, signalled more furious militancy, especially in the form of acts of arson, which continued unchecked for the next year and a half until the outbreak of war. 'Fresh stages of increasing violence', Emily Davison had impressed on a Cardiff street meeting a few months earlier, 'were the only method of reminding the Government of their broken pledges and dastardly treatment of the women's cause. Logic was no use, and until the vote was gained they were going to shock the public who elected the traitorous legislators.' The momentum had to be maintained; thus the campaign had moved on from destroying mail and window smashing; now 'incendiarism was the only possible outcome'.[78]

The first such incident in Wales occurred in April 1913 when a bonfire of materials, accompanied by suffragette literature and messages, apparently failed to ignite under the grandstand of Ely racecourse, Cardiff.[79] In August, Abergavenny cricket club was the target, early discovery of a pavilion fire preventing widespread damage, though a nearby hayrick was largely destroyed. Various papers relating to the women's cause, some in the Welsh language, were found at both locations. The arson attacks coincided with the holding of the National Eisteddfod in the town, where, given recent experi-

---

[77]   NA, HO 45/10695/231366, assistant commissioner of police, special branch, to Home Office, 21 February 1913. Ever loyal to the Pankhurst leadership, Rachel Barrett rejected any dissent to the strategy of Emmeline and Christabel. Thus, her response to the ruthless expulsion of key WSPU figures, Emmeline and Frederick Pethick-Lawrence, over the question of escalating militancy in 1912 was a curt, 'the Lawrences are just the Lawrences & this is the movement'. Journal of H. W. Nevinson, MS Eng. misc. e 617/3, 28 January 1913.
[78]   *WM*, 8 November 1912.
[79]   Ibid., 8 April 1913; *The Suffragette*, 11 April 1913.

ence of the annual event and the likelihood of Lloyd George and Reginald McKenna being in attendance, elaborate precautions were taken. The main arena was guarded night and day, nearly eighty policemen reportedly being drafted in to reinforce the usual stewards. Rumours of plots and reprisals abounded locally; one resident, supposedly encountering a suffragette disguised as a nurse, informed her that 'if any of the London tactics were adopted here, the Abergavenny Bull Dogs were determined to carry them to the river, and give them a good ducking'.[80]

That same week, arson of a similar nature took place in north Wales, where prompt action by a caretaker confined fire damage at Caernarfon county school to some windows and a door, but a haystack in close proximity was almost completely destroyed; again, an assortment of literature, in Welsh and English, testified to the work of suffragettes or their male sympathizers. A week later, an attempt to burn two unoccupied houses in Bangor was suspected of being similarly motivated.[81]

In early November, 'arsonettes' were apparently at work in Newport, leaving behind a 'votes for women' flag and other items in an abortive attempt to set fire to the county council offices, while a few weeks later two small fires brought limited damage to floor boards and window frames at the newly built Caerleon Training College, messages and a lady's handbag again indicating the incendiaries to have been suffragettes.[82] The end of 1913 saw a series of hayrick fires in the Cardiff district and others near Penarth and Newport, the total damage running into hundreds of pounds.[83] 'This year which has seen such a succession of outrages closes with only one Suffragist offender still in prison', bemoaned one south Wales

[80]   *South Wales Argus*, 7 August 1913; *Abergavenny Chronicle*, 8 August 1913; *Free Press of Monmouthshire*, 8 August 1913; *WM*, 8 August 1913; *SWDN*, 8 August 1913; *The Suffragette*, 15 August 1913.
[81]   *NWC*, 15 August 1913; *CDH*, 15 August 1913; *Yr Herald Cymraeg*, 19 Awst 1913; *North Wales Observer*, 22 August 1913; *Holyhead Mail*, 22 August 1913; *The Suffragette*, 22 August 1913.
[82]   *WM*, 5, 29 November 1913; *South Wales Weekly Argus*, 8 November, 6 December 1913; *The Suffragette*, 14 November, 5 December 1913.
[83]   *WM*, 5, 18 December 1913; *The Suffragette*, 12, 26 December 1913; 2 January 1914.

newspaper. 'Cardiff women are thinking of you' was a reference to her, on a note left at one of the burnt hayricks; at the same time, 'Messers Asquith and Co.' were warned that there would be 'no peace for the wicked'.[84] The only example of suffragette arson in Wales in 1914 seems to have been the attack on Colwyn Bay pier at the very beginning of August. Observing smoke issuing from the pavilion in the middle of the night, two patrolling policemen were able to extinguish the flames swiftly. There was clear evidence of arson, while a pair of ladies' gloves and a copy of *The Suffragette* implicated militant women.[85]

Shortly before the outbreak of war (and the prompt cessation of the WSPU's campaign of violence), the *Morning Post* published 'a census of the damage wrought by militant suffragists, or attributed with much probability to them, since the beginning of 1913'. During that eighteen-month period, the newspaper recorded that suffragettes had set fire to eight churches and tried to set fire to nine others; exploded bombs in six churches and deposited bombs which failed to explode in six others; they set fire to thirty-six houses and tried to set fire to eighteen others; they fired twenty-two cricket or football pavilions and tried to burn twenty more; they burned nineteen schools, railway stations and timber yards, and tried to burn four other schools; they made ten attempts to set railway carriages on fire, exploded seven bombs in buildings that were neither churches nor dwelling-houses, and made twenty-four other attempts to use bombs; they allegedly damaged well over four thousand letters and made ten attacks on pictures in public galleries. The material damage, leaving aside the works of art, was estimated at £384,000. The article also afforded detailed evidence to substantiate the home secretary's contention that: 'Since the beginning of 1913 the number of individual offences has been greatly reduced. On the other hand, we see that the seriousness of the offences is much greater.' The year 1912 had seen the highest total of offences with innumerable window smashings in the West

[84]   *CT*, 3 January 1914.
[85]   *North Wales Weekly News*, 6 August 1914; *Welsh Coast Pioneer*, 6 August 1914; *NWC*, 7 August 1914; *The Suffragette*, 7 August 1914.

End of London; but the damage done was little in excess of £5,000. In 1913 and 1914 the cost of damage soared as window breaking gave way to arson.[86]

Suffragettes insisted that the only human life threatened in their acts of destruction was their own. And, indeed, given the dangers involved in arson, cutting through telegraph wires and other daring exploits, it is surprising that there were not serious injuries and fatalities. Most of the perpetrators also escaped undetected. In south-east Wales, where a considerable number of 'outrages' took place, local WSPU branches strenuously denied involvement and it is certainly hard to envisage meetings of overwhelmingly middle-class ladies plotting and executing these deeds. The only activist convicted in Wales was Margaret Mackworth, who was sentenced to a month's imprisonment for placing a dangerous substance in a Newport pillar box in June 1913. However, as her autobiography makes clear, this was not part of a local conspiracy, her fellow committee members being 'uncommonly reluctant to be convinced' of the wisdom of her proposal; rather, she was intent on making a single individual gesture of commitment to such tactics and approached the crime with a great deal of anxiety:

> My heart was beating like a steam engine, my throat was dry, and my nerve went so badly that I made the mistake of walking several miles backwards and forwards past the letter box before I found courage to push the packets in. Then, as they were rather bulky, I had to force them a bit before they would drop.[87]

Another participant in such militant acts was the Cardiff suffragette, Edith Lester Jones, who recalled her deeds in an interview broadcast on BBC radio more than half a century later, in 1965:

> I did a pillar box … I filled an envelope with the filthiest mixture I could find. I know it had treacle and ink and soot. I didn't want to injure anybody's postal orders or anything. I wanted to annoy the authorities, and I did annoy them.
>   … then the organisers in Cardiff … advised me to do a little bit of arson … . We tried to burn a house down on Cyncoed … I came in

---

[86]   *Morning Post*, 13 July 1914.
[87]   Rhondda, *This was My World*, 152–4. See also below, 211–12.

disguise through Cardiff, and then we went at night and she had the fuse, Miss Bach [another Cardiff member]. I broke the window in the approved way with a stone in brown paper, which you popped through the window and you get in afterwards, you see ... And we saw, to our joy, a table underneath by the staircase laid out with rolls and rolls of paper. So she said, 'What a splendid idea, light the fuse here'. We, none of us, knew anything about fuses. She lit it and a sheet of flames shot out, and so I dragged her backwards through the window, and we escaped across the fields and looked back, hoping to see flames going up to the sky. You see it was empty. Therefore, we were doing nothing but lighting a torch as a symbol. The thing is a suffragette could get hurt but nobody else must ever be hurt.[88]

Local activists may well, of course, have been responsible for other attacks on property in Wales. Equally, the culprits could have been outsiders, perhaps WSPU 'mice', as they were called, who seem to have carried out missions in different parts of the country; spelling errors on messages left at the arson attack on Caernarfon county school in August 1913, for example, seemed to indicate 'the work of persons not very conversant with the Welsh language'.[89] Certainly, when incidents occurred, the press often spoke of the appearance of 'female strangers' in the area, while a number followed in the wake of public engagements undertaken by Cabinet ministers, notably Lloyd George, who tended to be pursued around the country by suffragettes.

It was in the interests of the WSPU leadership, in its strategy of pressurizing the government, to accept the blame for as many 'outrages' as possible. But clearly some claims were based on little factual evidence and simply do not stand up to scrutiny. Local investigation into arson attempts on Abercarn church in April 1913 indicated that they were most likely 'the work of mischievous spirits who, perhaps, wished to give colour to the rumour that the militants were to visit the district last week'.[90] Similarly, later in the year, Caernarfonshire police concluded that a small bag of gunpowder and

---

[88]   Edith Lester Jones interviewed by Dilys Breese, recorded on 31 March 1965 and transmitted on 16 April 1965. Audio copy of this interview in possession of author.

[89]   *NWC*, 15 August 1915.

[90]   *South Wales Gazette*, 18 April 1913.

length of fuse found in a Llanrug chapel pulpit, along with a directive to the minister, 'Preach "votes for women", otherwise look out!' was a hoax stemming from an internal feud.[91] In Cardiff, an explosion at St Michael's Theological College early in 1914, for which the WSPU was eager to accept responsibility, turned out to be caused by gas, while in April a supposed suffragette attempt to set alight the grandstand at Ninian Park football ground found no comment whatever in the local press.[92] Lastly, conjecture blaming militant women for the destruction, by fire, of Coedpoeth railway station, near Wrexham, the following June, was subsequently dismissed.[93]

Some 'copy-cat' acts of deception came before the courts. In August 1913 one youth was accused of setting fire to a shed near Abergavenny, attempting to put the blame on suffragettes by leaving behind an appropriate slogan.[94] A few weeks earlier, two 'boy militants', aged ten and eight, were convicted at Swansea of putting lighted matches in a letter box, their parents being fined 10s.; less fortunate was the thirteen-year-old Anglesey boy sentenced to four strokes of the birch for a similar offence.[95] There were other pranks elsewhere in Wales too.[96] The press also sought amusement in the cause, frequently through drawing analogies. Reporting a breach of the peace in the Rhondda in June 1913, for example, the *Glamorgan Free Press,* under the headlines 'Tylorstown Amazon – Like a Wild Cat – Broke the Door in with her Shoulder', began its report thus: 'The militant suffragettes in search of derring-do would do well to keep an eye on Tylorstown. They would find some very promising material . . .'[97] In similar vein, an Aberbargoed police constable, giving evidence in court

---

[91]   *CDH,* 5 September 1913; *NWC,* 5 September 1913; *The Suffragette,* 5 September 1913.

[92]   *WM,* 12 January 1914; *SWDN,* 12 January 1914; *The Suffragette,* 16 January, 1 May 1914; *Bristol Times and Mirror,* 27 April 1914.

[93]   *WM,* 22 June 1914; *Wrexham Advertiser,* 27 June 1914; *The Suffragette,* 3 July 1914.

[94]   *WM,* 4 September, 4 November 1913.

[95]   *NWC,* 13 August 1913; *SWDN,* 4, 6 August 1913. A few months later, two thirteen-year-olds in Kent were given six strokes of the birch for cutting a railway signal wire and leaving a placard reading 'Votes for Women'. *WM,* 7 January 1914.

[96]   As in incidents in Llanelli and Clydach, near Brynmawr, in 1913. *WM,* 14 March 1913; *Monmouthshire Weekly Post,* 12 April 1913.

[97]   *Glamorgan Free Press,* 19 June 1913.

against a woman accused of being drunk and disorderly, depicted her as 'kicking and scratching and biting like a Suffragette'.[98]

By 1913 the spectre of suffragettes evidently loomed large in the public mind. In April of that year, a group of women geology students carrying hammers were mistaken for suffragettes at Carmarthen fair, while the following month, two ladies seeking to gain admittance without tickets to a Welsh Church disestablishment meeting addressed by Reginald McKenna in Holyhead were presumed militants; set upon by an angry mob, pelted with missiles and chased out of town, they turned out to be innocent visitors.[99] Around the same time, police had to dispel rumours that an attempted derailment on the Llandudno and Colwyn Bay tramway was the work of suffragettes and, later that summer, in response to threats against property, towns and villages in Caernarfonshire organized their own night watchmen to protect chapels and other buildings.[100]

Suffragettes often determined to continue their protests during arrest and imprisonment. Magistrates frequently found proceedings disturbed by what they saw as irrelevant explanations of the accused's motivations. Some went even further. While awaiting her court case at Porthmadog in

---

[98]   *Glamorgan County Times*, 17 October 1913. 'In those days', recalled one Harlech man, 'the very name of Suffragette was something mysterious, even unpleasant. We'd say, "Here comes a suffragette", and run like blazes!' Oliver Wynne Hughes, *Every Day was Summer: Childhood Memories of Edwardian Days in a Small Welsh Town* (Llandysul, 1989), 4.

[99]   E. Vernon Jones, 'A champion of women's rights', 5; *WM*, 24 May 1913; *CDH*, 23, 30 May 1913. Scrupulous precautions accompanied the Holyhead meeting: 'The hall and cellars underneath, and all the adjoining rooms were searched before the meeting started. A cordon of police was on duty around the building, and the windows were barricaded to prevent a possible attack with stones and other missiles.' *Holyhead Chronicle*, 30 May 1913.

[100]   *North Wales Weekly News*, 16 May 1913; *CDH*, 29 August 1913. See also J. Ifor Davies, *The Caernarvon County School: A History* (Caernarfon, 1989), 246. Newspapers also reported 'special precautions being taken to prevent damage being done to the [Caernarfon] Castle' (two women carrying parcels being denied admittance on one occasion) and 'a strict vigil' being kept on various mansions in the county. *CDH*, 11 June 1913; *NWC*, 23 May 1913; *Holyhead Mail*, 23 May 1913. Again, the immediate reaction to an attempted train wreck at Blackwood, by placing stones on the line, was that it was 'another criminality of the suffragettes'. *Monmouthshire Weekly Post*, 19 April 1913.

June 1914, 'Phyllis North', one of the two Cricieth window smashers,

> barricaded herself in the cell by means of the bedstead, mattresses, and every movable thing she found in the room. The police were for about 15 minutes unable to get her out. They used iron bars, a saw and other implements to force the doors open.

Later, in court, when being removed from the dock, 'she clutched the rails, pushed her legs between the posts and twisted them in such a way that the four constables who were struggling with her could not extricate her'.[101] At Caernarfon Quarter Sessions a few weeks later, her fellow window smasher, 'Georgina Lloyd', attempted to jump out of the dock and had to be forcibly dragged back by three wardresses and two wardens; she then continued to struggle, shout and kick throughout the hearing, refusing to answer any questions.[102] Katherine Gatty proved to be a similarly difficult problem for the Abergavenny magistrates, having to be carried into court ('in the arms of two stalwart constables ... an operation which, judging by her smiles, gave her considerable gratification', maliciously suggested the local reporter) and thereafter displaying 'the insatiable appetite for display'. On being removed to Usk Prison, she declined to give up her possessions and she had to be forcibly deprived of her own clothes and put into prison dress.[103] Rachel Barrett also struggled against the wearing of prison clothes at Canterbury at the beginning of a nine-month sentence following her conviction for conspiracy, along with other members of *The Suffragette* newspaper staff, in June 1913.

The largely middle-class activists found the experience of prison profoundly shocking. 'It was a dark and very dirty cell. Someone had been sick down one of the walls, and it smelt like a urinal', recalled Margaret Mackworth. 'Its loneliness', she went on, 'its sense of being padlocked in, was sheer taut

[101] *NWC*, 5 June 1914. See also *CDH*, 5 June 1914; *North Wales Observer and Express*, 5 June 1914; *Holyhead Mail*, 5 June 1914; *Yr Herald Cymraeg*, 9 Mehefin 1914. Both culprits used aliases, 'Phyllis North' being Olive Wharry and 'Georgina Lloyd' (presumably a play on the name 'Lloyd George') being Emily Fussell.

[102] *CDH*, 3 July 1914.

[103] *Abergavenny Chronicle*, 23 August 1912; *VW*, 30 August 1912.

misery and there was a lot of dull drudgery too ...'[104]
'Degrading', 'fearful', 'terrible', concluded Welsh women
held in Holloway Gaol, highlighting 'the ghastly silence and
isolation', the lack of ventilation, hygiene and basic comforts,
the strict discipline and the poor quality of food, 'a filthy mess
not fit for pigs'.[105] Katherine Gatty found conditions there
similarly 'ghastly! The lavatory accommodation was absolutely
inadequate. The whole block was infested with mice & co. –
there was no heating apparatus at all.'[106]

In prison, extremists sometimes resorted to the hunger
strike. When first adopted in July 1909, the government's
response was to release such individuals, for fear of a suffragette death. With the spread of the tactic in subsequent months
and with the authorities appearing increasingly foolish,
forcible feeding, through the mouth or the nose, was introduced in September. Many found the horrors of this almost
unbearable but, showing immense courage and at serious risk
to their health, continued to resist food and even drink. Here
is 'Georgina Lloyd' describing her experiences at Caernarfon
Gaol:

> On Wednesday June 3, Miss Phyllis North and I arrived at Carnarvon
> Prison on remand and immediately started the hunger-and-thirst strike.
> Never once was I tempted to take food, but the anger and pain of the
> thirst strike is indescribable. I was afraid at times I should be forced to
> give in, but seemed again and again to be helped and sustained by some
> invisible force, and always at moments of deepest depression this feeling
> of outside help would return to brighten me up and the fight would be
> continued with renewed vigour.
>
> When out exercising on Thursday morning the Governor came to
> say he had orders to take our finger-prints. We both of course protested,
> and I struggled so much I fainted and had to be carried back to my cell.
> On the Friday I again fainted while exercising, and was carried in by
> wardresses and Miss North. On Saturday morning we were both forcibly

---

[104] Rhondda, *This was My World*, 121, 154. Her cousin, Florence Haig, recorded a
diary on sheets of dark brown prison toilet paper. Museum of London, Florence
Haig Papers; *Church Times*, 1 March 1968.

[105] Katherine Gatty to Mrs Arney, 14 March 1912, cited in June Purvis, 'The
prison experiences of the suffragettes in Edwardian Britain', *Women's History Review*,
4, 1 (1995), 109–10.

[106] *SWDN*, 22 December 1906, 1 January 1907; *WM*, 11 January, 21 February
1907.

fed. I struggled as much as I could, but was too weak to make an effective protest.

On Monday June 15, we were fed at 6 o'clock in the morning, and Miss North taken away by train to Liverpool. On Tuesday I followed.

On Wednesday, July 1, we were taken together by motor to Carnarvon. On Thursday, after the trial I began to struggle more and more against the feeding. To stand up calmly in one's cell waiting for the fight to begin is too dreadful for description. I was picked up bodily by one of the doctors, put down on to the bed and a blanket was wrapped tightly around me. In spite of six people sitting on me and holding various parts I could *not* be kept quiet. I was amazed at my own powers of resistance. My mouth was forced open and the food poured in. However, much of the food was spilt each time over my clothes and face and hair, down on to the cell floor and the bed, and over the bed and over the doctors and wardresses.

Twice the tube went down the wrong way and each time my voice would go entirely, and for a while I could not speak above a whisper . . .

On Sunday morning a doctor from the Home Office arrived, examined us, and watched the feeding process. I am sure the public would not tolerate forcible feeding for one moment could it but witness some of the scenes that take place. The whole proceedings are absolutely revolting. On Sunday I got fed three times, as the second time no food could be got down.

On Monday, July 6, Miss North was taken away to Holloway, and that afternoon the Governor came to tell me I was to be released the next day. He said all arrangements were being made. Although he knew my sister's address in London, he did not trouble to let her know of my coming till the next day; the consequence was I was left alone in a small commercial hotel feeling very ill and weak and very lonely until nearly twelve o'clock Tuesday night.

I am extremely thin and feel quite exhausted, and very run down after the fight.[107]

One of the most fiercely determined of suffragette prisoners was Katherine Gatty. Her conviction for window breaking at Abergavenny in August 1912 occurred only a few weeks after being released from Holloway Gaol, where she had been forcibly fed thirteen times. On imprisonment at Usk she immediately adopted the hunger strike and was forcibly fed twice before transfer to Holloway.[108]

[107] *The Suffragette*, 24 July 1914.
[108] *VW*, 30 August 1912. Kitty Marion, the actress suffragette and one of the

From April 1913, suffragettes were subject to the notorious Prisoners' (Temporary Discharge for Ill-Health) Act. Popularly known as the 'Cat and Mouse Act', this allowed hunger strikers to be temporarily released on licence until fit to resume their sentences, at which time they could be rearrested. From April 1913 until July 1914 Mrs Pankhurst was in and out of prison ten times. Similarly, Rachel Barrett was imprisoned and released three times during June and July 1913, having gone on hunger and thirst strikes, before escaping to an Edinburgh nursing home. She returned to London in December 1913 and for six months never left her bed-sitting room for fear of detectives, except to take exercise on her flat roof, all the while working on producing the weekly issue of *The Suffragette*.[109]

Suffragette courage was also evident in the face of public hostility, manifest from the early days of WSPU campaigning. Thus, speaking in Cardiff in the summer of 1907, Adela Pankhurst was subjected to 'concerted action by youthful hooligans of both sexes'; in the teeth of 'a fusillade of orange peel, banana skins and other missiles', she was forced to abandon the meeting, and 'under police protection ... was escorted to a tramcar, followed by a hooting and cheering crowd'.[110] Such 'escapes' became commonplace throughout Wales during subsequent years. In August 1909, for example, a holiday crowd of several thousands refused a hearing to suffragettes on the beach at Aberystwyth, heckling and gravel-throwing, culminating in a rush at the makeshift platform and the shredding of the WSPU flag; only the intervention of a police inspector and some male sympathizers saved the ladies from being driven into the sea.[111] Smaller gatherings could be equally threatening. A few months later, the *Aberdare Leader* reported thus on the reception given to Annie Kenney and Margaret Mackworth at the town's Liberal Club:

hecklers at the 1912 National Eisteddfod in Wrexham, served six prison sentences, and in one period of fourteen weeks and two days in early 1913 was force-fed 232 times. Crawford, *Women's Suffrage Movement*, 378.

[109] Barrett, *Draft Autobiography*. While in prison, she adopted the hunger-and-thirst strike.

[110] Arncliffe-Sennett Collection, vol. 1, February–July 1907, undated and untitled newspaper cutting.

[111] *Cardigan and Tivy-Side Advertiser*, 6 August 1909.

A number of youths and men were armed with bells, trumpets, and whistles which they used with a vengeance ... Cabbages were thrown into the hall through the windows and these were in turn hurled on to the platform. Bloaters and tomatoes were also thrown at the speakers. Mice were let loose in the body of the hall, and the presence of these creatures naturally caused no little panic among the many ladies present. Several chairs were broken, the wall-paper was greatly damaged and a window-pane was smashed. The fumes of sulphuretted hydrogen became well nigh intolerable, and violent sneezing throughout the hall testified to the presence of cayenne peppar and snuff.[112]

Clearly, the threat of serious physical injury was often real, not least in the clashes with police in the large London demonstrations, as most notoriously displayed on 'Black Friday' (18 November 1910) when women protesters were brutally treated. Among the 119 women arrested on this occasion were two of Margaret Mackworth's aunts, both giving Welsh addresses: Charlotte Haig (of 'Thatched Cottage, Llanwern, Newport') and Janet Boyd (of 'Pen Ithon, Radnorshire'). Another relative, Cecilia Haig, a cousin from Edinburgh, was also present at the demonstration and, it was claimed, died 'after a year's painful illness brought on in consequence of the terrible treatment to which she was subjected ... assault of the most disgraceful kind'.[113]

There are plenty of examples in Wales too, particularly involving suffragette attempts to target Lloyd George. One of his interrupters at Swansea in 1908 recalled the reaction of the assembly thus:

I felt as if I had put a match to powder magazine ... I saw a vast sea of faces vociferating hate at me, and waving sticks and umbrellas from the galleries above, shouting 'Turn her out'. Near me stood a steward, his face as white as a sheet, in a pouncing attitude as of one waiting to seize a wild beast. In front of me sat a clergyman who turned around and ground his teeth at me while his wife tried to scratch my arms ... I was hustled down the alleyway, shouted at by everyone, pinched, pulled, pummelled, kicked, and with my hat a ruin and my clothes pulled awry.[114]

---

[112] *Aberdare Leader*, 27 November 1909. See also *Merthyr Express*, 27 November 1909; Rhondda, *This was My World*, 121–3 (where the author mistakenly recalls the location as Merthyr); *Time and Tide*, 6 February 1843.

[113] *VW*, 18, 25 November 1910, 5 January 1912. See also Rhondda, *This was My World*, 166.

[114] Codd, *So Rich a Life*, 57–8.

The most dramatic episodes occurred in north Wales in 1912. First, there was the abuse meted out to Lloyd George's hecklers while delivering a speech at a disestablishment rally at Caernarfon in May. The *North Wales Chronicle* recorded the scenes thus:

> When they emerged from the Pavilion the Suffragists bore unmistake-able evidence of severe handling. The women's hair was dishevelled, and in some cases their dresses were badly torn. They were received by a large threatening crowd, who quickly surrounded them ... the women were subjected to a measure of brutality which was out of all proportion to any provocation they might have offered. Not content with leaving the interrupters in the hands of the appointed stewards, men who were in their near vicinity turned upon them, one woman being deliberately struck with an umbrella, while another received a blow in the face with a man's fist.[115]

In September, there was a ferocious public reaction to the persistent disturbance of Lloyd George's presidential address at the National Eisteddfod in Wrexham, the *Western Mail* describing the events thus:

> it was outside the pavilion that the worst scenes of retaliation took place. The police were helpless to protect their charges from the infuriated mass, which had developed into a mob outside the doors. Each of the women were [*sic*] smacked on the face, each one lost her hat, each one had bundles of hair torn ruthlessly from their roots, and each one suffered indignities. Blood flowed from the face of one of the women, the scalps of all of them bled owing to the uprooting of hair, and it was recorded by a credible eye-witness that the knife was used against one of the women. It was seen to gleam in the sun and to descend on the breast of the woman, but happily the cut was not serious. The police were helpless, and the assailant was not arrested. The coats, dresses, and blouses of the five women were torn more or less badly – and indeed one of them was almost stripped of her upper garments, and she presented a most sorry spectacle.[116]

---

[115]   *NWC*, 24 May 1912. See also Bangor University, Belmont MSS, 300, diary of Henry Lewis, 18 May 1912.

[116]   *WM*, 6 September 1912. See also below, 210. Similar fury had been aroused by protests at the 1909 National Eisteddfod, held in the Albert Hall, London, when suffragettes persistently interrupted Prime Minister Asquith's speech. One Eisteddfod official personally tore the 'Votes for Women' banner to shreds, while stewards and members of the audience bundled the offending women (sixteen in all) out of the building. Ibid., 17, 18 June 1909; *VW*, 18 June 1909.

Again, a few weeks later, 'scenes even more violent' occurred when protesters frequently interrupted Lloyd George's speech at the opening of an institute in his native village of Llanystumdwy:

> The crowd became enraged at their conduct and the meeting was at one time in a state of panic. The women fared badly, only being rescued with difficulty. It was stated that their clothes were torn from their backs, their hair was pulled out in bunches, and they were beaten about the head. One of them was flung clean over a hedge ... Some of them fell to the ground, and were trodden on.[117]

Protests were not, of course, unexpected and metropolitan police officers had been brought in to reinforce the local constabulary. Would-be hecklers were also well aware of the prospective dangers: 'If the Suffragettes do come to this hamlet tomorrow it will be at the risk of their lives. There will be an enormous gathering of Welshmen and Welsh-women collected – men from the quarries, the hills, and the pastures to whom Mr. Lloyd George is something more than a man, to whom he is a national institution.'[118]

The events made front-page coverage in many of the national daily newspapers, vivid reports being supported by photographic evidence; the *Daily Express*, for example, spoke of 'a real live suffragist hunt ... athletic quarrymen bearing home the trophies of rent skirts and torn strands of hair', and contended that only the intervention of the police 'saved the lives' of the four women who heckled the chancellor.[119]

By escalating militancy, especially after 1912, suffragettes thus often found themselves subject to intense public anger, hostility and violent attack. And it was, of course, letter burnings, window smashing and arson, hunger strikes, force feeding and the 'Cat and Mouse Act' and the manhandling of activists by police and public which dominated the widespread press coverage and subsequently evoked so many of the

---

[117] *WM*, 23 September 1912.
[118] *Daily Mail*, 21 September 1912.
[119] *Daily Express*, 23 September 1912. See also NA, HO 45/10689/228470, Disturbances: meeting in Wales attended by Lloyd George, suffragettes assaulted by crowd; Manchester University, John Rylands Library, MML / 5/ 21 and 46; Morris, "Merched y screch a'r twrw"; Holt, 'The battle of Llanystumdwy'; Jones, 'Lloyd George and the suffragettes at Llanystumdwy'.

memories. Yet such drama is emphatically only part of the suffragette story. Most WSPU members busied themselves in far more mundane campaigning activities, as Margaret Mackworth recalled of the movement in Newport:

> We formed a local branch of the Women's Social and Political Union, we ran a shop where one could buy suffrage literature, sold our weekly paper in the streets on market days, marched in poster parades, carried out door-to-door canvassing, wrote articles and letters for the local papers, and, above all, held meetings, meetings of all shapes and sizes, meetings in the shop, meetings in little halls, drawing-room meetings, street corner meetings (hundreds of street corner meetings) and occasionally meetings in the large Town Hall ... What people remember now seems to be chiefly the actual breaking of the law ... It did get broken, of course, but not, after all, so very often. I can only remember four or five people going to prison from our local branch in all the time we worked together.[120]

'A great deal of our work which wasn't law breaking at all was apt to be classed as militant', she added. And, indeed, this was so, because the highly demonstrative, dramatic, unconventional nature of suffragette agitation, the taking of the issue to the streets, was in such stark contrast to earlier activity. Neither law breaking, nor indeed militancy, were requirements of WSPU membership. Most did not themselves engage in illegal or violent action. Local WSPU members everywhere were able to find their own level of militancy, which often went no further than 'reminding Cabinet Ministers of what was expected of them', or church and theatre protests. 'Suffragette militancy' is a broad, imprecise term; it was multi-faceted, and must, of course, be seen in the context of the time.

Activists threw themselves into educational, propaganda and campaigning work with a commitment and zeal fired by a fierce sense of injustice and frustration, which led them to defend passionately those who did adopt extremism and also to castigate the press for 'focussing on broken windows rather than broken Cabinet promises'. 'No one should criticise anyone else's methods', argued Sybil Thomas, 'it is up to each

---

[120] *Time and Tide*, 6 February 1943.

individual activist.' Similarly, while eschewing violence herself, Fannie Margaret Thomas had 'the greatest respect for the noble women who were even prepared to die for the cause'.[121] Both were addressing meetings during the FCSU campaign in mid Glamorgan in April 1913 and such an attitude enabled them actively to support initiatives by militant and constitutional societies alike. The involvement of WSPU supporters in other organizations, such as the Church League for Women's Suffrage, the Actresses' Franchise League and the NUWSS, was common.

At best, it appears, the WSPU inspired just nine branches in Wales, some of limited duration.[122] Nevertheless, much of the populace came into contact with its vibrant campaigning and some with its militant actions. By 1914, few were unaware of suffragette fervour and notoriety. The dynamism for a women's suffrage movement in Wales sprang from the WSPU's initial inroads there from 1906, through its countless meetings, its holiday campaigns, its electoral activity, its dissemination of written material and, of course, its militancy, while, as we shall see, its offshoot, the Women's Freedom League, enthusiastically and conspicuously took up the torch in certain areas. The main constitutional body, the NUWSS, founded in 1897, made only slow progress in Wales, with just four branches by the end of 1909, and it was not until the immediate pre-war years that it emerged as the principal organization. Even then, to quote one NUWSS publicist, 'much of the enthusiasm expended in the ranks of the constitutional movement was generated and fed by the battles and sufferings of the militants'.[123] The role of the WSPU in awakening consciousness, in creating suffragists as much as suffragettes, in imposing the single issue of the vote on a disparate women's movement and in demanding public focus on a forty-year-old campaign must not be underestimated. The sentiments of one Cardiff activist must stand for many

---

[121] *Porthcawl News*, 24 April 1913; *Glamorgan Gazette*, 25 April 1913.
[122] The nine were at Barry, Cardiff, Caernarfon, Carmarthen, Llanelli, Maesteg, Newport, Pontypool and Ton-du (list compiled from WSPU *Annual Reports* and newspaper references).
[123] *Woman's Leader*, 14 March 1930.

others: 'I did not realise the importance of the women's vote till the militant movement began. I was not in the least opposed to it but did not see that it mattered ... militancy opened my eyes.'[124]

[124] SFC, 58.87/ 72, Lettice Floyd to Edith How Martyn, 10 May 1932. Lettice Floyd was a close friend of WSPU organizer Annie Williams, assisting her in Cardiff and elsewhere. In her two years at Cardiff she proved a stalwart of the local WSPU branch, helping to run the shop, selling papers, raising funds, donating generously herself and participating in protests; arrested on a number of occasions, she was imprisoned twice and forcibly fed. Ibid., 58. 87/ 73, 1 February 1931, 26 March, 10 May 1932; A. J. R., *Suffrage Annual*, 241–2; Crawford, *Women's Suffrage Movement*, 224–5.

III

THE WOMEN'S FREEDOM LEAGUE, 1907–1914

During its lifetime the WSPU suffered a series of schisms. The first, and most serious, occurred in September 1907 and led to the foundation of the Women's Freedom League (WFL). At the heart of the split was the conflict between the belief of Emmeline and Christabel Pankhurst in the need for an autocratic organization and the strong desire of others for internal democracy.[1] The dissension climaxed with Mrs Pankhurst's decision to cancel the annual conference scheduled for October 1907 and impose an authoritarian style of leadership. A number of prominent activists, including Teresa Billington-Greig, Charlotte Despard, Alice Abadam and a former student at Aberystwyth and WSPU secretary, Edith How Martyn, promptly resigned and set up a new provisional committee. Another member of the initial WFL executive committee was Marie Winton Evans, a London Welshwoman who had been imprisoned earlier in the year.[2] This pressed on with the conference, which ratified a democratic constitution and elected a national executive and officers. Some six weeks of confusion, during which two bodies laid claim to the title WSPU, ended with the seceders giving way and adopting the name WFL in November.[3]

The choice of name was significant, symbolizing the wide-ranging ambitions of the protagonists. In common with the many other suffrage societies that came into being in the decade before the First World War, the aim of the WFL was 'to secure for Women the Parliamentary Vote on the same terms

---

[1]   Five years later, the league suffered its own rift, centring on the alleged autocratic behaviour of the president, Charlotte Despard, seven members of the national executive committee resigning following a 'special conference' in April 1912. *The Vote*, 4 May 1912. There were also local resignations over this issue, including Swansea's Emily Phipps, one of Wales's most prominent activists, though she was later to rejoin. *South Wales Weekly Post* (*SWWP*), 8 February 1913.

[2]   *SWDN*, 21, 22 March 1907; *WM*, 21, 22 March 1907; *CT*, 6 April 1907. For Edith How Martyn, see Hilary Frances, 'Martyn, Edith How (1875–1954)', *ODNB*.

[3]   *WF*, 10, 17, 24 October, 14, 28 November 1907.

as it is or may be granted to men'. Uniquely, however, its constitution added two further objectives: 'to use the power thus obtained to establish equality of rights and opportunities between the sexes; and to promote the social and industrial well-being of the community'. Thus, the WFL did not disband either with the partial winning of the vote in 1918 or with the granting of equal franchise in 1928; it continued until 1961, representing over half a century of campaigning.

Thirty-one of the fifty-two WSPU branches then in existence were represented at the conference of October 1907, though apparently only a dozen committed themselves to the new self-governing organization.[4] The one Welsh WSPU branch founded by this time, in Cardiff, appears to have mirrored the national rift for, while a local WSPU continued to function, a number of prominent members broke away and established a WFL branch; the former remained in existence until the outbreak of war, the latter until the post-war years. By 1908 the league had fifty-three branches in England, Wales and Scotland but by 1914 total membership was only 4,000. As such, it was always the smallest of the three main suffragist societies. Nevertheless, unlike the WSPU, it created and retained a democratic structure, with annual conferences and an elected national executive committee and president (who was Charlotte Despard until 1926). Furthermore, the WFL retained its ILP roots, which the WSPU abandoned in 1906.

On inception, the league's immediate priority was to establish itself as an independent suffrage society, militant yet distinct from the WSPU. Thus, in its early months, several novel tactics were introduced that were designed to attract publicity and emphasize women's voteless status. Members used the police courts to protest against female subjection to 'man-made laws', visited Cabinet ministers at their homes and resisted the payment of taxes; the latter, developing the long-standing suffragist argument of 'no taxation without representation', remained very much part of the WFL campaign over the next seven years (as well as inspiring the formation of a separate organization, the Women's Tax Resistance League, in 1909). Militancy certainly extended to arrest and imprison-

---

[4]   Ibid., 10 October 1907; *The Vote*, 9 December 1909.

ment. During 1908, twenty-nine of the total of 142 suffragettes imprisoned were WFL members. One of the most publicized of the year's protests occurred in October when three league members interrupted a House of Commons debate while chained to the grille of the ladies' gallery; simultaneously, others caused disturbances elsewhere in the building, four-teen women subsequently being gaoled.[5] A further thirty-nine league members were imprisoned during 1909, twenty-six of them in February for obstruction during 'raids' on Downing Street and the House of Commons.[6] The precise nature of its militancy was to be a perennial topic of debate within the WFL.

The league was also innovative in its methods of propa-ganda. In November 1907, the first women carrying sandwich boards to advertise the campaign were to be seen on the streets of London. The following summer, the first suffrage caravan toured south-east England, a mode of operation which henceforth became an established feature of the league's calendar. Another tactic was the overnight placarding of ministers' houses and public buildings with thousands of proclamations demanding the immediate enfranchisement of women. More spectacular was the showering of central London with handbills from a balloon in January 1909, while later in the year the league conducted a fifteen-month contin-uous picket of the House of Commons in an effort to persuade the prime minister, Asquith, to meet a deputation. His repeated refusal induced more direct protest when two activists poured chemicals into the ballot box at the Bermondsey by-election in November in an attempt to deface voting slips.[7] In 1912, two members harangued MPs from a boat on the River Thames while they were taking tea on the terrace of the House of Commons.

[5] WFL, *Annual Conference Report*, 1908, 5; *The Vote*, 9 December 1909; Pankhurst, *The Suffragette Movement*, 293–4.
[6] Among those arrested (twice) was Mary Gwyther, a dental nurse from Cardiff. *SWDN*, 19, 20 February 1909; *WM*, 19, 20 February 1909; *South Wales Echo*, 19 February 1909; *CT*, 20 February 1909; *The Times*, 19, 20 February 1909; *WF*, 25 February 1909.
[7] Stella Newsome, *The Women's Freedom League, 1907–1957* (London, 1958), 4–7; *The Vote*, 4 November 1909.

Such actions largely took place in London but the league, of course, aspired to be a national body, which necessitated the building up and organization of regional strength. Accordingly, from 1908, speakers visited other areas of the country in order to stimulate activity. In May, Charlotte Despard came to south Wales, holding meetings in Cardiff, Caldicot and Pontypridd. Accompanied by National Union of Women's Suffrage Societies (NUWSS) leader, Millicent Fawcett, their reception was indicative of the hostility facing any public advocate of women's suffrage, even before the WSPU's adoption of window smashing and other attacks on property. In Cardiff, they arrived at the meeting hall 'after having spent about an hour in the streets dodging crowds of hooting young hooligans' and then completely failed to obtain a hearing; 'amidst one of the wildest scenes ever witnessed in the city . . . the crowd smashed the windows of the hall, captured the banners and mottoes of the Suffragists, smashed the furniture, and stormed the platform'.[8] At Caldicot, the speakers struggled to make headway against 'an antagonistic opposition', the meeting prematurely terminating in the face of a counter-resolution and amid 'general disorder, the company hooting, ringing bells and making other discordant sounds'.[9] Similarly, the Pontypridd meeting was broken up by 'unrestrained hooliganism'. Here, Charlotte Despard's 'throbbing anticipation of the evening's tumult before us' proved all too prophetic, as the local press vividly recounted:

> A scene without a parallel in the annals of Pontypridd took place, on Wednesday night, at the New Town Hall, where a public meeting in support of women's suffrage was to be held . . . Before a single person appeared on the stage the place was in a regular bedlam, with bells ringing and general cheers filling the air. It can safely be said that the din of the whistles, mouth organs, trumpets, alarm clocks and other instruments surpassed anything heard in the town or the Rhondda Valleys before. When Mrs Gregory, one of the chief promoters, made an appearance there were hundreds of the audience on their feet shouting frantically, whilst the ladies – for whose exclusive use the

[8] *WF*, 28 May 1908; *CT*, 16 May 1908; *Daily Chronicle*, 12 May 1908, cutting in Arncliffe-Sennett Collection, vol. 3, 38; David Rubinstein, *A Different World For Women: The Life of Millicent Garrett Fawcett* (Columbus, Ohio, 1991), 160. Four arrests were made.

[9] *Chepstow Weekly Advertiser*, 16 May 1908.

galleries had wisely been reserved – held their handkerchiefs to their
noses to stave off the effects of snuff and stuffs which were thrown about
to cause sneezing . . . Not only was there trouble inside the hall, but the
people waiting to get into the building had to undergo the unpleasant
experience of a bombardment with rotten fruit and refuse from the
market. Some of the stewards had their clothing spoilt, and the
policemen's clothing was not improved by the fusillade. A box of
bloaters was found, and having been broken open the fish were thrown
about amongst the crowd.[10]

The episode gave the area a lasting notoriety, daunting to
activists. 'To attend a Suffrage meeting in Pontypridd', observed
one NUWSS organizer in 1912, 'seems almost an act of
heroism. This feeling dates from a time some years ago, when
a Suffragist meeting was broken up by men who trooped
down the valleys for that purpose.'[11]

A succession of WFL representatives visited Wales over the
years, travelling from place to place, addressing meetings and
seeking to generate interest and support. The summer of
1909 saw the first extensive effort made. In the north, prominent league members from Liverpool and Manchester took
their campaign into largely untouched communities along
the coast and inland – to Colwyn Bay, Llandudno and Conwy,
to Llanwrst, Penmaenmawr and Llanfairfechan, to Bangor,
Caernarfon and Bethesda, to Menai Bridge, Beaumaris and
Holyhead. As so often, the call for assistance stressed a
rewarding combination of labour and leisure:

> Work amongst ideal conditions of climate and scenery, with an oppor-
> tunity for learning Welsh, are the attractions which the North Wales
> Summer Centre offers . . .Those who have not yet fixed their summer
> holidays would do well to consider Llanfairfechan, where they can enjoy
> sea and mountain air and give substantial help to the cause at the same
> time . . . Members who cannot speak might offer their services as house-
> keeper or cook. The duties in this respect will not be arduous.[12]

Local sympathizers played valuable roles in organizing meetings but the principal figures were English suffragettes; time

[10] *Glamorgan Free Press*, 15 May 1908. See also *Pontypridd Observer*, 16 May 1908;
CT, 16 May 1908; *WF*, 21, 28 May 1908; Cook and Evans, 'Petty antics', 167–8;
Masson, 'Women versus "the people"', 6–8.
[11] *The Common Cause* (*CC*), 29 November 1912.
[12] *WF*, 10, 24 July 1909.

and again, the request was for Welsh-language speakers. Meanwhile, in the south, league activity centred on Swansea, reaching out to the holiday bays of the Gower, to industrial towns like Llanelli, Neath, Gorseinon, Skewen, Ystalyfera and Brynamman, and further afield to Carmarthen, Llandeilo and even Llandrindod Wells. In the south-east, Cardiff was the natural focus with meetings also being held in Barry, Penarth, Cowbridge and Newport.

Audiences were often large, sometimes numbering several thousands. Organizers' reports no doubt regularly exaggerated the enthusiasm elicited, sometimes to the point of idealism, as in this account of a Bethesda meeting in September 1909:

> Never shall we forget the scene on our arrival in this picturesque little town. Hundreds of men and women crowded the streets, waiting in the rain, with an eager tensity that made one tingle. Up went our banner, and, followed by a cheering multitude, we wended our way to the hillside field, where, on a natural platform, we took our stand. There as we stood the public streamed and streamed till over 2,000 stood around us in a silence that could be felt. And if never before, we felt the true greatness of our work at that awe-inspiring moment.[13]

In reality, disruption, either for sport or through hostility to the cause, was rarely absent. Commonly, speakers had to battle to gain a hearing against all manner of disturbance. At Llanwrst, there was 'three-quarters of an hour's competition with bugles and gramaphones', while Menai Bridge's welcome entailed a 'lavish expenditure of eggs and energy'.[14] Countless instances of varying degrees of animosity could be cited; accordingly, the threat of physical injury was very real and often made police protection a necessity. While a WFL meeting was in progress in Penarth in November 1909, for example, 'the crowd outside charged the police and the hall, and the police had to clear the street before the ladies could get away in a cab by a side exit'.[15] Similarly, league activists touring mid and north-west Wales in September 1913 had to be escorted out of both Pwllheli and Llanidloes in the face of

---

[13]   Ibid., 9 September 1909.
[14]   *WF*, 26 August 1909.
[15]   *CT*, 13 November 1909.

violent crowds, the constables themselves sustaining injuries in the latter case.[16] On the other hand, authority could prove obstructive too, particularly in denying meeting places, as campaigners found in a number of Welsh towns; for some time, suffrage meetings were forbidden in the public parks of Cardiff, while one WFL organizer recounted how, at Penmaenmawr, she and her companions were 'pursued [by police] from the beach, where we had planted our flags well below high-water mark', and 'chased from pillar to post', before eventually obtaining the use of a farmer's field.[17]

The role of organizers was crucial to the development of all three main suffrage societies. One of their main functions was forming and invigorating branches, the key to sustained local agitation: 'The central organisation cannot reach every worker and sympathiser as efficiently as a local Branch ... it is branch work which sustains the League, welds its energies and makes it an effective fighting unit'.[18] References in *Women's Franchise* and *The Vote* indicate the existence, at one point or another between 1908 and 1914, of thirteen WFL branches in Wales: Aberdare, Aberdovey, Aberystwyth, Bangor, Barry, Brynmawr, Caldicot, Cardiff (renamed South Glamorgan for a period), Carmarthen, Llanelli, Maesteg, Montgomery Boroughs and Swansea. At no time, however, was more than half of this number operational. Indeed, those at Aberystwyth, Bangor, Carmarthen, Llanelli and Maesteg seem to have hardly got off the ground at all, while others were active for only a matter of months. The most durable were those in Caldicot, Cardiff, Montgomery Boroughs and Swansea.

'As a result of Mrs. Despard's recent visit to Cardiff new life has been infused into the Branch, and members are now working hard', recorded *The Vote* in November 1912.[19] And so often, of course, this was the reality – local enthusiasm fired by external stimulus, only to wane subsequently. Cardiff was the first branch formed in Wales, dating from the birth of the WFL itself, in September 1907. The second, at Caldicot, came into being a year later and remained active until the early

16 *WF*, 5, 12 September 1913; *Montgomeryshire Express*, 9 September 1913.
17 *WF*, 12 August 1909.
18 *The Vote*, 17 December 1910, 11 February 1911.
19 Ibid., 9 November 1912.

months of 1912, when its driving force, Louisa Corben, took up a prominent position in the Church League for Women's Suffrage. The branches at Swansea (founded in March 1909) and in the Montgomery Boroughs (founded in July 1911) were easily the most vigorous in Wales and, indeed, among the strongest in Britain.

'Is there no hope for the dead Branches?' asked one delegate at the 1909 annual conference. 'Four have died; can they not be resuscitated?' The response, from the league's chief organizer, Teresa Billington-Greig, was typically forthright: 'They have chiefly died from local indifference. The only thing is to send an Organising Secretary into the district. If you will help us raise the money we shall have them far more than resuscitated.'[20] Touring league agents like Muriel Matters, Alice Schofield and Anna Munro were instrumental not only in the formation of branches in Wales and elsewhere; their regular return was necessary to encourage vitality. Recognizing the need for a more permanent presence, the league introduced a scheme of district organizers into the various regions of Britain in May 1910 – four for England, two for Scotland and one each for Ireland and Wales; it was also hoped to save money, appoint women familiar with their areas and afford more local control over particular activities. The person appointed for Wales was Mary McCleod Cleeves, secretary of the Swansea branch and a national executive committee member, who, during the year she held the position, carried out a considerable amount of valuable work – arranging, chairing and addressing meetings around the country, campaigning in a number of constituencies in the general elections of 1910 and helping to set up several branches. Unfortunately, her tenure of office ended amidst a great deal of acrimony arising out of a clash with her fellow members at Swansea who claimed that she was assuming too much authority. Such became the depth of the bitterness that, following her split with the local branch, Mrs Cleeves first refused to give up its minute book and then, seething with indignation, burnt it and sent back the ashes. A full enquiry, involving the despatch of league officials from London to

---

[20]   WFL, *Annual Conference Report*, 1909, 4.

Swansea, resulted in Mrs Cleeves's resignation and her defec-
tion to the WSPU. The episode also led the national executive
to conclude that relationships generally between district
organizers and branches were unsatisfactory; shortly afterwards the whole scheme was terminated.[21]

The one other representative from Wales to serve on the
executive in pre-war years was the remarkably energetic Alix
Minnie Clark of Newtown (1874–1948), unquestionably the
driving force behind the league's considerable success in
Montgomeryshire. The daughter of a local ironmonger, she
was first drawn into WFL work during the 1910 general elections, rapidly rising to become one of the society's national
figures, organizing and speaking in propaganda campaigns in
Wales, England and Scotland, activities which she continued
throughout the war years and beyond the winning of limited
women's enfranchisement in 1918. She served on the league
executive from 1912 to 1928 and, like so many of her fellow
campaigners, remained immensely proud of her contribution
to the cause; WFL banners and photographs of meetings and
processions retained pride of place in the Weybridge home
she inhabited for many years, while her closest friends were
always those of 'the old days'. In the last weeks of her life, aged
seventy-four, in poor health and living in a nursing home in
Surrey, she was still posting a knitted parcel of clothes for the
league's 1948 spring sale.[22]

The degree of branch activity was, of course, largely
dependent on the energy and enthusiasm of local members.
This was certainly the prime factor in Swansea, where the
presence of a number of thoroughly committed individuals
ensured a flourishing organization which built up a large
membership, raised its own funds and sustained a range of
political and social activities for more than five years up to the
outbreak of war; indeed, the branch continued to function
into the 1930s. Its origin apparently lay in a typical WSPU

[21]   WFL, executive minutes, 24–25 March, 22–23 May, 18–19 June, 21–22 July
1911; Claire Eustance, '"Daring to be free": the evolution of women's political identities in the Women's Freedom League, 1907–30' (Ph.D. thesis, University of York,
1993), 69–70; *SWWP*, 8 February 1913.
[22]   *Women's Bulletin*, 14 May 1948; A. J. R., *Suffrage Annual*, 205; David Pugh, 'The
suffragette campaign in Newtown during the general elections of 1910', *The
Newtonian*, 7 (2001), 10–17.

protest and provides a good example of the effect of militancy in awakening female consciousness, as this recollection illustrates:

> She [Emily Phipps] introduced herself as the oldest of the old Presidents [of the National Union of Women Teachers] and then, in her forceful and witty manner, described the making of a militant suffragette. It was in 1908 when Lloyd George was speaking in Swansea, and Miss Phipps with Miss Neal decided to attend the meeting to hear the great man.
>
> Previous to this, she had given no serious thought to the question of Votes for Women. Of course, women ought to have votes, but why make all this fuss about it? In this frame of mind she went to the meeting.
>
> The Albert Hall, Swansea, was packed to the doors. The audience listened with rapt attention until, suddenly, a small voice said, 'We pay taxes'. And what was Mr. Lloyd George's reply? 'The lady says she pays taxes. I wonder how much she was paid for coming here this evening'. Then pandemonium; stewards rushed on the speaker, seized her roughly and flung her from the hall.
>
> While this was being done, Lloyd George called out, 'Fling them out ruthlessly; show them no mercy'. From that moment, Miss Phipps was a militant suffragette . . .[23]

During the following months, Emily Phipps and a handful of others held a number of preliminary meetings, secured the assistance of WFL organizer, Mary Manning, and in March 1909 founded a branch. In a year, membership rose from an initial twelve to 146, plus sixteen 'men associates', and by 1911 the branch had a well-developed administrative structure, comprising a president, an organizing secretary, correspondence secretary and literature secretary, a treasurer and two permanent subcommittees. Swansea was deemed sufficiently important for the whole national executive committee to visit the town in late September/early October 1910. The only other league branch in Wales comparable to Swansea in membership, drive and permanence was Montgomery Boroughs. Developing out of the considerable groundwork laid in two general election campaigns in the constituency in 1910, the branch was formally launched in July 1911 in the presence of WFL president, Charlotte Despard. It began with

---

[23] *Woman Teacher*, 5 October 1928. See also *SWDP*, 2 October 1908; *VW*, 8 October 1908; *WF*, 25 March 1909; Hilda Kean, *Deeds Not Words: The Lives of Suffragette Teachers* (London, 1990), 22–3.

a membership of twenty; by the end of the year it had risen to 120, principally based in Newtown, Welshpool and Llanfyllin but also taking in smaller communities throughout the county.[24] Most Welsh branches, however, attracted only a small membership, numbering just a few dozen.

Regular functions and activities were, of course, vital to maintaining members' enthusiasm. No Welsh WFL branch had its own offices; thus the venue was often an official's home, or perhaps a local schoolroom or chapel. Of first importance was 'missionary work', the constant drive to tackle public indifference and opposition and to attract members and support. 'We have held, during the year', recorded Swansea's first *Annual Report* in 1910, 'four Mass Meetings in the Albert Hall, thirty-six Branch Meetings, twelve Committees and six Speakers' Classes'.[25] Such vigour enabled activists to cover various parts of the town and surrounding areas, including the bustling industrial communities of the region, and, in the summer months, the popular coastal resorts to the west. The latter sometimes called for 'the holiday spirit', as at Tenby in 1909:

> Brilliant sunshine had brought the crowds to the shore to bathe. We met the situation by hiring a bathing machine, and from this novel rostrum we delivered our message to hundreds of interested listeners. In the audience was a Liberal MP who enlivened proceedings by cross-questioning.[26]

Montgomery branch members campaigned in accessible seaside resorts too, at Aberystwyth, Aberdovey, Barmouth and other places along the western seaboard. Inland, they took the cause into the 'unbroken ground' of the small rural towns and villages of mid Wales, while Cardiff stalwarts periodically ventured into the industrial heartland of the south, seeking to 'educate the miners with regard to Woman Suffrage'; a few active branches were founded here, as at Aberdare and

---

[24] WFL, *Annual Report*, 1911, 27–8; *The Vote*, 15 July 1911; *Montgomery County Times*, 8 July 1911; *Montgomeryshire Express*, 11 July 1911. See also Pugh, 'The suffragette campaign in Newtown', 10–17.

[25] Swansea University, Kirkland Papers, A1, *Report of the Swansea Branch of the WFL*, 1909–10, 4.

[26] *WF*, 19 August 1909.

Brynmawr, but, given the degree of labour unrest in the pre-war years, campaigners generally found the people 'indifferent, if not actually antagonistic'.[27] In many of these enterprises valuable oratorical skills and experience were provided by the league's national organizers who so often toured Wales. Such visits were sometimes used by branches to stage large public meetings, involving hired halls bedecked with banners and posters and advance publicity of a formal and informal kind:

> Swansea rubbed its eyes in the morning to see a dozen well dressed women ... walking in the road with umbrellas up and wearing the regalia of the League. The *raison d'être* of the umbrellas became apparent as each passed when huge bills announcing the forthcoming Albert Hall meeting in Swansea were seen pinned to the outside.[28]

Free from fear of disruption were the select gatherings of members and friends, the drawing-room meetings and the 'at homes', which, in spite of the term, could be sizeable affairs; 350 guests met for tea at one such function in Newtown in November 1911. Most common of all, however, were the open-air meetings, often of an impromptu, makeshift nature – a waggonette at Llanfyllin market, a huge beer barrel outside a Llanidloes hotel, a lorry at Cardiff docks, a rocky outcrop on Aberystwyth beach all provided the speakers' platforms.

Circulation of the League's own weekly newspaper was, of course, another important means of rousing and sustaining interest in the cause. 'The Vote is very popular', commented the Montgomery Boroughs' *Annual Report* in 1911, 'no difficulty is experienced in selling it, the members like it, and look forward each week to receiving it'.[29] In such a large and scattered branch, its role was a particularly valuable one; indeed, in 1914, several prominent local activists paid for a thousand copies of the special 'holiday number' for free distribution.[30] Montgomery Boroughs also produced one of the league's

---

[27] *The Vote*, 2 March 1912. See, for example, the hostility towards WFL representatives at Aberdare in July 1913. *Aberdare Leader*, 5 July 1913; *Mountain Ash Post*, 5 July 1913.

[28] *The Vote*, 8 October 1910.

[29] WFL, *Annual Report*, 1911, 28. Launched in October 1909, *The Vote* continued until 1933, when it was replaced by the much less substantial *Women's Bulletin*. For the first two years of its existence the league contributed a page to the weekly *Women's Franchise*.

[30] *The Vote*, 24 July 1914.

most prolific propagandists in Alix Clark; 'probably no individual ever sold more numbers of *The Vote* than she did, running into several hundreds a week', observed her obituary.[31] Outstanding efforts were singled out for praise elsewhere too but, essentially, obtaining new readers was deemed every member's responsibility. In some centres, branches deposited issues in public places, such as libraries, waiting rooms and hotels. At the same time, local leaders were mindful of the need to deepen knowledge of the movement among their 'converted'; thus, Swansea operated its own lending library for members.[32]

An enterprising method of educating the public was the staging of performances of suffragist plays, which often gained full and favourable coverage in the local press. 'An intellectual and spectacular treat', applauded the *South Wales Daily Post* of one such occasion, in May 1910, even though it could not accept the underlying message:

> The sceptic may not have been exactly converted to the side of the Suffragettes by the 'Pageant of Famous Women', as produced under the auspices of the local branch of the Women's Freedom League, but, nevertheless, the audience that crowded the Swansea Albert Hall on Thursday evening was highly delighted with the entertainment. Mere man can and does admire the important part that woman has played in the world's history. Miss Cicely Hamilton, the gifted authoress of the production, who played by far the most important part in it, was in herself a living witness to the fact that women as well as men possess brains ... The wisdom of giving votes to women is perhaps another matter, and this was the feeling of many who saw the pageant.[33]

The pageant, which moved on to Maesteg the following day, was a celebration of women's achievements and abilities throughout the ages. Other popular productions were farces, ridiculing the arguments of anti-suffragists. Typical of this type was Cicely Hamilton's *How the Vote was Won*, performed in Cardiff in November 1909.[34]

Cicely Hamilton was the most popular of the suffragist playwrights and a member of the WFL and the Women

---

[31]   *Women's Bulletin*, 14 May 1948.
[32]   *The Vote*, 3, 24 February 1912; WFL, *Annual Report*, 1911, 31.
[33]   *SWDP*, 6 May 1910. See also *Cambrian*, 13 May 1910; *Herald of Wales*, 7 May 1910.
[34]   *WM*, 11, 13 November 1909; *The Vote*, 18 November 1909.

Writers' Suffrage League. The latter, along with the Actresses' Franchise League, had been founded in 1908 with the aim of enlisting the theatrical profession in the campaign. Apart from the strong moral message of the plays, local branches naturally sought maximum propaganda value from the performances. Thus, for Swansea's production of the pageant, banners and placards hung from the balconies and walls, a large red dragon proclaiming 'Y Bleidlais i Ferched' ('The Vote for Women') added a Welsh flavour, and against the grand organ was the branch's own banner, designed and made by members, and bearing the league's motto (*Dare to be Free*) and its colours (green, white and gold); midway through proceedings, WFL president, Charlotte Despard, addressed the audience.[35]

The mixing of propaganda with enjoyment was an important feature of local suffrage activity and meetings commonly included recitations, piano solos, singing, dramatic sketches and refreshments. Swansea members enthusiastically took up morris dancing ('a pleasant social link which bring us all more closely together'), while in the summer months tennis occasionally preceded a speaker's address.[36] Social events also offered opportunities for fund-raising, a constant consideration of branches in order to meet local expenses and to satisfy the financial demands of league headquarters. Popular activities in this regard included jumble sales, cake and candy stalls, whist drives and garden parties. Sometimes more substantial efforts were made to raise money for 'the sinews of war', the best examples in Wales being the 'Green, White and Gold Fairs' held in Montgomeryshire, at Llanfyllin and Newtown, in July 1912. Using the spacious gardens of two local members, the various attractions included stalls, music, recitations, dancing and competitions, while speeches and the sale of literature ensured that the women's suffrage question was given a prominent airing. Thereby, in spite of vandalism prior to the Newtown function, the local league branch was able to advance the cause by a combination of 'business, pleasure and propaganda'.[37]

---

[35] *Cambria Daily Leader*, 6 May 1910. See also Masson, 'Votes for women', 35; eadem, 'The Swansea suffragettes', 69, 73–4.

[36] *The Vote*, 2 July, 17 December 1910.

[37] Ibid., 15 June, 6, 27 July 1912.

While the main preoccupation was the demand for the franchise, local activists concerned themselves with a diversity of wider issues. Addressing a public meeting in Cardiff in June 1913, Mary Keating Hill explained that 'the object of the League was to bring about a rearrangement of domestic service and to improve living conditions'; women could use their votes 'to raise the age of consent and marriage, to protect the lives of young girls, to enforce parental responsibility whether parents were married or unmarried, to make divorce laws apply equally to men and women and to bring other reforms affecting women'.[38] The programme of lectures and discussions at Swansea branch meetings offers striking evidence of the range of interests. Its *Annual Report* for 1911, for example, recorded addresses on early motherhood, the poor law, municipal lodging houses for women, and 'social reformers with a literary trend' in the shape of H. G. Wells and George Bernard Shaw. The provision of a municipal lodging house in the town was a particular concern. The lecture on this subject, by a branch member, was based on first-hand local investigation and was followed by a deputation to the health committee of the town council. 'We consider that we are a moral force in the town; our opinions are respected . . .', concluded the report.[39] Other topics debated by Welsh branches included the desirability of nursery schools and creche facilities to help the working mother, employment opportunities and conditions for women, reform of the laws relating to divorce and custody of children and legislation to protect girls from male sexual exploitation (the so-called 'white slave traffic').

Indeed, a recurrent theme of the league's campaign was the unjust operation of the legal system in relation to women. As part of its 'war against law', a column entitled 'How some men protect women' appeared in *The Vote* from February 1912, carrying reports designed to show 'not only how women suffer from acts of violence, but how slight a penalty the law exacts for such violence, in comparison with crimes against property'. In Wales, as elsewhere, league members attended

[38]   *WM*, 21 June 1913.
[39]   WFL, *Annual Report*, 1911, 3.

local courts and contributed newspaper cuttings of cases, involving attempted murder, rape, indecent assault, sexual abuse of children and other crimes.[40] All of this information sought to illustrate male oppression of women and to counter anti-suffragists' argument that women were adequately protected by the state.

The franchise was seen as the key to progress on all of these matters and, in spite of broader concerns, dominated branch discussions and activities. Thus, league branches in Wales canvassed local MPs, town councils, political associations and trade unions, urging them to declare support publicly for women's suffrage.[41] In pursuit of this fundamental aim, co-operation with other suffrage societies was not uncommon. In Wales, collaboration was particularly apparent in Swansea, where WFL and NUWSS branches sometimes came together in joint meetings and deputations, and members of both helped in the formation of a branch of the Church League for Women's Suffrage in 1913 and of the Free Church League for Women's Suffrage the following year.[42] There was clearly an overlap in personnel too, in Swansea and elsewhere in Wales. Membership of one of the religious or professional suffrage bodies as well as one of the three main societies was certainly commonplace throughout the whole movement. In Swansea, WFL members also belonged to the Church League, the Free Church League, the Women Teachers' Franchise Union and the Artists' Franchise League. The novelist, Flora Annie Steel, a league activist in mid Wales, was president of the Women Writers' Suffrage League, while another prominent figure with Welsh connections, Margaret Wynne Nevinson, public speaker and author of a number of league publications, was also a member of both the Church and Women Writers' Leagues. The daughter of an Anglican clergyman, a Welsh-speaking Welshman from Lampeter, she was a social worker in east London and a teacher before becoming a full-time

[40]   *The Vote*, 24 February, 23 March, 27 July, 12 October 1912, 10 January, 11 July 1913.

[41]   WFL, *Annual Report*, 1911, 31; *The Vote*, 20, 27 May 1911.

[42]   *The Vote*, 27 May 1911, 18 April 1913, 13 February, 20 March, 17 April 1914; *Church League Women's Suffrage Monthly Paper*, June 1913; *Cambrian*, 6 February 1914; *Free Church Times*, May 1914.

suffrage organizer.[43] Like many others, she had left the WSPU and joined the WFL on its inception in 1907; a minority, like Sybil Thomas of Llanwern and the Pontycymer elementary school headmistress, Fannie Thomas, remained active in both, such was their desire to promote women's suffrage in whatever way possible.

The WFL, like other suffrage societies, was also ready to work with a variety of local organizations in order to advance the cause. Meetings held under the auspices of branches of the Independent Labour Party, the Women's Labour League or socialist societies offered an opportunity for the problems of working-class women to be more fully debated and related to the suffrage campaign. Recruitment among this sector was altogether more difficult, however, and met with only limited success. Evidently, WFL membership in Wales remained very much like its branch leadership, thoroughly middle class.

At Swansea, Emily Phipps and her lifelong companion, Clara Neal, were local headmistresses. West-country women (the former from Devon, the latter from Cornwall), they both came to the town in the early 1890s and spent the remainder of their teaching careers there. Founder members of the Swansea branches of the National Federation of Women Teachers (NFWT) and the WFL, they remained very active in both organizations for most of their lives. In the words of one of Miss Neal's obituarists, theirs was 'a lifelong unbroken association' and she was 'to her chosen friend ... the light that never failed'.[44] The strong connection with the teaching profession was also evident in the support given to the branch by both the staff and students of Swansea training college; especially prominent were the principal's two daughters, Mary

[43]   See Angela V. John, 'Margaret Wynne Nevinson: gender and national identity in the early twentieth century', in R. R. Davies and Geraint H. Jenkins (eds), *From Medieval to Modern Wales: Historical Essays in Honour of Kenneth O. Morgan and Ralph A. Griffiths* (Cardiff, 2004), 230–45; eadem, 'Nevinson, Margaret Wynne (1858–1932)', *ODNB*; A. J. R., *Suffrage Annual*, 318; Crawford, *Women's Suffrage Movement*, 445–6.

[44]   *Woman Teacher*, 15 January 1937. See also ibid., 5 October 1928, 18 June 1943; *The Vote*, 1 May 1925; 25 April 1930; *South Wales Evening Post*, 5 January 1937; 6 May 1943; Kean, *Deeds Not Words*, passim; eadem, 'Phipps, Emily Frost (1865–1943)', *ODNB*; Alison Oram, *Women Teachers and Feminist Politics, 1900–1939* (Manchester, 1996), 209–11; Masson, 'The Swansea suffragettes', 74–5.

and Dorothy Salmon (the former was 'lady superintendent' at the college), and two lecturers, Winifred Hindshaw and Hilda Davies. Other activists engaged in paid employment worked in shops and businesses. Several others were married to notable local figures; Mary Cleeves was the wife of a coal exporter, while Ellen Seyler, another founder member and stalwart, was the wife of Swansea's public analyst and noted local historian, Clarence Seyler. Over the years, the branch committee of twelve divided almost evenly between single and married women. They were invariably from middle-class back-grounds, the one exception being Jennie Ross, a native of the west Midlands and sister of Emma Sproson, one of the few working-class women to become prominent in the WFL. A skilled tailoress, she settled in Swansea after marriage and became active in the local labour and cooperative movements. Most of the WFL branch committee, however, were members of the town's Women's Liberal Association.[45]

Branch membership at Swansea indicates the degree to which local suffrage involvement could be built around family and friendship links. Activists included a number of mothers and daughters, the most prominent of whom were Mary and Sylvia Cleeves, Emilie and Muriel Hutton, and Lilian, Dorothy and Gwendoline Knight, as well as various sets of sisters, such as the Salmons and the Knights, already mentioned, and Margaret and Jenny Kirkland. There was also the cooperation and support of male relatives – husbands, sons and brothers – either as 'men associates' or simply assisting with activities.[46]

In mid Wales, notable WFL activists tended to be of a higher social order and belonged to both Conservative and Liberal families. On its formation in July 1911, the leading officials of the Montgomery Boroughs' branch were Mrs Harriet Busch-Mitchell of Crosswood, Welshpool, as president, Mrs Courteney Scott of Pennant Hall, Abermule, as vice-president and Mrs Ada Felix-Jones of Llanfyllin as treasurer. Alix Clark,

---

[45] See Kirkland Papers, B1, *Petition of Women's Liberal Association for Swansea calling for 'extension of the Parliamentary Franchise to Women'*. For Emma Sproson, see Jane Martin, 'Sproson, Emma (1867–1936)', *ODNB*.

[46] Ibid., A1, *Report of the Swansea Branch of the WFL*, 1909–10. Among the sixteen 'men associates' of the branch at this time were three male members of the Cleeves family.

secretary of the Montgomery Boroughs' branch, has already been mentioned, while two other figures prominent in its activities were the novelist Flora Annie Steel and Mrs Frances Lewis, both of whom had been instrumental in the formation of a branch at Aberdovey, in neighbouring Merioneth, earlier in the year and which in reality seems to have merged with the new organization.[47]

The WFL was always eager to emphasize the economic interests of women and it was, no doubt, the inequalities between the sexes in their profession that attracted many teachers to the suffrage movement.[48] Membership of the league was particularly strong among members of the NFWT, at that time a pressure group within the National Union of Teachers (NUT), and this ensured that the issue of women's suffrage was raised at national conferences. Supporters first managed to get a motion expressing sympathy on to the agenda at the 1911 conference, held in Aberystwyth. Its reception, as described by Emily Phipps, indicates the degree of hostility to the cause present in this most respectable and moderate of professions:

> Then broke out the wildest scenes of disorder . . . Hundreds of men, massed at the back of the hall, prevented Mr Croft from obtaining a hearing. They stamped, howled, hurled insults at the speaker and at suffragists, and utterly refused to allow Mr Croft's speech to proceed. This continued without intermission for thirty minutes, at the end of which time Mr Croft had to resume his seat.[49]

The motion was decisively defeated, as it was in 1912, 1913 and 1914, outcomes that do not necessarily illustrate antisuffragism but reflect convictions on the proper function of the union. Nevertheless, an indignant Emily Phipps could

[47] For Harriet Busch-Mitchell, Ada Felix-Jones and Frances Lewis, see A. J. R., *Suffrage Annual*, 197, 279, 290. The Aberdovey branch was founded in January 1911, re-formed in March 1915 and apparently continued until 1921. *The Vote*, 14 January 1911, 16 April 1915; *ASR*, October 1912.

[48] See Kean, *Deeds not Words*, 19–21; Oram, *Women Teachers and Feminist Politics*, 118–24; Eustance, 'Daring to be free', 116–17. A Women Teachers' Franchise Union was founded in July 1912. For this organization and for a discussion of the whole issue, see also Susan Trouvé-Finding, 'Unionised women teachers and women's suffrage', in Boussahba-Bravard, *Suffrage Outside Suffragism*, 205–31.

[49] Emily Phipps, *A History of the National Union of Women Teachers* (London, 1928), 7. See also *Welsh Gazette*, 20 April 1911; *CN*, 21 April 1911; *Schoolmaster*, 22 April 1911.

later record that NFWT activists never managed 'to elicit an
official expression of sympathy for the principle of women's
suffrage, and a partial measure of enfranchisement was passed
in 1918 without there having been any official support, not
even a Resolution of sympathy, from the NUT'.[50] Nevertheless,
annual conferences became regular occasions for suffrage,
and indeed anti-suffrage, campaigns. The WFL was invariably
to the fore, public meetings, newspaper selling, poster parades
and other forms of propaganda serving to attract much
attention. League members were also involved in some of the
more heated exchanges during the conference debates on
women's suffrage and in the constant heckling of the first
address by a Cabinet minister to the NUT, that of Lord
Haldane in 1913, during which some nineteen women delegates were ejected.[51]

Welsh activists certainly played their part in these activities.
Alix Clark of Newtown was the league's organizer for a
number of conference campaigns, both before and during
the war, while Emily Phipps and Clara Neal of Swansea were
prominent members of the NFWT.[52] Members of this organization were determined to challenge the injustices facing
women within the teaching profession (especially the disparity
in pay and the marriage bar), and the suffrage was fundamental to this. 'The vote was a sign of equality, and they
wished their men folk to recognise their equality and joint
rulership', insisted Fannie Thomas of Pontycymer in her
inaugural presidential address at the 1912 NFWT annual
conference.[53] The federation itself had started as the Equal

[50]   Phipps, *History of the NUWT*, 13.
[51]   *The Vote*, 4 April 1913; *Schoolmaster*, 29 April 1913.
[52]   In 1920 the NFWT, which had remained a body inside the NUT, became the
National Union of Women Teachers (NUWT), which, with the acquisition of its
own offices and the launch of the *Woman Teacher*, quickly established itself on an
independent footing. Emily Phipps and Clara Neal served as national presidents of
the organization, during 1915–17 and 1927 respectively. Alix Clark was still
attending NUWT conferences a few weeks before she died in 1948, while other
teachers active in the WFL's suffrage campaign were Jenny Phillips, secretary of the
Aberdare branch, and Miss M. A. Judd and Miss Lewey, leading members in Brynmawr. For Miss Phillips's earlier involvement in the women's branch of the ILP in
Aberdare (as chair), see Masson, *Women's Rights*, 63, 76, 78–9.
[53]   *The Times*, 8 April 1912. A committed suffrage campaigner, Miss Thomas went
on to become an urban district councillor in Ogmore and Garw in the post-war
years. *Glamorgan Gazette*, 11 April 1919; Kean, *Deeds Not Words*, p. 91.

Pay League in 1904 and this remained one of its principal objects. 'In the Civil Service women doing the same work as men received from a half to two-thirds of what the men were paid', Emily Phipps told the 1913 conference. 'In the teaching profession they were paid anything from a half (never two-thirds) ... the vote was the only remedy for women's under-paid work.'[54] The vote was also vital for the futures of the pupils in their care. 'Why should they teach girls how to think for themselves and explain citizenship, and yet not hold out the hope of some day aiding by their vote the ideal they would like to attain?' asked Fannie Thomas. 'Did not all women teachers feel sorry to see young girls only just out of their hands about the streets, and would they not like to prevent this?'[55] She and others were also deeply concerned about the poverty of pupils. At the 1914 NUT conference, Clara Neal spoke of 'the waste of time, money and energy in trying to educate children who were deficient in food, clothing and decent housing accommodation', while Emily Phipps, as NFWT parliamentary candidate for Chelsea in 1918, urged 'progress and reform in the matter of housing, greater attention to education, improved laws to secure better health and pure food'.[56]

In common with other suffrage societies, the WFL looked upon parliamentary elections as excellent opportunities for vigorous campaigning. Alongside the WSPU and the NUWSS, it was particularly active in the Pembrokeshire by-election of July 1908, in opposition to the Liberal suffragist, W. F. Roch, on the basis that a Liberal government was refusing to sponsor a women's suffrage bill. League representatives addressed a large number of meetings and distributed literature across the wide constituency but their stance was a difficult one to advance. 'The Liberals are strong here, and ... they resent our opposition to their candidates', recorded one of their agents.[57]

---

[54] *The Vote*, 4 April. 1913. The league changed its name to the NFWT in 1907. Miss Phipps resigned from the NUT executive because of its continued support for unequal pay scales. Trouvé-Finding, 'Unionised women teachers and women's suffrage', 207, 225.

[55] *The Times*, 8 April 1912.

[56] *The Vote*, 24 April 1914; Kean, *Deeds Not Words*, 88.

[57] *WF*, 16 July 1908.

The year 1910, with its two general elections, saw much effort expended in this direction. In January, specific campaigns were mounted against Wales's two high-ranking Cabinet ministers, the chancellor of the Exchequer, David Lloyd George, in Caernarfon Boroughs, and the home secretary, Reginald McKenna, in North Monmouthshire, and against two outspoken anti-suffragist Liberals, Sir Samuel Evans in Mid Glamorgan and Sir J. D. Rees in Montgomery Boroughs. Organizers, appointed by the league executive in London, directed operations and drew on the assistance of local suffragists as much as possible. Committee rooms and shops were opened, daily meetings held, the press was courted and literature widely disseminated. In spite of activists' claims, their effect on the actual voting is impossible to assess, though they certainly forced candidates to pronounce on the women's suffrage issue and carried out a significant measure of propaganda work. 'We know that we have done real good in arousing interest on the question of Votes for Women in a district untouched before by any of the societies', wrote the organizer for Montgomery Boroughs.[58] And, indeed, by attracting large audiences to meetings at Newtown, Welshpool, Montgomery and Llanfyllin, and in recruiting committed local supporters, this electoral campaign, together with another later in the year, prepared the ground for a strong and vibrant WFL branch, which was to dominate the agitation in the mid Wales region. Elsewhere too, the suffragettes' energy in covering scattered centres of population with meetings and leaflets did much to tackle public ignorance of the movement.

Nonetheless, venturing into the Liberal strongholds of Wales was a hazardous experience. 'Our first meeting lasted five minutes and ended in a rush', reported one WFL activist from Newtown in January 1910, while later a crowd surrounded and stoned the house in which they were staying.[59] The antagonism was equally apparent in north-west Wales, where 'worshippers at the shrine of Mr Lloyd George' proved to be

---

[58]   *The Vote*, 29 January 1910. See also *Montgomeryshire Express*, 29 January 1910.
[59]   *The Vote*, 15 January 1910. See also *Montgomeryshire Express*, 11 January 1910; *Montgomery County Times*, 8 January 1910; Pugh, 'The suffragette campaign in Newtown', 13–15.

fierce adversaries, again to the extent of attacking the ladies' lodgings in Caernarfon, action which necessitated the intervention of police with batons.[60] When league representatives returned for the second general election of the year, in December, the police advised immediate withdrawal from the constituency. 'Prompt and uncompromising refusal!' was the response, though the authorities' fears were to prove justified when, on polling day, the increasingly menacing attitude of thousands of quarrymen who flocked into the town resulted in 'an ugly rush' on the Guildhall; 'I was nearly killed', recalled one activist.[61] Police protection was also required for those campaigning in Montgomery Boroughs, the only other Welsh constituency selected for concerted league action at this election (after which suffragettes celebrated the defeat of the Liberal incumbent and 'inveterate opponent of women's suffrage', J. D. Rees). In Cardiff Boroughs, too, WFL activists drew satisfaction from the defeat of the Liberal candidate, Sir Clarendon Hyde, having denounced his anti-suffragist stance in a series of open-air meetings.[62] Elsewhere, activity was confined to branch members questioning candidates in an effort to elicit firm commitments on the issue.

Another by-election in Mid Glamorgan in March 1910 (its third in five years) afforded a further opportunity to raise the twin cries of 'votes for women' and 'keep the Liberal out' in meetings throughout a large constituency. Wales organizer, Mary Cleeves, and other league stalwarts from Swansea were swiftly into the field, accompanied by a delegation from the national executive, all spiritedly but unsuccessfully seeking to defeat another Liberal suffragist, the local tinplate owner, F. W. Gibbins.[63]

In 1912, the league changed its electoral policy to supporting Labour in three-cornered contests, 'as a more effective weapon against a Government that denies justice to women'. Accordingly, it was active in East Carmarthenshire in

---

[60] *The Vote*, 29 January 1910.

[61] Ibid., 17 December 1910; SFC, 58. 87/68, *Recollections of Marguerite Annie Sidley*, 14 June 1931.

[62] *The Vote*, 26 November, 3, 10, 17, 24 December 1910; WFL, *Annual Report*, 1910, 23.

[63] *The Vote*, 26 March, 2, 9 April 1910.

August 1912, campaigning on behalf of Dr J. H. Williams. The WFL campaign urged the rejection of a Liberal candidate whose party had 'betrayed the cause of women's suffrage and . . . indicates with very clear signs its intention to continue its policy of tyranny and injustice to women in the future'.[64] Once again, however, Liberal principles, articulated on this occasion by the influential local Independent minister, the Revd Towyn Jones, comfortably overcame the Conservative challenge. The Labour Party performed poorly, coming bottom of the poll. Inadequate election machinery and failure to present a distinctive programme were key reasons, though one of its young constituency workers, James Griffiths (who in 1964 became Wales's first secretary of state), many years later vividly recalled another factor:

> One day there stalked – yes, that is the right word, stalked – into our committee rooms at Ammanford a tall lady, dressed in an unorthodox style, trilby hat, short hair, collar and tie, and with a cigarette at the end of a long holder. She introduced herself as Miss Nina Boyle [WFL organizer], of the militant suffragette movement. They had no members in the constituency so would be willing to join forces with us during the campaign, and if we would allow one of their speakers to address our meetings they would pay half the cost. The bargain was struck and for the rest of the campaign we shared our platform . . . We lost votes because of our youthful gallantry but were amply repaid by the experience.[65]

In fact, the league and the other women's suffrage societies succeeded in holding enthusiastic meetings over a wide area – in the villages along the higher reaches of the Tywi, in the small townships along the shores of Carmarthen Bay and in the more populous industrial centres of Llanelli, Ammanford, Brynamman and elsewhere. Public addresses were supplemented by 'a systematic canvass and a wholesale distribution of strongly-worded literature', as well as the questioning of candidates at their gatherings.[66] If women's suffrage never became a central election issue in East Carmarthenshire, it nevertheless enjoyed a significant and serious airing.

[64] A.J.R., *Suffrage Annual*, 115–16; *WM*, 21 August 1912.
[65] James Griffiths, *Pages From Memory* (London, 1969), 17–18. See also *The Vote*, 10, 17, 24, 31 August 1912, and below, 168–9.
[66] *WM*, 15, 17, 19 August 1912.

Nationally, the league was always ready to participate in the large suffrage demonstrations held in London. In June 1908 it was one of a number of organizations (though excluding the WSPU) to give support to the NUWSS procession, which stretched for two miles, numbered between ten and fifteen thousand women and was adorned by an unprecedented display of banners.[67] The next major public demonstrations were held during 1910–11, in support of the Conciliation Bills then before Parliament. In June 1910, the WSPU and the WFL organized the From Prison to Citizenship procession. Once again, between ten and fifteen thousand women, carrying 700 banners and marching to the accompaniment of forty bands, made an imposing spectacle. Among the many contingents was one comprising fifty women from Wales, largely members of WFL branches, half of whom were from Swansea and the remainder from Caldicot, Cardiff and Barry. They were headed by two of their number dressed in traditional Welsh costume and carrying 'the national banner' bearing a red dragon and carrying the inscription 'Y Bleidlais i Ferched' ('The Vote for Women'); others carried branch banners or flowers.[68] A few weeks later, the WFL was one of some twenty suffrage societies (though not the NUWSS) which again marched in splendid pageantry, in two processions converging on Hyde Park, where 150 speakers addressed the crowds from forty platforms. Welsh participants gathered around their own platform, where the principal speakers were WSPU compatriots, Rachel Barrett and Dr Helena Jones.[69] There was also significant Welsh support for the most imposing of all the suffrage demonstrations, the Women's Coronation Procession of June 1911, the one occasion on which all the societies joined together in a display of unity. Amongst the WFL contingents were representatives from forty-four branches, including five Welsh ones – those at Aberdare, Barry, Caldicot, Cardiff and Swansea.[70]

[67]   Tickner, *Spectacle of Women*, 85. A contingent from the CDWSS took part. *SWDN*, 15 June 1908; *WM*, 15 June 1908; *South Wales Echo*, 13, 15 June 1908; *CT*, 20 June 1908. See also below, 137.
[68]   *SWDN*, 20 June 1910; *CT*, 25 June 1910; Tickner, *Spectacle of Women*, 111–15.
[69]   *SWDN*, 25 July 1910; *CT*, 30 July 1910.
[70]   *The Vote*, 20 May, 10, 17, 24 June 1911.

These spectacles attracted widespread coverage in the press, much of it of a highly complimentary nature. 'An exquisite pageant', ran a *Western Mail* editorial in June 1910, 'the sweet strains of music, the exuberant gaiety of the flowers, the gorgeous silken banners, added to the formidable proportions of the procession and the remarkable variety of the interests represented, contributing to an effect which taxes the vocabulary of the word artist'. The writer went on, however, as did other commentators, to doubt the political effectiveness of such processions. 'In all its outward aspects the women's suffrage demonstration on Saturday was very successful', remarked the *South Wales Daily News*, 'but if the promoters think that it will soften the hearts of ministers and induce them to give facilities for the Women's Suffrage Bill they are greatly mistaken.' At other times the same newspaper was contemptuous:

> Saturday's Pageant did not advance a single argument for the Vote. On the contrary, it seems to us that it tended to bring the whole movement into ridicule ... 'Ex-prisoners' were there in all the unspeakable glory of martyrdom ... Many of those who took part in the procession would have been better employed at home.[71]

Such views contrasted starkly with the (misplaced) mood of optimism among the suffragists themselves.

From its inception, the WFL was at pains to identify itself as a militant society, but one whose militancy differed significantly from that of the WSPU. Particularly after 1911, when the latter embarked upon a campaign of window smashing, arson and other destructive acts, the league emphatically rejected violence and at times condemned the methods of its sister organization.

'Militant but not violent', as distinct from WSPU extremism and NUWSS constitutionalism, was the league's position and one reaffirmed repeatedly in leading articles in *The Vote* in the immediate pre-war years:

> 'Militant Suffragist' conveys no idea to-day save of an aggressive destroyer of public property ... Nevertheless, it must be remembered that the term 'militant' was earned and adopted by the advanced wings of the Suffrage movement long before a stone was thrown or a window

[71]   *WM*, 20 June 1910; *SWDN*, 25 July, 20 June 1910.

broken by any Suffragist; and the Women's Freedom League remains what it has always been, one of the militant Suffrage societies which no longer plead for, but demand insistently, equal rights for women with men within the King's dominions . . .

The first imprisonments took place for holding a meeting of protest against the brutally violent ejection of women from a Liberal meeting. Other militant demonstrations took place in Parliament-square, Downing-street, the House of Commons, Trafalgar-square, the police-courts, and elsewhere . . . In all of these the Freedom League played its part. The picketing of the House of Commons, the Grille protest, the Ballot-box protest, the Census and Tax Resistance campaigns, were Freedom League work. Freedom League workers were among the first prisoners . . .

The term 'militant', therefore, does not depend on the amount of damage inflicted, and was not brought into existence by throwing stones or burning houses. It marked the new departure in 1905; and though late events have somewhat overshadowed with their sensationalism the militancy of the Women's Freedom League it remains a militant society.[72]

Central to the league's philosophy was a strategy of civil disobedience and passive resistance. In April 1911 the focus of such protest was the decennial census; 'since they could not be citizens for the purpose of voting, they would not be citizens for the purpose of helping the Government to compile statistics', explained the Swansea stalwart, Emily Phipps.[73] Articles in *The Vote* urged all branches to take part, while visits from official representatives offered guidance and further stimulus. On census night, members from Cardiff, Swansea, Barry, Aberdare and Caldicot participated in the boycott. Some did so by joining all-night walking parties, some sheltered in non-resident premises, others assembled at houses where the occupier was a resister. In Swansea, Mary Cleeves opened her home to any would-be evaders; some ventured out to chalk and bill-post the town with the message, 'No Votes for Women, No Census'; the majority passed the time amidst impromptu entertainment. Most adventurously, five local members spent an uncomfortable night in a sea-cave on the Gower coast. The census protest proved effective in

[72]   *The Vote*, 4 December 1913.
[73]   *Woman Teacher*, 5 October 1928.

attracting press attention and in generating enthusiasm amongst the league membership, and indeed among WSPU and NUWSS activists too. Its success encouraged other forms of 'passive resistance'.[74]

Tax resistance had been undertaken by a small number of league members over the years; it now assumed a greater prominence in official policy and at branch level. In all, over 220 women undertook tax resistance. Mary Cleeves was one such protester. In October 1910 she appeared before Swansea police court charged with keeping a carriage without a licence; when she refused to pay the fine and costs, the vehicle was distrained. The court case, distraint and subsequent auction became the focus of a branch campaign, which received a good deal of publicity, the local press recording Mrs Cleeves's stance of 'no vote, no tax' and publishing photographs of the vehicle being taken away. A protest meeting disturbed the sale, at which another WFL member bought the carriage and promptly returned it to its original owner, who was then driven home in triumph.[75] The following March, shortly before leaving the league, Mary Cleeves was again defying the authorities, this time refusing to pay income tax.[76] Another resister with Welsh connections was the well-known novelist, Flora Annie Steel, who was distrained for non-payment of the rates on her cottage near Aberdovey in May 1913 and again in July 1914; on both occasions, levy of the amount by the sale of a manuscript chapter of one of her books was accompanied by well-publicized protests, involving banners, placards and a gathering of sympathizers.[77]

Early in 1910, with the formation of the Conciliation Committee and amid optimism that the government would actively support a measure to enfranchise women, the league, alongside the WSPU, had called a 'truce'; tax resistance would

[74] *The Vote*, 11, 18, 25 February, 4, 11 March, 8, 15 April 1911; *Woman Teacher*, 5 October 1928; WFL, *Annual Report*, 1911, 19, 31; Kean, *Deeds Not Words*, 25–6; Eustance, 'Daring to be free', 173–6.

[75] *Cambrian*, 21, 28 October 1910; *The Vote*, 29 October, 5 November 1910.

[76] *The Vote*, 25 March 1911.

[77] Ibid., 23 May 1913, 7 August 1914; *CN*, 21 July 1914; *VW*, 31 July 1914; Flora Annie Steel, *The Garden of Fidelity* (London, 1929), 265; Violet Powell, *Flora Annie Steel* (London, 1981), 123–4. See also Rosemary Cargill Raza, 'Steel, Flora Annie (1847–1929)', *ODNB*.

continue and a census protest would be introduced in 1911, but more explicit forms of militancy were suspended and remained so for almost three years. Such concessions made little impression on the public, however, and opponents continued to show their hostility. In July 1912, for example, a league meeting in Newtown was broken up and the speakers physically attacked and pursued by 'a yelling, savage mob, more like wild beasts than human beings', while a few days later, a fund-raising fair in the same town was wrecked in an overnight attack: 'Woodwork was smashed to atoms and decorative material, which adorned the stalls and which had involved many hours of patient labour, was torn to shreds.'[78]

Such episodes aroused a deep sense of outrage and, in the face of what many saw as government prevarication and duplicity, league strategy encountered increasing criticism from activists; 'all desire for militancy has died out of the so-called Militant Department', complained Alix Clark in 1912.[79] Eventually, in January 1913, following the collapse of the government's Reform Bill, the truce was abandoned, more than a year after the WSPU had terminated its truce. Within a few weeks, Swansea members were plastering the town with handbills condemning Asquith for betrayal of his pledges: 'DARE TO BE FREE!' they ran, 'Whereas the Prime Minister has Egregiously Failed to secure the fulfilment of his pledges, Militant Suffragists ... announce their intention to Defy and Resist Government without Consent.'[80] Thus, the years 1913 and 1914 saw the league adopt more open and direct anti-government protest and a return to the public demonstrations and arrests of the pre-1910 years.

Clearly, WFL militancy, in terms of tax resistance, census evasion and police court protests, had only a limited impact on Wales. As with the WSPU, however, such protest was not a league requisite; 'all members must approve, though they need not actually participate in, militant action', was the stipulation.[81] Local activists were certainly very ready to defend the

[78] *The Vote*, 27 July 1912. See also *Montgomeryshire Express*, 23 July 1912; *Montgomery County Times*, 27 July 1912.

[79] WFL, *Special Conference Report*, 1912, 22.

[80] *SWDP*, 3 February 1913; *SWWP*, 8 February 1913; Jennie Ross Papers (Swansea Museum), cited in Masson, 'Votes for women', 37.

[81] Kirkland Papers, A2, *Programme for the Pageant of Famous Women*.

more extreme actions of some of their comrades but, again like the WSPU, of much greater significance in Wales was the society's educative and propaganda role. Although branches often proved fairly short-lived, the league nevertheless took the women's suffrage campaign into a host of communities, holding hundreds of public meetings and carrying out other forms of 'persuasive work', and certainly in west Glamorgan and mid Wales its local enthusiasts were a considerable force, pioneering and dominating the suffrage agitation.

IV

THE NATIONAL UNION OF WOMEN'S SUFFRAGE SOCIETIES, 1897–1914

The Women's Freedom League (WFL) and the Women's Social and Political Union (WSPU) comprised the militant wing of the suffragist movement, although they developed into very different bodies in the years following the 1907 split. The National Union of Women's Suffrage Societies (NUWSS) spearheaded the constitutional wing, though most of the many other organizations, centred primarily on religious, professional and political party affiliations, which came into being in the pre-war period, also fell into this category. While the militants became associated with illegal and, in the case of the WSPU, violent methods of agitation, constitutionalists emphasized their commitment to strictly law-abiding tactics. This fundamental distinction cannot be applied unreservedly for the reality of the movement was more complex. Most members of the WSPU and WFL did not themselves engage in illegal or violent action, while many suffragists were members of militant and constitutionalist societies simultaneously, evidence that, certainly for a period of time, they did not 'view the two approaches to campaigning as either mutually exclusive or at odds with one another'.[1] Moreover, spurred by the example of the WSPU, by early 1907 the NUWSS had also adopted a much more demonstrative and vigorous style of agitation and taken the issue onto the streets, tactics which only a few years earlier would have been considered unconventional, shocking and, indeed, militant.

The foundation of the NUWSS in October 1897 saw the four most important regional women's suffrage societies, all of which dated from the late 1860s, assigned responsibility for a definite area of England and Wales, the names reflecting their geographical commission: the Central and Western Society

---

[1] Sandra Stanley Holton, *Feminism and Democracy: Women's Suffrage and Reform Politics in Britain, 1900–1918* (Cambridge, 1986), 4.

(formerly named the Central National Society), the Central and East of England Society (formerly the Central Committee of the National Society), the North of England Society (formerly the Manchester National Society), and the Bristol and West of England Society. An executive committee comprising representatives from the member societies headed the newly formed federation. Its outstanding figure was the fifty-year-old Millicent Garrett Fawcett, widow of the radical Liberal MP, Professor Henry Fawcett. Brought up in an actively feminist family, her interests stretched across the whole spectrum of the women's movement. Above all, however, she was a lifelong suffrage campaigner.

The other twenty-five members of the executive had similar characteristics. Mostly middle class and middle aged, with years of experience in the suffrage campaign and in other aspects of the cause, they were often active in women's party organizations and in local public affairs. A number had close connections with the male political world through family ties, including Eleanor Rathbone and Nora Philipps, the daughter and wife respectively of Liberal MPs for Welsh constituencies.[2] The bulk of the executive members were characterized by innate faith in the House of Commons, and a firm conviction that MPs would ultimately bow to reasoned argument and be persuaded of the justice of women's suffrage. Thus, in its early years the NUWSS continued the same patient tactics of its predecessor, the National Society for Women's Suffrage (NSWS). Its executive met regularly with parliamentary sympathizers (prominent among whom was the Liberal MP for Swansea District, Brynmor Jones) and deferred to their advice. Women campaigners remained, in the disdainful opinion of John Gibson in the *Cambrian News*, 'satisfied to sing hymns at their meetings and to drink afternoon tea on the Terrace of the House of Commons with the more or less spurious "champions" of their cause'.[3]

---

[2] William Rathbone, a Liverpool merchant, represented Caernarvonshire from 1880 to 1885 and, following redistribution, the northern part of the county (Arfon) from 1885 to 1895. For J. Wynford Philipps, see ch. I, n. 37.

[3] *CN*, 10 July 1908. David Brynmor Jones, a London Welshman knighted in 1906, was MP for Swansea District, 1895–1915. His wife was also a suffragist, active in the WUWLA and, for several years, served on the WLF executive.

Even though passage through all stages of the House of Commons was highly unlikely, the promotion of private members' bills was still perceived as the best means of attracting parliamentary and public attention; a majority of Liberal MPs voting in favour might also induce the government to sponsor a measure. Local societies were kept informed of parliamentary developments and urged to get up petitions and to write to, or wait upon, MPs; lists of members who 'have expressed themselves more or less favourably to their con-stituents' on women's suffrage were regularly published by the executive committee.

In its early years, the NUWSS was unable to make any parlia-mentary impact, and in the seven years following Faithfull Begg's moral success in February 1897, not one bill or resolu-tion came before the House of Commons. In March 1904, renewed interest was reflected in the passage of Sir Charles McLaren's motion, 'That the disabilities of women in respect of the Parliamentary franchise ought to be removed by legisla-tion'. Thereafter the issue was debated every year until the outbreak of the First World War, though a vote did not neces-sarily ensue, for a number of bills were 'talked out' by opponents.

Serving principally as a committee to coordinate the activ-ities of the member societies and to liaise between them and parliamentary sympathizers, the NUWSS, in its early years, bore no resemblance to the powerful organization it was later to become. Essentially, the societies in the national union were independent bodies, left free to carry out suffrage work along their own lines. The turn of the century was a quiescent period for the movement, the South African War of 1899–1902 dominating British politics. Just one suffrage meeting appears to have been held in Wales in these years, in Monmouth in November 1899, a foothold that was to result in Wales's first NUWSS branch in 1904, attached to the Bristol and West of England Society.[4] It never became a flourishing organization and its secretary, the former Women's Franchise League activist, Mary Maclaverty, regularly appealed for more

[4] *Monmouthshire Beacon*, 24 November 1899; *Women's Suffrage Record*, December 1904; 30 April 1905; NUWSS, *Annual Report*, 1903–4, 12.

members and funds. 'At present', she wrote in 1908, 'the Monmouth branch only just maintains its own needs, and is unable to assist the Parent Society.' Nonetheless, its handful of stalwarts kept the cause alive over a decade through intermittent activity, largely in the form of public meetings addressed by a succession of outside speakers. Millicent Fawcett came in March 1908, for example, leading one local enthusiast to express the hope that 'her splendid and kind championship will give impetus to the work which has been carried on in Monmouth for four years by a few members, under discouraging conditions'.[5]

The transformation of the NUWSS, by 1910, into the largest single organization campaigning for the enfranchisement of women can be traced to its sponsorship of a National Convention in Defence of the Civic Rights of Women in London in October 1903; thereafter, it began to exert more control over its affiliates in terms of formulating and directing policies and activities, and a new organizational scheme led to the establishment of a large number of committees, several of which quickly developed into branches (totalling thirty-one by 1906).[6]

The NUWSS questioned all candidates at the 1906 general election, receiving 415 expressions of support for some measure of women's enfranchisement, including twenty-three from Wales.[7] Later in the year, a by-election in Mid Glamorgan provided the opportunity for action against one of the most prominent Liberal anti-suffragists of the day, Samuel Evans. Encouraged by the prospect of a Labour candidature from the miners' agent and suffragist, Vernon Hartshorn, the NUWSS engaged appropriate speakers – Selina Cooper, Ethel Snowden and Isabella Rowlette, ILP, trade union and suffragist activists from northern England – to support him. In the event, a cautious South Wales Miners' Federation refused to endorse Hartshorn's candidature and no contest ensued.

---

[5] *Monmouthshire Beacon*, 13 March 1908; *WF*, 12 March 1908. 'There has been a small branch of the National Union in Monmouth for some years', ran a report of meetings addressed by Alice Abadam in February 1913, 'and now it is hoped to make a new beginning on a firmer basis.' *CC*, 2 May 1913.

[6] NUWSS, *Annual Report*, 1903–4, 5, appendix.

[7] *Women's Suffrage Record*, 31 December 1905.

Suffragist participation was dominated by WSPU disruption of Evans's meetings, tactics from which the constitutionalists publicly disassociated themselves.[8]

It was Evans's destructive role in the parliamentary initiatives earlier in the year which made him such a target of suffragists. He was involved in the 'talking out' of both Sir Charles Dilke's adult suffrage bill in March and Keir Hardie's resolution 'that sex should cease to be a bar to the exercise of the Parliamentary franchise' the following month. Hardie, a strong promoter of the cause inside and outside Westminster, spoke in both debates.[9] Evans was particularly prominent in the second, his lengthy recitation of a catalogue of familiar anti-suffragist arguments serving to prolong the debate and prevent a division.[10] Intense frustration at such treatment from MPs drove the WSPU towards more dramatic action. The 'talking out' of Hardie's resolution itself had brought a disturbance from incensed women in the ladies' gallery of the House of Commons, while the remainder of the year witnessed the beginning of regular heckling of Cabinet ministers and also demonstrations in and around Parliament with their accompanying arrests and imprisonments. At the same time, WSPU militancy during 1906 put pressure on constitutionalists to show that they were equally zealous and committed and that moral force methods could successfully arouse public interest in the cause. The next few years saw the NUWSS and its affiliates vigorously propel themselves into election activity, processions and other forms of agitation. The so-called 'Mud March' of February 1907, comprising some 3,000 women representing more than forty organizations, gave impressive notice of this animation. The novelty of women, from across the social spectrum, marching with banners and bands through the London rain aroused considerable public interest. 'The largest and most successful demonstration yet organised by the cause', acknowledged the *Western Mail*; 'a

---

[8]   Ibid., November 1906; *SWDN*, 10, 11 October 1906; Jill Liddington, *The Life and Times of a Respectable Radical: Selina Cooper, 1864–1946* (London, 1984), 186–7; John, *'Chwarae Teg'*, 8–9.

[9]   *Parl. Deb.*, 4th ser., 152, col. 1453, 2 March 1906; 155, cols 1570–2, 25 April 1906. No other Welsh MPs participated in the debates.

[10]   Ibid., 155, cols 1582–7, 25 April 1906.

most imposing ceremony', concluded the *South Wales Daily News*.[11] There was no evident Welsh presence, though Keir Hardie was one of the principal speakers.

At the same time, the NUWSS developed more of a presence in the country at large, its number of affiliated societies increasing from thirty-one to seventy during 1907–8 and to 130 during 1908–9.[12] A small number of these were in Wales. During the decade 1897–1906 only the one at Monmouth had been established, in December 1904. A second came into being in January 1907, at Llandudno. The initiative was very much a female one, as was explained at its first meeting: 'the question of Women's Suffrage has attained such importance in the last eight months that some of the ladies of Llandudno felt that it behoved them as intelligent women to discuss the matter and decide as to their attitude towards it'.[13] Male participation became pronounced, the branch including 'well known shopkeepers, businessmen, and professionals, members of the town council, clergy of the Church of England and some Nonconformist ministers'.[14] Cutting across party lines, it steadily and efficiently advanced the cause over subsequent years.

Two more branches were founded in 1908, in the wake of the brief tour by Millicent Fawcett and Charlotte Despard in May. These were at Cardiff (in June) and Pontypridd (in November); the third venue visited by the speakers, Caldicot, chose to form a WFL branch.[15] In the north, the Rhyl and District NUWSS branch came into being in December 1908.[16] The following summer, WSPU and WFL emissaries were very active in the northern coastal towns but, in the wake of the adverse publicity following suffragette disruption of the National Eisteddfod in June, it was the NUWSS that benefited in organizational terms. Branches were formed in Bangor and Colwyn Bay in late 1909 and at Caernarfon in March 1910 (the first two coinciding with visits from Eleanor Rathbone

11   *WM*, 11 February 1907; *SWDN*, 11 February 1907.
12   NUWSS, *Annual Reports*, 1907, 1908, 1909.
13   *Llandudno Advertiser*, 26 January 1907; *WF*, 23 January 1908.
14   Jones, 'Women's suffrage movement in Caernarfonshire', 80.
15   *WF*, 11 June, 26 November 1908.
16   *Rhyl Journal*, 12 December 1908.

and the last with one from Millicent Fawcett).[17] It was not, however, the local Welsh population which supplied most of the energy and enthusiasm and this served to limit the effectiveness of local work, as one agent observed in November 1910:

> I have just returned from my visit to the Welsh coast societies. In these towns the English residents, who form the bulk of the membership, leave home for lengthy periods in the summer and in most places the plans for winter work are just now under discussion. ... A Welsh speaking organiser must be found before Welsh speakers can be attracted in any number.[18]

Llandudno and Cardiff were among the provincial societies represented at the impressive NUWSS mass gathering of June 1908, each group headed by specially designed banners pronouncing their Welsh identity (a leek for Llandudno, a red dragon for Cardiff).[19] 'The most remarkable Women's Suffrage demonstration which has yet taken place in the country! That is the least that can be said of the procession of 10,000 women which marched from the Victoria Embankment to the Albert Hall last weekend', declared the *Monmouthshire Beacon*, its reporting typical of the flavour of local and national press coverage.[20]

The following month saw considerable NUWSS activity in the Pembrokeshire by-election, occasioned by J. Wynford Philipps's elevation to the peerage as Baron St David's. Affording valuable opportunities to publicize the cause and to press prospective MPs, by-elections became a key feature of the constitutionalists' campaign during 1908 and 1909, work being undertaken in thirty-one contests in these two years. In contrast to the WSPU and the WFL, both of which sought to put pressure on the government by opposing Liberal candidates everywhere, regardless of personal attitudes to the question, NUWSS policy was to support 'the best friend of women's

---

[17]   *WF,* 8 October 1908; *CC,* 23 December 1909; *NWC,* 17 December 1909; *Welsh Coast Pioneer,* 16 December 1909; *CDH,* 18 March 1910.

[18]   *CC,* 3 November 1910.

[19]   *Llandudno Advertiser,* 16, 30 May, 20 June 1908; *Women's Franchise,* 21 May, 11 June, 30 July 1908; *SWDN,* 15 June 1908, *South Wales Echo,* 13, 15 June 1908; *CT,* 20 June 1908. The Cardiff contingent comprised NUWSS and WFL members.

[20]   *Monmouthshire Beacon,* 19 June 1908.

suffrage', whichever his party, in order to elect as many sympathetic MPs as possible; particular emphasis was placed on the
educational value of by-election campaigns as opportunities to
arouse public support and organize local societies. In
Pembrokeshire, the national union's position was clearly established at the outset: 'Mr Lort-Williams (Conservative) and
Mr. Roch (Liberal) have both answered all the six questions
put to them . . . in the affirmative. We have therefore to confine
ourselves to propaganda work.'[21] Accordingly, the group of
activists sent by the union executive addressed gatherings in
towns and villages across a wide constituency. In what was by
now standard suffragist practice, meetings were announced by
the town crier or by the chalking of pavements; others were
more impromptu, tackling dockers at the start or end of shifts,
haymakers after a long day in the fields, or passengers on the
Pembroke Dock to Neyland steamer. The canvassing of individuals, the distribution of leaflets and the display of bills and
posters in hired shop windows supplemented speech making.

The outcome of the Pembrokeshire campaign gave the
NUWSS a good deal of satisfaction. A MP 'pledged to do all he
can to support the Woman's cause' had been returned, the
issue had been brought to the attention of large numbers of
people to whom it had been 'practically new', a 'fair hearing
and sympathy' had been received and a 'Pembrokeshire
Society' had been inaugurated in Tenby (though this was to
prove only transient). The *Pembroke County Guardian* reflected
on the contest thus:

> We have just emerged from one of the fiercest election fights which this
> generation, at any rate, has seen . . . there has been such a recrudes-
> cence of political activity, and the furbishing up of reasons for a
> particular faith, and such light shed upon current politics as cannot fail
> to exert a beneficial influence upon the county for some time to
> come.[22]

Women's suffrage had been very much part of that ferment,
even though no enduring agitation was to emerge in the area.

While by-election work, mass meetings and demonstrations
represented new and important elements of NUWSS strategy

[21] *WF*, 9 July 1908.
[22] Ibid., 23 July 1908; *Pembroke County Guardian*, 24 July 1908.

during 1907–9, the traditional reliance on private members' bills continued. Thus, in March 1907, a few weeks after the 'Mud March', considerable effort was directed towards winning support for W. H. Dickenson's Women's Enfranchisement Bill, which sought to open the existing property qualifications to women, both single and married. Two of Wales's MPs contributed to a parliamentary debate that focused largely on the scope of the bill's terms. Osmond Williams, Liberal member for Merioneth, argued the female case on civil rights grounds: 'Did our sense of natural justice not dictate that the being who was to suffer under laws should first personally assent to them; that the being whose industry government was to burden should have a voice in fixing the character and amount of that burden?'[23] Like so many of its predecessors, the bill was talked out, precluding a vote, the central figure being the Liberal MP for Montgomery Boroughs, J. D. Rees, an inveterate enemy of the cause. Anxious that 'the Member for Merionethshire was likely to convey a wrong impression to the House of the opinions of the men and women of Wales', Rees entered into a long and rambling speech in which he extravagantly protested 'against this attempt to force a revolution', denouncing proposals which would 'in effect and in the end hand over the management of affairs to the women of the country'.[24]

Early in 1908, a similar bill sponsored by Henry York Stanger fared substantially better and succeeded in passing its second reading by 179 votes, though it was denied parliamentary time to proceed further by the anti-suffragist Herbert Asquith, who succeeded the ailing Campbell-Bannerman as prime minister in April. Nevertheless, the positive response of the House of Commons (for the first time since 1897) greatly heartened the NUWSS, seemingly justifying both its faith in the Liberal Party (which supplied the vast majority of votes in support) and its by-election stance. Three of Wales's MPs participated in the debate, each speaking against the bill. J. D. Rees and Ivor Guest (Liberal MP for Cardiff Boroughs) did so

[23] *Parl. Deb.*, 4th ser., 170, col. 1142, 8 March 1907.
[24] Ibid., cols 1160–3. Rees was Liberal MP for Montgomery Boroughs from 1906 until 1910, during which year he joined the Conservative Party, becoming MP for East Nottingham in 1912. He was knighted in 1910.

out of anti-suffragist conviction, Clement Edwards (Liberal MP for Denbigh Boroughs) from the opposite standpoint, condemning 'its limited and property-mongering character'; as an advocate of adult suffrage, he rejected a 'pettifogging and ridiculous Bill', which sought to enfranchise 'well-to-do women ... who would do little or nothing to extend the same right and privilege to the working women of the country'.[25]

Outside Parliament, the recruitment of an expanding team of paid NUWSS organizers afforded more extensive and systematic coverage of the country in order to generate local activity. The first extensive campaigning in Wales by any of the three major suffrage societies occurred in the summer of 1909, each despatching speakers and organizers to various areas. In the south, NUWSS efforts were concentrated in the Cardiff area, where a branch society had been established the previous year; in May and June a full-time organizer, Helga Gill, directed a month's work in the town, during which drawing-room meetings, public meetings, dissemination of literature and fund-raising served to educate local members in the techniques of campaigning and lay the foundations for what was to be a very strong Cardiff and District Women's Suffrage Society (CDWSS).[26]

More adventurously, Miss Gill also directed a horse-drawn caravan tour through north and mid Wales during August and September 1909. One of only two such tours conducted by the movement in Wales (both organized by the national union), the enterprise began inauspiciously. Shortly after crossing the border from Chester there occurred one of the numerous and varied accidents which so beset this form of campaigning, the tethered horse almost strangling itself: 'had it not been possible to cut the cord at once the unfortunate Rosinante would now have been cropping celestial food in the Elysian fields', observed one of the party. Next, the holding of meetings at Wrexham and Ruabon was 'absolutely forbidden' by the police on public order grounds: 'These are mining districts, and have the reputation of being terribly rough and strongholds of Liberalism.' At the village of Trefor, near

[25]   *Parl. Deb.*, 4th ser., 185, cols 261–6, 279–84, 28 February 1908.
[26]   *CC*, 10 June 1909.

Llangollen, an attempted meeting 'was made impossible by gangs of roughs, who gathered in force. Our placards were torn to ribands, brick-bats were collected, and the uncontrolled excitement of the whole populace was enormous.' Similar hostility was demonstrated in Llangollen itself and in such circumstances the campaigners were confined to the distribution of literature and house-to-house, shop-to-shop, canvassing.[27] Continuing westwards, a change of strategy proved beneficial:

> We have altered our mode of procedure, and instead of holding a meeting, or attempting to hold one, the day of our arrival, we prepare the ground by making friends with the people in the shops and cottages, the very porters of the railway, and the station staffs, besides the clergy of all denominations. The result is that we are regarded as ordinary human beings, and the inhabitants are only too eager to hear what we have to say . . .[28]

Accordingly, even though the Bala meeting was broken up by an unruly crowd and the speakers escorted away by the police for their own safety, they were well received elsewhere, at Glyndyfrdwy, Corwen, Llanuwchllyn, Rhydymain, Dolgellau, Barmouth, Tywyn and various villages along the way. The presence among the party of a fluent Welsh speaker, Magdalen Morgan, a Merthyr teacher, and the availability of free literature in the Welsh language were vital to effectiveness in many of these communities.[29]

During the summer of 1909 both NUWSS and WFL activists had to contend with the Welsh public's reaction to the WSPU's disruption of the National Eisteddfod in London in June 1909, when sixteen women were ejected for heckling the prime minister, Asquith. 'Nothing could do their cause more injury in Wales . . . than this foolish outburst at the Eisteddfod, which is even more sacred to Welshmen than any political cause ever yet invented', argued the *Western Mail*, reflecting widespread press condemnation.[30] 'Everywhere we are met with the same cry', reported Helga Gill from her caravan tour; '"Why did you break up our Eisteddfod?" and it is, in many

---

[27] Ibid., 19 August 1909.
[28] Ibid., 26 August 1909.
[29] Ibid., 2, 9, 16 September 1909; *Seren*, 28 Awst 1909.
[30] *WM*, 17 June 1909.

cases, hard to explain that we had nothing to do with that incident.'[31] The NUWSS quarterly council, assembled in Nottingham in July, duly gave attention to the problem, accepting that 'Wales knew little of the Suffrage movement, and did not distinguish between this Union and the one which had disturbed its Eisteddfod', and, as part of its aim of 'making known this Union and its methods' to the inhabitants of Wales, agreed to hold its next such gathering in Cardiff.[32]

By the time the council convened, escalating WSPU militancy had brought to a head the tensions of the past year between the two organizations. Until the summer of 1908, relations had been largely amicable, moderates generally (though not universally) recognizing the enormous propaganda contribution of the militants to the cause. 'Much as we deplore their [the suffragettes'] attitude', wrote the stalwart Monmouth suffragist Mary Maclaverty in February 1908, 'we have somewhat unwillingly to acknowledge that the country at large has for the first time been roused to take in the idea that qualified women want the recognition of the vote.'[33] Earlier, Millicent Fawcett, in a well-publicized letter to *The Times*, had responded to the WSPU imprisonments of October 1906, by contending that 'far from having injured the movement, they have done more during the last twelve months to bring it within the region of practical politics than we have been able to accomplish in the same number of years'.[34]

Growing WSPU extremism in the latter half of 1908 and a proliferation of violent incidents during 1909 wholly changed attitudes. A few days before the NUWSS council met in Cardiff in October 1909, Mrs Fawcett expressed her concern to a suffragist colleague: 'I feel the present crisis to be most serious & that strong steps ought to be taken in the most authoritative manner to dissociate the NU' [from WSPU activities].[35] In her opening address to the gathering, she told delegates that

---

[31]   *CC*, 19 August 1909.
[32]   Ibid., 15 July 1909.
[33]   *Monmouthshire Beacon*, 7 February 1908.
[34]   *The Times*, 27 October 1906.
[35]   Millicent Fawcett to Helena Auerbach, 1 October 1909, quoted in Rubinstein, *Different World for Women*, 164.

recent militant tactics had been 'a cause of great pain and dismay', and subsequently deplored 'the justification and glorification of stone throwing'. Accordingly, the Cardiff conference saw the passage of a key resolution:

> That the Council of the National Union of Suffrage Societies strongly condemns the use of violence in political propaganda and, being convinced that the true way of advancing the cause of Women's Suffrage is by energetic, law-abiding propaganda, reaffirms its adherence to constitutional principles.[36]

At the end of 1909, the much divided nature of the movement was one element of a rather gloomy outlook for the enactment of a women's suffrage measure in the near future. The high hopes placed on the Liberals' assumption of office four years earlier had run into the sands, the NUWSS attaching a good deal of the blame to suffragette militancy which it now firmly believed to be alienating parliamentary and public support. A major source of pessimism was the obduracy displayed by Herbert Asquith, a convinced anti-suffragist whose opposition proved unexpectedly determined. Furthermore, Cabinet suffragists were evidently disinclined to press the question. Preoccupied with issues associated with his new role as chancellor of the Exchequer, Lloyd George adopted Asquith's line, forcefully arguing to a meeting of the WLF at the Albert Hall in December 1908 that suffrage should await the settling of larger, more urgent, questions and then be tackled as part of a general measure of electoral reform; amid constant interruptions from WSPU members, he added that only a reaction against militancy would prevent the enactment of a women's suffrage measure.[37] The divisions within the political parties compounded the impasse at Westminster.

In the unpromising political climate at the end of the decade, the NUWSS could none the less reflect upon its own advance as an organization. It was now a highly efficient national pressure group, possessing its own offices, administrative and campaigning staff, substantial funds, a literature department and a newspaper, *The Common Cause*. With some 130 affiliated societies and a membership of nearly 3,500, it

[36] *CC*, 14 October 1909; *CT*, 9 October 1909.
[37] *WM*, 7 December 1908.

was easily the largest of the suffrage organizations.[38] This was not yet mirrored in Wales, where the NUWSS had just seven branches at the close of 1909. Moreover, two of these, at Bangor and Colwyn Bay, had been formed only a matter of weeks earlier and the one at Monmouth had had a largely nominal existence since 1904. The other four, at Cardiff, Pontypridd, Llandudno and Rhyl, were firmly established. This picture is testimony to the national union's position as perhaps the least influential of the three main suffrage societies in Wales at that point. Over the next four years, however, it was to emerge as Wales's major suffrage organization, with several dozen branches in operation by the outbreak of the European war in August 1914, compared with the handful of WSPU and WFL branches.

Like the WSPU and the WFL, the NUWSS sought to advance the cause at the two general elections of 1910. Local societies were charged with questioning and obtaining pledges of support from candidates, as occurred in South Glamorgan and in Caernarfon Boroughs, and with carrying out propaganda work.[39] In the January election, NUWSS branches were also urged to collect signatures for voters' petitions, in an effort to demonstrate male support for the movement. At Llandudno, over half of the 1,400 voters who came to the poll signed, and similar efforts were made at Rhyl and St Asaph.[40] In total, over 280,000 signatures were collected around the country and a large number of petitions was presented to the House of Commons.

Across Britain, the general election results saw the Liberals' majority disappear and their retention of office was now dependent on the support of the Labour Party and the Irish nationalists. At the same time, the number of MPs supporting

---

[38]   In reality the number of its societies and total membership were larger than this for the lists included only those directly affiliated. The London Society for Women's Suffrage, for example, had thirty-four branches in 1909, yet only the London Society was listed as belonging to the NUWSS. Hume, *National Union*, 57.

[39]   *CC*, 8 December 1910; Glamorgan Record Office, D/DX 158/6/1, minutes of the Penarth WSS, 24, 29 November, 2 December 1910. The NUWSS dispatched one of its organizers, Helga Gill, to the Mid Glamorgan by-election of March 1910, to conduct propaganda in 'the constituency vacated by our old and bitter enemy, Sir Samuel Evans'. Ibid., 24 March 1910.

[40]   *CC*, 3, 17 February 1910; *Llandudno Advertiser*, 29 January 1910.

women's suffrage was certainly increased, though translating a Commons' majority into practical politics proved difficult in the extreme. Party differences presented the major obstacle and, in an attempt to overcome these, an all-party parliamentary Conciliation Committee was established early in 1910. For much of the next two years the NUWSS worked closely with the fifty-four-man committee and campaigned strenuously in support of the Conciliation Bills placed before Parliament in 1910, 1911 and 1912, while also demonstrating considerable (though misplaced) faith in the Liberal government's willingness to respond positively to the initiatives.

The first Conciliation Bill modestly sought to enfranchise about a million women who were local government electors – £10 householders, with the restriction that married women could not qualify with respect to the same property as their husbands. Welcomed by the various suffrage societies as 'an instalment of justice', and in the conviction that the House of Commons would not accept a more comprehensive measure, it nevertheless caused anxiety among many Liberal suffragists, including Lloyd George, who feared that the enfranchisement of propertied spinsters and widows would most benefit the Conservative Party. Although it secured a majority on its second reading (299 votes to 190) in July 1910, the bill was referred to a committee of the whole House, which made future progress highly doubtful. Confirmation of its demise in November left the entire women's suffrage movement bitterly disappointed. WSPU anger was signalled by a brief resumption of militancy with the clashes of 'Black Friday' and the violent episodes of subsequent days.

Three of Wales's MPs contributed to the lively second reading debate, Keir Hardie and Sir Alfred Mond speaking in favour of the bill, Lloyd George against.[41] Hardie welcomed 'a golden opportunity . . . not only [to] settle a long vexed question but [to] remove a thorny subject of discussion from the arena of politics and allow us to concentrate upon other matters of great moment', while also quelling 'the growing

[41] Walter Roch (Liberal MP for Pembrokeshire, 1908–18) also spoke a few weeks later in protest at the government's announcement that further facilities would not be given to the bill that session. *Parl. Deb.*, 5th ser., 19, cols 2601–2, 29 July 1910.

and clamorous demand on the part of women for their advancement'.[42] Mond's view was very much that of the Conciliation Committee and of suffragists widely: though far from ideal, the proposals offered the best chance of a practical settlement at that time.[43] In contrast, Lloyd George condemned the bill as undemocratic and objected to its being 'framed so nobody could move an amendment'; it amounted to the attempt of 'a committee of women meeting outside . . . to dictate to the House of Commons the way in which the question should be solved . . . a position that no self-respecting Legislature can possibly accept'.[44] A few weeks later, in August, he explained in detail his opposition in an address to the annual meeting of the Caernarfonshire WLA. 'It is a Bill', he insisted,' which would give a vote to every lady of property . . . but to barely one-tenth of working women', whereas his commitment was to 'women's suffrage all round'; whatever the case, he went on, a settlement of both the House of Lords question and Welsh disestablishment were priorities.[45]

Throughout the year the NUWSS did all it could to promote the bill, lobbying for parliamentary support and urging branches to stimulate and demonstrate popular enthusiasm in the country at large. In Wales, meetings were convened and resolutions passed in a number of localities, including Cardiff, Llandudno, Colwyn Bay, Rhyl, Bangor and Caernarfon. The Bangor society sent letters to each member of the city council, which subsequently came out in support of the bill. In Cardiff, leaflets were distributed, deputations waited upon local MPs and all other Welsh members were written to. Several dozen activists from Cardiff and Llandudno, the principal

---

[42]   Ibid., cols 140–5, 11 July 1910.
[43]   Ibid., cols 276–85, 12 July 1910.
[44]   Ibid., cols 305–9, 12 July 1910.
[45]   *NWC*, 12 August 1910; Jones, *Women's Suffrage Movement in Caernarfonshire*, 96–8. A deputation of representatives from the Caernarfonshire NUWSS branches subsequently waited on Lloyd George 'with the aim of laying before him their dissatisfaction with his attitude'. *NWC*, 30 September, 2 December 1910. From this point, the chancellor emerged as the *bête noire* of the WSPU: 'the Votes for Women cause has no more determined and mischievous enemy', proclaimed Christabel Pankhurst in an editorial headed 'The Wrecker' in August 1910; 'Mr Lloyd George's democratic pose is a sham by which he hopes to conceal his hostility to women's enfranchisement.' *VW*, August 1910. For Lloyd George and women's suffrage, see Jones, 'Lloyd George and the suffragettes', 1–33.

centres of NUWSS activity in Wales at this time, attended the large Trafalgar Square demonstration on the eve of the bill's second reading in July. At the same time, a deputation from women's Liberal federations and associations in Cardiff, Newport, Aberdare and Swansea unavailingly sought to shift Lloyd George's position. The Welsh National Conference of Liberal Women, meeting in Cardiff in November, called upon the government to grant facilities for the passage of a bill that was 'moderate, equitable and democratic'.[46]

Early in 1911 the Conciliation Committee produced a revised bill, which took into account criticisms of its predecessor. Proposing the inclusion of women householders regardless of the £10 qualification, the new draft offered a wider enfranchisement, while also ensuring it was open to free amendment.[47] With the NUWSS and the other suffrage organizations working in support (including the WSPU, which had once more reverted to a truce), the bill proceeded to pass its second reading decisively (by 288 votes to 88).[48] A divided Cabinet subsequently refused to grant parliamentary time for further progress during the current session but Asquith pledged to do so in the next.

The spectacular Women's Coronation Procession of June 1911, involving 40,000 suffragists representing all the societies, was testimony to the strength, unity and optimism across the movement that summer. Welsh women from all parts of Wales and from England took part in what the *North Wales Chronicle* described as 'the longest and most representative of any Women's Suffrage procession', embracing 'all classes of

---

[46] *CC*, 23 June, 21, 28 July, 13 October, 3, 10, 17 November 1910; *VW*, 11 November 1910; *SWDN*, 12 July 1910. The newly formed Bangor branch of the Men's League for Women's Suffrage sent a telegram to Lloyd George urging him to use his influence to obtain facilities for the passage of a Conciliation bill during the next parliamentary session. *NWC*, 25 November 1910.

[47] Having voted against the 1910 bill, Lloyd George now felt obliged to vote in favour.

[48] In a low-key debate, only Ellis Griffith among Wales's MPs spoke, arguing in its favour. *Parl. Deb.*, 5th ser., 25, cols 798–801, 5 May 1911. Ellis Griffith (later Sir Ellis Jones-Griffith) was Liberal MP for Anglesey, 1895–1918, and then for Carmarthen, 1923–4. From 1912 to 1915 he was under-secretary at the Home Office (and thereby responsible for the treatment of imprisoned suffragettes, including implementation of the 'Cat and Mouse' Act). See *Parl. Deb.*, 5th ser., 51, cols 452–6, 2 April 1913.

women, industrial and otherwise ... from musicians, clerks and sanitary inspectors, down to sweated labourers'. Most marched in the designated Welsh section, where the wives of a number of MPs (Ellis Griffith, D. A. Thomas, Llewellyn Williams and Walter Roch) took the lead in adopting a highly nationalistic tone, including traditional costume with distinctive sugar-loaf hats, choir, harpist and druid. Others took their places under the banners of one of the various suffrage organizations or of the Cardiff Progressive Liberal Women's Union or in one of the many other contingents such as of ex-prisoners (of whom there were 700), teachers, nurses and other occupational groups.[49]

As part of its propaganda campaign around the country the NUWSS urged branches to lobby public bodies and, during the year, 146 town, county and district councils were persuaded to pass resolutions in support of the bill.[50] In this respect, suffragists were particularly energetic in Lloyd George's native Caernarfonshire, eliciting formal backing from a large number of institutions. These included: Bangor City Council; Caernarfonshire County Council; Llandudno, Penmaenmawr, Llanfairfechan and Bethesda urban district councils; Pwllheli Town Council; Lleyn Rural District Council; Nefyn Parish Council; Pwllheli board of guardians; Pwllheli Free Church Council; Lleyn Temperance Association; branches of the Caernarfonshire Women's Liberal Association; habitations of the Primrose League; Caernarfon Labour Council; and eight trade unions in the Bangor district.[51] Similar work was undertaken in Cardiff, Penarth, Holyhead and Wrexham, while societies were equally active in Caernarfonshire, Cardiff, Carmarthen, Pontypridd and Newport in sending memorials to their local MPs.[52]

Lloyd George remained foremost among those Liberal and Labour suffragists who feared that the restricted enfranchisement of the Conciliation Bills would seriously damage their

[49]   *NWC*, 23 June 1911; *SWDN*, 19 June 1911; *WM*, 19 June 1911; *Manchester Guardian*, 19 June 1911; *Morning Post*, 19 June 1911; *Daily Sketch*, 19 June 1911.

[50]   NUWSS, *Annual Report*, 1911, 19–20.

[51]   Jones, 'Women's suffrage movement in Caernarfonshire', 95–6; *CC*, 13 April, 4 May 1911.

[52]   *CC*, 13 April, 4 May, 8, 15, June, 14 December 1911; minutes of the Penarth WSS, 10, 18 November 1910, 3 April 1911.

parties' future electoral prospects. He wrote emphatically to the Liberal chief whip in September 1911:

> I am very concerned about our pledges on the Female Suffrage question. We seem to be playing into the hands of the enemy. The Conciliation Bill could, on balance, add hundreds of thousands of votes throughout the country to the strength of the Tory Party . . . I think the Liberal Party ought to make up its mind as a whole that it will either have an extended franchise which would put working men's wives on the Register, as well as spinsters and widows, or that it will have no female franchise at all . . . We are likely to find ourselves in the position of putting this wretched Conciliation Bill through the House of Commons, sending it to the Lords, and eventually getting it through. Say what you will, that spells disaster for Liberalism . . .[53]

Others utterly rejected Lloyd George's assumptions, often drawing upon statistical evidence based on analyses of female local government electors. 'I have taken the trouble to make investigations in regard to my own Constituency', Keir Hardie told the House of Commons during the debate on the first Conciliation Bill in July 1910,

> over 2,000 of the 2,600 who would get the vote [in Merthyr Tydfil] are working women, widows for the most part whose husbands have been killed at their work or whose husbands have died comparatively young – widows, working spinsters, and others of that type who have the [municipal] franchise now.[54]

Similarly, a canvass undertaken by the Penarth Women's Suffrage Society in 1911 revealed that 'more than half the women on the municipal register are widows who work for their living by washing, taking in lodgers etc'; on the basis that Penarth was 'a residential neighbourhood', this was presented as 'strong evidence that the leisured class is in a minority among women municipal voters everywhere'.[55]

The Conciliation Committee, with the assistance of local NUWSS branches, conducted its own inquiries in 1911 in order 'to ascertain, on the exact basis of the Conciliation Bill in its

---

[53] Elibank Papers (National Library of Scotland), MS 8802, f. 308, David Lloyd George to Alexander Murray, Master of Elibank, 5 September 1911, quoted in D. Morgan, *Suffragists and Liberals: The Politics of Women's Suffrage in England* (Oxford, 1975), 82–3.

[54] *Parl. Deb.*, 5th ser., 19, col. 141, 11 July 1910.

[55] *CC*, 27 April 1911; minutes of the Penarth WSS, 24 February, 5 May 1911.

later form, what the distribution of classes would be among the women whom it sought to enfranchise'. The places chosen, as H. N. Brailsford, secretary and originator of the committee, went on to explain, were 'Dundee, a manufacturing town with several women's industries, which might be expected to show a high working-class percentage, and Bangor and Caernarvon, small residential towns with no industries, where the middle-class element is necessarily larger'.[56] In Dundee, 89.1 per cent of women householders were found to be working class, in Bangor and Caernarvon 75 per cent. 'The result of these elaborate canvasses', Brailsford concluded, 'is, in short, to confirm the conclusions of previous inquiries. On an average out of ten women enfranchised on the "Conciliation" basis, eight will belong to the working class.'[57]

These and earlier investigations, however, made no impression on Lloyd George, whose anxieties were shared by leading Liberal agents and officials. Determined on a more democratic substitute for the Conciliation Bill, his stance held sway in the Cabinet, for in November 1911 plans for a manhood suffrage bill, to which women's suffrage could be added, were announced. '[W]e have a chance', Lloyd George told a meeting of the National Liberal Federation in Bath, 'for the insertion in the Government bill of an amendment which will enfranchise not a limited class of women chosen just to suit the Tory canvasser, but for the insertion of an amendment which would include the working man's wife.'[58] The declar-

---

[56] The towns were the constituencies of the two principal opponents in the parliamentary debate on the 1910 Conciliation Bill, Winston Churchill (Dundee) and Lloyd George (Caernarfon Boroughs).

[57] *The Men's League Handbook on Women's Suffrage* (1912), 34–5, quoted in Constance Rover, *Women's Suffrage and Party Politics in Britain, 1866–1914* (London, 1967), 182–4; *NWC*, 24 November 1911. Ellis Griffith drew upon the same investigation when speaking in the Conciliation Bill debate of May 1911: 'in Dundee the leisured class is 7.5 per cent, while in Carnarvon and Bangor the percentage is 13. That gives an ample margin to represent the poor and the rich and the middle classes, and it gives us all a chance of securing their votes.' Not that these figures were central to Griffith's support for the bill: 'I am not very much concerned to enquire how these million women will vote . . . If the measure is a just one and this extension of the vote is right, we must leave our fortunes for the future.' *Parl. Deb.*, 5th ser., 25, cols 798–801, 5 May 1911.

[58] Grigg, *Lloyd George: People's Champion*, 299–301. 'I should deplore the extension of the franchise on the very narrow basis proposed by the Conciliation Bill', he told a deputation of Welsh suffragists in December 1912. *NWC*, 6 December 1912.

ation brought a mixed reaction from campaigners. WSPU leaders immediately sensed duplicity, a view seemingly confirmed by the chancellor's subsequent declaration that the Conciliation Bill had been 'torpedoed'. Christabel Pankhurst spoke bitterly of 'the Government's latest attempt to cheat women of the vote', denouncing 'the whole crooked and discreditable scheme' and singling out Lloyd George as chief conspirator.[59] 'We despised him for a false friend, a hypocrite, a traitor, whereas Mr Asquith we respected as a declared foe to our cause', recalled another prominent suffragette.[60] The WSPU now resumed militancy, which continued unabated and in an increasingly extreme fashion, until the outbreak of war almost three years later.

The NUWSS led a very different and far more widespread suffragist response: the prospect of a government reform bill open to women's suffrage amendments, plus the Conciliation Bill to fall back on, afforded grounds for considerable optimism, and a special council meeting in December 1911 resolved to 'keep all options open' and to work for both.[61] Once more, Welsh branches responded to the executive's call, organizing meetings, passing resolutions, lobbying MPs and councils, cooperating with other political associations and sending representatives to the impressive Albert Hall demonstration held in February 1912 in support of the third Conciliation Bill, then before the House of Commons.[62] In the event, even though comprising essentially the same proposals that had so decisively passed the same stage only ten months earlier, the bill was rejected at its second reading in March by fourteen votes, 222 to 208, a major setback to the NUWSS. '[W]e are all a little disheartened and finding our struggle somewhat uphill', confided the secretary of the NWF to E. T. John, one of its staunchest parliamentary supporters.[63]

---

[59]   *VW*, 10 November 1911.

[60]   SFC, *Kitty Marion Autobiography*, 207.

[61]   In the event, the government postponed the introduction of its Reform Bill, meaning that, much to the national union's dismay, the Conciliation Bill came before the Commons first.

[62]   *CC*, 4 January, 15 February, 7 March, 4, 11 April, 18 July, 13 December 1912; minutes of the Penarth WSS, 10, 17, 26 January 1912; Carmarthenshire Record Office, Carmarthen WSS minute book, 2 March 1912.

[63]   NLW, E. T. John Papers, 363, Jessie Beavan to E. T. John, 28 April 1912.

A number of factors contributed to the defeat. Irish nation-alists, fearful of the divisive effects of women's suffrage on the government and of vital parliamentary time being taken away from home rule by further progress of the bill, withdrew their support, while fifteen of the forty-two Labour Party represen-tatives, being preoccupied with a miners' strike, were crucially absent from the Commons. At the same time, suffragette violence appears to have had a considerable effect on the voting of both Liberal and Conservative MPs, increasing the number of opponents and abstainers.[64] In early March, the WSPU had for the first time resorted to attacks on private property, extensive window smashing at stores in central London resulting in several hundred arrests. Certainly the NUWSS leadership had no doubt about the damaging impact of militancy on their efforts and, coming in the wake of WSPU disturbance of its Albert Hall demonstration, many activists felt incensed. 'I resent the destruction of our work by the WSPU', wrote Helena Swanwick, editor of *The Common Cause*. 'When the National Union organises a great meeting and the WSPU attends it in order to interrupt and insult our guest and speaker [Lloyd George], I regard this as a clear act of hostility ...'[65] Parliamentary supporters were similarly frustrated. 'What really would help us most', observed E. T. John, Liberal MP for East Denbighshire, 'would be the cessation of militant action. If this could be arranged there would be some prospect of getting a comprehensive amendment to the Suffrage Bill carried in the Commons.'[66]

It was to this task that the NUWSS turned. During the course of 1912, hundreds of meetings were held around the

Seconding the bill, as 'an act of justice to women (and) an act of benefit to the State', and the only contributor to the debate among Wales's MPs, was Sir Alfred Mond, now one of the movement's most consistent advocates in parliament. *Parl. Deb.*, 5th ser., 36, cols 619–25, 28 March 1912.

[64]   Hume, *National Union*, 132–9; Pugh, *March of the Women*, 201. See also E. T. John Papers, 345, Jessie Beavan to E. T. John, 2 April 1912. Speaking in favour of a women's suffrage amendment to the Government of Ireland Bill later in the year, Walter Roch spoke of 'hon. Members of somewhat weak faith who, because windows were broken, broke their pledges by way of contrast'. *Parl. Deb.*, 5th ser., 43, col. 1082, 5 November 1912. Sir Alfred Mond also spoke for this (unsuccessful) amendment. Ibid., cols 1093–7.

[65]   *CC*, 3 October 1912; *Llangollen Advertiser*, 1 March 1912. The Llangollen WSS issued its condemnation in a public notice. *Yr Adsain*, 5 Mawrth 1912.

[66]   E. T. John Papers, 456, E. T. John to Jessie Beavan, 6 July 1912.

country, another big demonstration took place in the Albert Hall in November and branch societies lobbied MPs, party associations and public bodies, activities which were well supported by Welsh localities. A national union caravan tour in the late summer of 1912, the concluding stage of a three-month, 600-mile itinerary, also took in part of north-east Wales. Once again the NUWSS felt strongly that its efforts were seriously undermined by WSPU militancy, which from July onwards extended to arson. In south Wales, the latter half of the year saw pillar-box attacks and window smashing, while in the north activists had to contend despairingly with the public 'ferment' caused by suffragette interruptions at the National Eisteddfod in Wrexham and at Llanystumdwy in September, a major disestablishment demonstration in Caernarfon in May having met a similar fate. Unavailingly, the officers of the Cricieth society had written to the WSPU urging its members not to disturb the ceremonial opening of Llanystumdwy Institute, fearing the kind of violent scenes that in fact occurred.

> The suffrage cause is progressing steadily here under the auspices of the NUWSS. Militant methods will only injure the cause which both societies have at heart. Personal attacks, and abuse of Mr Lloyd George in his native village, on the part of strangers, will naturally not be tolerated, especially on an occasion such as this, which is not even political. Serious damage would be done to the suffrage cause if any attempt is made to prevent Mr Lloyd George and his guests from speaking.[67]

Indeed, meetings, especially in north Wales, were sometimes cancelled because of the hostility of communities, while elsewhere speakers met with constant disruption and vilification and risked physical harm. Welsh branches regularly issued formal condemnations of militancy, while on printed material, on banners and in public meetings they invariably stressed the words 'constitutional' and 'law-abiding', though they often made frustratingly little impression. The Penmaenmawr branch, for example, 'was decidedly antagonistic to militant tactics and all who joined that society did so on a law-abiding principle', while the president of the Newport WSS, Lady Tredegar, spoke of 'the inherent, absolute wrongness

---

[67] *NWC*, 20 September 1912; *CC*, 26 September 1912.

and immorality' of suffragette methods.[68] 'Welsh country-folk' seemed to interpret 'non-militant' as 'wicked window-smashers' (and 'non-party' as 'red-hot Tory'), complained one organizer.[69]

However much an irritant and a diversion, suffragists could hardly blame WSPU tactics for the sudden collapse of the government's Franchise and Registration Bill, when, in January 1913, the speaker of the House of Commons unexpectedly ruled the women's suffrage amendments out of order. The measure's prompt withdrawal, following earlier defeat of the Conciliation Bill, left NUWSS leaders and activists feeling betrayed by the Liberal Party and dispirited. 'I felt that what I had been working for for forty years had been destroyed at a blow', wrote Millicent Fawcett.[70] The disillusionment pervading the whole movement brought tactical reappraisal, all three major suffrage societies adopting a harder line. The NUWSS moved further towards an anti-Liberal electoral policy, while the militant societies responded with direct protest, the WSPU committing itself to greater extremism and the WFL abandoning its truce of almost three years.[71] The London-based Forward Cymric Suffrage Union (FCSU) was similarly incensed, a protest meeting reiterating its anti-government policy and expressing 'profound indignation at the way in which the Prime Minister has failed to carry out his solemn and repeated pledge' and rejecting 'with scorn the Government's offer of a private member's Bill next session'. The meeting also called upon Lloyd George to resign his Cabinet seat and launched a special fund 'to carry out a campaign in Wales among working men and women'.[72]

[68]   *North Wales Weekly News*, 6 June 1913; *WM*, 7 March 1914.

[69]   *CC*, 10 October 1912. Everywhere NUWSS speakers anticipated the worst. Fearing hostility in Abergavenny, Selina Cooper sought refuge in the cellar of the town hall until the time of the meeting. Lancashire Record Office, Selina Cooper Papers, diary entry, 17 April (though the date given is inaccurate).

[70]   Millicent Fawcett, *What I Remember* (London, 1924), 205–6.

[71]   In the House of Commons, Keir Hardie, speaking in opposition to the 'Cat and Mouse' bill in April, expressed the sentiments of suffragists across the spectrum in condemning the 'betrayal' and 'breach of faith by the Government' in regard to the cause. *Parl. Deb.*, 5th ser., 51, col. 423, 2 April 1913.

[72]   *Llandudno Advertiser*, 15 February 1913. During subsequent weeks the FCSU held meetings in several locations in Merioneth, in the Garw valley and in Porthcawl. *VW*, 4 April 1913; *Glamorgan Gazette*, 25 April 1913; *Porthcawl News*, 24 April 1913.

During 1913 and 1914 the few parliamentary initiatives in favour of women's suffrage aroused scant interest. Convinced, after the extinction of the Franchise Bill, that no private member's bill could pass the House of Commons, the NUWSS took no interest in W. H. Dickenson's bill of May 1913. Seeking to enfranchise women over twenty-five who were either house-holders or wives of householders (some six million in all), the measure was defeated by forty-seven votes, 268 to 221. Prominently representing the suffragist camp once again was Sir Alfred Mond, while, on the other side, a long-standing foe and former Liberal MP for Montgomery Boroughs, Sir J. D. Rees, was at his most belligerent in employing a battery of customary arguments to denounce the whole notion of women's suffrage.[73]

Home rule, the demand for which extended beyond Ireland to Wales and Scotland, presented another avenue for suffra-gists to press their claims before the House of Commons. Thus, the NUWSS worked closely with E. T. John, the driving force behind the resurgence of the issue of Welsh self-government at this time, and it pressed for the inclusion of women's suffrage in any measure. Although the Welsh Home Rule Bill of 1914 made no headway beyond a first reading, the proposed terms did indeed include a Welsh legislature elected by full adult suffrage.[74]

The NUWSS, in tandem with the Conservative and Unionist Women's Franchise Association, also lobbied in support of a Lords measure to enfranchise women in May 1914, the first time the upper house had debated and voted on the issue. Framed along the lines of the Conciliation Bill in seeking to grant the vote to those women on the municipal register, defeat by only forty-four votes on its second reading and the backing of several prominent Conservatives (led by its proposer, the earl of Selborne) gave suffragists grounds for optimism. Those voting in favour of the bill included Lords Aberconway, Glantawe, Glanusk, Pontypridd and St David's and the bishops of Bangor, Llandaff and St Asaph; those against included Lords Ashby St Ledgers (formerly Ivor Guest) and Raglan.[75]

[73]   Parl. Deb., 5th ser., 52, cols 1758–67, 1790–9, 5 May 1913.
[74]   E. T. John Papers, 737, E. T. John to Eleanor Rathbone, 2 June 1913.
[75]   Parl. Deb., 5th ser., House of Lords, 16, cols 133–4, 6 May 1914. The only peer

Essentially, however, the NUWSS focused on the country at large rather than on the parliamentary arena during 1913–14, by which time it had expanded into easily the largest of the suffrage organizations. By 1913, it had more than three times as many branches as the WSPU and WFL combined and was recruiting members at a rate of a thousand a month.[76] The increase in branches from thirty-one in 1907 to 130 in 1909 had brought a restructuring of the organization early in 1910 with the creation of federations comprising affiliated societies within defined regions. By the end of 1911 there were seventeen in all, two of which covered Wales – the West Lancashire, West Cheshire and North Wales Federation (NWF), formed in September 1910, and the South Wales and Monmouthshire Federation (SWF) a few months later.[77] Each federation was headed by a committee made up of one representative from each society in its area, together with one representative from the national executive, and these committees were to promote the formation of new branches within the federation and to coordinate activities between the societies. NUWSS growth after 1910 was dramatic. This was indicative of the success of the federation scheme and was an indirect result of WSPU tactics; the consciousness of many women was aroused by suffragette activities but they chose to demonstrate their support for the cause in a non-militant fashion. The number of branch societies increased from 207 in 1910 to 494 by July 1914.[78]

The NUWSS had a mere handful of five branches in Wales by the end of 1908 and two more a year later. By the close of 1910 the movement had spread across the north Wales coast with societies at Llandudno, Rhyl, Bangor, Colwyn Bay and Caernarfon; inland, Llangollen, 'a little Suffrage oasis in the midst of a desert of indifference', had a firmly established organization which was to remain active for the next eight

---

of Welsh connection to contribute to the debate was Lord Aberconway of Bodnant, who had long been active in the women's suffrage cause, just as his uncle, Jacob Bright, and his mother, Priscilla Bright McLaren, and other members of the family circle had been in earlier decades.

[76] Hume, *National Union*, 190; Pugh, *March of the Women*, 255.
[77] *CC*, 6 October 1910, 30 March 1911.
[78] Ibid., 10 July 1914. A few weeks later, *The Common Cause* was claiming 500 and then 602 branches. Ibid., 7, 14, August, 4 September 1914.

years.[79] A Merioneth society centred on Aberdovey also appears on the lists, though this seems to have had little more than a nominal existence. In south Wales, Cardiff was developing into the largest NUWSS centre outside London, while organizations also operated at Pontypridd, Penarth and Monmouth. Wales had twenty-seven branches by the end of 1911 and thirty-nine by the end of the following year, the substantial increase being to a large extent due to the efforts of the key regional agents, Edith Eskrigge in the north and L. F. Waring in the south. Caernarfonshire, targeted by leading suffragists because of the Lloyd George connection, had fourteen. Under the umbrella of the SWF, twenty branches extended from Chepstow in the east to Carmarthen and Lampeter in the west, and to Aberystwyth in the north. The movement was sometimes able to make a firm impression in the smallest and most remote of rural communities, a good example being Ffarmers, a village of scarcely a dozen houses eight miles east of Lampeter. Formed as a result of activity during the East Carmarthenshire by-election of August 1912, a branch was launched after the zealous local secretary had apparently 'scoured the countryside' for support.[80] There is also evidence of penetration of the industrial heartland, with branches being established at Merthyr, Bargoed, Ferndale and Treorchy. This development continued during 1913 and 1914. The nine added in these years included societies at Pontypool, Aberdare, Ebbw Vale, Ystrad Rhondda and Caerphilly. Working-class support is also indicated by branch formation in the slate-quarrying communities of Bethesda, Talysarn and Penygroes in Caernarfonshire. By the outbreak of the First World War in August 1914, some fifty NUWSS Welsh branches had been formed at one time or another.[81]

Inevitably, local societies varied considerably in size, durability and amount of activity. Some were undoubtedly ephemeral, springing into life in a burst of enthusiasm usually

[79] *CC*, 16 March 1911; *Llangollen Advertiser*, 15 April 1910.
[80] *CC*, 22 August, 31 October, 14 November 1912.
[81] Figures compiled from *The Common Cause* and *Annual Reports* of the NUWSS and London Society for Women's Suffrage (formerly the Central Society for Women's Suffrage).

following preparatory work by one of the regional organizers or speakers and then lapsing into abeyance within a short time. Branches at Bargoed, Bridgend, Dolgellau and Holyhead all had to be relaunched.[82] Flourishing national union societies undertook much the same sort of work as their WSPU and WFL counterparts, taking in a whole range of propaganda, fund-raising and social activities; some had their own shops and offices. Public meetings were, of course, a key element. Some were highly organized affairs, with considerable advanced publicity, decorated halls and experienced speakers. More often, they were held at short notice, frequently in the open air, on village greens, at steelworks and mills during dinner times, at cattle shows and markets, on seaside promenades and beaches. There were also the more select drawing-room gatherings, some specifically targeting groups such as teachers and clergymen. Speaking tours were conducted by prominent figures in the national campaign, by regional organizers and by local representatives. Local societies distributed literature, sold *The Common Cause*, canvassed from house to house, held debates and arranged study classes. Shops were opened at Cardiff, Penarth and Colwyn Bay; alternatively, market stalls were commonly used. Branches performed suffrage plays, provided musical and recitational entertainment, held whist drives, concerts, dances, Christmas functions, summer garden parties and tea and cake sales. Additional work included sending deputations to local MPs and councillors, petitioning, participating in elections and supporting major London demonstrations, where individual banners would be proudly displayed. Branch officers naturally sought as much coverage as possible for their activities in the press.

In north Wales, while the Llandudno society remained active, the Bangor branch assumed the leadership of the movement in the region in the years 1910–14. With its energetic secretary, Charlotte Price White, as the driving force, and supported by university and college academics, it carried out vigorous propaganda in the town and surrounding area (often through the Welsh language), raised money and

---

[82]   *CC*, 4 April, 6 June 1912, 3 April, 5 June 1914; *NWC*, 23 May 1913.

responded to every national executive initiative.[83] Less impact was made by the NUWSS in the north-east, though there were branches at Rhyl, Wrexham and Llangollen. A NWF caravan tour covering Flintshire and Cheshire in the late summer of 1912 was one attempt to increase interest and, certainly, the appearance of a second-hand parcels delivery van, its white tarpaulin cover painted with full title and mottoes of the national union and its determined band of sometimes rain-drenched enthusiasts setting up camp and venturing afield to publicize the cause, was guaranteed to stimulate a good deal of local curiosity. Meetings were held at Mold, Buckley, Flint, Northop, Caergwrle and Hawarden (where Helen Gladstone, daughter of the former prime minister, took the chair), but new branches failed to materialize, apparently because of the ill feeling generated by the WSPU militancy at Caernarfon in May and then at Wrexham and Llanystumdwy in September.[84]

The NWF, which directed NUWSS operations in the region, had eleven north Wales branches affiliated to it in 1912–13 (three remaining outside). Local representatives served on its executive and, in order that the Welsh societies should 'confer on purely Welsh affairs', a Welsh subcommittee (in which Charlotte Price White was the most prominent figure) operated from January 1912, meeting quarterly in different towns. Working in conjunction with local supporters, the federation despatched organizers to the localities and arranged speakers' tours and public meetings, while agitational work included pressing councils, political associations, temperance bodies and trade unions to pass women's suffrage resolutions and sending deputations and memorials to MPs. The appointment of area press secretaries reflected the importance of this

[83] Jones, *Women's suffrage movement in Caernarfonshire*, 92–4; Cook and Evans, 'Petty antics', 170–1; Bangor University, Bangor and District WSS minute book, 1912–14. Charlotte Price White studied at the university in the 1890s and subsequently married the town's electrical engineer. In 1926, she became the first woman member of Caernarfonshire County Council. Her son, Lieutenant-Colonel David Price White, a Bangor solicitor, was elected Conservative MP for Caernarfon Boroughs in 1945. Peter Ellis Jones, *Bangor, 1883–1983: A Study in Local Government* (Cardiff, 1986), 127–8.

[84] NWF, *Annual Report*, 1912, 13–14; *CC*, 10, 17 October 1912; *Flintshire Observer*, 13, 30 August 1912; *Flintshire News*, 29 August, 5 September 1912; *County Herald*, 30 August 1912. A branch society was formed at Mold (under the wing of the Chester society) the following year in the wake of the Flint Boroughs by-election.

line of work. A large number of north Wales papers, including Welsh-language ones, inserted 'suffrage news' on a regular basis. Most notably, the *North Wales Chronicle* was, in the words of one NWF report, 'our best friend'; it published a 'women's column', letters and the annual reports of local societies, covered meetings and offered sympathetic editorial comment on the non-militant campaign.[85]

In south Wales, NUWSS support was emphatically centred on the CDWSS, which became the largest branch in Britain outside London in 1912–13 (before losing that distinction to Glasgow). Founded in mid 1908, it had 700 members in November 1911, 920 by the spring of 1912, 1,100 by February 1913 and a peak of 1,200 at the outbreak of war. Highly organized, the society contained eight districts (including Barry and Penarth), each with its own officials and committee, which supplied representatives to a central executive. Fund-raising, membership recruitment, propaganda by means of lectures, public meetings and literature, and agitation, often in response to national developments, made up the bulk of the work.[86] By virtue of its numerical and financial strength, the CDWSS also played the leading role in the SWF, which had nineteen affiliated societies by mid 1913 and conducted similar functions to those of its north Wales counterpart.

None of Wales's other branches came anywhere near to Cardiff's in size. Scattered references to memberships afford an indication. Llandudno WSS was founded in 1907 with twenty members; a year later, there were 108 and by 1911 the total was 177, where it more or less remained.[87] The Bangor society began with just ten (growing to 'well over 100' during its first year), Merthyr with twenty-five (110 fifteen months later), Bridgend with around forty, Ystrad Rhondda with fifty, Bargoed, in the Rhymney valley, with fifty-three, Pontypool with fifty-eight, Aberystwyth with almost sixty, Ffarmers with seventy-eight (rising to 106 three months later) and Carmarthen with eighty-eight.[88] Newport WSS had nearly 200

---

[85]   NWF, *Annual Reports*, 1912, 1913.
[86]   *CC*, 30 November 1911, 4 April 1912, 21 February 1913; CDWSS, *Annual Report*, 1913–14, 6.
[87]   *Llandudno Advertiser*, 26 January 1907, 11 January 1908, 21 January 1911, 3 February 1912.
[88]   *NWC*, 2 December 1910; *CC*, 1 December 1910, 13 July, 2, 23 November 1911,

members in the summer of 1912, a year after formation; Swansea had 224 in March 1914.[89]

Everywhere NUWSS branches attracted male members and sympathizers, some of whom were active on local committees. Men also set up independent organizations – at least ten women's suffrage societies for men (or predominantly men) were formed in England in the decade before the First World War. By far the largest was the non-party and non-militant Men's League for Women's Suffrage (MLWS), founded in March 1907, which during its seven-year existence gained almost 1,000 members (especially businessmen, lawyers, clergymen, academics and writers) in various parts of Britain.[90] Branches were established around the country, including three in Wales – first at Cardiff, then others at Pontypridd and, later, Bangor. All three were small ('membership only reached eight or nine', in the Cardiff branch secretary's own admission) and evidently short lived, though the most committed members continued to work within the largely female local NUWSS branches.[91]

Yet essentially women were at the heart of NUWSS branches, and everywhere there were the stalwarts, such as Charlotte Price White in Bangor, Beatrice Stewart in Llangollen, Florence Wright in Llandudno, Mildred Spencer in Colwyn Bay and many others around Wales, who resiliently drove on local activity year after year. In some communities, such as Pontypool, Cardiff and Swansea, the campaign benefited from joint action between suffrage groups; indeed, some women

4 April, 14, 29 November, 6 December 1912, 2 May 1913; *Bargoed Journal*, 28 November 1912; *Porth Gazette*, 6 December 1913.

[89] *CC*, 4 July 1912, 6 March 1914; in Cricieth at the end of 1913, it was claimed that 'one-tenth of the population belong to the Suffrage Society'. Ibid., 16 January 1914.

[90] Angela V. John and Claire Eustance (eds), *The Men's Share? Masculinities, Male Support and Women's Suffrage in Britain, 1890–1920* (London, 1997), 10–13, 209. The league's parliamentary members included Walter Roch, Alfred Mond and D. A. Thomas. Another valued male supporter of the cause over many years was Edward Thomas ('Cochfarf'). See Cochfarf Papers (Cardiff Central Library), Box 7, letters from Erie Evans, Lucie Gregory, Jeanne Nautet and W. Watt. For Edward Thomas, see *Dictionary of Welsh Biography*, 945.

[91] *WF*, 29 October 1908, 28 January, 3 June 1909; *CT*, 23 January 1909; *Glamorgan Free Press*, 14 May 1909; *Men's League for Women's Suffrage Monthly Paper*, December 1910, June 1912; *NWC*, 25 November, 2, 9 December 1910. For Welsh men's support for women's suffrage, see John, 'Chwarae Teg'.

were members of more than one society.[92] Inevitably, cooperation between constitutionalist and militant supporters declined after 1911, as the former became increasingly frustrated by WSPU extremism. 'Work in North Wales has been rendered extremely difficult by the reversion to militant tactics of the WSPU', emphasized the 1912 federation report. 'It is impossible for anyone who has not worked in North Wales to realize the strength of the antagonism which is aroused by militant outbreaks, and the revulsion of feeling which they cause. In that part of the Federation ... the militant societies have become by far the greatest obstacle in the way of the success of our movement.'[93] Similarly, considerable resentment was caused in Cardiff in March 1914, when a government minister, F. D. Acland, the principal speaker at a large meeting jointly organized by the town's NUWSS and Church League branches and the Progressive Liberal Women's Union, was subjected to 'incessant interruptions' by WSPU members.[94]

A shortage of members confident enough to assume a prominent public-speaking role was another of the difficulties inhibiting societies. Some experience could be gained at branch meetings, while the problem was also tackled by the national union's summer school initiative. A number of these schools were organized around the country: one was held in north Wales, at Talybont in the Conwy valley, in August 1913, and was attended by women from various parts of Wales and England. Here, in a tranquil rural environment, a dozen or so students spent a week reading and discussing a variety of subjects, going well beyond the suffrage debate to include equal pay, divorce, women's parental rights, maintenance orders, sweated labour, factory legislation and a minimum wage. They attended classes, prepared and delivered speeches and ultimately practised oratory at meetings held in nearby villages.[95]

---

[92]   See June Hannam, '"I had not been to London"', 236–41; Pugh, *March of the Women*, 181–7.

[93]   NWF, *Annual Report*, 1912, 7. Desperately seeking to emphasize its law-abiding identity, in 1913 the Bangor society decided to erase the word 'agitation' from its rules, its methods now described as 'orderly propaganda and public discussion' only. Bangor WSS minutes, 17 November 1913.

[94]   CDWSS, *Annual Report*, 1913–14, 7.

[95]   *CC*, 5 September 1913; NWF, *Annual Report*, 1913, 26–8; *North Wales Weekly News*, 5 September 1913; *NWC*, 5 September 1913.

In parts of north and west Wales the language barrier had to be overcome. Certainly, Welsh-speaking assistance from supporters, such as Revd Ivan Davies of Llandrillo, the Davies sisters (Minnie and Bessie) of Lampeter and Magdalen Morgan of Merthyr, was vital to the success of touring English activists in these districts. In addition, national union leaflets were translated into Welsh by the Bangor society and sold to other branches for distribution.[96]

The most ambitious and effective propaganda enterprise undertaken by the NUWSS at this time was the 'Great Pilgrimage' of June and July 1913, when suffragists from all parts of Britain converged on London, having marched along eight different routes, holding meetings, distributing literature and collecting funds as they went. North Wales participation was a tributary of the 'Watling Street' route; a contingent set off from Cricieth in early July and, gathering members from the other national union branches along the coastal road, joined the marchers coming from north-west England at Chester. Though never more than forty in number, they were invigorated by a missionary-like spirit:

> A record of facts is dull and insipid. I wish I could bring before you some of the vivid scenes that lie splashed across my memory – the long procession winding slowly down the hill to Colwyn Bay with bristling pennants and banners blazing in the sun, and every window a flutter with hankerchiefs – the vast changing sea of faces on the sands at Rhyl, the silent listening group under the castle walls at Conway, and every morning the beauty of sea and hills, and the insistent call of the long white road between them.[97]

Meetings of several thousand people were held at Colwyn Bay and Rhyl, smaller ones at Bangor, Penmaenmawr, Conwy, Abergele, Prestatyn and Llandulais, the last specifically for the benefit of 200 quarrymen. Mocking, disruptive youths were a predictable and regular nuisance, though more deep-seated hostility was encountered too, most menacingly at Rhyl, where

[96] *CC*, 4 April, 13 June, 22 August 1912; NUWSS, executive minutes, 20 June 1912; *Yr Adsain*, 19 March 1912; *NWC*, 21 November 1913. For an example of a Welsh-language leaflet, see *Ychydig Resymau Paham y mae Merched Gweithiol yn Hawlio Pleidlais Seneddol* (Bangor, *c.*1912), Museum of London, 75.16/1.

[97] *CC*, 11 July 1913. See also NWF, *Annual Report*, 1913, 20–2; *NWC*, 13 June, 4, 11, 18 July, 1 August 1913, reprinted in Aaron and Masson, *Very Salt of Life*, 265–81.

local policemen had to escort the speakers from the sands in the face of a surging crowd.[98] Anti-militant sentiment lay behind much of the antagonism, and was an immense source of frustration to law-abiding campaigners.

In south Wales, the pilgrimage was heralded by a large demonstration in the centre of Cardiff on the eve of departure. The following morning a procession of around a hundred, some of whom had come from Barry, Penarth, Pontypridd and elsewhere, made its way out of the city towards Newport, banners, university gowns and a brass band adding vivid colour and spectacle to the event. As elsewhere, only a minority walked the twelve miles, though others made their way by bicycle, motor car or train. At Newport, a mass meeting welcomed the Cardiff 'pilgrims' and also those who had come from the western valley of Monmouthshire, from Blaenafon through Pontypool. The next stage of the journey was to Cheltenham and Bristol, where the party joined marchers from the south-west of England.

Both north and south Wales marchers encountered hostility in some communities as they made their way across central England – rotten eggs, stones and other missiles, as well as insults and heckling.[99] But, far more often, the demonstrators commanded respect and attention and the whole venture was widely and favourably covered in both the national and local press. Above all, it was applauded for asserting the law-abiding character of the cause; in the words of one south Wales editorial, 'the conduct of the pilgrims . . . assuredly helped to remove from the women's suffrage movement the opprobrium cast upon it by the insane acts of a section of its supporters'.[100] Time and again en route, speakers emphatically repudiated militancy, a theme particularly apposite in south-east Wales where the pilgrimage coincided with the much publicized arrest and conviction of Margaret Mackworth for her letter-box attack; accordingly, the Newport meeting centred overwhelmingly on a condemnation of suffragette 'criminal misbehaviour' and the 'stream of

---

[98]   *Welsh Coast Pioneer*, 10 July 1913; *NWC*, 11 July 1913; *Rhyl Journal*, 12 July 1913.
[99]   *CT*, 19 July 1913; *NWC*, 18 July 1913.
[100]   *Barry Dock News*, 18 July 1913.

anarchy' which was 'alienating hundreds of thousands of supporters and sympathisers'.[101]

Culminating in a huge rally of some 70,000 in Hyde Park on 26 July, each federation providing speakers for the twenty platforms, the pilgrimage was a resounding success. Particularly through its numerous open-air meetings, it brought hundreds of working men and women into contact with suffragism; indeed, a key development of the movement in the immediate pre-war years was the increased support from this sector of the population. This broadening of the NUWSS's social base stemmed to a large degree from the formal ties established with the Labour Party in the wake of the defeat of the third Conciliation Bill in March 1912. While pledges from Liberal and Conservative MPs evidently could not be relied upon, Labour's commitment to the cause seemed secure; all its MPs present had voted for the Conciliation Bill and the party's annual conference a few months earlier had resolved that no measure of franchise reform that did not include women would be acceptable. The aim was to put increased by-election pressure on a Liberal Party already lacking a majority in the House of Commons and induce it to make women's suffrage part of its programme. Negotiations with Labour Party officials moved quickly, a special NUWSS council meeting ratified the agreement and, by June 1912, a committee, named the Election Fighting Fund (EFF), was in place to implement the new initiative. It was agreed to support 'individual candidates standing in the interests of Labour in any constituency where the NU thinks it advisable to oppose a Liberal Antisuffragist'. Not all Liberals would be challenged (as was WSPU policy) and thus the NUWSS insisted that it was not abandoning either its non-party position or its support for 'the best friend' of women's suffrage; significantly, however, when deciding whom to support in future elections, the position of the respective political parties on women's suffrage, as

---

[101] *South Wales Argus*, 12 July 1913. For the pilgrimage in Wales, see *CC*, 20, 27 June, 11, 18, 25 July, 1 August 1913; *VW*, 4, 18 July 1913; *Welsh Coast Pioneer*, 12, 26 June, 3, 10, 17, 31 July 1913; *NWC*, 20 June, 4, 11, 18 July, 1 August 1913; *WM*, 11, 12, 14, 28 July 1913; *CT*, 19 July 1913; *Barry Dock News*, 18 July 1913; *South Wales Echo*, 12 July 1913; *South Wales Argus*, 14 July 1913; *Free Press of Monmouthshire*, 1 August 1913; NWF, *Annual Report*, 1913, 16–22; CDWSS, *Annual Report*, 1913–14, 6–7, 11.

well as that of individual candidates, would be taken into account.[102]

The task of cementing the relationship began with a major NUWSS presence at the annual ILP conference, held in Merthyr Tydfil later the same month. 'For the first time the women's question dominated the gathering', observed Philip Snowden. The theme of close cooperation between labour and suffragism was propounded by some of the union's most experienced speakers at a large open-air demonstration attended by over a thousand people on Whit Sunday and then again the following evening, while Snowdon, Keir Hardie and George Lansbury made emphatic women's suffrage speeches to the conference.[103]

The new departure was far from uncontroversial within the NUWSS. At executive level, opposition was led by Eleanor Rathbone (an influential figure among north Wales suffragists), who feared the alienation of long-standing Liberal and Conservative supporters. Her stance was supported by Wales's one executive member, Mabel Howell, secretary of the CDWSS, and, in the special council meeting, by other Welsh delegates, including Charlotte Price White of Bangor and Mary Collin of Cardiff. At the forefront of regional resistance was the Cardiff society, the immediate response of which was to send a circular letter to all branches urging rejection of the proposals. Its objections were largely based on scepticism of Labour's commitment. '*NO pledges* have been obtained from the Labour Party to vote against the 3rd reading of the Reform Bill if women are not included', emphasized Mabel Howell; 'we ought not to sacrifice our Union until we know exactly where they stand . . . Such identification at the present moment would lead to serious divisions among the local Societies'.[104]

---

[102] Hume, *National Union*, 144–5. See also CDWSS, *Annual Report*, 1912–13, 10–11. For detailed discussions of the EFF and Wales, see Masson, 'Divided loyalties', 113–26; and eadem, 'Political conditions', 369–88.

[103] *CC*, 6 June 1912; ILP, *Report of the 20th Annual Conference held at Merthyr Tydfil, 27th and 28th May 1912* (1912), 53–5, 94; NUWSS executive minutes, 18 April, 2, 16 May, 6 June 1912; *Labour Leader*, 31 May 1912; *Llais Llafur*, 1 Mehefin 1912; *Pioneer*, 1 June 1912; *Merthyr Express*, 25 May, 1 June 1912; Liddington, *The Life and Times of a Respectable Rebel*, 230; Jo Vellacott, *From Liberal to Labour: The Story of Catherine Marshall* (Montreal and Kingston, 1993), 178–9.

[104] NUWSS, Papers of Special Council Meeting, circular letter from CDWSS,

Cardiff's argument was that, despite the leadership's assurances to the contrary, the electoral pact did amount to abandonment of the national union's non-party stance, while association with Labour would offend a large number of suffragists with Liberal or Conservative party allegiances; 'this policy, if adopted in our area', argued Mabel Howell, 'would result in the loss of so many working members of our Society that the Society would be disastrously affected and its work in the locality very much crippled'.[105]

Other Welsh suffragists took a similar line. Accordingly, in June 1912, the SWF wrote to the national executive 'expressing our strong disapproval of the policy, and asking that it might not be put into effect in our area', apparently receiving the highly satisfactory reply that the policy would not be enforced in the region 'without full consultation with the Federation Committee'. Thus, Swansea branch members, receiving their annual report in February 1913, heard that 'during the summer some difficulty had arisen over the National Union's new policy of supporting Labour members. In Swansea and indeed all over South Wales that was unpopular, but after representations were made at the headquarters the new policy was not insisted upon.'[106]

The SWF's contention that 'Welsh Libl MPs were good Suffragists whilst the Labour Members were not so good' was far removed from the analysis of the EFF committee. 'Cardiff is in the mining district', wrote Mabel Howell to the NUWSS secretary, Kathleen Courtney; 'perhaps this accounts for the difference in our estimate of their value as supporters'. She was able to point to the miners' opposition to the Labour conference's women's suffrage resolution and also the fact that, of the thirteen Labour absentees from the Conciliation Bill division (who, she suggested, 'will not have been greatly grieved that circumstances made it possible for them to

7 May 1912. Such was the executive's concern that it responded by dispatching its own circular letter in reply to Cardiff's assertions. Ibid., 10 May 1912.
[105] Mabel Howell to Catherine Marshall, 27 June 1912, quoted in Masson, 'Divided Loyalties', 117. The SWF also protested against the executive's role at the ILP conference in Merthyr 'contrary to the wishes of the local society and without consulting the Federation'. NUWSS, executive minutes, 6 June 1912.
[106] CDWSS, *Annual Report*, 1912–13, 11; *Cambria Daily Leader*, 8 February 1913.

escape registering their vote'), four were from south Wales, with only Keir Hardie present to record his support.[107] The EFF committee, on the other hand, took a much more positive view of south Wales's five Labour MPs and a far less favourable one of its Liberals – five anti-suffragists and two 'rats'.[108] Nevertheless, in spite of the efforts of national union officers, the SWF was to remain apprehensive, suspicious and resolutely opposed to the EFF. Whether due to party, class, or family loyalties, the prospect of working for Labour candidates was thoroughly unpalatable to many south Wales suffragists.

Within a few months of its inception, resistance to the policy was manifest in the East Carmarthenshire by-election of August 1912, when the SWF immediately requested 'that the E.F.F. should not be put into action in their area without their wishes being taken into consideration'.[109] While the NUWSS executive was inclined to be conciliatory, 'on account of the unpopularity of the policy with the Federation', a majority of EFF members recommended 'that at all costs E. Carmarthen should be fought'.[110] In the event, local circumstances determined matters. Confusion and delay preceding the adoption of Dr J. H. Williams from Burry Port as the Labour candidate deterred the EFF from 'supporting a man who had no chance of making any impression'.[111] Instead, traditional NUWSS by-election work went ahead, with organizers and speakers undertaking several weeks of energetic propaganda in 'nearly every nook of the constituency'. Selina Cooper and Margaret Aldersley, experienced working-class activists from Lancashire, tackled the populated coal-mining communities of the Amman and Gwendraeth valleys, while Welsh-speaking local

[107] Catherine Marshall Papers (Cumbria Record Office), Mabel Howell to Kathleen Courtney, 13 July 1912, quoted in Masson, 'Divided loyalties', 116.
[108] Catherine Marshall Papers, D/MAR/3/19, cited in Masson, 'Divided loyalties', 116. The two 'rats' were presumably Clement Edwards (East Glamorgan) and Lewis Haslam (Monmouth Boroughs), both of whom voted against the 1912 Conciliation Bill but for either the 1910 or 1911 bill.
[109] NUWSS, executive minutes, 1 August 1912.
[110] NUWSS, EFF minutes, 2 August 1912.
[111] Ibid., 9, 14 August 1912; *Llais Llafur*, 3, 10, 17, 24, 31 Awst 1912; *South Wales Press*, 7, 14 August 1912; ILP, *Report of the 21st Annual Conference held at Manchester, March 1913* (1913), 18; Ioan Matthews, 'Liberals, socialists and Labour: politics in East Carmarthenshire 1906–12', *Carmarthenshire Antiquary*, XXXIV (1998), 90–1.

leaders such as Minnie Davies of Lampeter and the Llanelli branch secretary, Catherine Smith, gave vital support in the rural hinterland. In all, some ninety meetings were held in about forty or fifty locations – often in market places, on street corners, or in any suitable open space – while a great deal of written material, in Welsh and English, was disseminated. Scrutiny of the three candidates' views and pledges saw Dr Williams emerge as 'the best friend' of women's suffrage and during the latter part of the campaign NUWSS representatives, in the testimony of the *Labour Leader*, 'worked like Trojans' for his return.[112] The outcome was a poor third and, in reality, neither the national union, the WFL, the antisuffragists, nor any of the other pressure groups active in the contest made any significant impression against the chapel-honed oratory of the powerful Independent minister, the Revd Josiah Towyn Jones, who personified the enduring ascendancy of Welsh Nonconformist Liberalism. As one chastened NUWSS organizer bemoaned after the poll,

> One of the things an Englishman has to realise in Wales is that here religion and politics are inextricably connected. Politics are largely preached from the pulpit, and hatred of the Established Church makes Liberalism a camp entrenched with all the insurmountable bulwarks of religious fanaticism ... The Rev. Towyn Jones represents Disestablishment in East Carmarthenshire.[113]

The occasion of a by-election in Flint Boroughs a few months later, in January 1913, following the death of the Liberal incumbent, J. W. Summers, afforded another propaganda opportunity. Here there were no EFF complications, for the Labour Party did not field a candidate. Establishing committee rooms in Mold, where a nucleus of support had been created during the recent caravan tour, the small band of NUWSS workers and speakers, organized by the NWF, distributed literature, held nightly meetings and vainly sought to invigorate open-air audiences standing in 'inches of

[112] *Labour Leader*, 22 August 1912.
[113] *CC*, 29 August 1912. See also ibid., 1, 8, 15, 22 August 1912. James Griffiths's recollection of WSPU assistance for the Labour Party would appear faulty here. See Kenneth O. Morgan, *Wales in British Politics, 1868–1922* (3rd edn, Cardiff, 1980), 252. The NUWSS and the WFL gave support; the WSPU did not participate in the election.

melting snow'. Women's suffrage was not an issue in the contest, both candidates at the outset declaring in favour, with the victorious Liberal, Thomas Parry, pledging to vote for such amendments in Parliament.[114] No further by-elections occurred in Wales before the outbreak of war, during which the EFF policy was at first suspended and then terminated.[115]

Whatever reservations there were in Wales about EFF policy, the NUWSS considered it sufficiently successful across Britain to extend its commitment early in 1913, moving further in an anti-Liberal direction by determining that in future no government candidate would be supported and that at the next general election the parliamentary seats of anti-suffragist Liberals, particularly Cabinet ministers, would be attacked. Once again, the Cardiff society sought to forestall the decision, and its annual meeting in April reaffirmed its opinion 'that the new election policy of the N.U. will be detrimental to Suffrage work in Wales'; it once again recommended to the SWF that the national union executive be approached 'with a view of getting Wales exempted from the operation of the policy for the present'.[116] At the same time, north Wales branches were expressing similar reluctance to embrace the EFF, their federation requesting, in May 1913, 'that in view of the special national circumstances existing in North Wales . . . the new Anti-Government policy of the National Union should not be applied in any constituency without the consent of the Federation

---

[114]   NWF, *Annual Report*, 1913, 7, 32–3; *CC*, 17, 24 January 1913; *Flintshire Observer*, 16 January 1913. The Conservative candidate, Hamlet Roberts, in a written reply to Eleanor Rathbone, observed that 'the only issue in the forthcoming election is that of the Church'. NUWSS, executive minutes, 17 January 1913.

[115]   In late 1914 and early 1915, however, in the run-up to a contest in the Swansea District constituency, proposals for an EFF campaign against the possible candidature of Charles Masterman, an unseated Liberal Cabinet minister, were strongly opposed by the local NUWSS branch, backed by the SWF, again on the basis that it would offend the varied political allegiances of members and split the branch; 'electioneering policy on a previous occasion nearly caused the dissolution of the Swansea branch', warned its secretary. Masson, 'Divided loyalties', 121; eadem, 'Political conditions', 378. Elsewhere, too, Welsh branches remained adamantly opposed to the EFF; Llangollen's delegate to an NWF meeting in 1916 was instructed 'to take up an attitude antagonistic to the pro-Labour policy'. NLW, MS 22636B, Llangollen WSS minutes, 27 June 1916.

[116]   NUWSS, executive minutes, 6 February 1913; CDWSS, *Annual Report*, 1913–14, 8.

Committee'.[117] In all likelihood this was a reference to the controversy surrounding the government's efforts to deliver Welsh disestablishment, the bill being defeated in the House of Lords in February and then being reintroduced in June. Eleanor Rathbone and her allies on the national union executive (who included Mabel Howell) had continued to raise objections to the implementation of EFF policy during 1912 and 1913, a stance which was to culminate in April 1914 in her resignation and that of three other members. An 'urgency resolution' from the Cardiff society, expressing 'deep regret' at the departures, swiftly followed.[118]

Among the anti-suffragist ministers targeted by the EFF was the home secretary, Reginald McKenna, in his North Monmouthshire constituency; not surprisingly, this brought further problems with the SWF. Though declaring itself 'anxious to contest Mr. McKenna's seat', the federation resisted the introduction of EFF officials. In February 1913, it was being reported to central headquarters that 'the National Union organizers were having great difficulties in S. Wales owing to the objection to the E.F.F. policy in that district'; this brought a forthright response from the executive, notifying the federation that 'N.U. organisers cannot suppress the policy of the N.U. and ... if it were impossible for them to fulfil these conditions in S. Wales it would be necessary to withdraw the organisers'.[119] After insisting that 'the work was too urgent to admit of further delay', EFF machinery swung into operation in the constituency during 1913, Mary Hilston taking up the position of full-time organizer, setting about forging links with working-class bodies and being backed by a phalanx of well-established speakers, who addressed meetings throughout the two industrial valleys, the Ebbw and the

---

[117] NUWSS, executive minutes, 15 May 1913. For north Wales, see also *Llandudno Advertiser*, 25 January 1913; Bangor WSS minutes, 2, 27, 30 March 1914.

[118] NUWSS executive minutes, 20 June, 19 September 1912; CDWSS, *Annual Report*, 1914–15, 5.

[119] EFF, *Report to NUWSS Council*, n.d. [July 1913], quoted in Holton, *Feminism and Democracy*, 109; NUWSS, executive minutes, 2 January, 11 February, 17 April, 5 June, 3, 31 July 1913; NUWSS, EFF minutes, 20 December 1912, 20 February, 17 April, 5 June, 3, 31 July 1913; *CC*, 2 May, 10, 24 October 1913; Liddington, *Life and Times of a Respectable Radical*, 242–3; Masson, 'Divided loyalties', 122–6; *Free Press of Monmouthshire*, 25 April, 11, 25 July, 17, 24 October, 12 December 1913.

Llwyd, and in the sizeable agricultural town of Abergavenny. Well before the end of the year, Labour's prospects at the next general election were being viewed optimistically by both trade union and women's suffrage activists. The EFF committee felt able to claim: 'Until our organisers began their campaign the Labour forces in North Monmouth were content to be represented in Parliament by a Liberal. Our work has been two-fold, in rousing discontent amongst Labour and converting the Trade Unions to Women's Suffrage.'[120] Such developments were far removed from the initial scepticism of many. 'I do not like this policy and the more I think of it the less I like it', wrote Helga Gill on her resignation as NUWSS organizer in south Wales early in 1913; 'What an empty threat it is. Can't you see McKenna trembling in his shoes at the bare idea of the N.U. opposing him.'[121]

EFF work in the constituency continued during 1914, with the focus on propaganda and registration. In July alone, representatives reported seventeen open-air meetings and twenty-two resolutions passed by organizations representing 19,050 workers – 'one Church; two Steel Forges; three General Workers' Unions; one Dockers' Union; one Trades Council; and fourteen Miners' Lodges'. 'A live interest in the question of Women's Suffrage has been demonstrated', wrote the secretary of the Pontypool Trades and Labour Council. 'Prior to that the question has never been given serious consideration by the branches of the different Trade Unions.' At the same time, organizers' diligence in helping to form ward committees and to trace Labour supporters and get them on the register meant that 'thousands of men will be voting Labour at the next election who have never been in a position to vote before'. 'The Suffrage Society has worked a miracle here', commented a North Monmouthshire Labour Party official.[122] Ultimately, of course, this apparent success was not put to the test because war prevented the anticipated general election of 1915.

[120] *CC*, 7 August 1914; *Free Press of Monmouthshire*, 10, 17 July 1914; *Abergavenny Chronicle*, 10 July 1914.
[121] WL, Edith Eskrigge Papers, 7/ EES/ 2, Helga Gill to Edith Eskrigge, 5 March 1913.
[122] *CC*, 10 October 1913, 7 August 1914.

The EFF was a major facet of the whole NUWSS strategy of popularizing the cause amongst working men and women. It was to enlist such sympathy that the NUWSS launched its Friends of Women's Suffrage scheme in 1912, offering enrolment by simply signing a card pronouncing approval of women's enfranchisement to those either unable to afford the membership fee or who were perhaps reluctant to join formally a suffrage society. By early 1914 around 40,000 Friends had been recruited. Local figures are scarce, though reportedly the Rhondda had 100 by the autumn of 1912, Bangor WSS had enrolled 210 by November 1913 and the Newport WSS 180 in the Maindee district of the town alone by the same date.[123]

In pursuit of the same objective of widening support for the cause, the national union engaged more working-class speakers and organizers and dispatched them to industrial districts. Selina Cooper, who had been active at various times in north-east Wales on behalf of the NWF since its inception in 1910, became a frequent visitor to the south Wales mining valleys. Others closely involved in the labour movement, such as Ada Nield Chew, Isabella Ford, Ethel Snowden and Fenner Brockway (editor of the *Labour Leader*), also spoke on women's suffrage platforms in Wales.

Trade unions, which afforded 'an unequalled opportunity of getting in touch with the working people in the neighbourhood', were inevitably targeted. Following an NUWSS council directive of May 1913, federation and local activists waited upon officials and addressed branch meetings and as a result, across Wales, miners, quarrymen, tin plate workers, railwaymen, engineers, gasworkers, bricklayers, postal workers, municipal workers, bakers and others passed women's suffrage resolutions in the latter half of 1913.[124] Trades councils, ILP branches and women's guilds were similarly tackled. The convening of the annual conference of the ILP in Merthyr at Whitsun 1912 was made the occasion for vigorous activity by all three major women's suffrage societies, and this was followed by greater efforts to promote the cause in

---

[123] Ibid., 31 October 1912, 5 December 1913; *NWC*, 21 November 1913.
[124] NWF, *Annual Report*, 1913, 13–16; Bangor WSS minutes, 1 May, 28 October 1913, 13 January 1914; CDWSS, *Annual Report*, 1913–14, 9, 14.

the south Wales valleys. In particular, the NUWSS (and the WSPU) undertook campaigns in the Rhondda, local enthusiasts giving valuable support to visiting agents. The size and general demeanour of audiences, the formation of several NUWSS branches and the large number of Friends of Women's Suffrage enrolled were testimony to at least some impression being made in Wales's most densely populated working-class communities.[125] There was backing too from the ILP-controlled *Rhondda Socialist*, most vehemently from 'Matron', its anonymous women's columnist, who was scathing of a Liberal government which 'refuses ... even the smallest measure of granting the suffrage to women' and promoted 'one-sided legislation – more votes for men and a shove back to serfdom for women'.[126] The growth of the Women's Co-operative Guild (WCG) and its continued support for women's and adult suffrage also helped to draw working-class women into the campaign. In Wales, while only a handful of branches functioned in the early years of the century, the period 1909–14 saw the foundation of eighteen new ones and considerable local activity on a wide range of issues.[127]

EFF, federation and branch activity, the large number of meetings, public speaking tours, electioneering work, the dissemination of literature, often in the Welsh language, and support for national initiatives meant that the NUWSS mounted a significant campaign in Wales in the immediate pre-war years. Considerably augmenting its effectiveness, moreover, was an array of other constitutionalist organizations, based on religious, occupational or party political associations, and often serving to bring more men into the campaign.

By 1914 there were six distinct religious societies, providing for a wide range of persuasions, three of which made some impression in Wales.[128] Seeking to unite Anglicans in the cause

---

[125]   *CC*, 6 June, 4, 25 July, 31 October, 14, 22, 29 November 1912, 3 January 1913.

[126]   *Rhondda Socialist*, January 1912, in Aaron and Masson, *Very Salt of Life*, 224–5. See also ibid., 165–7, 226–7.

[127]   Gillian Rees, 'The Women's Co-operative Guild and women's suffrage', in Boussahba-Bravard, *Suffrage Outside Suffragism*, 144–52; Thomas, 'A democracy of working women', 32–5.

[128]   The Church League for Women's Suffrage, the Free Church League for Women's Suffrage, the Catholic Women's Suffrage Society, the Friends' League for

was the Church League for Women's Suffrage (CLWS). Formed in December 1909, it had over 5,000 members by the end of 1913, including 425 clergymen, and 103 branches.[129] Growth was most marked from 1912, a year during which membership, number of branches and activities increased considerably, a journal was launched and a full-time organizer appointed for the first time – Louisa Corben of Caldicot, formerly active in the WFL. 'Well known as a pioneer of Suffrage work in the county of Bristol and Monmouth', announced the *CLWS Monthly Paper*, 'we now have on the official staff a foundation-member of the League, who recognised its value and importance in days when we were not "respectable".'[130] From its inception the CLWS attracted scattered individual supporters in Wales and, in time, a number of branches too. The first was at Llanymynech, on the Montgomeryshire–Shropshire border, in May 1912; Cardiff, Swansea and Newport followed in 1913. The employment of a Wales organizer, Helen Davies of Ebbw Vale, in May 1914, brought a rush of activity over the next few months, especially in north Monmouthshire (where she reported 'overwhelming suffrage ignorance and indifference'). Meetings were held and groundwork laid at Abergavenny, Abertillery, Blaenafon, Ebbw Vale, Tredegar and elsewhere. Two new branches appeared at this time, in Ebbw Vale and Bangor, and the Newport one was revived. By the outbreak of war, Wales probably had several hundred Church League members, including twenty or so clergymen (and many more prepared to sign petitions).[131]

With 'education and prayer' as the watchword, propaganda was conducted through conferences, meetings and the

Women's Suffrage, the Scottish Churches League for Women's Society and the Jewish League for Women's Suffrage.

[129] CLWS, *Annual Report*, 1913, 1. Louisa Corben remained active in the campaign until its conclusion, serving on the executive of the Church League's successor, the League of the Church Militant, and being appointed its campaign organizer in 1925. *Church Militant*, 15 April 1926; *Annual Report*, 1926–7.

[130] *CLWS Monthly Paper*, August 1912.

[131] *Montgomery County Times*, 11 May 1912; *Llangollen Advertiser*, 17 May 1912; *WM*, 22 September 1913; *CLWS Monthly Paper*, May, July, September 1913, May, June, July, August 1914. The Cardiff branch began with thirty-two members in April 1913, rising to eighty-eight by the end of the year; Swansea grew from ten to fifty-three during the same period. Ibid., May, August 1913; CLWS, *Annual Report*, 1913, 17, 34.

distribution of literature, while divine worship was dedicated to the cause. Church people were inevitably key figures; thus, in late 1913, for example, the Cardiff and Newport branches distributed hundreds of copies of the *Monthly Paper* to clergymen, girls' friendly societies, mothers' unions and other church workers and groups.[132] Certainly, local vicars became involved in all five Welsh branches, holding official posts, chairing public meetings and leading special intercessory services. To them, women's suffrage accorded with fundamental Christian principles.

The CLWS was always careful to steer clear of controversial, divisive issues within the movement; thus, it 'neither discussed "militancy" in its changing forms, nor the election policies propounded and employed by various leagues, nor any kindred matters'.[133] As such, it offered an alternative or additional, rather than a rival, identity for suffragists, an avenue through which various activists, both militant and non-militant, could work together. In both Cardiff and Swansea joint ventures involving CLWS, NUWSS and WFL branches were common during 1913 and 1914, while individuals were clearly members of more than one local suffrage society.[134] For example, Beatrice Stewart, the driving force behind the Llangollen WSS, and Alix Clark, a WFL stalwart in Montgomeryshire, were involved in the Church League. So too was Sybil Thomas of Llanwern who supported almost every suffrage initiative.

Considerably smaller than the CLWS was its Nonconformist counterpart, the Free Church League for Women's Suffrage (FCL), formed in 1912. Like the other religious leagues, it was non-party and undertook little political action, confining itself largely to work of a spiritual and moral nature, by means of branch societies, religious services, meetings and lectures, and by the distribution of its own journal and other literature. Some thirty branches were established around the country,

---

[132]   *CLWS Monthly Paper*, November 1913.
[133]   Ibid., April 1914.
[134]   Ibid., June, August, December 1913, March, May 1914. For a detailed study on this theme, see Krista Cowman, '"Crossing the great divide": inter-organizational suffrage relationships on Merseyside, 1895–1914', in Eustance, Ryan and Ugolini (eds), *A Suffrage Reader*, 37–52.

including two in Wales, at Treorchy and Swansea.[135] The former, founded in 1913, was the inspiration of the Revd Jamieson Williams and his wife (both ILP activists), who were also involved in NUWSS activity in the Rhondda. The Swansea branch was formed in April 1914, with an initial membership of fifty, by local WFL activists.[136]

The FCL evidently made little impact in Wales. Nor did the Catholic Women's Suffrage Society (CWSS), established in 1911 but spawning only a dozen branches or so before the war. One was at Cardiff, established after the annual National Catholic Congress was held there in July 1914; but with the outbreak of European hostilities imminent, its work immediately became war related.[137] Wales did, however, provide the Catholic society's most able and energetic activist in Alice Abadam. Born in 1856, the youngest daughter of Edward Abadam of Middleton Hall, Carmarthenshire, she was a convert to Catholicism in her early twenties. Her early adult life was of a philanthropic nature, including church and social work and visiting Carmarthen Prison. Moving to south London in 1904, she became an ardent suffragist, undertaking an immense amount of public speaking on behalf of the cause, often tackling the question from a moral and religious dimension and emphasizing the theme of social purity in the manner of Josephine Butler. During the decade before 1914 she travelled all over the British Isles addressing hundreds of meetings under the auspices of various suffrage societies. Joining the WSPU in 1906, she was an original committee member of the WFL in 1907 but left later that same year. She was essentially a constitutionalist, being active in the NUWSS, CLWS, CWSS, Women Writers' League and the Actresses'

[135] *FCL Times,* June 1913, May 1914; FCL, *Annual Report,* 1913 (Bodleian Library, NLOWS, Newspaper Cuttings, vol. 30). Among listed vice-presidents were Annie Mary Dobell, headmistress of Pontypool County Girls' School, Revd Jamieson Williams of Ystrad Rhondda and Lady Aberconway.

[136] *FCL Times,* May 1914; *Cambrian,* 10 April 1914. See also *Rhondda Socialist,* 16 March 1912.

[137] CWSS, *Annual Report,* 1914, 3, 9; ibid., *Annual Report,* 1915, 7; *Welsh Catholic Herald,* 18 July 1914; *Catholic Citizen,* 15 November 1928. Also active in the CWSS was Walter Roch, Liberal MP for Pembrokeshire 1908–18, and his wife, Florens (daughter of Sir Ivor Herbert, Liberal MP for South Monmouthshire, 1906–17), who was a member of its national committee and its third chairman (1916–20).

Franchise League, while she also became first secretary of the Federated Council of Suffrage Societies, founded in November 1912 'to determine a united policy and action which all the constitutional societies might adopt'.[138]

A range of suffrage groups based on particular occupations represented another supplementary campaigning channel for professions such as actresses, artists, writers and teachers. London based, their impact in the provinces was confined to scattered individual subscribers and to producing propaganda plays, sketches, songs, poems and posters, all readily adopted by local branches of the various women's suffrage societies to enrich their campaigning.[139]

The women's suffrage movement in Edwardian Britain also embraced organizations closely linked to the political parties. The Conservative and Unionist Women's Franchise Association (CUWFA), formed in November 1910, was the creation of activists within the NUWSS who sought to convert their party to women's suffrage. By the outbreak of war in August 1914, it had about sixty-five branches. None was in Wales, to which the association gave no attention.[140]

At the same time, Liberal women suffragists maintained pressure on their party leadership and a succession of organizations within the WLF – the Union of Practical Suffragists, the Forward Suffrage Union and the Liberal Women's Suffrage Union – urged the withholding of assistance to anti-suffrage parliamentary candidates. Annual meetings of the federation brought heated, acrimonious debate between radical suffragists and party loyalists, Welsh women being prominent in the

---

[138]   *Carmarthen Journal*, 5 April 1940; *Catholic Citizen*, 15 April 1940; *Welsh Catholic Times*, 5, 12 April 1940; *The Times*, 3 April 1940. Marilyn Timms, 'Alice Abadam and inter-war feminism: recovering the history of a forgotten suffragist' (MA thesis, Ruskin College, University of Oxford, 2003), 7–10.

[139]   A number of women with Welsh connections were involved in the different 'professional' organizations. Alice Abadam, Margaret Nevinson and Flora Annie Steel spoke on behalf of the Actresses' Franchise League and also held executive positions in the Women Writers' Suffrage League. Dorothy Salmon of Swansea was involved in the Artists' Franchise League.

[140]   A strong supporter of 'the direct and active participation by women in the affairs of State' and a member of the Conciliation Committee was William Ormsby-Gore, elected for Denbigh Boroughs in January 1910, one of only two Conservative MPs in Wales. See *Conservative and Unionist Women's Franchise Review*, November 1910.

former camp. A conference of representatives from WLAs throughout Wales, meeting in Cardiff in November 1910, over-whelmingly passed the following resolution:

> Should the present Government fail to give satisfactory reply to the application which the Conciliation Committee will make this autumn for facilities for its Suffrage Bill, this conference recommends all Liberal women to confine themselves to suffrage work until the vote be won, and, in pursuit of this object, suggest that they support only those Liberal members who voted for the Bill, and shall refrain from opposing members of other parties who voted for it.[141]

'Revolt of Welsh Liberal Women' ran the newspaper headlines, and certainly those in attendance, who included leading Welsh suffragists from across Wales, were in uncompromising mood. 'It was time Liberal women made a stand' and 'Wales should take a lead in the matter' were the prevalent sentiments. Implementation of the conference resolution immediately caused controversy in Cardiff, where many members of the WLA refused to help the candidature of the anti-suffragist Sir Clarendon Hyde in the December 1910 election. Failure to resolve the electoral policy of the association led to a formal split a few months later, with hard-line suffragists, including the president, four vice-presidents and eight executive members, resigning en bloc and establishing a new society, the Cardiff Progressive Liberal Women's Union.[142]

Elsewhere, some Liberal women gave their support to the new NUWSS strategy of electoral alliance with the Labour Party through the EFF, while others simply ceased involvement altogether. 'Delay in giving Suffrage to women was dangerous to Liberalism as it made women leave the Party', warned a senior figure in the Cardiff association in 1911.[143] Mary Salmon, who spent twenty-one years as an executive member of the Swansea WLA, was a case in point:

---

[141] *SWDN*, 1, 2, 4 November 1910; *VW*, 11 November 1910; *CC*, 10 November 1910; *The Vote*, 12 November 1910. See also Masson, *Women's Rights*, 74.

[142] *CC*, 8 December 1910, 23, 30 March 1911 *CT*, 18 March 1911. For more details on the split, see Masson, 'Women versus "the people"', 14–17; Aaron and Masson, *Very Salt of Life*, 250–2, 260–4. Hyde was defeated in the election by the Conservative, Lord Ninian Stuart, who had declared in favour of women's suffrage.

[143] WLF, *Summary of Federation News*, 1 May 1911.

I have long felt it was time that the Liberal women should refuse to do the dirty work at election and other times, while the Government behaved so badly . . . I have at last quite come to the end of my patience, and in great disgust at the last failure of the House of Commons to keep its pledge to women, and at Mr. Asquith's attitude generally, I have last week resigned from this Association and severed myself from the party altogether until women are enfranchised . . . Several other women here are intending to follow my example and withdraw from party politics.[144]

'Women are leaving us in shoals', reported one Liberal activist, and indeed, in the period 1912–14, WLF membership declined from 133,215 to 115,097 and the number of branches dropped from 837 to 769. The number of associations in Wales affiliated to the WLF (which had revived from a low of five in 1908) fell from twenty-nine in 1911 to fourteen in 1914.[145] In the wake of the split over election policy, membership in Cardiff fell dramatically, from 845 in 1910 to 150 in 1912. Generally, in Wales, memberships were small in the years immediately preceding the First World War. Aberdare, for example, had twenty-seven members in 1914. The clear exception was the Swansea WLA, which grew from 1,025 members in 1910 to 2,075 in 1915.[146] Here, women's suffrage was always at the forefront of the agenda; visiting the town in 1912, NUWSS organizer, L. F. Waring, observed that 'the Liberal Women's Federation . . . is commonly regarded as a Suffrage Society'.[147] Elsewhere, significant numbers of disgruntled Liberal women now seem to have put their own enfranchisement first and transfered their organizational allegiance. 'As Cardiff WLA collapsed', writes Ursula Masson, 'the C&DWSS waxed mightily, reaching a membership of over one thousand – as the WLA had once done. It can reasonably be said that the suffrage societies replaced women's Liberal organisation in Cardiff and South Wales.'[148]

[144]   VW, 14 February 1913. At the same point, she also gave up her long-time membership of the NUWSS and joined the WFL, acknowledging militancy as 'necessary', though rejecting the destruction of property.
[145]   Pugh, March of the Women, 143; Linda Walker, 'Party political women: a comparative study of Liberal women and the Primrose League, 1890–1914', in Jane Rendall (ed.), Equal or Different: Women's Politics, 1880–1914 (Oxford, 1987), 169; Holton, Feminism and Democracy, 119–20; WLF, Annual Reports, 1908–14.
[146]   Masson, 'Divided loyalties', 119.
[147]   CC, 15 February 1912. An NUWSS branch was not formed in Swansea until relatively late, in May 1912. CC, 6 June 1912.
[148]   Masson, 'Women versus "the people"', 17.

As a succession of parliamentary initiatives collapsed after 1910, the dominant mood among Liberal women was one of increasing exasperation and disillusionment at the government's lack of commitment to the suffrage cause. At the same time, the WLF was vigorous in promoting the issue. 'There can be no real peace or accord in Liberal ranks until the Women's Suffrage question is settled righteously', concluded the resolution sent by the WLF executive to the government in January 1913.[149] The federation lobbied government ministers and MPs, by deputation and in writing, and urged local affiliates to do likewise; it passed resolutions and dispatched them to politicians and the press, published and distributed leaflets and pamphlets, participated in the Women's Suffrage Joint Committee (made up of various constitutional suffrage societies) and courted Men's Liberal Associations. Wales certainly gave support to this work. A series of WLA conferences in both north and south Wales in 1912 and 1913 gave prominence to women's suffrage, while individual associations promoted the issue locally. A large deputation of activists from across Wales, including the wives of several MPs, waited on the Welsh Parliamentary Party in December 1912, seeking support for the women's suffrage amendments to the government's Franchise and Registration Bill; all but five of the twenty-six MPs were apparently in favour.[150]

There was pressure too within the Labour Party to adopt women's suffrage. Most obviously, the ILP gave consistent support. In Wales, as elsewhere, suffrage speakers frequently addressed branch meetings, while local activists often gave considerable assistance to campaigners.[151] Similarly, the Women's Labour League (WLL), founded in 1906, promoted the demand as one of its objectives. Its total of 112 branches in 1911 included ten in south Wales.[152] While women's suffrage

[149] WLF, *Annual Report*, 1913, 28.

[150] Ibid., 20–9; ibid., *Annual Report*, 1914, 26–8; *Summary of Federation News*, 1 December 1910, 1 November, 1 December 1912, 1 January, 1 February 1913; *NWC*, 6 December 1912, 18 April 1913; *VW*, 6 December 1912; *The Suffragette*, 6 December 1912. In Caernarfon, a joint committee of the WLA and the WSS was established. *Montgomery County Times*, 15 March 1912.

[151] See, for example, the campaign by Annott Robinson, organizer for the suffrage committee of the Fabian Women's Group, in the Rhondda in March 1912. *Rhondda Socialist*, 16 March 1912.

[152] Christine Collette, *For Labour and for Women: The Women's Labour League*,

sometimes figured in their activities, the chief concerns of branches were undoubtedly social welfare issues and local government representation.

For years the Labour Party's commitment to adult suffrage was entrenched, a demand viewed by the leadership of the NUWSS, like that of the WSPU, as a diversion, the 'trick' of male politicians, and unrealistic in the immediate term. But there was significant support for the more democratic strategy. One expression of this was the People's Suffrage Federation, founded in 1909 and drawing support from across the labour movement, including trade unions, and branches of the WCG, the ILP and the WLL.[153] The long-standing conflict within the Labour Party was eventually resolved in 1912 when it became the first major party to adopt women's suffrage as official policy and the EFF alliance with the NUWSS came into being.

Taking all these developments into account, by 1914 organized suffragism across Britain could, for the first time, lay claim to being a mass movement, at the head of which was the NUWSS. On the eve of the First World War in August 1914 it had some 500 branches, over 54,000 subscribing members (growing at a rate of 800 a month) and over 46,000 affiliated (non-paying) supporters, Friends of Women's Suffrage. Annual revenue had increased from £5,500 in 1910 to over £45,000 in 1914. While relations with militant campaigners were clearly strained, it was at one with the vast majority of women's suffrage societies that then existed. The NUWSS had also taken the cause to the working class by forging close links with the Labour Party and through cooperation with trade unions, trades councils and the WCG.[154]

1906–1918 (Manchester, 1989), appendix 2, 204–17; Thomas, 'A democracy of working women', 35–6. See also Margherita Rendel, 'The contribution of the Women's Labour League to the winning of the franchise', in Lucy Middleton (ed.), *Women in the Labour Movement: The British Experience* (London, 1977), 57–83; Pat Thane, 'Women in the Labour party and women's suffrage', in Boussahba-Bravard, *Suffrage Outside Suffragism*, 35–51.

[153] People's Suffrage Federation, *Annual Report*, 1909–10. Among the affiliations were several ILP branches in south Wales and Newport Trades Council. Yet another organization was the Working Women's Suffrage Union, on behalf of which Dr Erie Evans, vice-president of the CDWSS, spoke. CDWSS, *Annual Report*, 1912–13, 20.

[154] Hume, *National Union*, 197, 223–3, 229–31; Pugh, *March of the Women*, 254–6, 278–9.

Mirroring these developments, the NUWSS had, by 1914, expanded into what was easily Wales's largest suffrage organization, with local branches covering much of the country; *The Common Cause* listed twenty-eight and four sub-branches in operation at the outbreak of war.[155] Working-class support had also been aroused by implementation of the EFF strategy in the North Monmouthshire constituency, and by organizers visiting and establishing branches in the south Wales valleys and in the slate communities of Caernarfonshire and penetrating the trade union movement. In addition, the NUWSS had worked hard to mitigate public hostility (so pronounced in Wales) engendered by suffragette militancy, which constitutionalists believed was seriously undermining their campaign after 1911.

In Wales, as in Britain as a whole, the educational and propaganda activities of the NUWSS and the other societies, both militant and non-militant, had been far reaching in the decade before 1914 and had done much to prepare public opinion for the enactment of women's suffrage. The national union, in particular, had succeeded in advancing the cause among politicians in the Liberal, Conservative and Labour parties. Yet, crucially, these efforts proved insufficient to overcome the intractable political obstacles to legislative progress at Westminster, while a further complication was an anti-suffrage campaign at its most vigorous.

---

[155] *CC*, 31 July 1914.

V

THE OPPOSITION TO WOMEN'S SUFFRAGE

'We most heartily wish these ladies a miserable New Year, and, if we had known them a week sooner, we should have wished them a wretched Christmas.' Thus the persistently anti-suffragist *Saturday Review* greeted the editor and contributors of *Revolution*, an American women's rights newspaper, in 1869.[1] Opposition to women's suffrage was often instinctively hostile and blatantly prejudicial. But much of it was considered and cogently articulated. Certainly it was entrenched and influential throughout the Victorian and Edwardian period and, as the suffragist agitation gathered momentum, was incorporated into a permanent and formidable movement after 1908, when both male and female organizations – subsequently amalgamated into the National League for Opposing Woman Suffrage (NLOWS) – were founded.[2] Anti-suffragist sentiment and activity undoubtedly made an impact in Wales. A number of its MPs emerged as outspoken suffrage opponents, unfavourable opinion was expressed in newspapers, periodicals, public meetings, pamphlets and books, and the NLOWS campaigned vigorously in parts of Wales, generating branch associations in much the same way as did its rival societies.

Opposition to women's suffrage came from across the political and social spectrum, all three major parties being divided on the issue. There was also the very important distinction, within the Liberal Party in particular, between staunch opponents of the principle of women's enfranchisement and those (such as Lloyd George) who rejected the various bills on the grounds of social class or marital status. The diversity of the outright anti-suffragists was reflected among Wales's MPs. A

---

[1] *Saturday Review*, 2 January 1869, cited in Margaret Hamilton, 'Opposition to woman suffrage in England, 1865–1884', *Victorians Institute Journal*, 4 (1975), 62.

[2] For the anti-suffrage movement, see Brian Harrison, *Separate Spheres: The Opposition to Women's Suffrage in Britain* (London, 1978); Julia Bush, *Women Against the Vote: Female Anti-Suffragism in Britain* (Oxford, 2007); Hamilton, 'Opposition to woman suffrage in England'; Pugh, *March of the Women*, especially chs 2, 7; idem, 'Pott, Gladys Sydney (1867–1961), *ODNB*; Riley, 'Opposition to women's suffrage'.

prime example from the political right was the Conservative member for Pembrokeshire, John Henry Scourfield. The adversary of a whole range of progressive causes, including the development of the railways, the abolition of capital punishment, the secret ballot, disestablishment of the Welsh Church, nonconformist agitation over burial laws and the extended use of the Welsh language in courts, he was one of the foremost opponents of the early women's suffrage bills.[3] Scourfield spoke in four successive parliamentary debates in the years 1870–3 and in 1875 was a leading figure in the formation of a cross-party committee of MPs designed to rally opposition to women's enfranchisement.[4]

An early anti-suffragist of a very different political hue was George Osborne Morgan, Liberal MP for his native Denbighshire from 1868 until his death in 1897 and a member of Gladstone's governments of the 1880s. A radical on nonconformist issues, he was by no means opposed to women's demands generally. He supported increased educational opportunities for women and reform of the married women's property laws, though, like Scourfield, he strongly opposed repeal of the Contagious Diseases Acts, condemning a 'miserable agitation ... that was a disgrace to the country, as it flooded gentlemen's breakfast tables with abominable literature, not addressed to themselves only, but also to their wives and daughters'.[5]

---

[3] Changing his surname from Philipps on inheriting his uncle's estates in 1862, Scourfield served as MP for Haverfordwest from 1852 to 1868, before transferring to the more secure and prestigious Pembrokeshire seat, which he held until his death in 1876 (shortly after being knighted).

[4] J. H. Scourfield's prominence among the opposition ensured Pembrokeshire received a good deal of attention from early suffragists. Speakers visited the county in 1871, 1872 and 1874, often entertaining audiences by ridiculing his parliamentary contributions in 'a mercilessly satirical manner'. See *Haverfordwest and Milford Haven Telegraph*, 27 November 1872; Miller, *An Uncommon Girlhood*, 387.

[5] *Parl. Deb.*, 211, col. 56, 1 May 1872. He ardently supported the continuation of the acts on public health grounds, arguing that the measures 'have done much, very much, to alleviate the severity and check the growth of one of the most terrible diseases to which humanity is scourged'. Ibid., 278, col. 799, 20 April 1883. Morgan's central role, as judge-advocate-general, in the passage of the Married Women's Property Act of 1882 was noted in a *Punch* caricature ('just the man for the ladies'). *Punch*, 7 October 1882. When supporting reform in this area, he was anxious to assure fellow MPs that it would not lead to 'the development of "the women's rights question", and looming behind that a Parliament in petticoats'. *Parl. Deb.*, 3rd series, 214, cols 676–7, 19 February 1873.

Conspicuous in the resistance to the women's suffrage initiatives of the early 1890s was another north-east Wales Liberal MP, Samuel Smith, the stern Scottish Presbyterian and Liverpool-based cotton merchant who represented Flintshire from 1886 to 1906. He detailed his objections in letters to the press (one of which was published as a pamphlet) and spoke in the parliamentary debate on the bill introduced by Sir Albert Rollit in April 1892.[6] Similarly resolute in his opposition at this time was the political heavyweight Sir William Harcourt, MP for West Monmouthshire (1895–1904), chancellor of the Exchequer in Gladstone's last administration (1892–4) and leader of the Liberal Party (1896–8), though he spoke in only one parliamentary debate on the issue, in 1897.

Wales provided several prominent parliamentary anti-suffragists during the Edwardian era too. Samuel T. Evans, Liberal MP for Mid Glamorgan, 'talked out' two women's suffrage measures in 1906, much to the anger of suffragettes both inside and outside the House of Commons. J. D. Rees, Liberal representative for Montgomery Boroughs and an impassioned foe of women's suffrage, employed the same obstructionist tactic to defeat Dickinson's bill the following year and continued in similar vein in subsequent debates. Two other Liberal members, Ivor Guest (Cardiff) and David Davies (Montgomeryshire), gave their support to the organized anti-suffragism of this period, while one of the staunchest opponents in the pre-war Liberal cabinets was the North Monmouthshire MP, Reginald McKenna.

'Antis', as suffragists contemptuously dubbed them, drew on multifarious arguments, which were often very persuasive and influential in the context of the time and served to convince people from all walks of life in Victorian and Edwardian society, including women themselves. Many of the objections proved highly durable and were repeated inter-

---

[6] *CN*, 28 March 1890; 1 May 1891, 22, 29 April 1892; *Letter from Samuel Smith, M.P.*; Rover, *Women's Suffrage and Party Politics*, 179–80. Smith did make a valuable contribution to one aspect of the women's movement, actively supporting the successful campaign (led by W. T. Stead, editor of the *Pall Mall Gazette*, and Josephine Butler) to raise the age of consent from thirteen to sixteen in 1885. Samuel Smith, *My Life-Work* (London, 1903), 172–3. See also G. Le G. Norgate, 'Smith, Samuel (1836–1906)', revised H. C. G. Matthew, *ODNB*.

minably over the many years of the campaign. Thus some of the arguments of J. H. Scourfield in the early 1870s were still being advanced four decades later. In this respect, one of the most frequently voiced claims was that most women did not want the franchise, a theme of all four of Scourfield's parliamentary speeches on the issue. 'The great mass of the women of this country did not desire to have this so-called privilege conferred upon them', he insisted in 1871, and he did not see

> why, because a small set of demonstrative women persisted in setting up what they claimed as the rights of their sex, the House should force upon the more numerous and more retiring of the female community what they did not wish for, and would, if given to them, probably repudiate.[7]

Similarly, Osborne Morgan, in the parliamentary debate of 1872, argued that enfranchisement 'was advocated by only a small knot of earnest women, who had been brooding over real or imaginary wrongs', and he insisted that he 'could not consent to make a revolution for the sake of a handful of fanatics'.[8] Time and again in later years, 'antis' denied that activists were typical of their sex. 'They are not representative women', said Sir J. D. Rees in 1913, 'and there is little peace, light and refreshment about them, but continual agitation, worry, and trouble.'[9] Accordingly, suffragist organizations, like the many other extra-parliamentary agitations mounted in this period, were looked upon with great suspicion and much distaste. 'One of the nuisances of the present day', said J. H. Scourfield in the parliamentary debate on women's suffrage in 1871, 'was the tyranny which was attempted to be exercised by societies who professed to represent the opinion of the country.'[10] Thus, he and others rejected both petitions and public meetings as reliable criteria for measuring public

[7] *Parl. Deb.*, 3rd ser., 206, cols 87–8, 3 May 1871.

[8] Ibid., 211, col. 56, 1 May 1872.

[9] Ibid., 5th ser., 52, col. 1762, 3 May 1913. To Colonel Cornwallis-West, lord lieutenant of Denbighshire, presiding over an anti-suffrage demonstration in Rhyl in 1909, it was 'the discontented unmarried woman who was at the bottom of the agitation that had lately been upsetting the country'. *Rhyl Journal*, 24 April 1909.

[10] Ibid., 3rd ser., 206, col. 87, 3 May 1871. Samuel Smith lamented in much the same fashion in 1891: 'Every fragment of political opinion in the country is now worked up by means of leagues and paid secretaries.' *Mr Samuel Smith, MP, and Women's Suffrage* (1891), 4.

opinion. 'Antis' were also able to point out that for many years membership of suffrage societies remained small, numbering no more than a few thousand until well into the Edwardian period. Feminine indifference was a perennial problem for the suffragist movement. Crucially, too, within the opposition's ranks were well-known women like the novelist Mary (Mrs Humphry) Ward, the philanthropists Octavia Hill and Beatrice Potter (later Webb), the public servant Violet Markham and, above all of course, Queen Victoria. For many years, female 'antis' were reluctant to organize themselves against their own enfranchisement, recognizing that political campaigning would be a contradiction of their case; 'the same reason that prevented women from desiring to have these privileges conferred upon them prevented them from getting up an agitation in opposition', explained J. H. Scourfield in 1870.[11]

Opponents of women's suffrage emphatically rejected any notion of the vote as a natural right; rather, it was a privilege exercised by sections of the community for the public good. And in this respect, 'antis' contended very vigorously that enfranchisement would benefit neither women themselves nor the state; indeed, it would be harmful to both. At the heart of the suffrage debate was the widespread belief in 'separate spheres', the notion that God and/or Nature had created the two sexes as fundamentally different, not only in physique but in temperament and moral and intellectual qualities, intending them to fulfil distinct roles in society. In the words of one Blaenafon opponent, woman's 'proper position was on the hearth, where she could rule as queen, and bestow that care in the proper upbringing of her children which nature intended her to do'.[12] Critically, 'antis' deduced from this that politics should be a male preserve, women being, it was said, too emotional, too sensitive and too irrational for such key decision-making, contentions which received a good deal of backing from the medical profession, especially with the advent of suffragette militancy. The most notorious of the assertions about female psychology and physiology was the claim by the eminent bacteriologist, Sir Almroth Wright,

[11]   *Parl. Deb.*, 3rd ser., 201, col. 210, 4 May 1870.
[12]   *Pontypool Free Press*, 22 February 1907.

that women were prone to hysteria, in a letter to *The Times* in March 1912, later published as a pamphlet entitled *The Unexpurgated Case against Woman Suffrage* (1913).[13] Women's specific talents, it was widely insisted, were designed for the home and the rearing of children and, in public affairs, were suited only to religious, charitable and educational work. In an age when childbearing was both frequent and dangerous and women's domestic role was often very much a full-time one, the belief that politics lay outside women's sphere was highly plausible.

Contemporaries could also point to the conduct of elections, especially to the drunkenness and disorder that commonly characterized contests even after the introduction of the secret ballot in 1872, and insist that exposure to this was wholly improper for the female character. 'The great mass of the sterner sex have far too much respect for the weaker one than to wish to see them embroiled in the tumult and wild excitement of political strife', contended the *Star of Gwent* in 1881. 'When they [women] wish to take part and lot in proceedings frequently characterised by violence, uproar, and vulgar personalities, they must be protected from themselves.'[14] Thus, of particular concern to J. H. Scourfield and others (including William Gladstone) was the requirement of personal attendance at the poll, 'a practical evil not only of the gravest, but of the most intolerable character', while the zeal and persistence of election agents would subject women to a great deal of 'annoyance and persecution', which to many Victorians and Edwardians was tantamount to indecency.[15] Accordingly, in the words of J. D. Rees, the suffrage carried 'the germ of the degradation of womanhood', sullying the natural feminine virtues of sweetness, charm and grace.[16]

---

[13]   '[W]oman has a finer and more highly-strung constitution than men', wrote Samuel Smith. *Mr Samuel Smith, MP, and Women's Suffrage*, 7. 'The arguments against female suffrage are many and are chiefly founded on the anatomical and physiological differences between the two sexes, and so are scarcely capable of being discussed in a popular journal as yours', wrote one Barmouth 'anti', voicing a widespread sentiment. *Barmouth and County Advertiser*, 31 December 1908.

[14]   *Star of Gwent*, 18 March 1881.

[15]   *Parl. Deb.*, 3rd ser., 101, col. 212, 4 May 1870; ibid., 211, col. 35, 1 May 1872. See also ibid., 4th ser., 3, col. 1484, 27 April 1892 (Samuel Smith).

[16]   Ibid., 5th ser., 2, cols 1425–6, 19 March 1909. See also Wallace, *'Organise!'*,

'Antis' could be deeply disparaging of female intellect and character. A *Cardiff Times* editorial in 1872, for example, spoke of 'the incompleteness of the average female mind', while the *Brecon County Times* correspondent, covering a Neath meeting the same year, was contemptuous: 'Two places only are suitable for women, viz. the cradle and the grave'.[17] More often, however, they went to the other extreme, eulogizing women in the most extravagant of terms. A striking example was the absurdly romantic nature of much of the vicar of Usk's public lecture in Monmouth on 'Women's Rights' in 1872:

> I would not rob the fairest and sweetest portion of God's creation of her real rights by putting her in the wrong place – I would not take away all the sweetness and scent of so fair a flower by casting it forth to the rough handling of the political world. I don't wish to see so delicate a piece of workmanship exposed to all the tussle and scramble of the ... balloting booth ... I know where woman shines forth most beautifully, and most beneficently ... in her home circle, in her family, and in that society around her, where she need shine with no borrowed lustre, no lurid illustration, but with a glory all her own, in her proper power and strength. Woman in her own sphere illumines like the sun in our system, and sheds light and diffuses a radiance and warmth which woman out of her sphere which God has assigned her, never could do. And if they burden you with politics, your sun is clouded with sackcloth, your glory is departed.[18]

Accordingly, the sight of women engaged in public speaking – and the early suffrage campaigners were the first ladies ever seen on a lecture platform by the majority of the audiences – was guaranteed to elicit strong condemnation in the Victorian period. This emanated not just from the male sex but from females too, as a columnist in an issue of the *Nineteenth Century* in 1884 vividly illustrated:

> Women who are exhibiting themselves, their persons, talents, and opinions, upon platforms ... are unconsciously helping to lower the standard of womanhood in the eyes of the world at large ... We present ourselves before our children or our younger sisters as talking-machines, as specimens of what they too may become when by aid of

163–4, quoting *Cardiff and Merthyr Guardian*, 11 June 1870; Masson, *Womanly Duties*, 8, quoting *South Wales Radical*, 21 May 1892.

[17] *CT*, 23 November 1872; *Brecon County Times*, 23 November 1872.

[18] *Monmouthshire Beacon*, 23 November 1872.

our example they shall have rid themselves of all latent feelings of refinement and quietness, and dislike of being stared at bodily and spiritually by the multitude.[19]

The prejudice was particularly strong among chapel elders and churchmen, many of whom argued that it was wrong to challenge principles ordained by God. 'From beginning to end the Bible teaches in the most explicit form the subordination of woman to man', declared Samuel Smith. 'I look with dread upon this movement [for the emancipation of women]. It is at bottom directed against those organic laws for the guidance of the sexes which the Creator has laid down.'[20] Likewise, the Revd Stephen Baker, the vicar of Usk, counselled vehemently: 'Oh! ye restless agitators for women's rights, do not try to subvert the order which your wise Creator has long ago settled for the best; are ye wiser than Omnipotence?'[21]

Alongside the argument that the franchise would be detrimental to women themselves was the widely held view that it would, as J. D. Rees put it, 'destroy the comfort and happiness of the English home' by introducing family discord between husband and wife and also neglect of women's essential role as loving and attentive wives and mothers.[22] It was on this basis that the *Cardiff and Merthyr Guardian* urged Rose Crawshay to reconsider 'before she sows the seeds of politics among the female population of her part of the country' in 1870.[23] Anti-suffragist propaganda frequently presented the spectre of the man returning home from a hard day's work to find that his wife had gone to a political meeting, abandoning domestic chores and children. By the end of the century, increasing concern about a declining birth rate and a deterioration in the quality of the British population as middle-class couples began limiting family size added fuel to this argument.

[19] *Nineteenth Century*, XV (March 1884), 414. In Wales, the first generation of women temperance workers in the late nineteenth century experienced similar antipathy. See Ceridwen Lloyd-Morgan, 'From temperance to suffrage?', 148–50, citing Ceridwen Paris (Alice Gray Jones), *Er Cof a Gwerthfawrogiad o Lafur Mrs Mathews* [*sic*], (Liverpool, 1931), 14–15.

[20] *Parl. Deb.*, 4th ser., 3, cols 1477–8, 27 April 1892.

[21] *Monmouthshire Beacon*, 23 November 1872.

[22] *Parl. Deb.*, 5th ser., 2, col. 1428, 19 March 1909. See also ibid., 4th ser., 3, col. 1484, 27 April 1892 (Samuel Smith).

[23] *Cardiff and Merthyr Guardian*, 11 June 1870.

Another central claim of opponents was that the enfranchisement of women was unnecessary, as their interests were already adequately cared for in the existing system. The contention of H. A. Bruce, home secretary and former MP for Merthyr Tydfil, speaking in the House of Commons in 1872, that 'women were well represented by husbands, brothers and fathers, who were not indifferent to their welfare' was a widespread one.[24] In similar vein, during her son's 1906 election campaign, Lady Wimborne argued to the Cardiff WLA that suffragists 'minimised the enormous influence they [women] already exercised in the home', which more than compensated for the absence of direct representation.[25] And, indeed, in the late nineteenth century, 'antis' could legitimately point to the positive response to women's demands of an exclusively male parliamentary system. Thus, by 1891, Samuel Smith could forcibly argue thus:

> the injustices which women suffered have been remedied one after another, the Contagious Diseases Acts have been abolished, the Married Women's Property Act and the Guardianship of Children Act have given to wives and mothers reasonable control over their property and children. Parliament of late years has shown itself most willing to remove any wrongs under which women labour, and to legislate for their welfare as far as it is practicable to do so.
>
> Public opinion fully supports Parliament, and in the matter of higher education, university training, medical education, literary work etc. we see that the door is being steadily opened wider and wider ... Therefore the claim of women to the franchise, based upon unequal laws, is no longer tenable.[26]

Equally fundamental to the anti-suffragist case were the 'physical force' arguments. Most obviously, there was an insistence that, as women could not fight to defend their country in time of war, or contribute to the maintenance of law and order, they did not merit full citizenship. 'The principle of our constitution', wrote one Portmadog 'anti', 'is that every citizen who helps by means of the franchise to return the member, and thus makes our laws, should share in the

---

[24] *Parl. Deb.*, 3rd ser., 215, cols 235–6, 30 April 1873.
[25] *SWDN*, 9 January 1906.
[26] *Mr Samuel Smith, MP, and Women's Suffrage*, 2. See also *Parl. Deb.*, 5th ser., 2, col. 1426, 19 March 1909 (J. D. Rees).

responsibility of carrying those laws into execution.'[27] 'The sexes are not equal', insisted Margaret Williams from Anglesey in a wide-ranging essay entitled 'Why women's suffrage would be a national danger'. 'The man is physically superior – all the rough and heavy work of the world is done by men – they are the soldiers, sailors, policemen – engineers etc.: they can personally enforce the laws they make.'[28] Women were thus held to enjoy special privileges and immunities that justified their exclusion from the franchise, as Henry Bruce argued in the parliamentary debate of 1873:

> Women are altogether exempt from police and military duties. If our safety is threatened by foreign foes, it is to men alone that we must look for defence; if by internal disturbance, every man among us is liable to be called upon to peril life and limb in defence of public order. If women were as independent as their advocates assert, how is it that we have special legislation treating them as dependent creatures, restricting their employment in manufactories and mines? The only justification upon which it is based, is the conviction that women are dependent upon men, and that it is necessary to protect them.[29]

Women's enfranchisement, it was further argued, would seriously impede a vigorous foreign policy and inhibit governments from going to war, thereby losing the respect of both other powers and subject peoples (especially Muslims) within the empire. The threat to Britain's imperial power and prestige was a commonly voiced objection. As Samuel Smith put it in 1892: 'We are trustees for the greatest Empire the world ever saw, and we cannot afford to sap its foundations by reckless innovations.'[30] Certainly, leading imperialists, such as Lord Curzon, Lord Cromer and Joseph Chamberlain, were prominent anti-suffragists, while this argument evidently influenced women too. A further development of the 'physical force' theme stressed the danger of women combining politically to impose legislation on men, who would then refuse to obey it. Constitutional crisis and anarchy would ensue because women did not have the physical power to enforce the law.

[27]   *CN*, 3 April 1874.
[28]   Margaret Williams, 'Why women's suffrage would be a national danger', Bangor University, Bangor MS 26003 (n.d.), 2.
[29]   *Parl. Deb.*, 3rd ser., 215 , col. 1235, 30 April 1873. See also ibid., 101, col. 201, 4 May 1870 (J. H. Scourfield); 5th ser., 52, col. 1760, 5 May 1913 (J. D. Rees).
[30]   Ibid., 4th ser., 3, col. 1484, 27 April 1892.

One reason why these perceived dangers carried strong weight was because throughout the period there were many more women than men in British society. 'Antis' argued that, however limited the initial female enfranchisement, it would eventually end in complete adult suffrage. Sir William Harcourt's opposition to the 1897 bill on these grounds was often repeated over the years:

> There are in this country 1,200,000 more women than men. This is practically a Bill for the ultimate enfranchisement of that majority . . . is it not perfectly clear that where you have a majority of 1,200,000 those who possess that majority must in the long run have the determining voice? This is a very fundamental change in the constitution of the country.[31]

The 'thin end of the wedge' argument was extended to fore-warn of other consequences, including women MPs and 'petticoat government', which would focus on 'feminine', moral issues such as strict temperance legislation. Ultimately, the fear was social revolution and, as Samuel Smith put it, 'absolute equality between the sexes in all the relations of life'.[32] At various times, anti-suffragist MPs from Wales offered doom-laden prophesies of national disaster. In almost every one of a number of anti-suffrage speeches in Parliament, J. D. Rees anticipated revolutionary consequences, while others spoke of 'a war of the sexes' (Osborne Morgan), 'a terrible leap in the dark' (Samuel Smith), 'a momentous change' (Sir William Harcourt) and 'a gigantic experiment' (Ivor Guest).[33] 'If we abandon the caution of the Anglo-Saxon race, and plunge into wild experiments like woman's suffrage', wrote Samuel Smith, 'I much fear that dark days will befall this nation, and that the splendid fabric of centuries will totter to its fall.'[34]

'Antis' were also compelled to tackle the suffragist case, of course. Margaret Williams countered the frequently voiced 'taxation and representation' argument thus:

[31]   Ibid., 95, cols 1226–7, 3 February 1897. See also ibid., 5th ser., 2, col. 1426, 19 March 1909; 52, col. 1760, 5 May 1913 (both J. D. Rees).
[32]   Ibid., 4th ser., 3, col. 1477, 27 April 1892.
[33]   Ibid., 3rd ser., 111, col. 56, 1 May 1872; 4th ser., 3, col. 1484, 27 April 1892; 45, col. 1228, 3 February 1897; SWDN, 9 January 1906.
[34]   Mr Samuel Smith, MP, and Women's Suffrage, 8.

It sounds just enough – but it must be looked upon from other points of view. The taxes we pay are not the price of a vote – rather we pay tax in order that we may share all the privileges of civilization at home – & we get full value for our money too – we pay that our soldiers and sailors may keep us safe from foreign invasion – for the police – & all the machinery of law and order.[35]

While stock anti-suffragist arguments were voiced time and again, over a period of a half-century and more the relative importance of different arguments varied significantly. Moreover, political and social changes introduced new dimensions into the debate. In particular, the emergence of women as members of school boards, poor law guardians and councillors at various levels presented a new challenge to the 'anti' case. Most commonly, the response was to argue that women's participation in local government was simply giving 'full scope for the exercise of talents peculiarly their own' in matters such as education, health and housing, but then to insist that this had no implications for national politics.[36] There was 'an enormous difference between the two franchises', argued Samuel Smith in 1892. 'Local Bodies possess merely administrative and no law-making powers, but the Imperial Parliament possesses absolute authority over the lives and property of all within the realm, and indirectly governs 300 millions of people outside the United Kingdom.'[37] Significantly, the *Appeal against Female Suffrage* of 1889 was not based on a narrowly domestic perception of women's role in society but recognized and applauded increased involvement in elective local government, education and the professions. Rather, the central claim was that 'the emancipating process has now reached the

[35]   Williams, 'Why women's suffrage would be a national danger', 3.
[36]   *Star of Gwent*, 18 March 1881. See also Williams, 'Why women's suffrage would be a national danger', 1.
[37]   *Parl. Deb.*, 4th ser., 3, col. 1472, 27 April. 1892. See also ibid., 45, col. 1226, 3 February 1897 (Sir William Harcourt); Wallace, *'Organise!'*, 162–3. ' *Gwaith Dynes* yw gofalu am y plant, y cartref, yr ysgol, y tlotai, yr ysbytai, y parciau cyhoeddus; llaeth, bwyd, a'r dwfr, etc', ran one of the antis' Welsh-language leaflets. 'Gall wneuthur hyn drwy gyfrwng y cynghorau lleol, ynghlyn [*sic*] â'r rhai y gall bleidleisio eisioes. ('Women's work is childcare, the home, the school, the workhouses, the hospitals, the public parks; milk, food, water, etc. This can be done through local councils by those who already have the vote'.) Granting women the national vote, on the other hand, would 'dinistrio'r Ymherodraeth, a difetha y wlad' ('destroy the Empire, and ruin the country'). *Yn erbyn pleidlais i ferched* (*c*.1912), NLW, Box XJN, 1156–60.

limits fixed by the physical constitution of women, and by the fundamental differences which must always exist between their main occupation and those of men'.[38] Precisely the same stance was adopted by the Women's National Anti-Suffrage League at its formation in 1908.

International developments also had a bearing on the suffrage debate in Britain. The Rocky Mountain state of Wyoming enfranchised women as early as 1869, and ten further states of the USA did so by 1914. In the southern hemisphere, women were granted the vote in New Zealand in 1893, followed by Australian states over the next decade. In Europe, the pioneers were Finland in 1906 and Norway in 1913. While British suffragists drew on evidence from these countries to advance their case, 'antis' rejected such comparisons as irrelevant, often with a lofty disdain. To Samuel Smith, Wyoming was a 'newly formed State on the outskirts of civilization', while J. D. Rees was damning of North America, Australasia, Scandinavia or anywhere else that suffragists cared to mention: 'The supporters of women's suffrage ransack the world for precedents. Are Englishmen to go for examples to the agricultural solitudes of Wyoming, the mines of Colorado, or the polygamous plains of Utah?' He was appalled at the notion of the great British empire looking 'to parochial daughter countries like New Zealand' for enlightenment – 'As if we should learn from our Colonies!' Finland, meanwhile, was patronizingly described as 'a very nice little country' with 'very good fishing', but its people were 'enormously inferior to the people of this country' and 'the women there did as their husbands told them to'; therefore, conditions were 'wholly different' and hardly an example for Britain to follow.[39] In more reasoned fashion, opponents denied that colonies were a valid analogy because they did not have responsibility for their own defence and foreign policy, and also emphasized that no great European power had yet adopted women's suffrage. Moreover, this was an age of increasing international tension and suspicion, which was to

---

[38]   *Nineteenth Century*, XXV (June 1889), 789–90.
[39]   *Parl. Deb.*, 4th ser., 3, col. 1479, 27 April 1892; 185, cols 282–3, 28 February 1908; 5th ser., 2, cols 1424–5, 1427, 19 March 1909; 52, cols 1763–4, 5 May 1913.

erupt in war in 1914. 'We are surrounded by jealous and often hostile States, armed to the teeth', warned Samuel Smith, 'and we need more wariness and trained skill in piloting the ship of State than any country since the world began.'[40]

Opponents of women's suffrage therefore drew upon every conceivable argument to gather support for their case. In organizational terms, however, resistance remained intermittent and limited until well into the Edwardian period, though parliamentary 'antis' first had mobilized their support at an early stage. Against a background of heavy petitioning in support of the private member's bill of April 1875, two whips were issued requesting attendance in the House of Commons to vote against – one signed by four Liberal MPs, the other by four Conservatives (including J. H. Scourfield). Sufficiently alarmed by the size of support for the bill, these members went on to set up a committee 'for the integrity of the franchise, in opposition to the claims for the extension of the Parliamentary suffrage to women', comprising twenty-seven MPs (Scourfield being the only one from Wales). This body did not seek to 'promote outdoor organisation or agitation' in the manner of the suffragists of the day, but it appears to have successfully mounted parliamentary opposition to the bills and resolutions of 1876–9 through systematic canvassing of MPs. It lapsed at the end of the decade when members seem to have concluded that the threat of women's suffrage had abated. The creation of the committee attracted the attention of the London press, but passed unnoticed further afield.[41]

Fears that the Conservative Party leadership, for reasons of self-interest, might take up women's suffrage seem to have been behind the next initiative by 'antis', the publication of a petition, *An Appeal against Female Suffrage*, signed by 104 women, and an accompanying article by Mary (Mrs Humphry) Ward in the *Nineteenth Century* in June 1889. The majority were titled ladies (such as Lady Wimborne), or the wives of well-known politicians (like Mrs Osborne Morgan) or

[40] *Mr Samuel Smith, MP, and Women's Suffrage*, 8. See also Williams, 'Why women's suffrage would be a national danger', 3–4.
[41] *WSJ*, 2 August 1875; Blackburn, *Women's Suffrage*, 139–41; Rover, *Women's Suffrage and Party Politics*, 170; Riley, 'Opposition to women's suffrage', 9–11, 109–12.

of eminent writers; only a few, most notably Mary Ward and Beatrice Potter, had gained an identity through their own achievements.[42] While critics promptly seized upon this and derided the signatories as ladies who 'have but fed on the roses and lain in the lilies of life', supporters accepted their lack of distinction, arguing that 'it was just because we were obscure . . . that we ventured to think we might be fairly representative of a large body of women'.[43] In spite of the criticisms, the *Appeal* attracted a good deal of attention and was valuable in strengthening the anti-suffragist contention that the majority of women did not want the vote. It did not, however, signal the launch of a permanent movement or organization, though some 'antis' certainly mooted this; that had to wait another eighteen years.[44]

Male 'antis' at a parliamentary level remained concerned about Conservative Party intentions in the early 1890s. A Conservative, Sir Albert Rollit, introduced the private member's bill of 1892 and, indeed, a few months earlier the annual conference of the National Union of Conservative and Unionist Associations carried a women's suffrage resolution by a large majority. Anti-suffragists were sufficiently alarmed by these developments to publish and circulate a letter from William Gladstone to Samuel Smith expressing his opposition to the bill and then to issue a whip urging MPs of both parties to vote against. 'We have so long stood almost alone in actively opposing this folly', commented *The Times*, 'that we note with mingled gratification and surprise the sudden awakening of a large and representative body of politicians to dangers which they have hitherto appeared to ignore.' Among the twenty signatories were two representatives from Welsh constituen-

---

[42] Mrs Humphry Ward, 'An appeal against female suffrage', *Nineteenth Century*, XXV (June 1889), 781–8. There were three names on the list with clear Welsh connections: Beatrice Potter (living at 'The Argoed, Monmouth'), Lady Wimborne (wife of Ivor Bertie Guest, 1st Baron Wimborne, owner of the Dowlais Iron Company) and 'Mrs Osborne Morgan' (wife of the East Denbighshire MP).

[43] *Nineteenth Century*, XXVI (August 1889), 348. The same article carried an additional 2,000 names in support of the *Appeal*, including twenty-two with Welsh addresses (half of whom were from Montgomeryshire).

[44] For a full discussion of the 1889 *Appeal*, see Bush, *Women Against the Vote*, ch. 6. See also Harrison, *Separate Spheres*, 115–17; Pugh, *March of the Women*, 150–2; Riley, 'Opposition to women's suffrage', 112–16; Blackburn, *Women's Suffrage*, 178–9.

cies, Sir William Harcourt and Sir Edward Reed, Liberal MP for Cardiff.[45]

The first nationwide organization of 'antis' was formed in response to the striking advance of the women's suffrage campaign during the Edwardian period. Its origins lie in a flurry of correspondence in *The Times* between December 1906 and February 1907 inspired by the dramatic Women's Social and Political Union (WSPU) protests in and around Parliament and the accompanying arrests and imprisonments. A women's committee was formed to organize a counter-protest in the form of an anti-suffrage petition, which generated 37,000 signatures within a fortnight and stimulated moves towards a permanent society.[46] The petition's success was to a large degree due to the zeal of the committee's secretary, Ermine Taylor, a barrister's daughter in her early twenties, living in Abergele and London, who was also closely involved in the protracted deliberations among women themselves and with a committee of MPs led by the then Cardiff member, Ivor Guest, before an association came into being.[47] It was, declared the promoters,

> of fundamental importance for the national welfare that the spirit of sex antagonism which is being aroused by much of the Women's Suffrage propaganda, should be combated by recognition of the fact that the respective spheres of men and women are neither antagonistic nor identical, but complementary.[48]

The Central Organising Committee comprised twenty women (including Ermine Taylor and Lady Evans, wife of the prominent parliamentary anti-suffragist Samuel Evans, MP for Mid Glamorgan) and eleven men (including Guest). When the Women's National Anti-Suffrage League (WNASL) was formally inaugurated in July 1908, Guest, serving as treasurer, was initially the only male member on the executive.[49] Wales

[45]   *The Times*, 21 April 1892.

[46]   Ibid., 20 February 1907; Bush, *Women Against the Vote*, 168–70; Harrison, *Separate Spheres*, 118.

[47]   See James Papers (Herefordshire Record Office), M45/ 1457, 1464, 1470, 1497, 1499, letters from Ermine Taylor to Lord James of Hereford, 1907–8; M45/ 1458, 1493, 1496, 1500, 1510, letters from Ivor C. Guest to James, 1907–8.

[48]   Ibid., M45/1460, printed circular (undated) headed 'National Anti-Suffrage Association'.

[49]   For the formation of the WNASL, see Bush, *Women Against the Vote*, 169–78;

had one representative among the eighteen ladies – Ermine Taylor, who served as a member until mid 1910.

Late in 1908 male anti-suffragists set up their own separate body, the Men's Committee for Opposing Female Suffrage. Originally comprising thirty-eight MPs, peers and other public figures, it expanded during the following year into a League with an executive and a council of 300 members but failed to attract anywhere near the level of support of the women's organization. By December 1908, when the first issue of the *Anti-Suffrage Review* was published, the WNASL had twenty-six branches, six organizing secretaries employed to tour the country and 2,000 subscribers to the central body as well as branch members. The initial involvement of Ermine Taylor ensured the formation of an early Welsh branch, under the name 'North Wales No. 1', located in Denbighshire.[50] A second was founded in Newport, Monmouthshire, in April 1909 and a third in Cardiff in November of the same year; three remained the sum total in Wales until the summer of 1912.[51] Meanwhile, the WNASL itself grew to 104 branches by December 1910, at which point it was amalgamated with the newly created NLOWS; this organization, in turn, went on to reach a peak of 286 branches and some 42,000 members by the summer of 1914.[52]

A total of nineteen NLOWS branches (plus one sub-branch and a girls' affiliate) were eventually formed in Wales, most during 1912 but with the number in decline by 1914. Their

Harrison, *Separate Spheres*, 118–19; Riley, 'Opposition to women's suffrage', 117–20. Ivor Churchill Guest (1873–1939) was Liberal MP for Cardiff from 1906 to 1910, becoming 1st Baron Ashby St Ledgers in 1910 and succeeding to the title of 2nd Baron Wimborne in 1914. See D. George Boyce, 'Guest, Ivor Churchill, first Viscount Wimborne (1873–1939)', *ODNB*. An inevitable target for suffragette wrath, one Cardiff activist told a local WSPU meeting in March 1907 that 'Mr Ivor Guest's opposition to the women's suffrage movement was very curious, seeing that the only person in the Guest family who had achieved any distinction was a woman – Lady Charlotte Guest' [his grandmother]. *WM*, 21 March 1907. A more dramatic display of feeling was the demonstration at Guest's family home, Canford Park in Dorset, on August Bank Holiday, 1909. *Southern Guardian*, 7 August 1909; SFC, 57. 87/ 73, Lettice Floyd to Edith How Martyn, 1 February 1931.

[50]   *Rhyl Journal*, 17, 24 April 1909.
[51]   *Anti-Suffrage Review* (*ASR*), December 1908, May, December 1909; *The Times*, 22 July 1908.
[52]   For detailed figures on growth, see *ASR*, July 1914; Bush, *Women Against the Vote*, 184–9, 212–13; Harrison, *Separate Spheres*, 122; Pugh, *March of the Women*, 153.

geographical distribution was very uneven. Thirteen were located along the west and north-west coasts, between Aberystwyth and Rhyl, with two more inland in the slate-quarrying communities of Blaenau Ffestiniog and Corris. Beyond this region, the only branches were in the major urban centres of Newport and Cardiff and in the old woollen towns of Montgomeryshire, Newtown and Welshpool. Elsewhere – either in the southern coalfield, in the industrial north-east, the rural hinterland, or the south-west – scarcely any anti-suffrage meetings were convened.

During 1912 the number of NLOWS branches in Wales increased from three to seventeen, the key stimulus being a lengthy campaigning tour, conducted by league 'organising secretary', Gwladys Gladstone Solomon, from north Cardiganshire through Merioneth and Caernarfonshire. At mainly open-air meetings between May and November, Mrs Solomon explained the objects of the league and argued the case against women's suffrage in a large number of communities. Local activists increasingly aided her efforts, the Bangor branch secretary, Miss Hughes, being especially valuable as a Welsh-language speaker. There was some opposition at meetings, including heckling, but nothing on the scale often endured by promoters of women's suffrage, and appropriate resolutions were carried almost everywhere, except most notably at one meeting in Bangor which was 'captured' by local suffragists. Eleven new branches came into being and a good deal of written and visual propaganda distributed – leaflets, the *Anti-Suffrage Review*, postcards, badges and such like.[53] Mrs Solomon returned to north Wales in August 1913, holding meetings in a number of towns and initiating two more branches, at Holyhead and Llanfairfechan.[54]

Significantly, Mrs Solomon's 1912 tour of west and north Wales coincided with the highly publicized suffragette disruptions of both the National Eisteddfod in Wrexham and Lloyd George's opening of the Llanystumdwy Institute in September 1912. Certainly, in their public speeches and in the press,

[53] *ASR*, July-December 1912; *NWC*, 8 November 1912; *NWC*, 4 October, 8, 15 November 1912; *Holyhead Chronicle*, 4 October 1912; Belmont MS 300, diary of Henry Lewis, 4 November 1912.
[54] *ASR*, October 1913; *NWC*, 29 August 1913.

Mrs Solomon and her supporters capitalized on these episodes, repeatedly expressing disgust at suffragette conduct, and in all likelihood organizing work was made easier; 'there is a demand for a branch of our League anywhere the public have had the misfortune to experience militant suffragism and its attendant anarchy', wrote the *Anti-Suffrage Review*.[55]

From the outset the 'anti' campaign struggled with financial problems. Subscriptions, even from an increasing membership, were insufficient and fund-raising relied heavily on the efforts of Lords Curzon and Cromer, who, largely through personal approaches, succeeded in obtaining donations of £20,000 during the summer of 1910 and backed this with a public appeal. All this, however, fell well short of the estimated £100,000 required 'to form a large and comprehensive League' and financially the 'antis' remained poorly equipped to mount a campaign comparable to their better-off suffragist opponents.[56]

The vast majority of NLOWS members were women, who also undertook the bulk of local work. The 'North Wales No. 1 branch' began with a committee of twelve, eleven of whom were women. Of the thirty-six branch officials appointed in Wales, twenty-six were women, seventeen of whom were unmarried. Some were evidently upper class – most obviously Mary Cornwallis-West (wife of the wealthy landowner and former Liberal/Liberal Unionist MP for West Denbighshire, Colonel William Cornwallis-West of Ruthin Castle), Lady Llangattock, Lady Turner and Lady Clarendon Hyde, the presidents of the branches at Rhyl, Newport, Caernarfon and Cardiff respectively. The first public meeting of the branch centred on Rhyl boasted 'many influential and fashionable

---

[55] *ASR*, October 1909, quoted in Harrison, *Separate Spheres*, 176. Welsh-language leaflets urged men and women to join the NLOWS and 'dangoswch eich bod yn anghytuno â'r arferiad gwrthun o falurio ffenestri' ('show that you disagree with the odious practice of breaking windows'), *Yn erbyn pleidlais i ferched*.

[56] Among the principal donations were £500 each from Lord Ashby St Legers (formerly Ivor Guest) and David Davies, Liberal MP for Montgomeryshire (1906–29). *Conservative and Unionist Women's Franchise Review*, April–June 1913; WL, 298/3, *Correspondence, Papers and Press Cuttings relating to Anti-Suffrage Opinion, Activities and Organisations, 1907–14*; Curzon Papers, F112/32, Lord Ashby St Ledgers to Lord Curzon, 10 and 20 July 1910; Lord Cromer to Lord Curzon, 11 August 1910. See also Harrison, *Separate Spheres*, 126–7; Riley, 'Opposition to women's suffrage', 123–4.

country folk in North Wales', including the lords lieutenant of both Denbighshire and Flintshire, while at the inaugural meeting of a branch in Monmouthshire Lady Llangattock expressed the hope that their efforts would be supported 'by all the principal ladies of the county'.[57] The 'secretary, treasurer and everything else' of the Newport and Monmouthshire branch was Margaret Protheroe of Malpas Court, daughter of the lord of the manor and principal landowner of the district; her deputy was the daughter of the vicar of Llangybi. Organized anti-suffragism everywhere was certainly middle and upper class rather than working class. The membership fee was 5s. a year, with 1s. to be an associate. The holding of a number of meetings at factory gates, timber yards and quarries in Wales was obviously an attempt to broaden appeal; working-class enrolments were duly highlighted in branch reports but were rare. Branches varied in size and vitality. 'Newport and Monmouthshire' was undoubtedly Wales's largest, with probably several hundred members (the vast majority of whom were women). Cardiff and Bangor also appear to have been fairly strong, but some branches must have had just a handful of members.

The league also sought to appeal to youth and, with the anti-suffrage pioneer Ermine Taylor of Abergele as president, the Girls' Anti-Suffrage League was founded in January 1911 'to bring together girls of the upper classes for the purpose of giving social entertainments to collect funds for the League, and with leisure time to undertake work that may be helpful in forwarding the Anti-Suffrage cause' (though 'working-girl associates' were also recruited). It never achieved the prominence of the 'Young Hotbloods' (as they were nicknamed) in the WSPU or the Young Suffragists in the National Union of Women's Suffrage Societies (NUWSS), however, at best only five branches being established. One of these was in Newport, though its independent existence, beyond assisting in the activities of the adult branch, amounted to little more than the occasional drawing-room meeting.[58]

---

[57] *Rhyl Record and Advertiser*, 24 April 1909; *Monmouthshire Weekly Post*, 1 May 1909.
[58] *ASR*, April 1912.

To a large degree, anti-suffragists replicated the activities and tactics of their opponents. The NLOWS closely monitored political developments regarding suffrage bills at Westminster, sent deputations to ministers, lobbied MPs and organized some major events in London. In its effort to rally public opinion against suffragist claims, the league executive despatched organizers and speakers to the provinces to arouse enthusiasm and stimulate branch associations, disseminated literature and initiated specific propaganda and agitational campaigns. In reality, however, the 'antis' scarcely competed with the suffagists in techniques of propaganda and agitation. The NLOWS did establish a nationwide network of branches but these rarely displayed the energy and continuity of suffragist societies. While local secretaries were instructed to send reports of activities to the central office for insertion in the *Anti-Suffrage Review*, little or nothing was reported on most of Wales's nineteen league branches beyond their foundation, almost certainly reflecting inactivity. Indeed, three (Welshpool, Holyhead and Llanfairfechan) never even appeared on the official list of branches, and elsewhere local executive posts were frequently left vacant.

Easily Wales's strongest and most energetic anti-suffrage society was in Monmouthshire, focused on Newport but attracting wider support from industrial communities like Pontypool and Griffithstown and from the rural parts of the county to the east, as far as Chepstow. An active organization operated here for more than five years, from April 1909 into the First World War period, stimulated in part no doubt by the vigour of the suffragette and suffragist campaigns in the area. It was sufficiently strong to set up sub-branches in different areas of Newport, to undertake a range of activities and implement national initiatives, and periodically to instigate intensive local propaganda campaigns in which several of its own female members emerged as highly competent speakers.[59]

---

[59] '[W]hat lady would not defend the dignity of her sex and show her disapproval of the suffragette party who thus brought discredit on womanhood', wrote Lady Llangattock on the birth of the local WNASL branch. *Monmouthshire Weekly Post*, 1 May 1909. For references to sub-branches, see ibid., 31 May 1913.

The most obvious method of agitation against women's suffrage was the public meeting. 'Antis' displayed their strength at a number of large events in London between 1909 and 1913, though none was comparable to the scale and spectacle of those of the huge suffragist demonstrations of the period. The greatest of the NLOWS rallies was held in the Albert Hall in February 1912, attended by 9,000 people. Prominent politicians dominated the proceedings, reciting familiar anti-suffrage arguments in a series of speeches, while others, including the prime minister, Herbert Asquith, sent telegrams of support. The most effective contribution of the evening came from Violet Markham, a leading female 'anti', who condemned women's unenthusiastic use of the political rights and votes they already possessed in local government.[60] Several large meetings were held in Wales, most notably in Newport in 1909 and 1912 when 'antis' attempted to match the sense of occasion so often created by their opponents; prominent national figures in the movement acted as principal speakers, local dignitaries gave their support from the platform, flags and decorations brightened the halls and musical entertainment enlivened the proceedings.[61]

Many smaller indoor and outdoor meetings, some pre-arranged, some spontaneous, were also held by the 'antis' in Wales, but their number was severely handicapped by a perennial shortage of speakers. Suffragist heckling was certainly a hazard but a greater obstacle was the reluctance of female supporters to figure prominently in agitation, the limitations of women's public role being seen as a central tenet of the 'anti' case. NLOWS annual reports emphasized 'the impossible burden' placed on 'the small band' of speakers supplied by central office and urged local branches to take steps to produce their own. Nor did the league have the financial means to create a comprehensive structure of local organizers and itinerant speakers in the way that the WSPU, the Women's Freedom League (WFL) and NUWSS did. While scores of suffragist speakers travelled Wales and organizers

[60]   *ASR*, March 1912.
[61]   Ibid., January 1909, June 1912; *South Wales Weekly Argus*, 11 December 1909, 11 May 1912; *Monmouthshire Weekly Post*, 1 May, 11 December 1909.

were often based in regions for a considerable time, injecting much-needed enthusiasm into branch life, Gwladys Gladstone Solomon was the only league representative to spend any length of time in Wales, conducting tours in 1912 and more briefly in 1913, and leading a concentrated campaign in the Newport area in late summer 1911 when she addressed eleven open-air and three public meetings in two weeks.[62] The number of anti-suffrage meetings convened in Wales, including the small private gatherings in drawing rooms, totalled a few hundred at best; the various suffragist societies held thousands, though over a longer period of time of course.

Mrs Solomon's visits to north and west Wales targeted the seaside resorts during the holiday season, though she also addressed meetings at a number of local quarries. In Newport and elsewhere attempts were made to reach out to working-class audiences by holding dinner-hour meetings outside works and factory gates. Essentially, though, the anti-suffrage movement operated most commonly and comfortably through social functions such as drawing-room meetings, garden parties and dances. The grand fete organized by the Newport NLOWS branch in June 1914 was typical. Held in the grounds of one of its committee members, the usual array of stalls was supplemented by music, dancing and sketches. The political dimension was provided by the welcoming notice declaring 'Women do NOT want votes' and by several speeches centring on the theme that 'women's suffrage would mean the destruction of their home institutions'; a policeman stationed at the gates ensured against interruption by local militants. The fete was part of an intensive four-day agitation during which the branch organized a variety of meetings in the town and district.[63] Another specific campaign in Wales focused on the National Union of Teachers (NUT) annual conference held in Aberystwyth at Easter 1911, when the league congratulated itself on 'rebutting the first attempt to force the question of votes for women through Conference'.[64]

---

[62]   *ASR*, October 1911.
[63]   Ibid., July 1914; *South Wales Weekly Argus*, 13 June 1914.
[64]   *ASR*, May 1911.

The 'anti' movement gave a great deal of attention to substantiation of one of its central arguments – that the women's suffrage agitation was engineered by a vociferous minority and that there was no real public demand for such a change. Two techniques were adopted in particular, the petition and the canvass. The origins of the WNASL lay in the formation of a committee to promote an anti-suffrage petition in 1907. 'Antis' continued to put vigorous efforts into this tactic in subsequent years, most notably in 1908 when over 337,000 signatures were collected, a larger total than any suffragist petition since 1874. More enterprising was the systematic canvassing of female local government electors. The NLOWS received returns from ninety-four districts throughout the country, which, with a few exceptions, emphatically indicated that the majority of women were opposed to enfranchisement. The only result from Wales was supplied by the Newport branch, which, by a mixture of house-to-house interviews and postcard replies during 1910–11, recorded 844 'antis', 113 suffragists and 76 neutral (with 258 'no replies'), 'conclusive proof of the strong anti-suffragist sympathy existing in Newport'. Suffragist societies, of course, challenged and contradicted the whole canvass. Whatever its flaws, by statistically contesting the suffragist claim to represent the majority of women in the country, the initiative was a significant and timely boost to the 'anti' propaganda campaign.[65]

Another way in which 'antis' sought to demonstrate the strength of opposition to women's enfranchisement was to engage in public debates with suffragists and a number of these took place in Wales. In Newport (on three occasions), Swansea, Cricieth, Colwyn Bay and Bangor, NLOWS speakers took on representatives of one of the various suffrage societies, the individuals involved being sometimes local activists, sometimes outside agents. The events invariably aroused a good deal of enthusiasm – large meetings, partisanship (with rival supporters sporting the ribbons and rosettes of their societies) and substantial press coverage.[66]

The NLOWS was by no means as evident in electoral activity as the suffragist societies, though there was some participation in by-elections. In the Carmarthen Boroughs contest early in 1912, an official league representative, H. B. Samuels, was dispatched to Llanelli, where he held meetings and distributed literature, while the fervent 'anti', Sir J. D. Rees, speaking in support of the Conservative candidate, scornfully denounced women's suffrage, as he had frequently done in Parliament and in speeches at public meetings elsewhere in Wales.[67] Essentially, of course, electioneering on the part of female 'antis' ran counter to their ideology. Far more common were low-key deputations to parliamentary candidates, as was done by Newport women in June 1914.[68]

In terms of written material, whereas the suffragists established a number of periodicals, the 'antis' had just one, the monthly *Anti-Suffrage Review*, serving as the organ of the WNASL and subsequently the NLOWS. Significantly, however, they could rely on strong support from established national newspapers, most obviously *The Times* and the *Morning Post*, while by 1914 nearly two hundred local newspapers were regularly publishing anti-suffrage notes sent out from league headquarters.[69] In turn, branches were expected to send reports, articles and letters to the local press and to respond to opponents' claims. As for literature, Welsh-language leaflets arguing the case against women's suffrage were published and circulated, and newspapers frequently carried advertisements for the purchase of leaflets and pamphlets, as well as conveying information regarding the signing of anti-suffrage petitions locally.[70]

Generally, however, the Welsh press showed scant interest in developments in organized anti-suffragism. Local meetings were certainly reported, often very fully, but drew no editorial

1914; *NWC*, 14 March 1913; *South Wales Weekly Argus*, 25 October 1913; *CC*, 2 January 1914; *Cambrian*, 6 February 1914; Bangor WSS minutes, 14 February, 10 April 1913. See also Bush, *Women Against the Vote*, 217–18.

[67] *South Wales Press*, 17 January 1912; *Llanelly Mercury*, 18 January 1912; *Carmarthen Weekly Reporter*, 26 January 1912. See also *Montgomeryshire Express*, 18 January 1910; *ASR*, June 1911; *WM*, 4 May 1911.

[68] *ASR*, July 1914.

[69] Harrison, *Separate Spheres*, 151–4; Pugh, *March of the Women*, 229–30.

[70] See *Yn erbyn pleidlais i ferched*; *Barmouth and County Advertiser*, 14 January 1909.

comment, while the large NLOWS meetings in London usually passed unnoticed. An exception was the *Cambrian News*, which championed the cause of women's enfranchisement for decades. In typical style, its editor, John Gibson, bitingly greeted the formation of the NLOWS thus: 'There is in existence a men's league for opposing woman suffrage. Many women support this league. The creed of this league is that womanhood suffrage would be against the best interests of the country. The worst thing we know against women is that they should have brought into the world the sort of men who started this league.'[71] Of much greater news value to the press was coverage of suffragette militancy, frequently accompanied by editorial condemnation (though this did not necessarily entail rejection of the principle of women's enfranchisement). But essentially the key controversies focused upon in the Welsh press in the immediate pre-war years were labour unrest and disestablishment.

Whatever the variations and limitations of press coverage, the strength and determination of anti-suffragists over many decades clearly represented a major reason for the inability of women to win the franchise before the First World War. Vociferous in their objections in Parliament, in the press and at public meetings throughout the period, their influence benefited greatly from contemporary attitudes and relationships. Indeed, such was the confidence that 'antis' had in their case that they felt it unnecessary to organize themselves until 1908. Thereafter, they developed a powerful campaign, while a number of other factors also served to buttress their position and frustrate the suffragist cause.

In the first place, certainly after 1912, suffragette militancy developed into a major complication, alienating both the public and politicians, attracting adverse press coverage and acting as a diversion from the central issue of women's enfranchisement. From the earliest days of the campaign, opposition at public meetings in Wales and elsewhere commonly expressed itself in disruption by nuisances. Hostility to the extent of violence, however, was rare before the advent of militancy, but then became widespread, extending, by association, to

---

[71]   Quoted in *VW*, 16 September 1910.

law-abiding suffragists too. It was present from the early WSPU ventures into Wales in 1906 and was most glaringly apparent in the assaults on hecklers at the Wrexham National Eisteddfod and at Llanystymdwy in September 1912. In its coverage of the former, the *Western Mail* carried a cartoon by J. M. Staniforth headed 'The Biters Being Bitten'. Surveying a thoroughly battered group of suffragettes, an angry 'Dame Wales' observes: 'it serves you right! Shame on you to come to my Eisteddfod an' make disturbance, an' bait my bachan Lloyd George, look you!'[72] This was its editorial theme too, and a typical one across the Welsh press:

> the whole responsibility lies with the suffragettes themselves. The British public has up to now regarded their wanton conduct with generous patience, not because they have condoned the militant movement in the slightest degree, but on account of a large measure of sympathy for the cause they espouse. Forbearance has more than once been tested to the breaking point. But the temper exhibited at Wrexham yesterday was a new and salutary experience for them, though one readily confesses that the punishment was hopelessly out of proportion on this particular occasion.[73]

The lack of sympathy extended to hunger-striking suffragettes whose suffering was widely seen as self-inflicted. Postcard replies to the efforts of the Cardiff WSPU branch to generate protest against forcible feeding in the summer of 1913 were indicative. Cardiff Wesleyan Mission found it 'impossible to comply to the request. If women will not take food when it is offered them they must put up with the consequences.' Another local organization was even more contemptuous:

> We have not heard of any Tortures being inflicted upon the Women of this country, except the abominable execrable outrages perpetrated by female hooligans, who are a disgrace to their sex, and to their nation and who ought to receive punishment to the utmost of the law.[74]

Reactions to the death of Emily Wilding Davison, following her dramatic intervention in the Epsom Derby of June 1913, revealed a similar attitude. While militant sympathizers

---

[72]   *WM*, 7 September 1912.
[73]   Ibid., 6 September 1912.
[74]   SFC, Z6084e, postcard to Cardiff WSPU branch from Cardiff Wesleyan Mission, 5 July 1913; Z6084f, postcard to Annie Williams, unsigned, July 1913.

pointed to 'one of the most fearless deeds in the annals of human daring', contemporary press accounts invariably offered a very different perspective. Reports in Welsh newspapers spoke of 'a sort of "hari-kari" . . . a mad deed', which, like the extremism of other 'poor, deluded Davisons', would do nothing for the legislative prospects of women's suffrage.[75] Most unattractive was the tasteless sensationalism generated by the tragedy, epitomized in the triumphalism of one Rhondda cinema manager on securing 'the film which audiences around the country had been craving for'; it afforded, the advertising insisted, 'a clear and full view of the suffragette outrage by which Miss Davison lost her life . . . racecourse incident and funeral procession will be shown in one picture at the Porth Grand Cinema on Monday, Tuesday and Wednesday. No one should miss this wonderful picture.'[76]

Public reaction to Margaret Mackworth's 'letter-box firing' in Newport, and her subsequent arrest and imprisonment, provides another example of the complications of seeking publicity through militant protest. A guilty plea led to a £10 fine and £10 costs, or a month in the county gaol at Usk. Here, she promptly adopted a hunger strike and was released five days later, whereupon her fine was paid anonymously. She had not been forcibly fed and her release, even under the terms of the 'Cat and Mouse Act', was unusually early, family influence no doubt proving significant. The whole episode certainly attracted considerable interest and press coverage. Suffragette activists crowded into Newport police court in a display of solidarity, while local WSPU gatherings inevitably applauded 'Mrs Mackworth's sacrifice for the cause' and her 'bold and aggressive . . . eminently courageous action'.[77] At the same time, much of the publicity was adverse. A NUWSS public meeting in the town a few days after the conviction denounced militants for letting loose 'a stream of anarchy, crime and law breaking . . . entirely disastrous to the cause'.[78]

[75] *South Wales Worker*, 21 June 1913; *Carmarthen Journal*, 20 June 1913. The *Daily Express* concluded that 'a brilliant career . . . had withered like Dead Sea fruit under the malignant influence of militancy' and ended in 'pathetic loneliness' and 'an ignominious death'. *Daily Express*, 11 June 1913.
[76] *Porth Gazette*, 28 June 1913.
[77] *South Wales Argus*, 12 July 1913; *WM*, 18 July 1913.
[78] *South Wales Argus*, 14 July 1913.

Similarly, a typical letter in the local press condemned those of the 'idle rich', who 'for evident self-gratification ... spend their time in burning the letters of poor and other folk who had not done them the slightest harm'.[79] Equally vehement were the numerous accusations of 'one law for the rich and another for the poor', as reflected in the sentiments of another correspondent:

> So Mrs Mackworth is out of prison. She has given her digestive organs a rest, and I am sure she will feel all the better for it. The postman, the telegraph messenger, and the telephone operator will be kept busy for a while delivering congratulatory messages praising her heroism, her self-sacrifice etc. etc. – which, by the way, consisted of a nice lunch in the Chief's office, an apology from every one connected with the case, and a ride to Usk in a motor car. Such martyrdom is enough to cause a smile on the face of an owl.[80]

Indeed, the chief constable was subsequently required to explain to councillors the alleged preferential treatment: lunch, he insisted, had been sent across by her parents from the Westgate Hotel, while the 'black maria' had not been used for fear of a suffragette demonstration. During the course of the controversy, which lasted several weeks, Sybil Thomas tried vainly to emphasize her daughter's deprivation and suffering in prison.[81]

The public's difficulty in, or indeed indifference to, distinguishing between suffrage societies added to the complexity. The tendency was to 'tar everyone with the same brush' and immediately to assume that campaigners were WSPU militants; thus activists from the WFL, the NUWSS and other organizations often fared badly too. A Metropolitan Police report on meetings held by half a dozen different societies on the same day in Hyde Park in June 1914 recorded that 'the utmost hostility was shewn towards every section of the Suffrage movement ... [and] police experienced consider-

[79]   Ibid., 16 July 1913.
[80]   Ibid., 18 July 1913.
[81]   For full details of the whole affair, see *South Wales Argus*, 26 June, 11, 12, 14, 15, 16, 17, 18, 19 July 1913; *WM*, 27 June, 12, 16, 18, 25, 26 July 1913; *Free Press of Monmouthshire*, 27 June, 4 July 1913; *The Suffragette*, 4, 18 July 1913; *The Times*, 28 June, 12 July 1913; Nominal Register, vol. 22, 1912–13, 236, 11 July 1913 (HMP Usk); Rhondda, *This was My World*, 152–61; Eoff, *Viscountess Rhondda*, 30–1.

able difficulty in maintaining order and protecting the speakers from violence'. The NUWSS gathering, in particular, was 'surrounded by a howling mob of at least 3,000 persons' and everywhere 'the crowds strongly resented the protection afforded to the speakers and the fact that truncheons were drawn'. Such episodes deepened the divisions and resentments in the suffrage movement.[82]

In earlier years, militancy had arguably done much good for the cause, in terms of publicity, arousing interest and awareness and making women's suffrage prominent in British politics. In 1909 the *Western Mail* could assert that 'had it not been for the courageous agitation of the Suffragettes the question would have remained purely academic and unimportant'.[83] By 1912–14, however, there is strong evidence that the balance had shifted significantly and WSPU extremism had become a distraction and an impediment. As the *North Wales Chronicle* explained:

> Very few people are bothering now about the rights of the women to a vote, suffrage or anti-suffrage, the benefits or the drawbacks of granting votes to women. The sole concern is whether the 'malignants' should be deported, or allowed to die in prison, or be forcibly fed – what punishment is most likely to deter militant criminals and put a stop to their outrages.[84]

To anti-suffragist opinion, militancy was welcomed as a boost to their efforts. Thus, the *South Wales Argus* commented almost gleefully in 1912: 'The latest window-smashing campaign, however angry we may be feeling about it just now, may have the happy effect of saving the country from petticoat government.'[85] Suffragists, meanwhile, were left deeply frustrated. Even that most steadfast of campaigners, John Gibson of the *Cambrian News*, was, by 1909, highly critical of 'the Pankhurst policy of pin-pricks': disruption of the National Eisteddfod in London in that year was 'foolish, aggravating the whole of Wales', interfering with public meetings was 'nagging and irritating', the election strategy was 'childish and

---

[82]   NA, HO 45/24665, Suffragette meetings in Hyde Park, 21 June 1914.
[83]   *WM*, 8 June 1909.
[84]   *NWC*, 12 June 1914.
[85]   *South Wales Weekly Argus*, 9 March 1912.

utterly ineffective', and the indiscriminate window smashing was 'outside the range of sanity' – all were delaying the enfranchisement of women.[86]

The Welsh press overwhelmingly adopted this condemnatory stance. Typical was the insistence of the *Barry Dock News* that suffragette methods had alienated public support: 'nothing is more certain than that these insane tactics are putting back the clock, and deferring the day when public opinion will support women's claim to the vote'.[87] Certainly, anti-suffragist arguments about the nature of women appeared more plausible. 'Beyond dispute', wrote a prominent Pontypridd Conservative, 'militancy is not merely the excrescence, but the very root and branch of Suffragism. It is the acute development of those qualities in the female character, which unfit many women for the responsibilities of political power.'[88] Opponents were equally quick to accuse Parliament of bending to coercion. 'I think it deplorable', objected J. D. Rees in 1909, 'that this Bill should come forward at a time when the supporters of Women Suffrage are engaged in conspiracies to break the law and to worry and harry their fellow citizens ... destroying letters, biting and kicking warders, and attacking policemen'.[89] House of Commons voting was also adversely affected, for backbenchers turned out in growing numbers to oppose women's suffrage bills in 1912 and 1913, while the 'Cat and Mouse Bill' was passed by a huge majority in 1913. Lloyd George had no doubt about the role of militancy in strengthening the opposition camp. 'I think this Parliament has been ruined so far as suffrage is concerned', he told a suffragist deputation in October 1913, 'it has been antagonised; its mind is poisoned'.[90] An individual example in point was the refusal of

---

[86]   *CN*, 9 July, 20 August, 15 October 1909, 19, 26 August 1910, 21 April, 21 July 1911, 1, 8 March, 13 September 1912, 15 August 1913.

[87]   *Barry Dock News*, 13 February, 22 May 1914. There were a few dissenting voices. 'But for the tactics, hysterical and bizarre, employed in recent years, the question of female suffrage would be as dormant, so far as the bulk of the people are concerned, as the eugenic movement', insisted the *South Wales Daily Post*. 'Let us be fair to ourselves by not shirking disagreeable certainties.' *SWDP*, 5 February 1913.

[88]   L. Gordon Lenox, *A Political Text Book and Glossary, and the Great European War, 1914–15* (Pontypridd, 1915), 211.

[89]   *Parl. Deb.*, 4th ser., 52, col. 1759, 19 March 1909.

[90]   *VW*, 31 October 1913.

the Cardiff MP, Lord Ninian Crichton Stuart, to address the annual Catholic congress on women's suffrage held in the town in 1914, on the basis that 'the methods employed by those attempting to gain votes made it impossible for him to identify himself in any way with the movement'.[91]

The effects of suffragette militancy were largely responsible for the confidence that permeated anti-suffrage ranks by the summer of 1914, a mood captured in Lord Curzon's buoyant address to the annual council meeting of the NLOWS in June:

> the Anti-Suffrage cause stands in a stronger position at the present moment in all parts of the United Kingdom than it has done at any time during the past twenty years. (Cheers.) This has been due, perhaps, in the main to the tactics, and I may add to the errors, of our opponents, for which in passing let me give them a hearty vote of thanks ... Incendiarism, bombs, the mutilation of priceless works of art, brawling in religious buildings, the burning of churches, rioting in the streets, violence in the police courts, insults to the King, these are the methods which appear to be thought necessary to propagate a cause which we are told is associated with the highest ideals and aspirations of woman-hood, and which is intended to raise the standard and tone of public life in this country. Our Suffragist opponents are continually telling us that they are marching to a triumph. It seems a curious thing, if that be the case, that it should be necessary to mark the roadway with the ruins of golf links and cricket pavilions, still more with the ashes of the House of God. These wild women are in a sense the most capable recruiting sergeants that we could have, and every one of them is an unconscious agent for our cause.[92]

One further aspect of the pre-war political situation requires emphasis. Militancy developed and escalated at a time when parliamentary suffragists were already facing formidable practical difficulties in their quest to translate support for the general principle of women's enfranchisement into legislative reality – the intellectual debate had essentially been won by then. Most obviously, from 1908 Britain had a determinedly anti-suffragist prime minister, Herbert Asquith, who headed a Cabinet and a party deeply divided on the issue. Beyond this, there were the complexities of framing the precise details of a measure, as the Conservative suffragist,

[91]   Catholic Women's Suffrage Society, *Annual Report*, 1914, 3.
[92]   *ASR*, July 1914; Harrison, *Separate Spheres*, 198–9.

W. A. Ormsby-Gore, MP for Denbigh, recognized in 1910: 'Though there is in the present House of Commons a majority friendly to the cause of Women's Suffrage, it is quite another thing to get that majority through the division lobbies upon a concrete proposal in favour of it.'[93]

Two key issues – the marital status and the social class of those proposed for enfranchisement – provided much of the ground for resistance. For tactical reasons, the early suffragists confined their demand to spinsters and widows who met the required property qualifications – that is, single, independent women. This caused divisions within suffragist ranks, which 'antis' were able to exploit in addition to raising specific objections (which were often shared by suffragist sympathizers too). Were not wives equally deserving of the vote and did not they need it to remedy the special grievances which suffragists contended they had? How, it was asked, would giving the vote to well-off spinsters and widows aid the majority of women? Was not loss of the franchise on marriage patently absurd? Would not marriage be discouraged and divorce encouraged? Most telling was the accusation that the proposed bills would principally enfranchise the less deserving kind of woman. Simply to dispense with the sex discrimination barrier – the principle upon which all the bills supported by the suffragists before 1918 were based – would essentially involve the enfranchisement of women householders and £10 lodgers. But the latter would mean, as Samuel Smith explained, the inclusion of

> a multitude of young women ... enormous numbers of shop girls, factory girls, sempstresses, barmaids, etc ... [who] would completely swamp the women householders ... [and] along with this class would come in an appalling number of fallen women, whose numbers have been estimated in London as high as sixty thousand.

Politicians, as Smith recognized, would thus be open to the very uncomfortable charge that 'we made marriage a disqualification; that we emancipated the harlot but disfranchised the wife'.[94]

---

[93] *Conservative and Unionist Women's Franchise Review*, November 1910. He was a supporter of the Conciliation Bills of 1910–12, which unsuccessfully sought a compromise solution on women's suffrage.

[94] *Mr Samuel Smith, MP, and Women's Suffrage*, 4. Another anti-suffragist, P. B. Smollett, MP for Cambridge, made the same point in the 1875 debate: 'Under this

Repetition of such criticisms was damaging to the suffragist case, though late nineteenth-century changes in married women's property law obscured the distinction between propertied single women and dependent wives. In time, objections based on marital status became less pronounced. Fears of class bias in women's enfranchisement remained prominent, however. In Liberal and Labour circles it was widely believed that the suffragist measures campaigned for before 1914 would benefit the Conservatives. As early as 1870, the Liberal MP, Thomas Love Jones-Parry, explaining to Lydia Becker why he had voted against Jacob Bright's bill, wrote thus:

> In the county I represent (Carnarvonshire), the women are all Liberal in politics and Non-conformists in religion – that is, the vast majority of them; and this may be said of all North Wales.
>
> On the other hand, in England, and particularly in boroughs such as Bath, women are Conservative under great influence, which always tends to fetter freedom of thought.
>
> I reluctantly, for these reasons, voted (against my own interests) to prevent women being made capable of doing what I consider politically wrong in many places, *i.e.*, voting against the Liberal party.[95]

Although, by the Edwardian period, equal franchise bills would no longer solely affect widows and spinsters, many Liberals remained convinced that adult suffrage would benefit their party far more. This was very much the view of the Denbigh MP Clement Edwards, who rejected the 1908 measure as 'limited and property-mongering ... a Bill which would shut out 89 per cent of the married working women of this country'.[96] Lloyd George's considerations were much the same. As a young MP, he was dismissive of Rollit's 1892 proposals: 'The Women's Franchise Bill is before the House & the Division is now taking place. As I am not in favour of enfranchising widows and spinsters without giving a vote to married women at the same time I take no part in trotting around the

Bill, elderly virgins, widows, a large class of the *demi-monde* and kept women ... would be admitted to the franchise, while the married women of England – mothers, who formed the mainstay of the nation – are rigidly excluded.' *Parl. Deb.*, 3rd ser., 223, col. 449, 7 April 1875.

[95] *WSJ*, 1 June 1870. Osborne Morgan also believed that 'votes for women would be a great Conservative gain', on the basis that 'every woman was a Tory at heart'. *Parl. Deb.*, 3rd ser., 111, col. 55, 1 May 1872.

[96] *Parl. Deb.*, 4th ser., 185, cols 262–3, 28 February 1908.

lobby at all. I am in favour of the general principle.'[97] Twenty years later, as chancellor of the Exchequer, his conviction that limited suffrage extension would seriously harm the Liberal Party's future electoral prospects was evident in his strong opposition to the Conciliation Bills.

The details of particular women's suffrage measures therefore left the issue embroiled in party conflict. In mounting their case, 'antis' made the most of these difficulties just as they did of suffragette militancy. As a result, the obstacles impeding women's suffrage legislation proved insurmountable before 1914. It required the far-reaching political and social changes of the war years to remove them and produce at least a compromise solution.

---

[97]   Kenneth O. Morgan (ed.), *Lloyd George: Family Letters, 1885–1936* (Cardiff, 1973), 48. His stance had been quite different when as a sixteen-year-old he had attended a local women's suffrage meeting, addressed by Lydia Becker, in Porthmadog in 1879, recording his thoughts thus: 'Very few real arguments. She proved too much, which proved nothing. The earth would be a paradise were women to have the suffrage. She was rather sarcastic. Mr. Breese rose to oppose her, and made a half-hour speech. Very good. As for myself, I do not see why single women and widows managing property should not have a voice in the adjustment, etc, of the taxes.' Herbert Du Parcq, *The Life of David Lloyd George*, I (1912), 33–4.

VI

THE IMPACT OF THE FIRST WORLD WAR

'Armageddon in Europe!' excitedly wrote the young Vera Brittain in her diary entry for Monday, 3 August 1914. 'On Saturday evening Germany declared war upon Russia & also started advancing towards the French frontier ... The great fear now is that our bungling Government will declare England's neutrality.'[1] She worried unduly, for Britain entered the conflict the very next day, following the German invasion of Belgium.

The reaction of many suffragists, both militant and constitutional, was instinctive and predictable: war was a calamity, the inevitable result of a man-made world founded on physical force. 'Would that we had won our scrap of paper [the ballot] before the War', bemoaned the Forward Cymric Suffrage Union (FCSU) leader, Edith Mansell Moullin.[2] WSPU representatives around the country elaborated on this theme. Thus, the south Wales organizer, Annie Williams, told Pontypool branch members that

> The war ought never to have been ... If five years ago the men had enfranchised the women and given them a share in the government of the country it is possible that there would have been no war to-day ... emancipating woman would have resulted in the attainment of a higher state of civilisation.[3]

On 10 August, the home secretary, Reginald McKenna, announced the unconditional release of all suffragette prisoners (as well as those gaoled for offences connected with labour unrest). Three days later, in a circular letter to her members, Mrs Pankhurst declared the suspension of all

---

[1] Alan Bishop (ed.), *Chronicle of Youth: Vera Brittain's War Diary, 1913–1917* (London, 1981), 84. In later life, Vera Brittain became a prolific writer and speaker and a passionate campaigner for the causes of peace and feminism.

[2] *Woman's Dreadnought*, 26 December 1914.

[3] *Free Press of Monmouthshire*, 12 February 1915. Helena Jones argued in similar vein: 'with women enfranchised, there would have been no war'. *Suffragette News Sheet*, September 1916.

agitation.[4] In early September, Christabel Pankhurst returned from her exile in Paris to signal the Women's Social and Political Union's (WSPU) fervent anti-German campaign and the subordination of women's interests to war propaganda. Not all activists were prepared to accept the jingoistic line of Mrs Pankhurst and her eldest daughter, but a number of prominent figures certainly did, most notably 'General' Flora Drummond and Annie Kenney. With remarkable swiftness, suffragette leaders were transformed from public enemies to fierce nationalists. As the Conservative Party leader and three times prime minister, Stanley Baldwin, recalled years later when unveiling a statue to Mrs Pankhurst at Victoria Tower Gardens in the shadow of the Houses of Parliament: 'The World War came. In the twinkling of an eye, at the sound of the trumpet, the revolutionary died, and the patriot was born, and the militant suffragettes laid aside their banners.'[5] Patriotism was all, women's suffrage was sidelined. The WSPU, in the words of Sylvia Pankhurst, 'now entirely departed from the Suffrage movement. Giving its energies wholly to the prosecution of the War, it rushed to a furious extreme, its Chauvinism unexampled amongst all other women's societies.'[6] In October 1915, *The Suffragette* became *Britannia* and, in November 1917, the WSPU was rechristened the Women's Party.

The unwavering path chosen by the WSPU leadership during the war was emphatically not that trodden by all suffrage activists, even within the WSPU itself. Wartime responses were complex but broadly fell into three categories: those who supported the war effort through voluntary welfare work or by taking on new forms of paid employment; those who worked for peace; and those who 'kept the suffrage flag flying'. These responses were not mutually exclusive and individual priorities shifted during the course of the war.[7]

[4]   SFC, Z6078, circular letter from Emmeline Pankhurst, 13 August 1914. With typical extravagance, Mrs Pankhurst asserted that WSPU members had selflessly stopped their agitation 'when victory was practically within their grasp'. Her Aberdare audience was told that 'the news of the women's truce, and the decision to throw in their lot with the nation was received with great disappointment in Berlin'. *Merthyr Express*, 16 October 1915.

[5]   *The Times*, 7 March 1930.

[6]   Pankhurst, *Suffragette Movement*, 594.

[7]   Cheryl Law, *Suffrage and Power: The Women's Movement, 1918–28* (London, 1997), 13–14.

While never approaching the excesses of the WSPU leadership, the National Union of Women's Suffrage Societies
(NUWSS), after an increasingly acrimonious struggle with its
internationalist and pacifist wing, adopted the strongly patriotic stance determined by its president, Millicent Fawcett.
Interpreting the conflict as the preservation of democracy
against German militarism, she uncompromisingly avoided any
association with the peace movement and placed the NUWSS
solidly behind Britain's war effort, suspending suffrage
campaigning until franchise reform returned to the political
agenda in late 1916. The National League for Opposing
Women Suffrage (NLOWS) also decided to 'abandon for the
time being all outside propaganda work' on the outbreak of
war.[8] In contrast, other organizations – the Women's Freedom
League (WFL), the East London Federation of Suffragettes
(ELFS) and the United Suffragists most notably, but also
others, including the FCSU – resolved to continue the franchise campaign.

The British government's immediate priority following the
declaration of war was the creation of a large army to with-
stand the German tidal wave sweeping across Belgium and
into France. As Britain had no military conscription until 1916
a huge recruitment drive sought to attract volunteers. Much
of the propaganda targeted women, whose supreme duty, it
was urged, was to dispatch their menfolk ('husbands, sons and
sweethearts') to the armed forces. Such sentiments were
loudly echoed in the national and local press. In late 1914,
under the headline 'Young Men, to Arms', the advice being
conveyed by the *Abergavenny Chronicle* to its female readers ran
thus:

> Women are the best recruiting sergeants and they should do all they
> can to encourage young men to enlist. Let the young ladies lay down
> the dictum that there shall be no gladsome smiles or kisses for the
> young men who will not serve their country, and there will at once be a
> stampede to join the colours. It is 'up to' the young ladies of
> Abergavenny to give an exhibition of self-sacrifice and to show how
> effective are their powers of persuasion.[9]

[8]   *ASR*, September 1914. For the impact of war upon organized anti-suffragism,
see Bush, *Women Against the Vote*, ch. 10.
[9]   *Abergavenny Chronicle*, 28 August 1914.

No woman was more active in the recruitment campaign than Emmeline Pankhurst, who travelled the length and breadth of the country addressing hugely enthusiastic public meetings, which were glowingly reported in the local press. To encourage volunteers, it was essential to whip up hatred of Germans, to demonize them by portraying an evil and barbaric people, guilty of unspeakable atrocities in Belgium. Thus man's foremost obligation was to take up arms and, if necessary, die for Britain and the empire. This was very much the message delivered by Mrs Pankhurst across south Wales in the autumn of 1915. In late September, for example, she assured a crowded Pontypool audience that unless Germany was defeated there would be 'no "land of my fathers" – the heritage of centuries would become a foreign province ... under German despotism'. The young men of the town were told that 'there were dearer things than life itself – honour, liberty, love of country. To lose one's life fighting for those things immortalised the man – he was doing the great and splendid thing.'[10] At Aberdare, she urged Wales to 'rally round the old flag as one man with only one aim – that of annihilating German militarism and its concomitant oppression and savagery'.[11] The image of future German atrocities in Britain was recurrent in the patriotic propaganda of the war; thus, pacifism would 'lead to exactly the same tortures in Swansea as had been suffered in Belgium', insisted Christabel Pankhurst on a visit to the town in November 1917.[12]

Similarly, the spectre of a victorious Germany was used by WSPU leaders to caution workers against industrial strikes:

> remember that if the Germans come the miners of South Wales will be among the first to suffer as the civilian people of Belgium have suffered! You miners will either be assassinated at sight, burnt alive in your home, perhaps after you have seen your wife violated or your baby stabbed by a bayonet, or you will be compelled to choose between being shot against a wall or working to get coal for the Germans.[13]

---

[10] *Free Press of Monmouthshire*, 1 October 1915.
[11] *Merthyr Express*, 16 October 1915.
[12] *Britannia*, 23 November 1917.
[13] *The Suffragette*, 3 September 1915.

The WSPU was also at the forefront of the campaign for military conscription, a mass meeting in London in early June 1915 urging the new coalition government to introduce 'universal obligatory national service for men and women'. Citation of 'German barbarism' added colour and vehemence to the platform speeches. Thus, in opening the proceedings, Mrs Pankhurst chose to read a letter from the former leading Welsh suffragette, Margaret Mackworth, a survivor of the sinking of the *Lusitania* by a German U-boat a few weeks earlier during which 1,200 lives were lost. Here was vivid testimony to 'the sort of fiends we are fighting'. The letter went on to recall:

> I do not think that I have ever seen so many small children on board a ship . . . The great majority of them perished, as was inevitable when no notice of torpedoing was given, and the whole ship had sunk in fifteen minutes. The brutality of the people who could make war on those defenceless babies seems to me a thing that we ought to give everything we have and are to fight and get rid of. Mad brutes of that type are very much too dangerous to leave at large.[14]

A prominent theme of the WSPU recruitment campaign was that women should take over the jobs of men, who would then be able to 'do the right thing'. Thus in a rousing speech at a Merthyr rally in October 1915, Flora Drummond was typically uncompromising: 'shop assistants, teachers and postmen, you are hiding behind the petticoats . . . the women can do your work . . . Don't be cowards. Come out and fight.'[15] A few months earlier, on 17 July, the WSPU had organized a 'Women's Right to Serve' demonstration in London, a procession of 30,000 women culminating in a deputation led by Mrs Pankhurst to Lloyd George, the newly created minister of munitions. It was termed a 'war pageant' and was reminiscent of earlier suffragette spectacles. Anxious to secure the wider employment of women at a time of national crisis – in the face of the opposition of trade unions and businessmen – the government provided financial support.[16] A year later the WSPU staged a second demonstration, urging a still greater

14 Ibid., 11 June 1915.
15 *Merthyr Express*, 23 October 1915.
16 *The Suffragette*, 23 July 1915.

national effort, war service for women especially in munitions and, among other demands, the now regular Pankhurst call for the internment of enemy aliens. Lloyd George, once 'crooked and discreditable', now 'that great Welshman', was again in attendance.[17]

The campaign for women munitions workers found an enthusiastic response in some localities; Mrs Pankhurst's visit to Pontypool in the autumn of 1915 led to the immediate setting up of a district munitions register, with some women apparently walking five or even ten miles to volunteer their names.[18] And, as in other parts of Britain, Welsh women took up this form of employment in increasingly large numbers as the war progressed. By 1918, for example, women comprised 83 per cent of the workforce at the Newport Shell Factory and 70 per cent at Queensferry.[19] Such sterling contributions afforded much satisfaction to the WSPU leadership. Accordingly, when Lloyd George visited Neath in August 1918 he was formally greeted by a procession of women workers – from munitions factories, tinplate works and the Land Army – carefully organized by the Women's Party, the renamed WSPU.[20]

The zeal of Emmeline and Christabel Pankhurst and other WSPU stalwarts was unremitting. Time and again in the years 1915–18 audiences in industrial south Wales (whose supply of 'Admiralty coal' was seen as crucial to the war effort) encountered their patriotic fervour. 'Germans, and others with pro-German sympathies have been cleared out of the Women's Social and Political Union, and if you have any in Swansea . . . get rid of them as quickly as you can', Mrs Pankhurst exhorted a huge audience in the town in October 1915.[21] On the rare visits to the rural hinterland, the message was equally forceful. Thus, at a mass meeting in Llandrindod Wells on 4 August 1917, marking the third anniversary of the outbreak of war, Christabel was at her most ferociously anti-German. In the course of what one local newspaper described as 'a mighty

[17] *Britannia*, 28 July 1916; *VW*, 10 November 1911.
[18] *Britannia*, 15, 22 October 1915.
[19] Deirdre Beddoe, 'Munitionettes, maids and mams: women in Wales, 1914–1939', in John, *Our Mothers' Land*, 193.
[20] *Britannia*, 16 August 1918.
[21] *SWDP*, 26 October 1915.

speech', the 2,000-strong gathering was told that 'the Kaiser was a criminal, a hardened criminal, but he had his partners in crime, the whole German people. Nothing must blind them to this fact.'[22] She went on to denounce talk of peace and compromise, urging renewed and sustained determination to secure complete victory.

To Christabel and her supporters, all pacifists were traitors and deserved imprisonment.[23] The activities of organizations like the Union of Democratic Control, the Fellowship of Reconciliation, the Women's International League for Peace and Freedom, the Women's Peace Crusade and the No Conscription Fellowship were 'insidious' and 'pernicious' and ought to be suppressed. Thus individuals like Sylvia Pankhurst and Emmeline Pethick-Lawrence, former suffragettes but now peace campaigners, were strongly attacked. So too were the Labour politicians Ramsay MacDonald and Keir Hardie. The fact that the latter was an old friend of the Pankhursts and had been the WSPU's staunchest parliamentary defender in the pre-war years counted for nothing. Thus, in July 1915 *The Suffragette* published a cartoon from *Punch* which depicted 'Keir von Hardie' receiving the Nobel peace prize in the form of a bag of money from the Kaiser.[24]

A few months later Hardie died, an exhausted and disillusioned man, saddened by the widespread working-class enthusiasm for war and by the fierce personal criticism and hostility he endured, even in his own Merthyr Boroughs constituency. A memorial service for Hardie at Aberdare in October 1915 did indeed offer a protest against militarism, but this was very much a minority sentiment; in fact, the preceding and succeeding evenings saw huge recruitment rallies in the town, addressed by Flora Drummond and

[22]   *Radnor Express*, 9 August 1917; *Radnorshire Standard*, 11 August 1917; *Britannia*, 17 August 1917.

[23]   Emmeline denounced conscientious objectors in south Wales in private letters to Lloyd George. David Lloyd George Papers, D/11/2/24–25 (House of Lords Record Office), cited in Laura E. Nym Mayhall, 'Domesticating Emmeline: representing the suffragette, 1930–1993', *National Women's Studies Association Journal*, 11, 2 (1999), 13.

[24]   *The Suffragette*, 30 July 1915. To Sylvia Pankhurst, it was 'a vile cartoon' and she wrote to her mother in protest. E. Sylvia Pankhurst, *The Home Front: A Mirror of Life in England during the First World War* (London, 1932), 228.

Mrs Pankhurst respectively.[25] In the subsequent by-election, the president of the South Wales Miners' Federation and Labour Party nominee, James Winstone, was defeated by Charles Stanton, industrial militant turned arch-patriot standing as an 'Independent Labour' candidate. The contest centred on their respective attitudes to the war, with Stanton fiercely in support and Winstone widely, though inaccurately, seen as an opponent. 'The miners' candidate is a Socialist of the Keir Hardie type . . . Socialist first and country after a long distance', asserted the *Merthyr Express*. To return Winstone, the newspaper continued, would be 'a smack in the face for the brave men who have gone and are still going from the borough to fight'.[26] The eventual result was seen both as evidence of the war fever enveloping all parts of the country and as a clear break with Merthyr's Labour tradition. Flora Drummond, once a devotee of Hardie, worked in the constituency as a member of Stanton's election team.[27]

Throughout the conflict, Mrs Pankhurst and her colleagues remained alarmed at what they perceived to be the strength of anti-war feeling across the south Wales coalfield (though in reality the evidence is far from conclusive). As early as October 1915, an irate Frances Stevenson, Lloyd George's long-time secretary, companion and eventual wife, noted in her diary:

> we do not *deserve* to win this war. Mrs Pankhurst has been holding recruiting meetings in S. Wales, and she says there are districts where the people simply don't care whether the Germans are beaten or not. She says they are sulky and difficult to handle and will not sing the national anthem.[28]

Indeed, in the closing stages of the war, a special Home Office report concluded that

---

[25]   *Aberdare Leader*, 16 October 1915.

[26]   *Merthyr Express*, 6 November 1915. The London press took much the same line. Stanton was 'thorough-going on the war, while around his opponent a halo of lukewarmness was shed. There is no room for lukewarmness.' *Daily Graphic*, 30 November 1915. 'The result of the by-election in Merthyr has real importance. It is as good a blow against Germany as anything in British politics could be.' *Evening Standard*, 27 November 1915.

[27]   Pankhurst, *Home Front*, 228.

[28]   A. J. P. Taylor (ed.), *Lloyd George: A Diary by Frances Stevenson* (London, 1971), 64.

The situation in Glamorgan, Carmarthenshire and Monmouthshire is highly discouraging. There is an active Socialist and pacifist party, a minority probably, but they do all the shouting ... and it would seem that the women alone, especially Mrs Drummond, are the only speakers who meet with any success in answering the talkers.[29]

Given the passions on both sides, heated clashes inevitably occurred, with rival speakers sometimes battling for supremacy. Such an occurrence at Trehafod in the lower Rhondda in October 1917 resulted in the two combatants, Flora Drummond and the prominent anti-war socialist, Arthur Cook, jostling each other, the latter having been bluntly told to 'go to Germany'.[30]

Flora Drummond was a frequent visitor to industrial south Wales during the war. So too was Mrs Pankhurst; Christabel Pankhurst, Annie Kenney and others appeared only occasionally. From late 1917 the WSPU/Women's Party had a permanent regional organizer in south Wales, Phyllis Ayrton. As in suffragette days, meetings were often hurriedly convened after chalking walls and pavements in advertisement; others, of course, received considerable advance publicity by poster and in the local press. Again, much of the speaking was done in the open air – at pitheads, at dockyard gates and at factories, in the dinner hours and before or after shifts. The theme was invariably the 'internal peril', emanating from 'peace cranks', the 'German canker' and later from the 'Bolshevists'.

The 'evil' was most visibly expressed, it was argued, in industrial militancy, and indeed unrest was endemic in the south Wales coalfield during the war years. A major strike over wage rates took place in July 1915; thereafter, discontent on a range of issues made threatened or actual stoppages common. WSPU speakers could always be relied upon to preach

---

[29]   NA, Home Office 45/ 263275 f. 334, quoted in Deian Hopkin, 'Patriots and pacifists in Wales, 1914–1918: the case of Capt. Lionel Lindsay and the Revd T. E. Nicholas', *Llafur: Journal of Welsh Labour History*, 1, 3 (1974), 30. Lloyd George too, writing privately at the end of the war, pointed out that the Pankhursts had been 'extremely useful' to the government in the industrial areas, where they had 'fought the Bolshevik and Pacifist element with great skill, tenacity and courage'. NLW, Lloyd George to A. Bonar Law, 21 November 1918, David Lloyd George Papers, F/30/2/55, quoted in Martin Pugh, *Women and the Women's Movement in Britain, 1914–1999* (London, 1992), 44–5.

[30]   *Glamorgan County Times*, 19 October 1917.

vigorously the government's patriotic message, though the miners were not always seen as the sole villains; in September 1915 the Welsh coal owners were sternly warned that 'the nation is fighting for its life and will stand no nonsense from you'.[31] The unrest was greatly encouraged by the revolutions in Russia in 1917. Having undertaken a lengthy summer visit there, Mrs Pankhurst claimed both first-hand knowledge of the developments and recognition of similar 'poisonous intrigues' at home, especially in the shape of the Unofficial Reform Committee of the south Wales miners: 'the Bolshevists, who brought Russia to ruin, are in our midst trying to work the same harm to this country'.[32] The war ended with Women's Party representatives strenuously seeking to counter strike action over food shortages in the Monmouthshire valleys – in Abertillery, Blaina ('little Germany'), Ebbw Vale and Tredegar. Miners were urged to 'stand by their comrades in the trenches', for a shortage of coal would seriously hinder the conduct of the war. If the men did come out on strike, women, it was suggested, 'should also down tools and refuse to do the housework'.[33]

How did the membership react to the direction in which Emmeline and Christabel Pankhurst took the WSPU? While not necessarily supporting the extremist views, most appear to have accepted the patriotic line. The names of the foremost Welsh suffragettes are traceable during the war years. Margaret Mackworth continued to subscribe to WSPU funds, gave full support to its demand for military conscription and endorsed the general views expressed in *The Suffragette*: 'it fills a gap in the fighting of the enemy that no other British paper would exactly do and it is taking ... just exactly the right line'.[34] Acceptance of the Germans as 'devils incarnate', however, was in part expediency, as she later explained:

> I knew very well, knew it quite consciously, that one could not carry on war without hating the enemy, and that one must let oneself go to unreasonable hatred and think the worst of the enemy for the time

[31]   *The Suffragette*, 3 September 1915.
[32]   *Britannia*, 12 July 1918.
[33]   Ibid., 7 June, 13 September, 1 November 1918.
[34]   *The Suffragette*, 11 June 1915.

being, even though a piece of one knew that one was believing many lies.[35]

Rachel Barrett was another to echo the leadership's sentiments and, indeed, some of the rhetoric, denouncing Germany as 'the most formidable embodiment of militarism in the history of the world'. At the outset, the invasion of Belgium had, in her eyes, made the moral case for war overwhelming:

> we, as a nation, are forced to choose between standing aside and watching an unprovoked assault upon a weaker nation which we have pledged ourselves to defend, and resisting that assault in the only way possible – by force of arms; ethically the choice offered us is between acquiescing in evil and actively resisting it.[36]

'An unconquered Germany . . . would be a perpetual menace to the liberties and peace of the world' and thus peace initiatives prior to 'complete victory for the Allies' were condemned as 'vain and possibly mischievous'. One such, 'An Appeal to the Women of Wales' published in the columns of the *Welsh Outlook*, was greeted thus:

> As a Welsh woman, I sincerely hope no woman of Wales will respond to the 'Appeal'. . . . Let women do their part, not by sentimentally prating of peace, and so playing into the hands of Germany, but by making shells, or otherwise doing their share of the nation's work, so that men may be set free to fight the foe without whose downfall all talk of peace is vain.[37]

Rachel Barrett was inevitably a contributor to the WSPU's 'Victory Fund', launched in late 1916 to sponsor the campaigns against 'a compromise peace', 'German and pro-German influence', 'pacifist intrigue' and industrial strikes.[38]

While WSPU branches ceased to function within a few months of the outbreak of hostilities, individuals readily responded to local war-related initiatives. At Pontypool,

---

[35]   Rhondda, *This Was My World*, 274.
[36]   *Welsh Outlook*, April 1915.
[37]   Ibid., October, December 1915.
[38]   *Britannia*, 3, 10, 17 November 1916, 6, 22 June 1917. Among the other subscribers were Mary Ann Butler of Panteg and Margaret Mackworth's cousin, Florence Haig. In the early years of the war, until 1916, the latter is listed as one of the secretaries of the WSPU, working alongside Mrs Pankhurst, Christabel and Annie Kenney, and in 1928 she was one of the pallbearers at Mrs Pankhurst's funeral. Crawford, *Women's Suffrage Movement*, 257.

members promptly became engaged in work connected with the Belgian Relief Service, the Prince of Wales Relief Fund and the organization of clubs for the dependants of soldiers and sailors.[39] And this was the general pattern. One specific scheme was the fund to help 'Welsh wives of German miners', launched by a WSPU stalwart, the north Walian Dr Helena Jones. Though British born, 'these victims of an Anti-Suffragist system' were classed as German subjects and, as such, faced destitution during the war.[40] The other suffrage societies, and the NLOWS, also became involved in relief work, pledging support to the mushrooming wartime organizations. The WFL immediately set up its own agency, the Women's Suffrage National Aid Corps, to help 'alleviate distress among the most helpless of the community' and urged branches to respond to the call. League representatives touring central Wales and the Swansea area in late 1914 publicized the appeal, while Brynmawr branch members swiftly formed themselves into a local aid corps.[41] In London, the FCSU immediately set about raising funds for Welsh families made destitute by the war.[42] In Monmouthshire, the NLOWS branch at Newport played a prominent role in organizing Red Cross activity.[43] Throughout much of the war, CLWS branches at Swansea and Cardiff gave support to local volunteer and charitable initiatives.[44]

NUWSS branches around the country were particularly active in relief work and throughout Wales members gave support to the various agencies, often taking on key organizational roles locally. The Cardiff and District Women's Suffrage Society (CDWSS), with a strong executive and its large membership extending to Barry and Penarth, committed itself to a wide range of activities. Workrooms were established to produce socks, shirts and other items of clothing for the

[39]   *Free Press of Monmouthshire*, 15 January 1915.
[40]   *VW*, 16 October 1914.
[41]   *The Vote*, 14 August 1914; 4 September, 27 November, 18 December 1914; *South Wales Gazette*, 28 August 1914.
[42]   *The Vote*, 28 August 1914.
[43]   *ASR*, September 1914.
[44]   *CLWS Monthly*, September, October, November, December 1914, January, April, December 1915, January, February 1916; CLWS, *Annual Report*, 1915. See also *Free Church Times*, August 1915.

men at the Front but much of the effort sought to mitigate the local suffering caused by the war. Within a few months, some thirty branch members were serving on relief committees and over a hundred had registered as voluntary workers to be allocated suitable jobs among the different bodies – as secretaries, interpreters, visitors and cooks. Aid focused on the families of soldiers and sailors, on unemployed women and 'foreigners in distress', including those 'stranded in Cardiff', British women designated 'aliens' through marriage and also refugees arriving from Belgium. A successful appeal to other NUWSS branches throughout north and south Wales raised nearly £300 to provide a 'women's suffrage bed' in the Welsh hospital near Southampton, a programme of lectures at branch meetings dealt with the various problems raised by the war, and French classes were organized for teaching the language to soldiers and nurses.[45] More typical of the NUWSS branches in Wales which survived the war years was the small Llangollen Women's Suffrage Society (around fifty members and a handful of committee members) which continued to meet regularly and whose relief work concentrated on raising money for war-related charities and organizing knitting and sewing groups to produce articles of clothing for the troops.[46]

In the early stages of the war, such work was an obvious channel for the patriotic feelings of members of the various suffrage societies. Increasingly, though, there were also opportunities for women to assist the national cause through employment, in the munitions industry and in all sorts of other occupations as replacements for men needed in the armed forces. 'Wales has responded with characteristic enthusiasm to the call for money, for munition workers, for women to replace men in offices and shops, and above all for helpers in hospitals', observed the South Wales and Monmouthshire

---

[45]   *CC*, 4 September, 13 November 1914; *Annual Reports of the Cardiff and District Women's Suffrage Society*, 1914–15, 1916. For relief work undertaken by NUWSS branches in various parts of Wales, see *CC*, 28 August, 11, 25 September, 4, 18 December 1914, 26 March, 2, 9 April, 7, 14 May, 30 July, 12 November, 10 December 1915, 11 February, 14 April 21 July 1916, 1 June, 27 July 1917. See also Beddoe, *Out of the Shadows*, 52–5.

[46]   Llangollen WSS minutes; *Llangollen Advertiser*, 20 November 1914.

Federation (SWF) *Annual Report* for 1916.[47] One prominent figure in the government drive to increase female employment was Margaret Mackworth, who in 1917 was appointed commissioner of Women's National Service in Wales, with responsibility for recruitment into agriculture, nursing and other jobs. Taking a particular interest in the Women's Army Auxiliary Corps, she addressed meetings throughout Wales, urging women of every class to make a positive contribution to the war effort, to rise to 'the best traditions in this hour of the nation's need'. In November 1917, Margaret was elevated to be chief controller of women's recruiting in the newly created Ministry of National Service.[48]

Many suffragists chose to combine welfare and relief work with campaigning for peace rather than manifesting patriotic fervour, a response that signalled conflict within the NUWSS. The executive's rejection of participation in the Women's International Peace Congress at the Hague in April 1915 brought matters to a head and a raft of resignations ensued. The Cardiff, Bangor and Llangollen branches and the SWF all expressed support for the stance of Millicent Fawcett and the leadership, Llangollen resolving that 'the NUWSS was formed for the political enfranchisement of women' and that it was 'unjustifiable to use the organization for pacifist propaganda', and this appears to have been the attitude of most Welsh suffragists.[49] A few months later, in September, ex-NUWSS executive members were prominent in founding the British branch of the Women's International League for Peace and Freedom (WILPF), which had been set up at the Hague Congress. An immediate call from a Cardiff member for sympathizers to join the 'English Society, or form ourselves

[47] NUWSS, *Annual Report*, 1916, 19.

[48] *Glamorgan County Times*, 9 November 1917; *SWDN*, 17 July 1917; Eoff, *Viscountess Rhondda*, 40–7. Her father, formerly D. A. Thomas and elevated to the peerage as Lord Rhondda in 1916, played a prominent role in Lloyd George's wartime coalition government, first as president of the Local Government Board and then as food controller. For details of the employment taken up by women in Wales, see Beddoe, *Out of the Shadows*, 57–69; Lisa Snook, '"Out of the cage?" Women and the First World War in Pontypridd', *Llafur: Journal of Welsh Labour History*, 8, 2 (2001), 75–87; *Project Grace, Unit 7, Women in the First World War*.

[49] NUWSS, executive minutes, 30 April 1915; Bangor WSS minutes, 2 June 1915; Llangollen WSS minutes, 29 May 1915.

into a separate Welsh one' may have elicited a positive response for the WILPF's first annual report recorded one of its thirty-four branches in Cardiff (comprising fifty members). It was still in operation a year later, but had apparently disbanded by the end of the war, at which point the league had fifty-one branches and 4,500 members.[50] The first 'chairman' of the British WILPF was the former editor of *The Common Cause*, Helena Swanwick, who now dedicated herself to the peace movement, and like many other such campaigners, endured the discomforts, frustrations and hostilities of conducting speaking tours in areas like industrial south Wales.[51] The WILPF cooperated closely with other groups in seeking an end to the war yet also supported the continued agitation for women's suffrage.

The other pre-war women's suffrage societies had their peace campaigners too. In the WFL there was most strikingly its president, Charlotte Despard, who served on the executive of the WILPF and in 1918 toured various parts of Britain, including Wales, speaking on behalf of the Women's Peace Crusade.[52] Among other suffragists involved in groups with internationalist and pacifist views were several prominent Welsh activists, including Edith Mansell Moullin, Alice Abadam and Helena Jones.

The anti-war strand in the WSPU was most strongly evident in the activities of Sylvia Pankhurst, who, from the beginning of the war, was intent on organizing opposition to it through her ELFS. The contrast between her attitude to the outbreak of hostilities and that of her mother and elder sister could not have more stark. And, while they were applauded everywhere by huge crowds and acclaimed in the national and local press on their recruiting tours of the country, Sylvia's activities

---

[50] *Welsh Outlook*, September 1915; WILPF, *Annual Reports*, 1916–18.

[51] H. M. Swanwick, *I Have Been Young* (London, 1935), 293–9. Much of the organizational work for Mrs Swanwick's tour of south Wales in late 1916 was undertaken by the young Brynmawr teacher and daughter of a Wesleyan minister, Minnie Pallister, who was to become one of the most important women in the ILP and a Labour parliamentary candidate in the 1920s. Claire Collins, 'Women and labour politics in Britain, 1893–1932' (Ph.D. thesis, London School of Economics and Political Science, University of London, 1991), 55, 211, 278–9; *The Vote*, 6 July 1923.

[52] A crusade group was set up by Minnie Pallister in Brynmawr. Collins, 'Women and labour politics in Britain', 211.

frequently met with fierce public hostility and press contempt. 'Peace Suffragettes Mobbed: An Old-Time Scene in Trafalgar Square', ran a 1916 headline, with the accompanying report describing the scenes thus: 'amid screams from the women and wild yells and cheers from the crowd, the banners and flags were torn from the hands of their bearers and distributed in fragments as souvenirs among the mob'.[53] An incensed Mrs Pankhurst cabled WSPU headquarters from the United States instructing an unequivocal response: 'Strongly condemn and repudiate Sylvia's foolish and unpatriotic conduct. Regret I cannot prevent use of name. Make this public.'[54] This was far from a universal response, however. Sylvia often drew large crowds on her visits to the south Wales coalfield, particularly as the war progressed.[55]

The ELFS was one of a number of suffragist organizations determined to continue the franchise struggle when war broke out, though its particular objectives became far removed from women's suffrage by 1918. It had been formed in May 1913, following Sylvia Pankhurst's campaign to arouse the interest of working-class women in that part of the capital in the issue of votes for women. Its highly democratic character, increasing links with the labour and socialist movements and Sylvia's criticism of the strategy of individualistic militancy led to a split with the WSPU early in 1914.[56] During the course of the war, the ELFS developed into an organization preaching a revolutionary brand of socialism to which the suffrage and indeed parliamentary democracy ultimately became marginalized. Changes of name reflected the process. In February 1916, it became the Workers' Suffrage Federation (WSF), emphasizing the commitment to adult suffrage, and later, in June 1918, a further change introduced the Workers' Socialist Federation. Its weekly journal, the *Woman's Dreadnought*, was retitled the *Workers' Dreadnought* in July 1917.

[53]   *Daily Chronicle*, 10 April 1916.
[54]   *Daily Express*, 20 April 1916.
[55]   *Amman Valley Chronicle*, 12 July 1917; *Woman's Dreadnought*, 14 July 1917; *The Pioneer*, 6 October 1917.
[56]   Interestingly, Sybil Thomas of Llanwern served as temporary treasurer of the ELFS in the early months of 1914. *Woman's Dreadnought*, 2 January 1915. (Her niece, Florence Haig, had been one of the thirteen women present at the meeting to form the organization in May 1913. Crawford, *Women's Suffrage Movement*, 257.)

The various organizations were small and had only limited political influence. Indeed, south Wales became the only base which the WSF established outside London. Sylvia Pankhurst herself often visited the region during the war years, lengthy articles in the *Dreadnought* (which built up a wide circulation in the coalfield) detailing her impressions and experiences. At times of industrial militancy she was vigorous in condemnation of 'a small master class'. Thus, in September 1915, striking miners across the coalfield were eulogized 'for the fighting of that system of greedy capitalism that sucks the very life blood from the poor and weak'. At Tonypandy, the men 'walked on air, their faces were radiant. One saw in them a vision of labour bursting its life long chains.'[57] She was also active at this time in the anti-conscription campaign in the Rhondda, where she established close links with the left-wing leaders of the south Wales miners.[58] By 1917, her programme had become very broad; in July, a gathering of some two thousand people in Ammanford gave enthusiastic approval to her demand for 'immediate peace on the basis of no annexations, no indemnities, to Adult Suffrage, the abolition of the House of Lords, and the substitution of an industrial Parliament, Socialism, and the immediate nationalisation of the food supply'.[59] By the end of the year she had placed herself solidly behind the Bolsheviks on their assumption of power in Russia.

A number of Women's/Workers' Suffrage Federation (WSF) branches were set up in industrial south Wales, invariably stimulated by a visit to the area from Sylvia. Of fifteen provincial branches listed in June 1916, three were in Wales – Brynmawr and Nantyglo, Cwmtillery and Pontardawe.[60] Branches were also apparently in the process of formation at Llanelli and Gorseinon at this time, while two more were established later – Mid Rhondda in the autumn of 1917 and Bargoed

[57] *Woman's Dreadnought*, 4 September 1915.
[58] Ibid., 6 November 1915; Pankhurst, *Home Front*, 221, 413; M. G. Woodhouse, 'Rank and file movements among the miners of south Wales, 1910–1926' (Ph.D. thesis, University of Oxford, 1969), 135–8.
[59] *Woman's Dreadnought*, 14 July 1917; *Amman Valley Chronicle*, 12 July 1917; WSF minutes, 29 June, 13 July 1917, E. S. Pankhurst Papers, *Women, Suffrage and Politics: The Papers of Sylvia Pankhurst, 1882–1960* (Marlborough, 1991).
[60] WSF minutes, 24 June 1916; *South Wales Gazette*, 14 July 1916.

early in 1918.[61] The most enduring seem to have been those at Brynmawr and Nantyglo, where the local secretary, Mrs S. J. Hayward, a miner's wife, was particularly hard working, and in Mid Rhondda. Both no doubt had small memberships, but they held branch and public meetings, circulated the *Dreadnought*, attracted press attention and, through local pressure, sought to defend working-class standards of living at a time when war presented 'peculiar opportunities . . . for profiteers to exploit the miseries of the people'.[62] Thus, aside from calls for adult or 'human' suffrage and an end to the war, local branches were especially concerned about shortages of food and its 'unfair and unequal distribution', demanding special allowances of both food and milk for expectant mothers and young children.[63]

Another organization determined not to abandon the suffrage cause despite the difficulties and demands of war was the London-based FCSU led by Edith Mansell Moullin. Notices placed in newspapers in England and Wales in August 1914 pronounced 'propaganda work as usual . . . as Welsh women are of the opinion that the present time is most opportune for pointing out the need of the voice of women in the government of all nations'.[64] Indeed, the union remained true to its word, its weekly Sunday afternoon meetings in Hyde Park during the summer months ensuring that the 'red dragon' banner was conspicuous in the continuing metropolitan suffrage campaign. The FCSU also cooperated in joint activities and protests with other societies, notably the United Suffragists and the ELFS. Following the resignation of its driving force, Edith Mansell Moullin, from its executive in April 1916 (on health grounds), the union was noticeably less prominent, though it was not disbanded until women gained 'the partial vote' in February 1918.[65]

---

[61]   *Woman's Dreadnought*, 27 May 1916; *Workers' Dreadnought*, 6 October 1917, 26 January, 23 February. 1918; WSF minutes, 19 January 1918.

[62]   Mrs S. J. Hayward writing in the *Workers' Dreadnought*, 8 December 1917.

[63]   Ibid., 8 December 1917, 12 January, 23 February 1918.

[64]   Ibid., 28 August 1914; *Woman's Dreadnought*, 22 August 1914; *VW*, 21 August 1914. At the beginning of 1916 the union claimed members 'in eight Welsh counties and in twenty-eight districts of London'. *Woman's Dreadnought*, 22 January 1916.

[65]   The FCSU was part of a deputation, including the WFL and other bodies, to

Throughout the war Edith worked for the blind at St Dunstan's. At some point she also 'joined the Pacifists'; certainly, very early in the conflict, a visit to a military hospital in Farnborough, near to where her son was serving in the Royal Flying Corps, seems to have made a telling impression on her.[66] An anti-war stance, long-standing concern for social questions related to the plight of 'the weak, the helpless and the oppressed' and, of course, belief that suffrage pressure should be kept up brought close contact with Sylvia Pankhurst's ELFS. She contributed, as she had done before the war, to the *Woman's Dreadnought*, her co-worker, Mary Davies, spoke on federation platforms and the FCSU's concerns now extended beyond the suffrage to such issues as equal rates of pay, high food prices and sweated labour.

Of the three principal pre-war women's suffrage societies, the one that remained thoroughly committed to the campaign throughout the war was the Women's Freedom League (WFL). At an emergency meeting in August 1914 its executive insisted on 'the urgency of keeping the Suffrage flag flying, and, especially now, making the country understand the supreme necessity of women having a voice in the counsels of the nation' (though it also undertook 'to abstain during the war from all forms of active militancy').[67] The league was the one suffrage organization to maintain provincial activity by carrying on with its propaganda visits to areas where it was strong. On the outbreak of war, it was in the midst of a campaign along the coastal resorts of north and west Wales. This continued, with the familiar daily meetings on the seafront at Aberystwyth, the distribution of suffrage literature and the selling of *The Vote*. Over the following months, a similar (month-long) campaign was conducted in Montgomeryshire and shorter ones in Swansea, Brynmawr and Cardiff.[68] This was clear confirmation of the league executive's rejection

---

Lord Rhondda, president of the Local Government Board, early in 1917, pressing for the inclusion of women in any franchise legislation. *The Vote*, 2 February 1917.

[66] SFC, 57.116/ 79, Notes on E. R. Mansell Moullin; *Woman's Dreadnought*, 31 October 1914.

[67] *The Vote*, 14 August 1914.

[68] Ibid., 7, 14, 28 August, 4, 11 September, 6, 27 November, 11, 18 December 1914, 1 January, 12, 19 February, 5 March 1915.

of the notion that suffrage should be kept in the background for the duration of the war: 'To desert the Cause because the situation has become particularly difficult is betrayal of the basest description.'[69] Several more local campaigns were sporadically conducted in parts of Wales in the years 1915–17, the most intensive being in Montgomeryshire and Aberystwyth, areas where the irrepressible Alix Clark of Newtown organized a large number of meetings and supervised the sale of hundreds of copies of *The Vote*.[70] Elsewhere, most conspicuously at Swansea and Cardiff, branches continued to meet and carry out activities. At the end of the war four Welsh branches of the league remained in existence (Aberdovey, Cardiff, Montgomery Boroughs and Swansea) out of a total of forty.[71]

WFL activity in Wales, as elsewhere, embraced continued suffrage propaganda, war relief work and the protection of women's interests. Central to the latter were the employment rights of women and, in particular, the issue of equal pay for equal work. As ever, suffragists linked economic injustice to votes for women. Thus, the opposition of Cardiff tramwaymen to the employment of female conductors in the spring of 1915 demonstrated 'in a compressed and quintessential form, the economic difficulties which surround the work of women in a community which refuses to recognise their citizenship'.[72] Equally important was the principle of an equal moral standard, which led to WFL involvement in another Cardiff controversy early in the war. Drawing on the wide-ranging powers vested in him by the Defence of the Realm Act (DORA), the commanding army officer for the district issued a curfew order stating that 'women of a certain class' were not allowed on the streets of the city between the hours of 7 p.m. and 8 a.m. Subsequently, in November 1914, five women were arrested and, following a military court-martial, imprisoned. To women's organizations this amounted to back-door revival of the hated Contagious Diseases Acts, which Josephine Butler and others had campaigned so strenuously to remove decades earlier.

[69]   Ibid., 29 January 1915.
[70]   Ibid., 19 February, 5 March, 16, 23 April, 7 May 1915; 2 June, 11, 18, 25 August, 1, 8, 15, 22 September 1916; 2 February, 6 April 1917.
[71]   WFL, *Annual Report*, 1915–17, 8, 32, 47–8.
[72]   *VW*, 30 April 1915.

In Cardiff itself the campaign was led by a relatively new organization, the United Suffragists, which sent representatives to the city, mobilized local opposition, led a public meeting and arranged a deputation to the central figure in the case, Colonel East. The vigorous protest was successful, securing the women's release and the quashing of the curfew. The United Suffragists, the WFL and other bodies followed this up with a demonstration in Trafalgar Square, highlighting not only the operation of unequal moral standards, as epitomized in the Cardiff episode, but also other legislative injustices towards women in welfare and employment; the only guarantee against discrimination between the sexes, it concluded, was the immediate enfranchisement of women.[73]

The United Suffragists had been formed in February 1914, disaffected supporters of the WSPU to the fore, and it presented itself as a wholly inclusive body open to men and women 'irrespective of any other society, militant or non-militant'. War prevented the development of its provincial aspirations and a total of only about eighteen branches was established, none of them in Wales.[74] Nevertheless, by single-mindedly maintaining its focus, the United Suffragists played a particularly important role in sustaining the suffrage campaign during the difficult war years.[75]

Two other suffrage organizations emerged during the course of the war, both representing former WSPU members opposed to the leadership's decision to suspend the franchise campaign in favour of anti-German extremism. A series of meetings in late 1915 strongly protested against the way in which union policy had been fundamentally changed and

[73]   VW, 4, 11, 18, 25 December 1914, 1, 8, 29 January 1915; The Vote, 4, 11 December 1914, 8, 15 January 1915; Woman's Dreadnought, 5 December 1914; Free Church Times, January 1914. See also Beddoe, Out of the Shadows, 70; Law, Suffrage and Power, 28–9.

[74]   There were some Welsh connections. Sybil Thomas (now Lady Rhondda) was a vice-president (and gave £2 a month to keep the society's journal, Votes for Women, going), while Dr Helena Jones was one of the society's speakers. VW, 9 October 1914, 9, 16 April 1915.

[75]   For the United Suffragists, see VW, 6 February 1914; Krista Cowman, '"A party between revolution and peaceful persuasion": a fresh look at the United Suffragists', in Joannou and Purvis, Women's Suffrage Movement, 77–88.

also demanded a full financial statement of accounts.[76] In December, the Suffragettes of the WSPU (SWSPU) came into being and the *Suffragette News Sheet* was launched, each monthly issue carrying the following explanation:

> This News Sheet is issued by a body of members of the old WSPU, who differ from their former leaders in thinking it right to continue suffrage propaganda during the war. They have, therefore, agreed to act together under the title *The Suffragettes of the WSPU*.
>
> Their constitution is entirely democratic and consists of an Executive and officials who are responsible to the members, and who are elected by the whole membership. The policy is therefore controlled by the members.[77]

The latter half of the statement represented a clear condemnation of Pankhurst autocracy, which had led to the use of the WSPU name, organizational structure and possibly funds for a purpose totally divorced from its original object. Thus, on the occasion of the women's war demonstration of July 1916, it was asserted that the union was 'never formed to organise processions other than connected with suffrage work'.[78] A few months later, the new body was again anxious to dispel the widespread belief that Mrs Pankhurst was still the voice of the suffragettes, a press announcement insisting that 'a large and increasing group of members of the WSPU joined the Society solely on account of its work on behalf of the enfranchisement of women' and wished to 'entirely dissociate themselves from the line Mrs Pankhurst has taken since the outbreak of war'.[79]

The *raison d'être* of the new association was thus to help sustain a women's suffrage campaign in spite of the war. As one of its most zealous committee members, Dr Helena Jones, emphasized:

> We (the Suffragettes of the WSPU) consider that our business as a Women's Suffrage Society is to obtain the removal of the sex barrier. This is the Alpha and Omega of our present existence ... we persist in

---

[76] *Jus Suffragii*, 1 November 1915; *The Vote*, 5 November, 10 December 1915; *VW*, 10 December 1915; Rosen, *Rise Up, Women!*, 253–4.

[77] The first thirteen issues have survived, December 1915 and March 1916–February 1917, in the WL, Emily Wilding Davison Papers, G6/1–13. There are two further issues (May 1917 and December 1917/January 1918) in the British Library, Arncliffe-Sennett Collection, vols 27 and 28 respectively.

[78] *Suffragette News Sheet*, August 1916.

[79] Ibid., September 1916.

the old demand – votes for women on the same terms as they are or may be given to men.[80]

During 1916–17 the SWSPU's small number of enthusiasts held indoor and outdoor meetings, lobbied MPs, wrote to ministers and cooperated with other suffragist organizations in demonstrations, deputations and fund-raising. Though it remained entirely a London body, making no overtures to the provinces, there was some Welsh influence. Helena Jones, now assistant medical officer of health in the Rhondda, was one important activist, figuring prominently as a public speaker and *News Sheet* columnist and condemning Mrs Pankhurst as having 'departed from her first love and gone over to the enemy'.[81] Edith Mansell Moullin was also involved, absolutely convinced of the need to 'keep the Suffrage flag flying in these terrible days ... with half the world bathed in blood and tears'.[82]

A second initiative 'among the London members who differed from Mrs Pankhurst's views' was taken in March 1916 with the formation of the Independent WSPU (IWSPU). Comprising entirely different personnel, the distinction between the two organizations is by no means clear. The IWSPU attracted pacifists too, while similarly maintaining a focus on the 'supreme importance of the Vote'. Advocating 'work in the spirit of the old WSPU', a prison badge decorated its banner, while its organ, the *Independent Suffragette*, echoed the rhetoric of old:

> This little paper embodies our ideals. It utters a war-cry to the world. By means of it friends and enemies know that we are not dead, but very much alive, and still maintaining our own demands, and that we shall never be silent till the goal is won. Members of the IWSPU ... Be alive! Be awake![83]

The IWSPU was certainly alive to the danger of wartime conditions bringing encroachments on rights that women had

---

[80] Ibid., December 1916. The full text of this article is reprinted in Aaron and Masson, *Very Salt of Life*, 286–7. See also ibid., 284–5.

[81] *Suffragette News Sheet*, September, December 1916. Another contributor to the *News Sheet* was Alice Abadam.

[82] Ibid., January 1917. See also, *Woman's Dreadnought*, 3 July 1915.

[83] *Independent Suffragette*, September 1916. Only five issues have survived, two at the British Newspaper Library and three at the WL.

already won and was thus involved, along with other suffrage organizations, in the successful protest against clause 40D of the Defence of the Realm Act, which had been so controversially applied in Cardiff. Familiar campaigning methods re-emerged, as one activist recalled: 'We sold our paper, full of details about the Bill, at street corners; we printed leaflets with rousing headlines, which we distributed outside public meetings; and, above all, a few of our members poster-paraded the London streets', often donning aprons carrying the slogan, 'Vice can never be made safe'.[84] While voicing aspirations of 'spreading our propaganda through the length and breadth of the kingdom', the IWSPU remained a small society, spawning only a few branches outside London.

The formation of the SWSPU and the IWSPU coincided with the re-emergence of franchise extension as a political issue. War had thrown the existing electoral register into confusion by disfranchising men in the armed forces and also many munitions workers who now failed to meet the one-year residential qualification, while there was also the delicate matter of servicemen risking their lives for their country but not possessing the necessary property qualifications to vote. Parliamentary concern was reflected in the (subsequently withdrawn) Service Voting bill of Lord Willoughby de Broke which proposed to enfranchise servicemen over the age of twenty-one. The various suffrage societies sprang into action, pressing the claims of women. Among them was the FCSU whose secretary, Edith Mansell Moullin, wrote to the bill's sponsor in November 1915:

> There are at least as many women in this Union engaged on war service, and doing their best for their country, as there are men, and there are multitudes doing the same. Why should they be left out? On what principle can this privilege be conferred on one sex but not upon the other? We Welsh people . . . appeal to you to amend your Bill so as to include women on the same terms as men.[85]

The following month, a joint letter, signed by eleven suffrage societies (including the FCSU) was sent to the prime minister, Asquith, insisting that women be included in any new

---

84   Zoë Proctor, *Life and Yesterday* (London, 1960), 120.
85   *VW*, 12 November 1915.

Registration Bill.[86] During 1916, as Cabinet ministers grappled inconclusively with the whole franchise issue, these societies continued in debate and collaboration. In May, the NUWSS rejoined the fray.[87]

Significantly, the NUWSS, which was still by far the largest of the suffrage bodies, had maintained its organizational structure intact during the war years and was now able to energize local societies in support of the suffrage cause. Both the SWF and the NWF continued to operate in spite of the difficulties.[88] Within the federations a considerable number of branches remained active, though focusing on support for the war effort rather than on suffrage work. In April 1916, *The Common Cause* was listing thirty-five NUWSS branches in Wales, though this was undoubtedly a highly optimistic figure.[89]

In the summer of 1916 local committees readily responded to exhortations from the NUWSS executive to exert pressure on politicians. Thus, in July the Llangollen branch sent the following resolution to its MP:

> This society considers that, after the splendid national services rendered by women during the present troubles, a parliament elected on a register excluding women would be absolutely destitute of moral force or authority and therefore presses for the grant of the suffrage to qualified women in any Franchise or Registration bill that may be passed at the present time.[90]

Similar resolutions, to the local MP, to the prime minister and members of the Cabinet, followed over the following months. Activists were also again busy in the local community carrying out suffrage propaganda.[91] By early 1917 the Bangor society

[86] Ibid., 3 December 1915; *Church League for Women's Suffrage Monthly*, January 1916.

[87] Holton, *Feminism and Democracy*, 145–51. All the main suffrage newspapers continued publication throughout the war years and new ones had come into being, thereby affording the societies an immediate platform.

[88] *CC*, 21 July 1916; NUWSS, *Annual Report*, 1916, p. 19; NUSEC, *Annual Report*, 1918, 52.

[89] *CC*, 24 April 1916. Reports and affiliation fees suggest half of this number is more realistic with active branches located in Cardiff, Newport, Pontypool, Abergavenny, Chepstow, Port Talbot, Neath, Merthyr Tydfil and Pontypridd in the south, and Bangor, Penmaenmawr, Cricieth, Colwyn Bay, Rhyl and Llangollen in the north.

[90] Llangollen WSS minutes, 25 July 1916. See also ibid., 6 June 1916.

[91] Ibid., 8 November, 9 December 1916, 31 January 1917; ibid., *Annual Report*, 1916–17.

was again pressing the issue, lobbying local organizations and prominent individuals to sign a women's suffrage memorial to Lloyd George.[92] In south Wales, Winifred Coombe Tennant, president of the Neath Society and national executive member, visited branches to urge members to press for the franchise 'as the present time is most critical', while in April 1917 the Cardiff and District Society appointed a paid organizer to undertake suffrage work.[93]

WFL branches, whose activities had become highly diversified during the war, moved back towards suffrage politics. In Wales, 'educational' campaigns in Aberystwyth and Montgomeryshire, in late summer 1916 and spring 1917 respectively, focused on the injustice of servicemen and male munitions workers obtaining the vote while women were left out.[94] In London, the league leadership closely monitored parliamentary developments and lobbied ministers in writing and by deputation.

Unable to reach agreement on electoral reform, in August 1916 the government set up an all-party conference, chaired by the speaker of the House of Commons. Its recommendations, published in the following January, included women's suffrage but rejected equal rights, opting instead for the enfranchisement of women who were either themselves 'occupiers' or the 'wives of occupiers' (thereby qualifying as local gov- ernment electors) and, to ensure a substantial male majority in the electorate, the imposition of an age limit, with Parliament deciding whether it be thirty or thirty-five. Suffragists were divided on the proposals, for they were emphatically not what the movement had been demanding ever since its inception in the 1860s – votes for women on the same terms as men – and would exclude the majority of female munitions workers (who would be too young to qualify). Indeed, the suffrage societies spent much time during 1916–17 debating whether to seek adult suffrage or women's suffrage. Eventually, however, virtually all the societies fell in behind Mrs Fawcett and the NUWSS and gave

[92]   Bangor WSS minutes, 7 February, 9 March 1917.
[93]   *CC*, 15 December 1916, 1 June 1917; NUWSS, executive minutes, 1 November 1917.
[94]   *The Vote*, 18, 25 August, 22 September 1916, 6 April 1917.

their acceptance to the recommendations, fearing that rejection would jeopardize women's suffrage altogether: 'we preferred an imperfect Bill which could pass to the most perfect measure in the world which could not', recounted Mrs Fawcett.[95] But acceptance often came amidst scarcely concealed contempt, as in the case of the SWSPU:

> Do not let us imagine too readily that the battle is won. Even if this unfair dole is ladled out to us, let us take it, bearing in mind that it amounts to an insult. There need be no kow-towing, no bowing and scraping about it. In taking it, we take a small part of what is our just due, wrongfully withheld from us for generations by men. We take it and we demand the rest.[96]

In March 1918, a deputation representing some twenty-five suffrage societies and other women's organizations personally assured Lloyd George (who had succeeded Asquith as prime minister a few months earlier) of their acceptance of the measure. One of the deputation, a 'Mrs Edwards, speaking on behalf of the women of Wales', extravagantly informed Lloyd George that their hopes centred on him, and that 'if they were successful, the Wales of the future will be cheerier and brighter than the Wales of the past, and that a crown of blessing would be placed on the Prime Minister's head'.[97] Rather less colourfully, local NUWSS branches conveyed the same message by petition.[98]

Lloyd George engineered Cabinet adoption of the entire Speaker's Report as a legislative proposal, and in the subsequent Commons debates on the Representation of the People Bill argued that women's war work had transformed public opinion and the 'devotion, zeal and courage' they had displayed made denial of the franchise an 'outrage ... ungrateful, unjust and inequitable'.[99] The women's suffrage

[95] Millicent Garrett Fawcett, *The Women's Victory and After: Personal Reminiscences, 1911–1918* (London, 1920), 146.

[96] *Suffragette News Sheet*, undated, quoted in *Parl. Deb.*, 5th ser., 93, col. 2217, 22 May 1917.

[97] *CC*, 3 February, 7 April 1917.

[98] See, for example, the memorial to Lloyd George from the Bangor and District WSS. Ibid., 27 April 1917.

[99] *Parl. Deb.*, 5th ser., 92, cols 492–4, 28 March 1917. Frances Stevenson recorded in her diary (2 April 1917): 'He had a tough fight in the Cabinet to get the thing through, as it deals a blow at the Tories. But he and [Arthur] Henderson [the

clause, with an age qualification of thirty, was accepted by the House of Commons in June 1917 and then by the House of Lords the following January. The resistance of many Conservatives, which at one point appeared formidable, fell away dramatically and the suffragist margin of victory at the committee stage in the Commons was overwhelming, 385 votes to 55. Many, concluding that women's suffrage had now become inevitable, no doubt feared retribution by female voters at the next election, while there was also evidence that opinion in the Conservative constituency parties favoured enfranchisement. Moreover, anti-suffragists could console themselves that the women's suffrage measure conceded was fundamentally moderate, leaving large numbers of women, including the more radical elements in all probability, excluded.[100]

The huge suffragist majority in the House of Commons greatly undermined opposition in the Lords, which was now of course the last hope for the 'antis'. Outside Parliament, the organizational structure of the NLOWS had been badly damaged by the war, more seriously than that of the women's suffrage organizations, and was ill prepared to respond to the re-emergence of franchise reform as a political issue in 1916. The agitation eventually mounted was too little and too late. In April 1917 a special league meeting, comprising representatives from sixty branches, registered an 'emphatic protest' against any consideration of women's suffrage by Parliament during the war and two subsequent public meetings in Hyde Park reiterated the message.[101] There was also much condemnation of suffragists, and the NUWSS in particular, for

Labour Party leader] arranged things between them before the Cabinet meeting, "You do the heavy truculent working man", said D. to Henderson, "& then I will do my bit & we will see if we cannot manage it together." And Henderson did.' Taylor (ed.), *Lloyd George*, 148.

[100] See Martin Pugh, 'Politicians and the woman's vote, 1914–1918', *History*, 59, (1974), 366–71; idem, *Electoral Reform in War and Peace, 1906–18* (London, 1978), 148–51; David H. Close, 'The collapse of resistance to democracy: Conservatives, adult suffrage and second chamber reform, 1911–1928', *Historical Journal*, 20, 4 (1977), 904–5; Harold L. Smith, *The British Women's Suffrage Campaign, 1866–1928* (London, 1998), 65–8. None of Wales's MPs voted against the women suffrage clause of the bill either on its second reading or at the committee stage.

[101] *ASR*, May, July 1917. There was no representation at the meeting from Wales, where NLOWS branches now seem to have been non-existent.

violating 'the political truce' and for 'driving the nation into a bitter controversy when all attention ought to be concentrated on the war'.[102] A formal letter of protest from the NLOWS had been sent to MPs and peers and to the press making this point in late 1916. Further letters and statements were circulated in national and provincial newspapers during 1917 and efforts were made to stir local branches into action. In the last few months before defeat, Mary Ward led a more vigorous and determined campaign, launching a Women's Memorial to the House of Lords, signed by over 2,000 women, and using the *Anti-Suffrage Review* and the wider press to reiterate long-standing anti-suffragist arguments.[103] Essentially, however, the league failed to mount any effective campaign in the face of political developments. 'One curious feature' [of the situation regarding women's suffrage], observed Sir Alfred Mond in June, 'is that there is no opposition, and has been no opposition of a vocal kind of any substance throughout the length and breadth of the country'.[104]

Concerted resistance in the upper chamber rested to a large degree upon the shoulders of Lord Curzon, leader of the House of Lords and president of the NLOWS. In the critical committee stage debate in January 1918 he delivered a long, powerful speech, rehearsing a catalogue of long-established arguments to denounce women's suffrage as 'a vast, incalculable, almost catastrophic change'. Then, remarkably, in concluding, he announced that, regardless of personal opinion, his responsibility as a Cabinet minister dictated that he must abstain in the division for fear of a dangerous clash with the Commons and advised fellow peers to do likewise. The women's suffrage clause subsequently passed through the Lords by the unexpectedly large majority of 134 votes to 71; much of the league's disappointment as it now moved towards dissolution expressed itself in bitter recrimination at Curzon's conduct.[105]

---

[102] Ibid., April, May 1917.

[103] See Bush, *Women Against the Vote*, 281–5; Harrison, *Separate Spheres*, 202–3, 209–10, 214–15; Riley, 'Opposition to women's suffrage', 155–6.

[104] *Parl Deb.*, 5th ser., 94, col. 1715, 19 June 1917.

[105] Harrison, *Separate Spheres*, 218–23; Bush, *Women Against the Vote*, 285–7; Pugh, 'Politicians and the woman's vote', 372–3; idem, *Electoral Reform in War and Peace, 1906–18*, 151–3; Riley, 'Opposition to women's suffrage', 98–9, 157–9.

The First World War impacted on the suffrage question in a number of ways. Women's vital contribution to the war effort as munitions workers and in other roles won universal recognition, accelerated social change, made female involvement in the public sphere appear less threatening and shifted opinion in favour of enfranchisement. 'It is idle to deny that the part played by women since the War began has profoundly affected public opinion in regard to their claims', wrote Winifred Coombe Tennant. 'It has brought sight to eyes that were blind and hearing to ears that were deaf.'[106] In a very different way, the uncompromising jingoism of the WSPU leadership won acclaim for women. Welcoming Christabel Pankhurst to Cardiff in the summer of 1918, for example, the *Western Mail* stressed that she and the Women's Party had 'done yeoman service to Great Britain during the war', especially in tackling industrial unrest.[107] The conflict certainly undermined some of the traditional arguments of the 'antis'. Thus, to Sir Alfred Mond, their most forceful contention that 'in a state of war women would not count, and men alone would be the deciding factor, had become a broken reed in their hands'. As an advocate of 'an act of justice long deferred', his reasons had simply 'become stronger and emphasized and more clearly silhouetted against the political sky than they were in peace time'. At the same time, he was witness to 'the striking change of the somewhat remarkable conversions which we see both in the House and outside it' and could delight in opponents 'having to assume the white sheet of repentance'.[108]

More important than the war's effect on 'anti' arguments was its transformation of the political situation and the removal of the main barriers to women's suffrage that were present prior to 1914. In the first place, franchise reform was taken up by the government in 1916 because of the need to revise the electoral register and to include servicemen on it; the opportunity was thus created for the promotion of the claims of women by supporters both inside and outside Parliament. Moreover, the crisis of war brought significant

---

[106] *Welsh Outlook*, December 1916.
[107] *WM*, 6 July 1918.
[108] *Parl Deb.*, 5th ser., 94, cols 1711–16, 19 June 1917.

political change, first in May 1915 with the creation of a coalition ministry and then, in December 1916, the replacement of Asquith, who had proved a major obstacle to women's enfranchisement, as prime minister by Lloyd George, who had consistently supported the demand in principle, if not the specific bills themselves. For years, women's suffrage had been dogged by party conflict over the precise terms of the legislation; there was now far greater scope for compromise and agreement. The coalition also greatly increased Labour Party influence and, in particular, brought its leader, Arthur Henderson, a committed suffragist, into Lloyd George's War Cabinet. Other ministerial changes during the war years, such as the removal of the anti-suffragist Reginald McKenna, were beneficial to the cause; even the elevation of Lord Curzon to the Cabinet placed constraints on his opposition to women's suffrage.

The campaigns of the suffrage societies prior to 1914 had thoroughly prepared the ground for enfranchisement. Their conduct during the war helped to secure it. At a national and local level, suffragists organized and undertook war-related work, thereby favourably influencing opinion. At the same time, some societies determinedly kept 'the suffrage flag flying' and, when franchise reform returned to the political agenda in 1916, these bodies, reinforced and spearheaded by a reinvigorated NUWSS, pressed for the inclusion of women in any new legislation. In addition, of course, the outbreak of war brought the cessation of suffragette militancy, which allowed politicians a means of dignified retreat. As the most important of such 'converts', Asquith pointed out in 1917:

> since the War began, now nearly three years ago, we have had no recurrence of that detestable campaign which disfigured the annals of political agitation in this country, and no one can now contend that we are yielding to violence what we refused to concede to argument.[109]

Some politicians may well have been influenced too by fear of renewed suffragette militancy at the end of the war, in a context of widespread working-class discontent and dangerous social unrest.[110]

---

[109] Ibid., 92, col. 470, 28 March 1917.
[110] See Harrison, *Separate Spheres*, 220–1. A letter from the IWSPU to the

The Representation of the People Act of 1918 gave the parliamentary franchise to women aged thirty and over who were local government electors or were the wives of such and university graduates could vote in university seats. Thus, after more than half a century of campaigning, the principle of women's suffrage had finally been established. At the same time, since the legislation enfranchised men at the age of twenty-one (indeed, nineteen if they had served in the armed forces), the legislation fell far short of equal suffrage. Ironically, the three million women between the ages of twenty-one and thirty excluded from the franchise largely comprised those whom the government had so handsomely applauded for their contribution to the war effort. Nevertheless, for politicians, the 1918 Act, making women less than 40 per cent of the electorate was a 'suitable compromise', a resolution that avoided 'the great danger' of adult suffrage whereby men would be outnumbered by some two million.[111] Moreover, it excluded young, often single, women in their twenties who were believed to be most susceptible to radical and feminist causes, whereas those over the age of thirty were likely to be married, have children and be mature and 'responsible'. The government estimated that the provision would add about six million voters to the register, of whom five million would be married women. The Welsh electorate expanded from about 430,000 to over 1,172,000, an increase of some 173 per cent.[112]

Speaker's Conference ended by warning the government to be 'fully alive to the consequences likely to follow any alteration of the franchise which ignores the claims of women'. *Independent Suffragette*, February 1917. Margaret Mackworth was later to argue that women had been enfranchised not 'as a reward for their magnificent war work' but because 'the Government and the country knew that if they did not get it, the end of the war meant a renewal of militant methods'. Rhondda, 'The political awakening of women', 563.

[111] See, for example, the speech of the Conservative member for Denbigh Boroughs, Colonel William Ormsby-Gore, *Parl. Deb.*, 5th ser., 94, cols 1839–41, 20 June 1917.

[112] Ibid., 5th ser., 93, col. 2135, 22 May 1917.

VII

THE CAMPAIGN FOR EQUAL SUFFRAGE, 1918–1928

'Self and several members of Staff voted', routinely recorded Mary Collin, headmistress of Cardiff High School for Girls, in her diary for 14 December 1918. In reality, this simple note masked both her 'rejoicing of this great change' and her personal sense of triumph, having been the first 'chairman' of the Cardiff and District Women's Suffrage Society (CDWSS), in which a number of her staff and past students had also been very active.[1] In keeping with such sentiments, the various suffrage societies commemorated enactment of the 1918 Representation of the People Bill with celebratory meetings, dinners and thanksgiving services in London, while provincial activists organized local and regional events. In Swansea, the town's main women's organizations came together in a 'mass meeting', to herald 'one of the greatest of Reform Bills ever passed' and the dawn of 'the new era in politics'.[2] In south-east Wales, the CDWSS, backed by the South Wales and Monmouthshire Federation of the NUWSS (SWF), invited Millicent Fawcett to 'honour the passing of the Act'. Formally welcomed at the railway station by the lord mayor, she was escorted to a civic reception before appearing as the principal speaker at a large public meeting attended by suffragists from across south Wales. The following morning, as the train carrying Mrs Fawcett passed through Newport, officials of the local National Union of Women's Suffrage Societies (NUWSS) branch formally expressed its 'appreciation of fifty years' work for the admission of women to citizenship' and presented her with flowers.[3]

[1] Catherine Carr, *The Spinning Wheel: City of Cardiff High School for Girls, 1895–1955* (Cardiff, 1955), 71, 192–8. For Mary Collin, see Deirdre Beddoe, 'Collin, Mary (1860–1955)', *ODNB*.

[2] *The Vote*, 5 April 1918; *Cambria Daily Leader*, 11 April 1918; *SWDP*, 11 April 1918; *Cambrian*, 12 April 1918; *Swansea and Glamorgan Herald*, 13 April 1918; *Herald of Wales*, 13 April 1918. For London commemorations, see *CC*, 25 January, 15 February, 22 March 1918; *VW*, February 1918; *The Vote*, 1 March 1918; *Britannia*, 22 March 1918.

[3] *CC*, 12, 19 July 1918; *WM*, 5, 6 July 1918; *SWDN*, 6 July 1918; *South Wales Argus*,

Speakers at the celebratory gatherings invariably reflected on the struggles of a marathon campaign and also appealed for women to use their newly acquired 'power and responsibility' to help transform society. Many suffragists, however, felt mixed emotions, triumph and aspiration mingling with a sense of disenchantment. Overshadowing everything of course was the continuing horror of war, but there was also the inescapable recognition that only partial success had been achieved. 'Let there be no abject expressions of fulsome gratitude', fumed Alice Abadam. For, amidst the joy of 'a famous victory so long and ardently fought for', she detected 'a sullen anger' at the restrictions. Most obviously, there was 'the absurdity' of the age qualification of thirty and accompanying this was the 'mere coverture vote': 'Out of the six millions of woman voters some five millions vote not by their own right, but in virtue of their husbands . . . To women of any spirit this condition for qualification of the vast majority could not possibly have been more distasteful.'[4] Elizabeth Andrews, who became the Labour Party's first women's organizer for Wales in 1919, wrote of the 'insult to our womanhood that we got Votes because we are **married to men**, not because we are intelligent human beings and citizens'.[5] In total, three million adult women aged under thirty remained unenfranchised, while a variety of restrictions excluded another two million over thirty.

The widespread discontent with the terms of enfranchisement ensured the continuance of the campaign. The immediate focus during the course of 1918, however, was the right of women to stand as parliamentary candidates, a demand expressed, for example, at the joint suffrage societies' celebration in Swansea in April. The issue was debated in the House

6 July 1918; NUSEC, *Annual Report*, 1918, 52. Christabel Pankhurst also spoke in Cardiff that same weekend, once again warning against pacifists and Bolsheviks – 'the poisonous intrigues of a mischievous minority' – and emphasizing the Women's Party's support for the imposition of a harsh peace on Germany. *WM*, 6, 8 July 1918.

[4] Abadam, *Feminist Vote*, 2–3. 'A partial prejudiced franchise', wrote Sylvia Pankhurst, 'extended to women, not graciously, but in a grudging spirit.' *Woman's Dreadnought*, 16 February 1918.

[5] *Colliery Workers' Magazine*, May 1927, in Elizabeth Andrews, *A Woman's Work Is Never Done* (Dinas Powys, 2006, repr. ed. by Ursula Masson), 102.

of Commons in October and a bill admitting women (over the age of twenty-one) as MPs was passed the following month, three weeks before the date of the first post-war general election.

Seventeen women stood in that election, among them were a number of leading suffragists, including Christabel Pankhurst, Charlotte Despard and Emmeline Pethick-Lawrence. The one success was Constance Markiewicz who was returned as a Sinn Fein MP in Dublin. Formerly active in the women's suffrage campaign in Ireland, she had become increasingly drawn into the nationalist movement. In prison at the time for her republican activities and, like all the other Sinn Fein MPs, refusing to recognize the Westminster parliament, she never took her seat in the House of Commons. The first woman to do so was Nancy Astor, who became Conservative MP for Plymouth in December 1919 following her husband's elevation to the peerage.

There was one female candidature in Wales, Millicent Mackenzie, a former professor of education at the University College of South Wales and Monmouthshire, Cardiff, who was resoundingly defeated in the newly created University of Wales seat. A vice-president of the CDWSS, she stood as a Labour candidate against the highly experienced Coalition Liberal, Sir Herbert Lewis, formerly member for Flint Boroughs (1892–1906) and Flintshire (1906–18) and a government minister, in order to 'emphasise the importance of the part that should be played by women in national affairs'.[6]

Among the women candidates in English constituencies was the prominent Swansea suffragist, Emily Phipps, who was still a headmistress in the town. Standing as a 'progressive independent' in Chelsea, on behalf of the National Federation of Women Teachers (NFWT) and backed by the Women's Freedom League (WFL), she strongly supported the popular demand for harsh punishment of Germany and the Kaiser for a 'deliberately planned' war and specifically appealed to women voters by calling for better housing, pensions for deserted or widowed mothers, child benefits, equal pay and

---

[6] H. M. Mackenzie (ed.), *John Stuart Mackenzie* (London, 1936), 116. She obtained 176 votes, 19.2 per cent of the poll. For Millicent Mackenzie, see also *Dictionary of Twentieth-Century British Philosophers*, vol. 2 (Bristol, 2005), 616–17.

equal legal rights. She vigorously threw herself into a 'fast and furious' campaign:

> Miss Phipps sweeps through artistic and industrial Chelsea like a whirl-wind. She speaks incessantly. She holds meetings for men only, meetings for women only, and meetings for both. She visits women voters in their homes. Her supporters patrol the streets with sandwich boards, after the manner of Suffragette days.[7]

Nevertheless, in her own words, she shared 'the general debacle' of women candidates and, in a two-way contest with the Conservative candidate, Sir Samuel Hoare, obtained just 2,419 votes, 21 per cent of the poll.

Eight women stood for Welsh constituencies in the next four general elections, in the last of which, in 1929, Wales's first female MP was returned, Megan Lloyd George, the former premier's youngest daughter being elected Liberal member for Anglesey. During the 1920s a number of suffrage activists in Wales contested parliamentary seats – Dr Olive Wheeler, as Labour candidate for the University of Wales in 1922, and, for English constituencies, Winifred Coombe Tennant (Liberal, Forest of Dean, 1922), Minnie Pallister (Labour, Bourne-mouth, 1923 and 1924), and Edith Picton-Turbervill (Labour, North Islington, 1922; Stroud, 1924; and, successfully, the Wrekin division of Shropshire, 1929).[8]

The 1920s saw a considerable widening of the objectives of the women's movement as a proliferation of organizations spearheaded a diversity of campaigns on such issues as women's employment, equal pay, an equal moral standard and the rights of married women. There was much debate on priorities and policies, and an ideological divergence emerged between 'old' or 'equality' feminists and 'new' (welfare) feminists, with the issues of birth control, family allowances and protective legislation (for women only) proving particularly divisive.[9] The disagreements, tensions and divisions of the decade, however,

---

[7] Phipps, *History of the NUWT*, 52–3; idem, *Englishwoman*, February 1919; *SWDP*, 5 December 1918; *Daily Mail*, 4 December 1918; Kean, *Deeds Not Words*, 88–9.

[8] See John B. Thomas, 'Wheeler, Dame Olive Annie (1886–1963)', *ODNB*; Deirdre Beddoe, 'Tennant, Winifred Margaret Coombe (1874–1956)', *ODNB*; Susan Pedersen, 'Turbervill, Edith Picton- (1872–1960), *ODNB*. For Minnie Pallister, see *The Vote*, 6 July 1923.

[9] For a full discussion of old and new feminism, see Harold L. Smith, 'British

should not conceal the degree of common ground among activists, and nowhere was this more evident than in the campaign for equal suffrage, where there was certainly unanimity of purpose, if not always of method.

Equal franchise, when it was finally attained in 1928, did not arrive simply as a matter of course. Rather, it was secured only after a continuous campaign of organized pressure spanning a decade, encompassing non-party feminist societies and women's organizations within the political parties. The former continued to direct and drive the agitation, which, while lacking the drama and spectacle of the Edwardian era, was nonetheless vigorous, especially in the latter stages. In 1919, in order to reflect a broader programme designed to widen its support, the NUWSS renamed itself the National Union of Societies for Equal Citizenship (NUSEC). With a 'special committee' in place from 1921 to focus on the matter, equal franchise continued to be the first item on its agenda, as it was of the other two main surviving societies of the pre-war movement, the WFL and the St Joan's Social and Political Alliance (previously the Catholic Women's Suffrage Society). New groups appeared early in the decade, most notably the Consultative Committee of Women's Organisations and the Six Point Group (SPG), both of which were established in 1921. Lady Astor initiated the former to coordinate the work of the women's societies on a range of demands, including equal franchise, while Margaret Rhondda (the former Margaret Mackworth, who had become second Viscountess Rhondda, as heir to her father's title, in 1918) founded the latter.[10]

Having been active in the Edwardian suffrage campaign, Margaret Rhondda emerged as one of Britain's leading feminists in the interwar years, establishing a number of women's organizations and pressure groups (including the Women's Industrial League, the Open Door Council and the Equal Political Rights Campaign Committee (EPRCC)) and

feminism in the 1920s', in idem (ed.), *British Feminism in the Twentieth Century* (Cheltenham, 1990), 47–65; Johanna Alberti, *Beyond Suffrage: Feminists in War and Peace* (London, 1989), 164–90; Law, *Suffrage and Power*, 161–77; Pugh, *Women and the Women's Movement*, 235–43.

[10] For the Consultative Committee, see Pugh, *Women and the Women's Movement*, 70–1.

launching an influential feminist journal, *Time and Tide*, in 1920. She also conducted a personal campaign to try to gain entry into the House of Lords, in an unsuccessful attempt to overturn a 1922 ruling against the admission of women. Focusing on a broad range of social reforms, the objectives of the SPG emphatically reflected Margaret Rhondda's position as a champion of 'old feminism'; nevertheless, equal franchise was not given a prominent place on its platform until a revision of its programme in 1926, whereupon the organization played a leading role in pressurizing the government into delivering suffrage legislation.

Of the very large number of organizations that actively supported the equal suffrage campaign in the 1920s, only the NUSEC, the WFL and the National Union of Women Teachers (NUWT), as the NFWT became in 1920, drew Welsh localities into the agitation. The SPG was always a small organization, whose activities were largely confined to London, where Margaret Rhondda herself spent most of her time. It attracted individuals and groups from around the country, including a small number from Wales, but made no effort to create branch societies.

In Wales, as elsewhere in Britain, many local women's suffrage societies folded amidst the adversities of war. Others discontinued their operations once the principle of women's enfranchisement had been established in 1918. The Llangollen WSS, having waged an active campaign from its inception in April 1910, held its last committee and annual general meeting in December 1918 and resolved thus:

> This society rejoicing in the success that has attended its efforts has decided to wind up its affairs and recommends its members to join the National Council for Women; that the funds in hand be given to the Central Fund of the NUWSS; that the Library after certain deductions be given to the Llangollen Free Library; that the banner . . . be given to the National Council.[11]

Others reviewed the situation and revised their future role. Thus, as early as May 1918, the Newport WSS took the lead in

---

[11]   NLW MS 22636, Llangollen WSS minutes, 17 December 1918. (The society had thirty-three subscribers in 1918, four of whom were men.) Llangollen had a branch of the National Council of Women.

bringing other local organizations into a Women Citizens' Association (WCA) in order to reflect more accurately its extended aims and concerns. A similar development occurred in Cricieth, while the Cardiff society simply reconstituted itself in the belief that

> now that a large number of women have been enfranchised, more useful work could be done by the Association which would make a direct appeal to all women citizens, and while carrying on the work of the NUSEC, as an affiliated Association, might devote itself more particularly to matters of local interest.

In Bangor, on the other hand, while giving its backing to the formation of a WCA in the town, the local WSS resolved to 'continue as hitherto working to obtain votes for women on the same terms as they are granted to men'.[12]

Affiliation fees indicate that about a dozen NUWSS branches in Wales survived the war and that this number subsequently dwindled still further, leaving just a handful in the early 1920s. 'The period of recovery [after the war] has been a long and trying one and many of our weaker Societies have succumbed', recorded the *Annual Report* of its successor, the NUSEC, in 1921. After 'a careful survey of the whole country' and 'a drastic revision of our index', the list of local societies numbered 131.[13] In some areas, the formation of WCAs initially caused 'a serious depletion in the ranks of Suffragists', with the same work being 'done by the citizens as was formerly done by the Suffragists, and generally by the same people'. The introduction of an affiliation system by the NUSEC sought to overcome such diffusion of feminist activity and this led to a period of growth. Out of a total of 162 local affiliates in 1924, Wales supplied eight, with those in south Wales organized into an area group.[14]

Most of the societies in Wales were WCAs and, as such, embraced a broad range of interests. Inevitably, they varied

---

[12]   *CC*, 2 August 1918, 16 January 1920; *Woman's Leader*, 1 April 1921; Glamorgan Record Office, D/DX 158/1, Cardiff and District Society for Equal Citizenship, 17 January 1921; Bangor WSS minutes, 11 April 1918.

[13]   NUSEC, *Annual Report*, 1921, 24.

[14]   Ibid., 1919, 50, and 1924, 27; WL, 2/NSE/E2/1, NUSEC, *Rules and Affiliated Societies, 1924*; *Woman's Leader*, 9 January 1925. The eight societies were at Abertillery, Bangor, Cardiff, Colwyn Bay, Ebbw Vale, Llandudno, Newport and Swansea, plus a 'local correspondent' in Merthyr Tydfil.

considerably in size and energy. Those in Cardiff and Newport were among the national union's strongest and could
be 'confidently relied upon to undertake systematic and
effective propaganda and Parliamentary work'.[15] Cardiff had
400 members in 1922 and Newport over 600. Much of their
activity centred on local issues, including public health and
housing, widows' pensions, prostitution, prison reform, the
dismissal of female teachers on marriage and women police.
The Cardiff association was particularly active in prison work,
organizing weekly classes for female inmates, and in campaigning for women's representation on public bodies, while
Newport members closely monitored court cases, giving
support to women and child offenders. During parliamentary
elections, women's meetings were arranged in the various
constituencies where candidates were questioned on their
views; alternatively deputations waited upon individuals or
sent them questionnaires. Nationally, support was given to
proposed legislation benefiting women, including equal
suffrage bills.

While considerably smaller than the NUSEC, the WFL
retained a network of branches scattered throughout Britain.
Of forty listed in 1919, four were in Wales – Aberdovey,
Cardiff, Montgomery Boroughs and Swansea.[16] While the
first two had disbanded by 1921, Montgomery and Swansea
continued operations throughout the decade and beyond.
Neither the national union nor the league was able to undertake the kind of provincial campaigning that the various
suffrage societies made so common in the pre-war years.
Throughout the 1920s, financial problems meant that the
WFL could afford just one or two paid organizers to cover the
whole country and, much as branches were urged to raise and
send money to headquarters in order to employ more, this
was never forthcoming. In turn, as one local official pointed
out, 'unless we can provide someone who will from time to
time go around and work up interest ... the branches in the
provinces will absolutely die of inanimation'. Visits to Wales
from league representatives were rare during the decade, in

[15]   NUSEC, *Annual Report*, 1921, 24.
[16]   WFL, *Annual Report*, 1915–1919, 47–8. A branch had also been in existence in
Aberystwyth in 1918. *The Vote*, 26 April 1918.

spite of pleas from stalwarts like Alix Clark of Newtown for the national executive somehow to 'get more life and more enthusiasm and more ideas into our branches'.[17]

The league's efforts to launch regional initiatives also came up against the restrictions imposed by authority in many parts of the country, especially in Wales. As Alix Clark, who was invariably prominent in such work, explained to the 1927 annual conference:

> I think it is almost impossible to hold a campaign in Wales ... we are hung up by police ... they allow you to hold public meetings, but in some hole and corner way and it is difficult to get a well attended meeting ... Before the war we had that wonderful battle-cry 'Votes for Women' when people would come out of curiosity, and when Votes for Women was a sensational thing. Then of course we got turned away, but we went to the next corner and the crowd would follow us ... Conditions are quite different now. They won't even allow you to sell your paper on the Promenade [in Aberystwyth]. Before we were allowed the very best place for our meetings, and the same in Rhyl and Llandudno.[18]

The parliamentary vote for women on the same terms as men remained the league's first object, but its broader aim 'to establish equality of rights and opportunities between the sexes and to promote the social and industrial well-being of the community' inevitably led to activity across a broad spectrum. Thus, the first post-war campaign of the Montgomery Boroughs branch in January 1919 involved a series of meetings in various towns focusing on an equal moral standard and protesting 'against any return to state-controlled vice'.[19] Montgomeryshire was one of the WFL's most flourishing outposts during the 1920s, each year its branch carrying out a substantial programme of campaigning and social activities. In March 1922, for example, well over 400 people attended an 'at home' in a Newtown theatre, its walls decorated with the league's colours and displaying topical banners and photographs. As in former days, musical entertainment and refreshment went hand in hand with political speeches, which appealed for support for equal franchise and other legislative

17 WFL, *Annual Report*, 1919, 40, 47.
18 Ibid., 1926, 12.
19 *The Vote*, 10, 31 January 1919.

demands and for the election of women to local public bodies. Opening proceedings, the chairman reminded the audience that 'the Women's Freedom League was the only women's organisation known among them'.[20] The election of branch members as poor law guardians and councillors reinforced this presence. Inevitably, one of those returned was Alix Clark, who proved an industrious and enterprising Newtown guardian, while remaining a vigorous WFL propagandist. In the latter regard, she revived the Aberystwyth summer campaigns in 1919 and 1920, organized regular campaigns at teachers' conferences around the country and, while serving on the national executive committee from 1918 to 1928, headed *The Vote* sales department.

In Swansea, WFL activity revealed a similar mix of local and national matters, and social and fundraising functions. As in mid Wales, the election of women to positions of influence was an important theme. Thus members participated in municipal and parliamentary contests and, in particular, campaigned in support of Leah (Lily) Folland, Liberal candidate in the Gower constituency at the 1923 general election. The branch also took the lead in bringing the town's women's organizations together into a consultative committee in 1925 in order to facilitate concerted action to secure measures of social reform.[21]

The most prominent WFL figures in Swansea were Emily Phipps and Clara Neal, close companions and founder members of the local branch in 1909. In the early 1920s the former remained a secondary school headteacher and very active in the women's movement but was also editor of the *Woman Teacher* and studying to become a barrister; on being called to the bar in 1925 she resigned her teaching post and moved to London to become the standing counsel for the NUWT. The twin causes of equal suffrage and equal status within the teaching profession dominated the whole of her political life. Clara Neal was no less committed, serving on the WFL executive from 1920 to 1930, and, like Emily, holding the office of president of the NUWT. Both certainly made full use of the public platforms provided by the two organizations to press the case for equal franchise. Emily, as editor of the *Woman Teacher* from its inception in 1919 until 1930, also repeatedly used this avenue to urge women teachers throughout the country to support public meetings, demonstrations and other strategies to advance the demand. During the 1920s the NUWT, reaching the peak of its strength with 8,500 members, emerged as a vigorous feminist organization, active across a range of issues and certainly prominent in the franchise campaign, undertaking its own initiatives and also cooperating closely with other societies.[22]

Feminist societies, at a national and local level, were naturally eager to demonstrate support for parliamentary initiatives on equal suffrage. Eight private members' bills were introduced between 1919 and 1928, every year except 1921. Despite strong support in the House of Commons, however, most were blocked by successive governments, which failed to provide sufficient parliamentary time. On each occasion, the NUSEC and the WFL, in particular, but with the backing of a host of other women's organizations, rallied their forces behind the measure, holding meetings in London, arranging deputations and memorials to politicians and attending the House of Commons with 'sandwich-board' parades on relevant days.[23] Locally, societies signed equal suffrage petitions and lobbied MPs; at election times, they pressed candidates to make pronouncements on the issue and to include a commitment in their published addresses. For a number of years, however, the agitation was essentially muted and, while feminist periodicals highlighted the activities, they passed largely unreported in the national press. From 1926 the campaign gathered momentum and the agitation became of a far greater scale and intensity and as a result attracted much wider newspaper coverage and comment, extending to the regional press in Wales.

[22]   See Sarah King, 'Feminists in teaching: the National Union of Women Teachers, 1920–1945', in Martin Lawn and Gerald Grace (eds), *Teachers: The Culture and Politics of Work* (London, 1987), 31–49. The NUWT was affiliated to the SPG, a fellow 'old style', egalitarian feminist organization.

[23]   For details of the various bills and of extra-parliamentary agitation in their support, see Law, *Suffrage and Power*, 185–98, 203–4, 208–18. See also *Equal Franchise, 1918–1928* (NUSEC, 1927).

Five of the equal franchise bills emanated from the Labour Party, acting upon its manifesto pledge at the 1918 general election. In the same vein, changes in its organizational structure sought to embrace the new female electorate. The new constitution of 1918 enabled women to join the party as individual members for the first time and introduced women's sections, the creation of which entailed the dissolution of the Women's Labour League (WLL). The Standing Joint Committee of Industrial Women's Organisations (SJC), which had been established in 1916 and comprised representatives from the main working-class women's organizations, including the Women's Co-operative Guild (WCG) and the WLL, was also now recognized as the Labour Party's Women's Advisory Committee. Committed to equal franchise, the SJC cooperated with the feminist societies in campaigning for the demand from 1919, although by 1926–7 party and class allegiance had greatly undermined gender solidarity.[24]

In the late 1920s, membership of the Labour Party women's sections reached a peak of around 300,000 in almost 2,000 local organizations. Women's sections and area advisory councils were established throughout Wales in the post-war years, bringing large numbers of women into the party and into the political arena for the first time. By 1933, there were 9,160 female members in Wales, 45 per cent of the individual party membership; in Cardiff, three-quarters of party membership in 1930 was female.[25] The principal concerns of Labour women in the interwar years were undoubtedly those most vital to their daily lives: economic and social issues such as maternity, child welfare, health, housing and unemployment. Nevertheless, Labour women certainly gave some attention to the question of their political and legal status, even if, in the words of Elizabeth Andrews, the Labour Party's woman organ-

[24]   See Smith, *British Women's Suffrage Campaign*, 71–4; idem, 'Sex vs. class: British feminists and the Labour movement, 1919–1929', *The Historian*, 47, 1 (1984), 32–3.

[25]   Pugh, *Women and the Women's Movement*, 130–1; Neil Evans and Dot Jones, '"To help forward the great work of humanity": women in the Labour Party in Wales', in Duncan Tanner, Chris Williams and Deian Hopkin (eds), *The Labour Party in Wales, 1900–2000* (Cardiff, 2000), 220–1; Lowri Newman, 'A distinctive brand of politics: women in the south Wales Labour Party, 1918–1939' (M.Phil. thesis, University of Glamorgan, 2003), 31–2; Pat Thane, 'The women of the British Labour Party and feminism, 1906–1945', in Smith, *British Feminism*, 125.

izer for Wales from 1919 to 1948, there was a danger that economic conditions would 'crush' the young married mother 'in body and spirit and make her apathetic to her power through the vote'.[26] When equal franchise bills were debated in parliament, the *Labour Woman* consistently urged women's sections to put pressure on their MPs through letters, resolutions and delegations, something that was evidently enthusiastically undertaken in some Welsh localities. Newport Labour women, for example, sent 'hundreds of messages' of support for the 1924 bill, only for their Conservative member, Reginald Clarry, to vote against.[27]

Significantly, a number of influential Labour women in Wales were long-standing suffragists. Elizabeth Andrews was involved in suffrage activity in the Rhondda in the pre-war years and in the 1920s used her column in the *Colliery Workers' Magazine* to urge women's sections to demand equal franchise; one of the last contributions, entitled 'Votes for Women', was a vigorous advocacy of the case and a rallying cry to ensure that the government carried out its suffrage pledge, 'for **Tory promises are like pie-crusts – made to be broken**':

> Let us therefore do all we can to help our younger women, as well as ourselves, for Political Equality. We can do this by creating public opinion, so that when the Bill is before the House, the House will realize that it must carry it through.[28]

Similarly, Rose Davies, the Aberdare ILP activist, moved in local suffragist circles before the war, and in the 1920s, as a member of the SJC and its spokesperson to women's sections and advisory councils in her region, she stressed 'the necessity for demanding equal suffrage for men and women'.[29] In Swansea, Elizabeth Williams was a founder member of the local WFL branch, as well as being active in a number of

---

[26]   *Labour Woman*, 1 October 1927.

[27]   Ibid., 1 April 1927.

[28]   *Colliery Workers' Magazine*, May 1927. For Elizabeth Andrews, see Ursula Masson and Lowri Newman, 'Andrews, Elizabeth (1882–1960), Labour Party Women's Organiser for Wales', in Keith Gildart, David Howell and Neville Kirk (eds), *Dictionary of Labour Biography*, XI (Basingstoke, 2003), 1–11; Andrews, *A Woman's Work*; Dot Jones, 'Andrews, Elizabeth (1882–1960)', *ODNB*.

[29]   For Rose Davies, see Ursula Masson, 'Davies, Florence Rose (1882–1958), Independent Labour Party activist, Labour alderman', in Gildart, Howell and Kirk, *Dictionary of Labour Biography*, XI, 39–47.

labour organizations, including the WLL, the ILP and, above all, the WCG, becoming its national president in 1918.[30] Winifred Griffiths, then a fledgling local labour activist and newly married to James Griffiths who went on to become an MP and Cabinet minister, chose the franchise as the topic for her first platform speech, at the general election of 1918 in the Llanelli constituency; she herself did not qualify because of the age limit. She recalled the meeting in a small mining village in the Swansea valley:

> It was held in a chapel vestry and my little speech about women's rights, and how unfair it was that we had not got equal voting rights with men, got a rather cold reception. The all male audience obviously had some doubts about even the women over thirty being allowed to vote. They did not seem at all enthusiastic about demanding any more freedom for their women folk.[31]

Given the Labour Party's consistent advocacy of equal franchise and its manifesto commitments, suffragist expectations were inevitably high when it formed its first ministry in 1924. In the event, the government proved distinctly unenthusiastic about implementing its support for the general principle and, although eventually agreeing to adopt the private member's bill then before the House of Commons, it did not allow sufficient time to proceed before its abrupt fall from power after just ten months in office. Feminists were left with a strong sense of betrayal.

In Wales, as elsewhere in Britain, Labour was rapidly superseding the Liberal Party in the 1920s. Labour representation at Westminster rose to twenty-one (out of thirty-six) in the 1923 general election and to twenty-five in 1929, while the number of Liberals fell to eleven and ten respectively. At the same time, the Liberal Party machinery and organization were collapsing in some constituencies, especially in the south Wales coalfield.

---

[30] For 'Mrs David (or H. D.) Williams', as she was most commonly known, see Andrews, *A Woman's Work*, 22; *WM*, 7 January 1932; *South Wales Evening Post*, 3 May 1943; *Herald of Wales*, 8 May 1943. She became Swansea's first woman JP in 1920, while her husband became the town's first Labour MP in 1922.

[31] Winifred Griffiths, *One Woman's Story* (Ferndale, 1979), 75–6, 109–12. As a leading figure in the Ystradgynlais women's section of the Labour Party and a member of the local board of guardians and rural district council in the 1920s, she was brought into close contact with the hardships and priorities of communities, particularly during and after the miners' strike of 1926.

Welsh women's associations certainly struggled in the aftermath of war, though there was a significant revival from the
mid 1920s. Local organizations were reformed and others
invigorated and a Welsh Women's National Liberal Federation,
under the presidency of Dame Margaret Lloyd George, was
launched in November 1926. It was affiliated to the Women's
National Liberal Federation, which always lagged far behind
its Labour and Conservative equivalents (746 branches and
66,200 members in 1924). Nevertheless, it gave its support to a
number of women's issues, including the coordinated equal
franchise campaign of 1926–8, while local associations were
also active on the question, particularly where leading party
activists, such as Charlotte Price White in Bangor and
Professor Barbara Foxley in Cardiff, were staunch suffragists.[32]

Like Labour, the Conservative Party sought to make itself
more accessible to female members by introducing organizational changes in the immediate post-war years. By 1924 the
Women's Unionist Organisation, established six years earlier,
had 4,067 branches and by 1928 female party membership
had grown to one million.[33] Women's annual conferences
debated feminist questions, including equal franchise, and
the Women's Advisory Committee relayed the various views to
government ministers. From the mid 1920s in particular, Lady
Astor sought to mobilize Conservative women to pressure the
leadership into delivering equal suffrage, to which it was now
pledged. The women's section of the Wales and Monmouthshire National Conservative and Unionist Council, with its
own executive and annual conference, was established in 1924
and within a few years this had developed rapidly into a very
significant organization, encompassing many thousands of
members, hundreds of local branches and a central committee
in almost every constituency.[34]

Although it did not appear in the manifesto, in the run-up
to the general election of 1924 the Conservative leader,
Stanley Baldwin, had declared his party in favour of equal
political rights for women, the question of franchise extension

[32]   *Liberal Women's News*, May, December 1926, January, June, September 1927.
See also Pugh, *Women and the Women's Movement*, 139–41.
[33]   Ibid., 62–4, 124–9; Smith, *British Women's Suffrage Campaign*, 71, 74–5.
[34]   *WM*, 19 May 1927; *NWC*, 20 May 1927.

to be settled by an all-party conference on the same lines as the 1916 Speaker's Conference. Following an overwhelming election victory, the Conservative government affirmed this position when another private member's equal franchise bill came before the House of Commons a few months later, while at the same time insisting that it could not deal with the matter immediately.[35]

Continued delay in implementing the equal franchise 'pledge' left the various women's societies impatient and frustrated, and also brought friction over strategy. Most strikingly, Margaret Rhondda and the Six Point Group (SPG) urged more vigorous action. From its inception, this organization had been critical of the reliance on private members' bills, backed by the lobbying of sympathetic MPs and supportive meetings, generally conducted in a low-key fashion. In so doing it implicitly rejected National Union of Societies for Equal Citizenship (NUSEC) tactics as ineffective in much the same manner that the Women's Social and Political Union (WSPU) had dismissed those of the National Union of Women's Suffrage Societies (NUWSS) and its predecessors years earlier:

> Private Bills are apt to absorb the energies of ardent reformers, to keep them happy and quiet and to distract them from what should be the main business of their lives ... making themselves so apparent, and if need be so unpleasant, to the powers that be that they decide to give them what they ask.[36]

This strident approach, insisting that the only route to success was to force the government into introducing a bill, reflected the strong ex-WSPU element in its membership.

From late 1925, Margaret Rhondda determinedly set about invigorating the suffrage campaign. First, she attempted – albeit unsuccessfully – to draw Emmeline Pankhurst back into the movement, 'for the last lap of Equal Suffrage', offering her a salary to work for the SPG. The former suffragette leader's prompt rejection suggested little enthusiasm for the cause.

[35]   *Equal Franchise*, 5–6; Law, *Suffrage and Power*, 203.
[36]   *Time and Tide*, 21 January 1921; 2 March 1923; Cheryl Law, 'The old faith living and the old power there: the movement to extend women's suffrage', in Joannou and Purvis, *Women's Suffrage Movement*, 206; Alberti, *Beyond Suffrage*, 186–7.

'The situation, both international and national, is exceedingly and increasingly serious and alarming', she replied. 'It seems to me undesirable to reopen the franchise agitation in such a world-crisis as this, especially as women have already enough voting power, if effectively employed, to secure the various ends to which the vote is a means.' Undeterred, Viscountess Rhondda pressed on with reviving the suffragette tactic of mass demonstrations in London and sought to rekindle the spirit of militancy. Such a strategy induced tensions within the campaign during 1926–8, as Eleanor Rathbone and the NUSEC continued their judicious lobbying of politicians, their propaganda and meetings around the country, while Lady Astor sought to generate pressure from Conservative women within the party structure and to press ministers privately, convinced that Baldwin would deliver his pledge on franchise reform unless there was a return of suffragette militancy – hence her opposition to bringing Mrs Pankhurst back into the campaign: 'the Government are certain to give equal suffrage without this', she informed Margaret Rhondda.[37]

The first half of 1926 saw a marked increase in suffrage agitation, signalling the start of a vigorous two-and-a-half-year agitation encompassing a very large number of organizations. Each of the principal feminist societies held significant events in London. An intensive winter campaign launched by the NUSEC among its affiliated societies around the country, culminating in a large meeting in London in February, set the momentum. With banners and mottoes, stewards and litera-ture-sellers, 'all', in Emily Phipps's words, was 'reminiscent of the old days when we made up our parties and travelled from all parts of the country to demonstrate at the Albert Hall'.[38] In succeeding months, the SPG held a dinner and reception to celebrate Emmeline Pankhurst's return to Britain after a

[37]   Mrs Pankhurst to Lady Rhondda, 30 November 1925, quoted in Ethel Smyth, *Female Pipings in Eden* (London, 1933), 260; Nancy Astor Papers (Reading University), MS 1416/1/1/261, Margaret Rhondda to Nancy Astor, 5 November 1925; Purvis, *Emmeline Pankhurst*, 338–9; Eoff, *Viscountess Rhondda*, 88–9; Harrison, 'Women's suffrage at Westminster', in Michael Bentley and John Stevenson (eds), *High and Low Politics in Modern Britain* (Oxford, 1983), 119; idem, *Prudent Revolutionaries: Portraits of British Feminists between the Wars* (Oxford, 1987), 75; Smith, *British Women's Suffrage Movement*, 77.
[38]   *Woman Teacher*, 5 March 1926.

seven-year absence and, then, the St Joan's Social and Political Alliance staged a major rally, while the Women's Freedom League (WFL) held regular public meetings.[39] At the same time, the Equal Political Rights Demonstration Committee, initiated and chaired by Margaret Rhondda, busily coordinated arrangements for a mass procession and rally in Hyde Park in July. Employing publicity techniques ranging from street poster parades to decorated motor cars to a preliminary press conference, and supported by some forty women's organizations, this signalled a revival of the old strategy of public display to demand fulfilment of the government's pledge on equal franchise.

Attracting around three and a half thousand marchers, the event was a major publicity success, the national and provincial press giving widespread coverage and portraying it as a rekindling of the spirit of the pre-war era. Typical was the report carried by the *South Wales Echo*:

> The old troublous times of militancy were recalled on Saturday when London saw the first suffrage procession held since the outbreak of war, the object of which was to demand the franchise for women on the same terms as for men. With none but peaceful intentions on this occasion, yet with determination writ plainly on their faces, veterans of the cause assembled on Victoria Embankment near Charing Cross Station. Many of their number, which included such famous suffragettes as Mrs Pankhurst, Mrs Despard, and Dame Millicent Fawcett, wore decorations, including prison badges, depicting a prison grille, and other members carried an historic collection of banners made during and after the active suffrage days.[40]

The report went on to detail the various contingents, including women MPs and candidates, mayors, councillors and JPs, feminist, professional and political societies, the 'under thirties' and groups from overseas. Welsh newspapers gave prominence to the role of Margaret Rhondda, who spoke on one of the fifteen platforms in Hyde Park, and also noted the attendance of her mother, Sybil (Viscountess) Rhondda, who had travelled from Monmouthshire, thereby marking her fourth decade of active involvement in the movement.

---

[39]   *The Vote*, 12 March, 7 May 1926.
[40]   *South Wales Echo*, 5 July 1926.

Speakers from a wide range of organizations tackled the question of political equality from all angles, with proceedings culminating in the passing of two resolutions from each platform, calling for an immediate government measure giving equal franchise at the age of twenty-one and for peeresses in their own right to have a seat, voice and vote in the House of Lords.

Among the organizations most strongly committed to the event was the National Union of Women Teachers (NUWT), whose specially established Demonstration Committee called for as much support as possible from the provinces and ultimately mustered a contingent numbering 700. Cardiff branch members, who travelled by early morning train and returned at midnight, were applauded for displaying 'the real NUWT spirit' and for their striking banner – a red dragon in the centre, daffodils in the corners and, over a rising sun, the motto, 'Deffro, mae'n ddydd' ('Arise, it is day').[41] The union had its own platform in Hyde Park, where Emily Phipps and Clara Neal of Swansea were two of the speakers, while the former gave a great deal of space to the demonstration in the *Woman Teacher.*

In size, the event fell a long way short of the great mass suffrage demonstrations of pre-war years but, as the *Manchester Guardian* pointed out,

> in those days more people were disengaged on Saturday afternoons, free to march in processions or to look on, and there were not the manifold distractions to take them out of London ... And it must be admitted much more enthusiasm was aroused to demand the very first recognition and instalment of a right than can be stirred up to demand its immediate extension.

At the same time, in areas like north and south Wales, public attention in preceding weeks was captured by the General Strike and the continuing miners' dispute and also by the women's peace pilgrimage. Nevertheless, in dramatic style and impact, the suffrage demonstration compared favourably with former occasions, the large banners and countless coloured

---

[41] NUWT, *Annual Report,* 1926, 4; *Woman Teacher,* 2, 9 July 1926. Among other local bodies represented was the Newport and District WCA, also proudly displaying its banner. *South Wales Argus,* 5 July 1926.

pennants, the bands and community singing, the procession of distinctly attired groups and the giant circle of platforms in Hyde Park presenting an impressive spectacle, and one that successfully achieved its chief object, 'proving that organised women will not be content with less than equal political rights nor tolerate delay'. 'An Army with Banners', 'Women's Spirited Call for Equal Suffrage', 'An Imposing London Demonstration' and 'Opening of New Intensive Campaign' ran some of the headlines.[42]

To Margaret Rhondda's *Time and Tide*, the demonstration marked the end of the period of 'political lassitude left by the war years' and 'the beginning of a fresh period of enthusiasm and courage, and the active prosecution of that intensive campaign to which women born to this generation are committed'.[43] Seeking to maintain the impetus thus generated, it was promptly decided to retain the coordinating role of the Demonstration Committee as the reconstituted Equal Political Rights Campaign Committee (EPRCC). The underlying differences which had been laid aside in July 1926, however, now resurfaced, and while the SPG, WFL, NUWT and the St Joan's Alliance supported this development, it was opposed by other bodies, most notably the NUSEC, whose leaders feared that Margaret Rhondda and her allies were hijacking the movement and might adopt damaging militant tactics. Certainly, both the SPG and WFL were making allusions to such action in this period, though it never materialized.

The agitation and pressure for equal franchise were overwhelmingly centred in London but they were supplemented by steady work in the provinces. Everywhere, it was essentially the stalwarts who remained at the heart of the struggle, the task of rousing young recruits to anything like the enthusiasm of the old suffrage days proving impossible. To a large degree, they did so out of principle. Many took the view of Vera Brittain that, for feminists, 'the vote has never been anything other than symbolic. Women still hold political demonstrations because the incompleteness of the English franchise is a

[42]   *Manchester Guardian*, 5 July 1926; *Daily Herald*, 5 July 1926; *The Times*, 5 July 1926; *Morning Post*, 5 July 1926. See also Law, *Suffrage and Power*, 209–13.
[43]   *Time and Tide*, 9 July 1926.

symbol of the incomplete recognition of women as human beings.'[44]

During 1926 the NUSEC and its affiliated societies organized over two hundred meetings nationwide focusing on the question, despite being in the midst of an internal power struggle between 'new feminists' and supporters of equal rights.[45] Cardiff and Newport Women Citizens' Associations, in particular, held public meetings on the suffrage issue, sometimes addressed by national union officers making periodic visits to Wales. In Swansea, WFL members regularly lobbied their MPs, individually and in deputations, when bills came before the House of Commons.[46] South Wales was represented at all the main London demonstrations. In Cardiff and Swansea strong NUWT branches were committed to promoting the cause and worked in cooperation with other local women's organizations. Members everywhere were inundated with circulars from headquarters urging action in every constituency, by convening meetings, using the press and putting pressure on MPs by whatever means – letter, postcard, resolution or deputation. 'Equal franchise', women teachers were told, 'is the key to our complete emancipation and that is why we think it worth while to spend our time, energy and money in trying to secure equal voting rights at the next election. The opportunity is now.'[47]

Equal franchise activity in north Wales was concentrated in Caernarfonshire, especially in the Bangor and Llandudno areas, both of which had provided strong support for the pre-war suffrage campaign. Both towns had branches of the

---

[44] Ibid., 22 July 1927.

[45] *Equal Franchise*, 6. Victory for the 'new feminists' led to a serious split in the NUSEC with the resignation of eleven executive members and also a great deal of deliberation among its local societies. A move by the Cardiff WCA to disaffiliate, for example, was averted only by assurances of considerable autonomy, though this did not prevent some rank-and-file resignations. Glamorgan Record Office, Cardiff WCA minutes, 10 May, 10 September 1926; Pugh, *Women and the Women's Movement*, 238–9.

[46] *Woman's Leader*, 15 May, 18 December 1925; 7 May, 3 December 1926; 20 May 1927; NUSEC, *Annual Report*, 1927, 33; WFL, *Annual Report*, 1927, 21–2; *WM*, 23 November 1926; *SWDN*, 23 November 1926; *Woman Teacher*, 3 December 1926, 20 May 1927.

[47] Institute of Education, NUWT Archive, Box 522, undated circular (autumn 1926). There were NUWT members across south Wales, though only a handful of branches.

NUSEC, which promoted the cause of equal franchise during 1927–8 by holding public meetings and lobbying local MPs. In the latter regard, a deputation of nine women from across the Caernarfon Boroughs constituency, representing a range of organizations including the Bangor and Llandudno Societies for Equal Citizenship, the Bangor branch of the National Council of Women, the Bangor Women's Liberal Association (WLA) and the Welsh Women's National Liberal Federation, waited upon Lloyd George in April 1927. He was urged to support personally equal suffrage at twenty-one and 'to use his great influence with the Liberal Party [of which he was leader] in favour of such a measure and against any complicating amendment to alter the age or to introduce other electoral reforms'.[48]

The delegation's chief spokeswomen were Charlotte Price White of Bangor and Gwladys Thoday of Llanfairfechan. The former had been the leading figure in the Bangor NUWSS branch and was now secretary of the city's WLA and president of its National Council of Women organization (as well as being a councillor). The latter, having been the 'local correspondent' of the NUSEC, was largely responsible for the formation of its Bangor and District branch in 1927. Highly educated herself, with a master's degree, she was married to the university's professor of botany. Both Charlotte Price White and Gwladys Thoday were also key initiators in the development of a vigorous women's peace movement in north Wales during the interwar years. This originated in local participation in the Peacemakers' Pilgrimage of late May–early June 1926, which to a large degree replicated the NUWSS enterprise of 1913. The link between peace and suffrage activism was clearly strong and indeed the Bangor NUSEC branch became a constituent of the Women's Peace Council. Suffrage activists gave ardent support to the pilgrimage, which generated fifteen major meetings and sixteen processions across north Wales in five days. In south Wales, too, the event aroused considerable enthusiasm as pilgrims set off from Cardiff, the culmination being a mass

---

[48]   NUSEC, *Annual Report*, 1927, 33; *NWC*, 22 April 1927. See also *CDH*, 22 April 1927; *Woman's Leader*, 17 December 1926, 29 April, 13, 20 May 1927.

rally in Hyde Park calling for international arbitration and conciliation rather than armed conflict. The whole enterprise also provided excellent opportunities for propaganda on equal suffrage and many speakers took the opportunity to promote the claims of unenfranchised women to have a share in national decisions relating to war and peace.[49]

As the campaign of meetings and lobbying continued throughout 1926 and 1927, the debate within the Conservative Party was played to a conclusion. Both male and female members were divided on the issue. The 1926 annual conference of the Women's Unionist Organisation defeated a motion calling for equal franchise at the age of twenty-one in favour of one at twenty-five. So too in Wales, when 300 delegates of the women's section of the Wales and Monmouthshire Unionist Council met at Llandrindod Wells in September. An overwhelming majority rejected the mover's argument that 'modern girls . . . in spite of their frivolity, short skirts and shingles, had in them that sense of patriotism and spirit of good citizenship that were inherent in every Britisher' and resolved that the age for equal franchise should be twenty-five.[50] Whether favouring twenty-one or twenty-five, or simply removing the property qualification ineligibilities for all over thirty, Conservative women were in general agreement that the government had made a promise to deal with the subject and, in the words of Lady Elveden of the party's Women's Advisory Committee, 'it will be very disastrous if the Prime Minister can be represented at the Election as not having redeemed a Pledge'.[51]

The party leadership faced a number of conflicting considerations. On the one hand, Conservative Central Office warned that equal suffrage at twenty-one would be electorally damaging, fearing that in industrial areas it would create large numbers of Labour voters among working women subject to

[49]   Sydna Ann Williams, '"Law not war – hedd nid cledd": women and the peace movement in north Wales', *Welsh History Review*, 18, 1 (1996), 63–91; *Woman's Leader*, 4, 11, 18 June, 22 October 1926; *Equal Franchise*, 6.

[50]   *WM*, 24 September 1926; *NWC*, 24 September 1926; *Brecon County Times*, 30 September 1926.

[51]   NA, HO 45/13020/474274, Gwendolen Elveden to Colonel Jackson, Conservative and Unionist Central Office, 16 November 1926.

trade union influence, adding that if the age for women's franchise was reduced to twenty-five, 'a large proportion … would be married and, therefore, much less likely to be led astray by extravagant theories'.[52] At the same time, it recognized that there were the practical difficulties of implementing such a solution, which would involve disfranchising, and thereby antagonizing, younger male voters, while also failing to satisfy female demands. Moreover, if the Conservatives did not grant equal franchise at twenty-one, then the next Labour government almost certainly would and would subsequently reap the electoral rewards.

Equalization of the franchise did not appear in the King's Speech of February 1927, but the following month the prime minister, Stanley Baldwin, met a deputation organized by the EPRCC and representative of fifty-six women's societies, including, most importantly, the NUSEC. The early months of the year saw intense behind-the-scenes lobbying of government ministers, by personal interview, telephone and written communication, backed by articles and letters to the press and the courting of editors, all designed to bring as much pressure as possible on Baldwin to implement his pledge.[53] In April the Cabinet reached a final decision: legislation granting equal franchise at the age of twenty-one during the next parliamentary session, without a preliminary all-party conference – a very clear majority prevailing over the forceful opposition of Winston Churchill and Lord Birkenhead, and in the face of considerable backbench hostility.[54]

Public announcement of the government's intentions produced a storm of condemnation from sections of the press. To the fore was the *Daily Mail,* the country's biggest circulation newspaper, which conducted a vehement and unrelenting campaign against 'the flapper vote folly', misleadingly portraying the proposed legislation as extending the franchise to 'girls' who were single, unreliable, irresponsible, immoral and politically ignorant. Wide-ranging criticism of the contemporary young woman, the so-called 'flapper', was

[52]   Smith, *British Women's Suffrage Campaign,* 78, 102 -3, memorandum to the Cabinet Equal Franchise Committee, 21 February 1927.

[53]   *Equal Franchise,* 6–8.

[54]   Close, 'The collapse of resistance to democracy', 914–17.

accompanied by the supposed effects of creating a female majority in the electorate, which would transfer political power to the female sex, threaten the very fabric of society and leave the British empire in ruins. Running alongside the anti-feminism of the *Mail*'s attacks was a fierce anti-socialism and the conviction that young women would vote overwhelmingly for the Labour Party and place it in power for many years.[55]

Echoes of this rhetoric can certainly be found in the Welsh press. 'Votes for 5,000,000 Girls of 21' ran the *North Wales Chronicle* headline.[56] The *Monmouthshire Beacon* evidently delighted in a frivolous depiction of young women to accompany its disapproval of 'the Flapper Bill':

> why should our attractive 'flappers' be called upon to worry themselves about what few of them, quite pardonably, do not understand? Why interfere with the grave reflections that centre around their selection of a new hat, or the consideration of how far they may go as regards the length, or otherwise, of their dainty frocks? These and many other – foibles if you like – are, after all, excusable, and more in harmony with their years than high and dry politics![57]

The *Western Mail* found 'no indication whatever that our young womenfolk ... are abating their interest in sport and amusement, romance and home-making, in order to devote their leisure to political activity circles'.[58] Other commentators adopted a much more measured tone but were nevertheless deeply uncomfortable about the enfranchisement of young women. To the *Merthyr Express*, the vote was being granted to 'hundreds of thousands who have never given a thought to politics, and until they have had some instruction will be muddled', while the *North Wales Observer* opposed franchise equalization on the basis that 'an interest in politics is on the whole more often found amongst young men than amongst young women'.[59]

---

[55]   See Adrian Bingham, '"Stop the flapper vote folly": Lord Rothermere, the *Daily Mail*, and the equalization of the franchise, 1927–28', *Twentieth Century British History*, 13, 1 (2002), 17–37; Billie Melman, *Women and the Popular Imagination in the Twenties: Flappers and Nymphs* (London, 1988), 27–37; Noreen Branson, *Britain in the 1920s* (London, 1975), 203–4.

[56]   *NWC*, 14 April 1927.

[57]   *Monmouthshire Beacon*, 22 April 1927.

[58]   *WM*, 21 February 1925.

[59]   *Merthyr Express*, 7 July 1928; *North Wales Observer*, 21 April 1927.

In the course of protesting against 'the flapper franchise' as 'a deplorable proposal' put forward 'with reluctance and without unanimity' by the government, the *Western Mail* insisted that there was 'far too much talk of democratic rights, and no corresponding regard paid to the fact that rights carry with them responsibilities, and that responsibilities cannot be discharged without preparation and fitness'. Suffrage extension merely on the basis of equality with men would thus be granting the vote to 'women of a correspon-ding stage of immaturity'.[60] This touched upon one of the prevalent arguments of the later 1920s, namely that an enlarged franchise would accentuate the current defects of democracy. As one speaker to the 1927 Conservative annual conference argued: 'There are too many unintelligent and hopeless electors on the registers already – both men and women – and the adoption of the resolution [women's suffrage at twenty-one] would be an aggravation of an existing evil'.[61] This sentiment contributed to equal franchise at twenty-five gaining such widespread support in both the Conservative and Liberal parties and in the press. To the *Carnarvon and Denbigh Herald*, this would 'protect the State against the immature vote' and, moreover, could be achieved without disfranchising anyone, simply by enacting that no new voters would be added until they were aged twenty-five.[62] After conducting a number of interviews in the area, the Cardiff *Evening Express* concluded that 'prominent women workers, particularly those closely identified with work among young girls, are strongly in favour of equal franchise at the age of 25, deploring the franchise at 21 on the ground that the majority of girls at that age have not thought deeply enough about the subject'.[63]

A great deal of anxiety inevitably surrounded the creation of a female majority in the electorate, which, it was feared, might initiate gender-centred change, while the large numbers of young, single women enfranchised would be

[60] *WM*, 14 April 1927, 21 February 1925.
[61] Ibid., 7 October 1927. See also Close, 'The collapse of resistance to democ-racy', 914.
[62] *CDH*, 22 April 1927.
[63] *Evening Express*, 14 April 1927.

more inclined to feminism than older, married women. 'Two millions of women will be brought to the polls in excess of the number of men, so that is something more than an equalisation of the sexes', declared an indignant *Merthyr Express*. 'When the weaker sex have learnt what the possession of votes for all public bodies may be made to achieve in action', warned the same editorial, 'men will perhaps read, mark, learn and inwardly digest its full interpretation.'[64] To the *North Wales Observer*, the 'magnitude' of the change – a female majority in '70 per cent of the constituencies' – made it 'nothing much short of a revolution in politics'.[65] So, too, the *Monmouthshire Beacon*:

> To add from four to five million women voters to the number on the register – and these, too, mostly inexperienced in their country's needs – is to take a serious plunge into the unknown. It means that women, as voters, will be in a majority. Having regard to what we believe to be the nature of our Flappers' sartorial embellishments at present, it may not, perhaps, be literally correct to say that for the future we shall, politically, be under 'petticoat' government, but, nevertheless, we shall be largely subject to the domination of the 'British Miss'. Is the country prepared to accept this condition of things?[66]

In the face of such concerns, feminists put considerable effort into reassuring opponents that the political divisions among women were as great as those dividing men, insisting that all the evidence since 1918 showed that women would not vote in the same way, against all men.

The *Monmouthshire Beacon* also argued, as had so many anti-suffragists over the decades, that there was no demand for the change, a view expressed most stridently by the *Western Mail*. Inaccurately, it contended that 'there is no organisation of young women which exists to agitate the subject', and it continued thus: 'There never was a more artificial political demand. The Government ... appear to have succumbed without a thought to the wiles of unrepresentative organisations of the feminist type.' Prime Minister Baldwin and the home secretary, Sir William Joynson-Hicks, were singled out as

---

[64]   *Merthyr Express*, 7 July 1928.
[65]   *North Wales Observer*, 21 April 1927.
[66]   *Monmouthshire Beacon*, 22 April 1927.

most culpable. Their pledges, the newspaper insisted, 'were of a vague kind and did not bind the Government to propose a minimum franchise age of 21'. It conceded that there were well-educated and professional women over the age of thirty who were 'deprived of the franchise because they are spinsters and own no furniture in the house where they reside' and that this was an anomaly. 'But the extension of the franchise to them would not entail the folly of granting it down to the age of 21.'[67]

The *South Wales News* accepted that the government's decision was probably arrived at reluctantly but, in contrast to the *Western Mail*, insisted that 'there was no escape from it without violating one of the most explicit pledges given by the Prime Minister at the time of the last General Election'. The newspaper acknowledged that, 'if the issue were an open question and free from established commitments', a strong case could be made out for fixing the voting age for both sexes at twenty-five. But, it went on, in 1918 it was felt that hundreds of thousands of soldiers under that age deserved the franchise and it was not practicable to go back on that decision, and 'logically if a male person of twenty-one years is entitled to vote, it is impossible to resist that demand for a similar concession to females who have reached that age'.[68] While accepting the inevitability of the extension, some observers nevertheless had their criticisms. *Baner ac Amserau Cymru*, for example, drew attention to the additional expense of a greatly enlarged electorate to parliamentary candidates and ratepayers, while *Y Cymro* and *Y Seren* regretted that women's suffrage was not part of wider franchise reform embracing a redistribution of seats and safeguards for minorities through some form of proportional representation.[69]

A number of Welsh newspapers were at pains to emphasize the prejudiced, misleading nature of much of the franchise debate and to negate the impression that the five million women to be enfranchised were 'all cocktail drinking, Charleston dancing flappers of 21', stressing that, aside from

[67]   *WM*, 14 April 1927. See also ibid., 21 February 1925.
[68]   *South Wales News*, 14 April 1927.
[69]   *Baner ac Amserau Cymru*, 21 Ebrill 1927; *Y Cymro*, 20 Ebrill 1927; *Y Seren*, 23 Ebrill 1927.

the two million women over thirty who would now be brought into the electoral system, the majority of the other three million would be well over twenty-one. 'These facts', concluded a number of editorials, 'rather discount the agitation about "flooding" the registers with "flapper" voters.'[70]

At the same time, some of the Welsh press took a generous view of younger women. In the opinion of the *Montgomeryshire Express*, 'much nonsense has been written on the political "flapper", whose modern ideas indicate ... a sprightliness of thinking which we hope will be usefully translated in the domain of affairs'.[71] To the *South Wales Daily Post*, it was

> easy to poke and to riddle with hostile reasons the idea of extending the franchise to young women, but precisely the same arguments apply to the franchise as at present conferred upon males of a considerably maturer age, and many young women of 21 and upwards are just as fit to vote as men of 45 and upwards are unfitted to vote.[72]

The *Cardiff Times* reflected on the post-1918 experience and concluded that 'none of the disquieting effects that were feared are likely to be realised. Women have exercised their rights as intelligently as men.'[73] Thus, extremist contentions about 'the hastening of the downfall of the Empire were mere repetitions of what had been urged on every occasion when the franchise has been extended. And yet the British Empire appears to flourish . . .'[74]

No Welsh newspaper gave fuller support to the bill than the *Carmarthen Journal*. Placing Baldwin in a Tory democratic tradition, the government was, declared an editorial, 'legislating for the happy and rightful conclusion of the chapter in our political history which began to be written when an earlier great Conservative leader, Disraeli, effected his extension of the Franchise' [in 1867]. It went on to recall women's contribution during the First World War:

[70]   *Woman's Leader*, 8 April 1927; *Free Press of Monmouthshire*, 22 April 1927; *County Echo*, 21 April 1927. See also Elizabeth Andrews in the *Colliery Workers' Magazine*, May 1927.
[71]   *Montgomeryshire Express*, 19 April 1927.
[72]   *SWDP*, 23 February 1925.
[73]   *Cardiff Times*, 27 November 1926.
[74]   *Montgomeryshire Express*, 3 April 1928.

when the War came there was an overwhelming demonstration before the eyes of the nation of the part played by women in every phase and sphere and function of the national life. We agree with Mr. Baldwin that to those who saw the part which women played in the War there seems something ridiculous, and we would add ungenerous, in refusing their claim to equal citizenship.[75]

Some Welsh newspapers came out firmly in favour of women's suffrage at twenty-one simply on the basis of 'justice and equality'. Thus, long-standing suffragist arguments continued to be deployed. Large numbers of unenfranchised women paid the full rate of income tax, were subject to laws in which they had no say and made a significant contribution to the country in all sorts of ways, thereby proving their fitness for the vote. 'No woman under 30', observed the *South Wales Argus,* 'be she a wife, a mother of a family, a doctor, a lawyer, a head-mistress of a school, etc., is considered to be a fit and proper person to be entrusted with the vote.' Other newspapers high-lighted the anomaly of denying the vote to women under thirty but allowing a woman of twenty-one to sit and vote in the House of Commons, concluding that 'it would be illogical of Parliament to continue such an absurdity'.[76]

The equal suffrage case was largely based on the principle of equity, but much too was made of the fact that under the present arrangements it was employed women, arguably those most in need of the vote, who were very likely to be unenfran-chised – one estimate was that only about one in fifteen women wage-earners had the right to vote in the 1920s.[77] Women working in industry were invariably young and unmarried and therefore did not meet the age qualification. But there were also the two million women over thirty, especially single professional women renting accommodation, who were disqualified by the technicalities of the 1918 Act. These were precisely those, in the words of Emily Phipps, who were 'in the van of political and social thought', well informed and inde-pendent rather than subject to their husbands' influence.

[75]   *Carmarthen Journal,* 6 April 1928.
[76]   *South Wales Argus,* 5 July 1926; *Free Press of Monmouthshire,* 22 April 1927; *County Echo,* 21 April 1927.
[77]   Eva Hubback, 'The case for equal franchise', *Fortnightly Review,* CCXXIII (1928), 529.

Analysing her own experience and that of other female candidates at the general election of 1918, Miss Phipps insisted that 'the bulk of the women on the register this first time were not the women who had done most in the political world before; they were, to a large extent, merely "voters' wives"'. In response to an NUWT questionnaire seeking to highlight local anomalies and injustices, Clara Neal reported in 1927 that seven lecturers over thirty (plus some younger ones) at the Municipal Training College did not meet the franchise qualifications, nor did the headmistress of Swansea High School and the senior woman doctor at the school clinic, all of whom lived in 'furnished lodgings' (rather than supplying their own possessions); her own sister, a successful business manager and a regular Conservative Party speaker, was in a similar position.[78] The NUWT leadership was in no doubt of the importance of equal franchise:

> Unequal voting rights between men and women of 21–30 place a most formidable handicap on young women in industries and in the professions. Where there is so much competition for attention and fair play, the interests of the voteless women are sacrificed to those of the voting men. If women teachers want equal pay, equal opportunities, equal consideration of their point of view on professional questions, equal chances of appointment to headships of Mixed Schools, etc., etc., the quickest way is to get women enfranchised on the same terms as men.[79]

The exclusion of such professional women enabled campaigners like Emily Phipps to quip that they were 'voteless because they have acquired neither of the two essentials – a piece of furniture or a husband'. Other categories of excluded women over thirty were shop assistants or domestic workers who lived in and daughters living at home.[80] Equal suffrage activists stressed that the concerns of wives and mothers, the principal beneficiaries of the 1918 terms, were often markedly different from those of their invariably employed 'unenfranchised sisters'. The interests of male and female workers sometimes clashed and, in such circumstances, married women were

[78] Institute of Education, NUWT Archive, Box 522, C. Neal to E. Froud, 6 March 1927.
[79] Ibid., undated circular (autumn 1926).
[80] *Englishwoman*, February 1919; *Woman Teacher*, 22 July 1927. For details of the 1918 Act as it related to women, see Law, *Suffrage and Power*, 182–3.

likely to identify with their husbands and sons. Parliament would thus discuss legislation affecting women workers, whose views were inadequately represented.[81]

Welsh members turned out in sizeable numbers to vote for equal suffrage in the parliamentary divisions of the post-war years: nine out of a total of thirty-six in 1920; thirteen in 1922 and 1924; eighteen (plus a teller) in 1928. Just two of Wales's representatives spoke in the various debates – John Hugh Edwards (Coalitionist Liberal MP for Neath) in 1919, and Goronwy Owen (Liberal, Caernarvonshire) in the final debate of 1928, when he simply commended the bill as 'a Measure of justice which has been long delayed', irrespective of the preponderance of female voters being created.[82] To Edwards, women were a stabilizing influence in an age of great industrial unrest, counteracting the revolutionary ideas, 'the rampant Bolshevism' being advocated in some quarters. 'The greatest bulwark you can have against any kind of Bolshevism in the land', he contended, 'was the innate sanity of women.' It was thus 'in the interests of the State itself that women should be admitted into the full exercise of the rights of public life and service'.[83]

No Welsh representative spoke against equal suffrage in the parliamentary debates of 1919–28 and only two of Wales's MPs registered votes in the opposition camp during this period – Leolin Forestier-Walker (Conservative member for Monmouth) in 1922 and Reginald Clarry (Conservative, Newport) in 1924. Indeed, it was Conservatives who provided the bulk of the votes against the equal franchise bills of the period and who demonstrated any resistance to the ultimately successful government measure of 1928, rather than the Liberal and Labour parties.[84]

With continued opposition within the Conservative ranks to equal franchise at twenty-one, and the *Daily Mail* and other newspapers fomenting opinion against reform, the feminist societies kept up the pressure on the government during the

---

[81] *South Wales News*, 14 April 1927. See also Smith, *British Women's Suffrage Campaign*, 70–1, 101, 104.

[82] *Parl. Deb.*, 5th ser., 215, cols 1395–7, 29 March 1928.

[83] Ibid., 114, cols 1598–1602, 4 April 1919.

[84] See Harrison, *Separate Spheres*, 231–2.

summer of 1927, their forces strengthened by the NUSEC's decision to join the EPRCC, though its proviso that it 'need never be committed to any course of action of which it does not approve' indicated continued suspicion of a revival of militant tactics.[85] Weekly open-air suffrage meetings in different locations in the capital, regular poster-parades through the streets, and the systematic lobbying of individual MPs at Westminster culminated in another major rally in July, which was again widely reported by the press around the country.[86] 'No fewer than 35 speakers addressed a mass meeting, described by Viscountess Rhondda, who presided, as "the last great suffragette demonstration that will probably ever be held", in Trafalgar Square, London, on Saturday afternoon', recounted the *South Wales News*. 'Brightly coloured banners of more than 40 organisations decorated the base of the Column, while one of the lions dominating the Square supported a placard bearing the words, "Gentlemen prefer blondes, but blondes prefer the vote".'[87]

Most of those attending were inevitably from London, but Wales was represented among the groups from the provinces. Speakers addressed the crowds from three platforms surrounding the central plinth. Margaret Rhondda, opening proceedings as 'chairman' of the EPRCC, and Emily Phipps, on behalf of the NUWT (which again played a central role in the event), were among the speakers who emphasized 'the necessity for such a demonstration to strengthen the Prime Minister's hand', the latter warning that 'his Party won't let him keep his promise unless a strong demand is shown'. Both also recognized the need to display 'the strong feeling and determination of the big numbers which stand united behind the demand for equal rights at twenty one ... in view of the activities of the stunt press'. As at Hyde Park a year earlier, resolutions were carried calling for the speedy fulfilment of the prime minister's promise and the right of peeresses to sit and vote in the House of Lords.[88]

85 *Woman's Leader*, 10 June 1927.
86 *SPG News Letter*, April/ May, June/ July 1927.
87 *South Wales News*, 18 July 1927.
88 *Woman Teacher*, 22 July 1927; *The Vote*, 22 July 1927; *Time and Tide*, 22 July 1927; *Woman's Leader*, 22 July 1927; *Observer*, 17 July 1927.

In the light of the continued differences within the Conservative Party, its annual conference, held in Cardiff in the autumn of 1927, assumed considerable significance. Here, both the WFL and the NUSEC held meetings and engaged in intense behind-the-scenes activity to secure a favourable decision.[89] As many as four resolutions were submitted in opposition to the central council's proposal of equal franchise at twenty-one, but the outcome was a very decisive victory for the leadership's position. To the *Western Mail*, this was now 'the only one practical settlement', while, as *The Times* explained, 'the delegates evidently felt that the honour of the Prime Minister and his Government were involved. The Prime Minister was "standing to his guns", and his supporters rallied, as they always do rally, to their leader on issues of that kind.'[90] Indeed, in the months following the government's spring announcement, rank-and-file Conservative opinion had swung into line at a succession of provincial conferences. The annual conferences of the Wales and Monmouthshire National Conservative and Unionist Council and its women's section did not even debate the question in Colwyn Bay in May 1927, while the national conference of the Women's Unionist Organisation, meeting a week later and attended by a large number of Welsh delegates, heard complimentary addresses on young women between the ages of twenty-one and twenty-five as a campaign to capture the prospective new voters was inaugurated.[91] Conservative MPs accepted the decision too, many unhappily, some with a display of enthusiasm. Reginald Clarry, the Newport member who had voted against a private member's bill in 1924, announced his 'conversion' in a speech to an equal franchise meeting in the town in February 1928. Partial enfranchisement of women had proved a successful experiment, he argued, and now 'cold, sheer and definite logic' demanded that '"the young ducks" were a section of the community whose presence they should not and could not ignore'.[92]

The first week of February 1928, marking the tenth anniversary of women's enfranchisement and seeing the opening of a

[89]   WFL, *Annual Report*, 1928, 9; *WM*, 5, 8 October 1927.
[90]   *WM*, 7 October 1927; *The Times*, 7 October 1928.
[91]   *WM*, 19, 21, 27 May 1927; *NWC*, 20 May 1927.
[92]   *South Wales Argus*, 7 February 1928.

much anticipated new parliamentary session, brought a burst of suffragist activity. Alongside a celebratory dinner arranged by former militants, and meetings held by various women's organizations, there were even a few escapades reminiscent of 'the old spirit'. On the morning of the King's Speech, the Young Suffragists, a group of under-thirty campaigners, submitted a petition to 10 Downing Street and then sought to enter Buckingham Palace to deliver a letter, while later in the day a parade of motor cars, driven and occupied by women and brightly decorated with posters demanding equal voting rights at twenty-one, boisterously followed a route down Whitehall and round Parliament Square for some two hours.[93]

The prime minister's confirmation that evening that a franchise bill would be forthcoming was promptly welcomed by the twenty-four constituent associations making up the EPRCC, which, taking nothing for granted, also resolved to monitor closely developments during subsequent months. The expected announcement aroused little excitement in the press. To the *South Wales News*, it was 'the only important legislative business on the agenda', but, 'as this is not likely to be contentious, being a fact already accepted by all parties, Parliament should have a nice, quiet, sleepy time ahead'.[94] What negative comment there was echoed the sentiments of the *Merthyr Express*, namely that it was 'keenly disappointing that such a measure should have been given preference to the more urgent need of grappling with the far more serious problems of unemployment and the reduction of rates and taxes'.[95]

By the time the Representation of the People (Equal Franchise) Bill came before the House of Commons in March 1928, the debate had, in the words of the *Western Mail*, 'been fully forestalled and discounted by previous discussions' and there was 'an air of indifference that was astonishing'; the crucial struggle, that within the Conservative Party, had already taken place. A handful of intransigent backbenchers spoke out, but 'the opposition generally appeared to lack spirit as well as hope' and 'the result was a foregone

---

[93]   *The Vote*, 10 February 1928; *WM*, 8 February 1928; *SPG News Letter*, January/ February 1928.
[94]   *South Wales News*, 8 February 1928.
[95]   *Merthyr Express*, 11 February 1928.

conclusion'.[96] Presenting the bill for the government, Sir William Joynson-Hicks estimated that 5.25 million more women would be enfranchised, thereby creating a female majority of two million (52.7 per cent of the total electorate). Of the new voters, roughly a third would be women over thirty, nearly another third married women between twenty-one and thirty, and another 27.5 per cent in the latter age bracket of unmarried women 'earning their own living'.[97] Welsh newspapers published lists of the estimated number of male and female voters in the various constituencies and concluded that the latter would invariably constitute a majority.[98] The bill passed its second reading in the Commons by a huge majority of 387 to 10, though the paltry opposition vote in no way mirrored the extent and depth of anti-feminist sentiment. To the *North Wales Chronicle*, 'the half a dozen stalwart members of the so-called Die Hard variety' who maintained their hostility were voicing 'the views of a very large section of the Conservative Party, who think the policy a mistake, but are accepting the inevitable in loyalty to the Prime Minister'.[99] In all likelihood too, the voting reflected the tactical judgement of MPs who, realizing that the measure was certain to succeed, sought to safeguard their political futures. The bill was duly endorsed in the House of Lords by a majority of 114 to 35. A continuous campaign, stretching back to the presentation of the 'Ladies' Petition' by J. S. Mill sixty-two years earlier, had thus finally reached its conclusion.

[96]   *WM*, 30 March 1928.
[97]   *Parl. Deb.*, 5th ser., 215, col. 1369, 29 March 1928. 'Who is to-day going to object to women over 30, who, under the present franchise, have not the vote, being given it?' asked Joynson-Hicks. 'Who is going to object to married women, who have their responsibilities? Who is going to object to unmarried women who are working and earning their own living side by side with the men in the factories and shops being added to the register?'
[98]   In reality, men remained in a majority in exactly half of the thirty-six Welsh constituencies at the 1929 general election – in the fifteen south Wales coalfield seats, in Swansea East, Wrexham and the University of Wales. The increase in the female electorate in Wales (excluding the university seat) was from 40.4 per cent in 1924 to 49.9 in 1929. For detailed figures on the Equal Franchise Act, see John Graham Jones, 'Wales and the general election of 1929' (MA thesis, University of Wales, 1980), 63–4, appendix G.
[99]   *NWC*, 30 March 1928.

EPILOGUE

'Thus quietly ends a struggle which began over sixty years ago and which in its time of stress between 1905–14, when the real question of victory or defeat was being decided, took its heavy toll from those who shared in it.' So observed Margaret Rhondda's *Time and Tide*, as the Equal Franchise Bill was making its way to the statute book in June 1928. The same issue also recorded the death of Emmeline Pankhurst, 'the woman who more than anyone else in the world was responsible for the victory [the bill] embodies': her funeral occurred on the day of its passage through the final stage in the House of Lords.[1] *Tide and Tide*'s testament chimed with much of the press comment at the time. To the *South Wales Daily Post*, Mrs Pankhurst was 'one of the great political figures of British history ... there is no gainsaying the tremendous change she brought about, nor the courage and energy with which her campaign was pressed'. Recalling 'the whirlwind of furies and termagants' perpetrated by the militant suffragettes, they were rewarded with, and justified by, 'triumphant success'.[2] To the *Western Mail*, Emmeline Pankhurst 'more than any other woman in the country secured the recognition of the right of women to vote' and, in the process, dramatically brought 'her world-famous agitation' to south Wales.[3]

Royal assent to the bill in early July led *Time and Tide* to evaluate responsibility for the success of the campaign, a leading article, entitled 'To the Victors – the Laurels', presenting a suffragette interpretation of events that did scant justice to the non-militants:

> Many people were present in the House of Lords to watch the ceremony. Representatives of almost all the women's organisations of to-day

---

[1] *Time and Tide*, 22 June 1928. Mrs Pankhurst had been present in the ladies' gallery for 'the triumph of her life', the decisive second reading vote in the House of Commons, a few months earlier. *WM*, 30 March 1930.

[2] *SWDP*, 15 June 1928.

[3] *WM*, 15 June 1928.

heard the words *Le Roi le Veult* pronounced in reply to the reading out
of the title of the Representation of the People (Equal Franchise) Act.
But those to whom the passage of the Equal Franchise Bill of 1928, just
as that of 1918 was in reality chiefly due, were not there.

... although in Great Britain, Equal Franchise was given in two
parts, the action of one group was in the final event responsible for the
whole reform – that of the militants whom Mrs Pankhurst led from 1905
to 1914. It was those nine years that won women the franchise. In 1918
the immediate fear of the resumption of militant methods at the end of
the war was – behind the scenes – frankly on men's tongues. And to-day
although militancy ceased many years ago, its memory (as those who
saw the great crowds at Mrs Pankhurst's funeral must have realised) is
still amazingly fresh in men's minds. Those nine years took heavy toll of
the women who fought through them but – they won the vote. . .

It is very easy for the descendants of those who twenty years ago had
not the courage to allow themselves to be thought violent and outrageous, or the insight to realise that the time had come when that
sacrifice was demanded of them, to suggest to-day that it was they, who
through thick and thin remained sweetly reasonable, who *really* won the
vote . . . But the vote was not won by sweet reasonableness, it was won by
self-sacrifice and courage, and – above all – by that most difficult of all
forms of courage, the courage to appear violent, unreasonable, ugly.

... a most effective and necessary piece of work and the one which
probably did much to ensure the granting of the Franchise during this
Parliament was the big Hyde Park Demonstration of 1926, organised by
the Equal Political Rights Campaign Committee, in which practically all
the women's organisations took part. It was effective mainly because –
entirely pacific as it was – dimly, delicately, faintly, it recalled to men's
nostrils the odour of militant days . . .[4]

'[F]ull of suppressions of the truth and suggestions of the
false', was the sharp response of Eleanor Rathbone, president of the National Union of Societies for Equal Citizenship
(NUSEC) (which, along with its predecessor, the National
Union of Women's Suffrage Societies (NUWSS), had not even
rated a mention in the article).[5] Indeed, a few months earlier,
she had told an audience in Newport (which had been a
important Women's Social and Political Union (WSPU)
centre) that 'the votes for women campaign had experienced

[4] *Time and Tide*, 6 July 1928.
[5] Ibid., 20 July 1928.

a chequered career. It was a debatable question whether they gained a great deal in the militant suffrage programme.'[6]

Amidst the equal franchise celebrations, however, she and other constitutionalists gave generous acknowledgement to the very considerable contribution of suffragette militancy to the triumph. In a glowing tribute to Mrs Pankhurst, entitled 'Death of a Hero', the *Woman's Leader*, the successor journal to the NUWSS's *Common Cause*, also provided a balanced assessment of the WSPU, questioning the 'terrorism' element of its multifaceted militancy, but applauding its 'flame of genius for dramatic effect ... the stage management of its vast meetings and processions, the exploitation of its situations', which captured public attention and aroused women's consciousness – 'many a sober-minded suffragist carried to the offices and committee rooms of the constitutional societies fire kindled at the feet of Mrs Pankhurst'. '*Of course militancy helped*', the piece concluded, '*Immeasurably and indespensably.*'[7]

Locally too the note of harmony was evident in the final triumph. In Swansea, all the town's main women's organizations came together in a celebratory Women's Franchise Victory Dinner in October 1928, when members of the Women's Freedom League (WFL), National Union of Women Teachers (NUWT) and NUSEC branches, with the old WSPU stalwart 'General' Flora Drummond as a special guest, spent an evening of convivial reminiscence.[8] Here, the divide between the two wings of the movement had never been significant.

Elsewhere, the competing claims of militant and constitutional suffragists were being vigorously pressed. Within a few

---

[6] *South Wales Argus*, 7 February 1928; *South Wales Weekly Argus*, 11 February 1928.

[7] *Woman's Leader*, 22 June, 6 July 1928. See also ibid., 14 March 1930.

[8] Swansea NUWT branch minutes (Institute of Education, NUWT Archive, DC/UWT/F/12/1/1), 9 July, 24 September, 15 October 1928; *SWDP*, 20 October 1928; *Cambria Daily Leader*, 20 October 1928; *Herald of Wales*, 20, 27 October 1928; *Cambrian*, 19 October 1928; *Woman Teacher*, 26 October 1928; *The Vote*, 26 October 1928. As in 1918, the national campaigning organizations held a series of victory celebrations, to which they invited provincial representatives, while many local societies arranged their own. *Woman's Leader*, 22, 29 June, 6, 13, 27 July, 3 August, 2 November 1928; *The Vote*, 13 July, 3 August, 2 November 1928; *South Wales Weekly Argus*, 14 July 1928; NUSEC, *Annual Report*, 1928, 24.

months of the attainment of equal voting rights, a former NUWSS executive member, Ray Strachey, published the first real attempt to produce a history of the women's suffrage movement. While acknowledging a WSPU contribution, *The Cause* presented both enfranchisement instalments principally as triumphs for constitutional methods. Far more influential was the appearance of Sylvia Pankhurst's *The Suffragette Movement* in 1931, which located the campaign emphatically around the WSPU and the Pankhursts. The initiative had indeed already been seized by this camp with the foundation of the Suffragette Fellowship in 1926, 'to perpetuate the memory of the pioneers and outstanding events connected with women's emancipation and especially with the militant suffrage campaign'. Thereafter, such diehards established a narrative of the suffrage movement focused narrowly on the WSPU's campaign of window smashing, arson, imprisonment and hunger striking (to the exclusion of the WFL's brand of passive resistance militancy). So effectively did they do this that a perception of the whole suffrage movement as the preserve of Emmeline Pankhurst's WSPU dominated both media coverage and historical accounts for several decades. It was not until the final quarter of the twentieth century that the imbalance was redressed and constitutionalists took their rightful place in the historiography of the movement, and there was recognition that the WSPU itself amounted to much more than either militancy or the Pankhursts. The relative importance of militancy and constitutionalism, of the WSPU, the NUWSS and other organizations, continues to be a matter of debate.

Within two years of Mrs Pankhurst's death, the enterprise and perseverance of fellowship members succeeded in erecting a life-size statue to her in Victoria Tower Gardens, in the shadow of the Houses of Parliament; Stanley Baldwin performed the unveiling ceremony before a crowd of several thousand in March 1930, amid much publicity.[9] From the late 1920s until the 1980s, the fellowship organized several

---

[9] *Woman's Leader*, 14 March 1930; *Manchester Guardian*, 6, 7, 8 March 1930; *The Times*, 7 March 1930; *WM*, 7 March 1930; Purvis, *Emmeline Pankhurst*, 356–7; Pugh, *Pankhursts*, 409–11.

commemorative gatherings a year and for much of that time produced a yearly *News Letter* (from 1947 entitled *Calling All Women*), which carried news of women's political progress and, more especially, personal reminiscences, obituaries and reports of memorial events. It also brought together an archive of records and memorabilia, including a prisoners' roll of honour. In addition, a large number of former suffragettes produced autobiographies and, inevitably, the dramatic appeal of militancy drew the attention of journalists, authors and broadcasters.[10]

Several WSPU militants from Wales were prominent in fellowship activities. Margaret Rhondda, who served as treasurer of the Pankhurst Memorial Fund, was one of three speakers at the unveiling ceremony, while the most dedicated of all Welsh suffragettes, Rachel Barrett, played an important role in raising money for this and the other commemorations. According to her obituary, 'the statue to Mrs Pankhurst in Victoria Tower Gardens stands as a permanent memorial to Rachel's organising ability'.[11]

Margaret Rhondda was the only suffrage activist from Wales to publish an autobiography substantially detailing her experiences. Referring exclusively to 'the militant movement' – and not even acknowledging the existence of constitutionalism – she described her political awakening and her subsequent role as Newport branch secretary; hostile public meetings figure prominently and the personal story culminates in lawbreaking, imprisonment and hunger striking. The account concludes with excessive claims for the achievement of the suffragette campaign:

> that militant fight before the war . . . was only ostensibly concerned with changing the law. The vote was really a symbol. And the militant fight itself did more to change the status of women – because it did more to alter our opinion of ourselves – than ever the vote did. In actual fact, in

---

[10] See Laura E. Nym Mayhall, 'Creating the "suffragette spirit": British feminism and the historical imagination', *Women's History Review*, 4, 3 (1995), 319–44; Brian Harrison, 'The act of militancy', in idem, *Peaceable Kingdom: Stability and Change in Modern Britain* (Oxford, 1982), 26–81; idem, *Prudent Revolutionaries*, 320–4; idem, 'Women's suffrage at Westminster', 80–122; Hilda Kean, 'Searching for the past in present defeat: the construction of historical and political identity in British feminism in the 1920s and 1930s', *Women's History Review*, 3, 1 (1994), 57–80.

[11] *Women's Bulletin*, 18 September 1953; Purvis, *Emmeline Pankhurst*, 355.

those years we were changing the attitude of a country – nay, of the world; for in that fight England led the way. The other nations followed after.[12]

Radio and television broadcasts played a major role in crystallizing public memory of the suffrage movement around Emmeline Pankhurst, the WSPU and militancy. One example was the interview given by the former Cardiff suffragette, Edith Lester Jones, on the Welsh Home Service in 1965, when she recounted her memories of more than half a century earlier, including the local 'spadework' of selling newspapers in the streets and organizing meetings, rubbing shoulders with the Pankhursts, and, most particularly, 'doing a pillar box' and 'a little bit of arson'.[13]

The Suffragette Fellowship began the militant monopoly of the history of the movement from the late 1920s onwards. For the majority of campaigners, however, the priority in the immediate aftermath of the 1928 triumph was focusing on the practicalities of future action rather than preoccupation with the past. At a Victory-and-After Luncheon celebration, organized by the Equal Political Rights Campaign Committee (EPRCC) in London in October, and attended by over two hundred suffragists, militant and non-militant, the basis of every speech was that the vote was only the first step towards full equality between men and women; 'victory was the beginning of a fresh struggle for real equality in municipal, national, and international life'. 'I wonder', declared Margaret Rhondda, chairing the gathering, 'how many more generations are going to use up their lives before we can put the whole thing behind us, and forget that there was ever any difference of status, freedom, or opportunity based on the difference in sex.'[14] More specifically, her *Time and Tide* was asking:

---

[12]   Rhondda, *This Was My World*, 118, 299–300.

[13]   *Calling All Women*, February 1966. A drama teacher and actress, Edith Lester Jones became involved in the Actresses' Franchise League when training in London and was then prominent in the Cardiff WSPU on her return home. She was also president of the Cardiff WLA at the time of its split over women's suffrage in 1911. A former pupil of Cardiff High School for Girls, she recounted her suffrage experiences to its sixth form in 1968. Ibid., February 1969.

[14]   *The Vote*, 2 November 1928; *Woman's Leader*, 2 November 1928. The EPRCC continued beyond the achievement of equal franchise, working for equal political rights, equal economic status and an equal moral standard. Operating until at least

What about the exclusion of women from the House of Lords? What about the barring of women from the diplomatic service? What about the dismissal of women on marriage, and equal pay for equal work in the Civil Service? What about the whole body of restrictive legislation? We are a long way from equality of treatment between men and women even so far as actual legal enactments go.[15]

Elsewhere, amid the commemorations of the summer and autumn of 1928, feminists remained well aware of the inequalities that remained. At Swansea's Victory Dinner in October, the prominent Neath suffragist, Winifred Coombe Tennant, reminded her audience: 'We have a long way to go before we get equal citizenship, which is a very different thing from equal voting rights.'[16] Similarly, in October 1928 the South Wales Area Group of Women Citizens' Associations (WCAs) held a conference in Cardiff to consider their future work now that the chief aim of equal franchise had been attained. Attended by members from Aberdare, Abertillery, Ebbw Vale, Cardiff and Newport, the conference went on to focus on the issues of restrictive legislation, married women and paid work, and the responsibilities and opportunities of the new voter.[17]

For all such intent, however, further advance was hesitant. From 1929 onwards women comprised a majority of the British electorate, but the consequent sex division anticipated by many did not follow. Women did not organize themselves into a distinct political party, nor did they act independently of male voters; the *Western Mail* was proved right in its assertion that 'women electors are Conservatives or Liberals or Labourists, they are not feminists'.[18] Women were also slow to win adoption as parliamentary candidates. In Wales, six women had contested seats between 1918 and 1928, ten did so between 1929 and 1939, 1.7 and 3.3 per cent respectively of the total candidatures. Only one was successful, Megan Lloyd George serving as Liberal member for Anglesey from 1929 to

1930, Margaret Rhondda remained 'chairman'. The WSPU and Wales connection was also evident in the appointment of Rachel Barrett as secretary in 1929. EPRCC, executive minutes, 1927–30.

[15] *Time and Tide*, 6 April 1928.
[16] *The Vote*, 26 October 1928.
[17] *WM*, 22 September, 3 October 1928; NUSEC, *Annual Report*, 1928, 21, 25.
[18] *WM*, 30 March 1928.

1951.[19] In spite of the repeated efforts of Margaret Rhondda ('the persistent peeress'), women remained excluded from the House of Lords until a few months after her death in 1958.[20]

Feminist organizations found progress equally difficult in the 1930s. NUSEC membership declined rapidly after 1928. Its *Annual Report* for that year recorded that some of its affiliated societies

> have been in a more or less moribund condition and others decided to cease activities when the goal of equal franchise was reached. The list of societies which have passed out of existence during the year is therefore larger than usual and we greatly regret the passing of some of those which have a long and honourable history of devotion to 'the Cause'.[21]

In 1929, Wales had six affiliated societies, five located in the south-east and the sixth at Bangor in the north. Of the total of forty NUSEC affiliates in 1938, three were from Wales – Abertillery, Cardiff and Newport, which still operated as a South Wales Area Group.[22] Organizational decline was accompanied by a dilution of feminist objectives, especially at a local level. In Cardiff the WCA focused much of its work during the decade in support of the League of Nations Union and the 1934 Peace Ballot, while also concerning itself with such issues as road safety for pedestrians, the appointment of women JPs and the provision of public lavatories.[23]

The WFL, sustained by a small, dedicated leadership, proved resilient and for several decades continued to press its broad programme of social equality. By 1940, however, the number of its branches had dwindled to a dozen or so and membership to a few thousand, making the league little more than a London-based pressure group.[24] The SPG and

---

[19]   See J. Graham Jones, 'Lady Megan's first parliamentary contest: the Anglesey election of 1929', *Transactions of the Anglesey Antiquarian Society and Field Club* (1992), 107–22. She was later Labour MP for Carmarthen from 1957 until her death in 1966.

[20]   Eoff, *Viscountess Rhondda*, 81–8; Law, *Suffrage and Power*, 111–12.

[21]   NUSEC, *Annual Report*, 1928, 23–4.

[22]   Ibid., 1929 and 1938.

[23]   Pugh, *Women and the Women's Movement*, 242.

[24]   The branches in Swansea and Montgomeryshire remained active into the 1930s.

the NUWT continued their campaigns too, but the most flourishing organizations of the decade were the essentially
non-feminist women's institutes and townswomen's guilds,
both of which focused on women's traditional domestic role.
Symptomatically, both the *Woman's Leader* (the organ of the
NUSEC) and *The Vote* ceased publication in 1933, while *Time
and Tide* surrendered much of its feminist edge after the franchise victory of 1928. In contrast, the 1930s saw a striking rise
in the popularity of weekly magazines, such as *Woman's Own*
and *Woman*, which focused on the pleasures of home and
family life.[25]

While the women's movement thus entered a period of
decline after 1928, it certainly did not disappear and many
suffragists were active in subsequent campaigns, such as those
for equal pay and family allowances and the peace movement.
Nevertheless, equal voting rights clearly marked the end of an
epoch. When, in 1867, John Stuart Mill proposed that women
be granted the parliamentary franchise and thereby instigated
the first women's suffrage debate in the House of Commons,
some MPs greeted the idea with ridicule and there was a good
deal of amusement, while the press coverage was often
mocking and condescending. In 1928, in the last debate on the
subject, with the success of the Equal Franchise Bill assured, it
was women MPs who revelled in the banter and the humour,
while much of the press expressed serious concerns about
female voters forming a majority at the next general election,
in 1929. That same year, the Cardiff Women Citizens' Association held a Suffrage Relics Exhibition, displaying banners,
photographs, posters, placards and other mementos associated
with the city's role in the campaign. Outlining the history of the
items, the veteran activist Mary Collin expressed the hope that
'these treasures might be placed in the National Museum of
Wales'.[26] The women's suffrage movement had truly passed
into history.

[25]   See Martin Pugh, 'Domesticity and the decline of feminism, 1930–1950', in
Smith, *British Feminism*, 144–64.
[26]   *WM*, 26 April 1929.

BIBLIOGRAPHY

1. Unpublished manuscripts
2. Official papers
3. Newspapers and journals
4. Contemporary pamphlets
5. Annual reports
6. Works of reference
7. Secondary works
8. Unpublished theses

1. UNPUBLISHED MANUSCRIPTS

Aberdare Public Library
Aberdare Women's Liberal Federation Minute Book, 1891–1907 (W. W. Price Collection).

Bangor University
Bangor MS 25800, Bangor and District Women's Suffrage Society Minute Book.
Bangor MS 26003, Margaret Williams, 'Why women's suffrage would be a national danger'.
Belmont MS 300, Diary of Henry Lewis.
Papers of William Jones, MS 5471, fo. 43 (Circular from Lord Cromer, president of the NLOWS, 15 December 1909); and fo. 60 (Circular from the Cymric Suffrage Union, *Etholfraint i Ddynes*, 12 Medi 1911).
A Petition addressed to the Right Hon. Henry Herbert Asquith, Prime Minister and first Lord of the Treasury, to place the Welsh writer, Gwyneth Vaughan on the Civil List for a substantial subsidy (n.d., *c.*1909) [X/GEN.67 VAU].

Bodleian Library, Oxford
John Johnson Collection: JJ/SJC/11.86, seven boxes of women's suffrage material, covering the NLOWS and various suffrage organizations.
Journals of H. W. Nevinson: MSS Eng. misc. e. 610–28.

Bristol University Library
Women's Liberal Federation Collection.

British Library
Add MS 47,449–55: Letters of Mrs E. C. W. Elmy.
Add MS 49976: Olive Wharry's Prison Notebook, 1911–14.
Arncliffe Sennett Collection.
Lord Curzon Papers (India Office Collection).

British Library of Political and Economic Science
Mill-Taylor Collection.
Women's Co-operative Guild Papers.

Cardiff Central Library
'Cochfarf' Papers (Edward Thomas, 'Cochfarf').
Miscellaneous Photographs (suffrage).

Carmarthenshire Record Office
Carmarthen Women's Suffrage Society Minute Book [Acc. 4495].

Cumbria Record Office
Catherine Marshall Papers.

Cyfarthfa Castle Museum, Merthyr Tydfil
Diaries of Rose Harriette Thompson Williams (née Crawshay).

Girton College, Cambridge
Helen Blackburn Collection.

Glamorgan Record Office, Cardiff
Records of the Cardiff Women Citizens' Association, including material on
    the Cardiff and District Women's Suffrage Society and the minutes of the
    Penarth Women's Suffrage Society [D/DX 158].

Gloucestershire Record Office
Diaries of Emily and Mary Blathwayt [D 2659].

Gwynedd Archives, Caernarfon
Guy Hughes Papers, Section 1 – Gwyneth Vaughan Papers [XD/85/1].

Herefordshire Record Office
Lord James of Hereford Papers [M 45].

Institute of Education Library, University of London
NUWT Archive, including minute books, correspondence and leaflets, and
    material relating to the Six Point Group and the Equal Political Rights
    Campaign Committee.

International Institute of Social History, Amsterdam
E. S. Pankhurst Papers [available in microfilm, *Women, Suffrage and Politics: The Papers of Sylvia Pankhurst, 1882–1960* (Adam Matthew Publications, Marlborough, 1991)].

Lancashire Record Office, Preston
Selina Cooper Papers.

Manchester Central Library
Women's Suffrage Collection.

Manchester University, John Rylands Library
Manchester Men's League for Women's Suffrage Archive.

Museum of London
Florence Haig Papers.
David Mitchell Collection.
Suffragette Fellowship Collection.

National Archives, Kew
HO 45/10689/228470, Disturbances: meeting in Wales attended by Lloyd George, suffragettes assaulted by the crowd.
HO 45/10695/231366, Disturbances: suffragette activities and meetings, 1912–13.
HO 45/13020, Elections: equal franchise for men and women, 1924–28.
HO 45/24665, Suffragettes: amnesty of August 1914, index of names of persons arrested, 1906–14.
HO 144/1119/203651, Disturbances: suffragist disturbances, 1911–13.
MEPO 2/1016, The Suffragette Movement: disturbances and convictions, 1906–07.

National Library of Wales, Aberystwyth
(a) General Manuscripts
19865C, Minute Book of the Aberystwyth Women's Liberal Association (1894–8).
21971B, *Letters of Well Known Women* [to Leonora Philipps].
22636B, Papers of the Llangollen Women's Suffrage Society.

(b) Deposited Collections
Samuel T. Evans Papers.
William George Papers.
E. T. John Papers.
D. A. Thomas Papers.

(c) Welsh Political Archive
Political Ephemera, XJN 1156–60.

Reading University
Nancy Astor Papers.

Swansea Museum
Jennie Ross Papers.

Swansea University
Kirkland Papers.

Wellcome Library for the History and Understanding of Medicine, London
Florence Fenwick Miller, *An Uncommon Girlhood* (draft autobiography).

Women's Library (formerly Fawcett Library), London Metropolitan University
(a) Papers of Individuals
Teresa Billington-Greig.
Emily Wilding Davison.
Edith Eskrigge.
Millicent Garrett Fawcett.
Edith How Martyn.
Harriet McIlquham.

(b) Records of Organizations
Catholic Women's Suffrage Society / St Joan's Social and Political Alliance.
Central National Society for Women's Suffrage.
Central Society for Women's Suffrage.
Consultative Committee of Societies for Women's Suffrage.
Consultative Committee of Women's Organisations.
Equal Political Rights Campaign Committee.
London Society for Women's Suffrage.
National Union of Women's Suffrage Society.
Six Point Group.
Women's Freedom League.
Women's National Anti-Suffrage League.
Women's Social and Political Union.
Women's Tax Resistance League.

2. OFFICIAL PAPERS

Census Returns of England and Wales, 1871, 1881, 1891, 1901.
Parliamentary Debates, House of Commons, 3rd, 4th and 5th series.
Parliamentary Debates, House of Lords, 5th series.

3. NEWSPAPERS AND JOURNALS

Aberdare Leader
Aberdare Times
Abergavenny Chronicle
Abergavenny Mail
Aberystwyth Observer
Yr Adsain
Amman Valley Chronicle
Anti-Suffrage Review
Baner ac Amserau Cymru
Bargoed Journal
Barmouth and County Advertiser
Barry Dock News
Barry Herald
Brecon and Radnor Express
Brecon County Times
Brecon Reporter
Bristol Times and Mirror
Britannia
Calling All Women
Cambria Daily Leader
Cambrian
Cambrian News
Cardiff and Merthyr Guardian
Cardiff Times
Cardigan and Tivyside Advertiser
Cardigan Observer
Carmarthen Journal
Carmarthen Weekly Reporter
Carnarvon and Denbigh Herald
Catholic Citizen
Catholic Suffragist
Chepstow Weekly Advertiser
Chronicle for Mid and South Glamorgan
Church League for Women's Suffrage Monthly Paper
Church Militant
Clarion
Colliery Workers' Magazine
Conservative and Unionist Women's Franchise Review
Contemporary Review

Co-operative News
County Echo
County Herald
County Observer
Y Cronicl
Y Cymro
Daily Bristol Times and Mirror
Daily Chronicle
Daily Express
Daily Herald
Daily Mail
Daily Mirror
Daily Sketch
Daily Telegraph
Denbighshire Free Press
English Woman's Journal
Englishwoman
Englishwoman's Review
Evening Express
Y Fellten
Fishguard, Goodwick and County Times
Flintshire News
Flintshire Observer
Fortnightly Review
Free Church Times
Free Press of Monmouthshire
Gentlewoman
Glamorgan County Times
Glamorgan Free Press
Glamorgan Gazette
Halstead Gazette
Haverfordwest and Milford Haven Telegraph
Yr Herald Cymraeg
Herald of Wales
Hereford Times
Holyhead Chronicle
Holyhead Mail
I.L.P. News
Illustrated London News
Independent Suffragette

Jus Suffragii
Labour Leader
Labour Record and Review
Labour Woman
Liberal Women's News
Liverpool Daily Post
Llais Llafur
Llandudno Advertiser
Llanelly and County Guardian
Llanelly Mercury
Llanelly Star
Llangollen Advertiser
Manchester Guardian
Men's League for Women's Suffrage Monthly Paper
Merthyr Express
Merthyr Guardian
Merthyr Pioneer
Merthyr Telegraph
Mid Glamorgan Herald
Monmouthshire Beacon
Monmouthshire Merlin
Monmouthshire Weekly Post
Montgomery County Times
Montgomeryshire Express
Morning Post
Mountain Ash Post
National League Journal
Newtown and Welshpool Express
Nineteenth Century
North Wales Chronicle
North Wales Observer and Express
North Wales Weekly News
Pembroke County Guardian
Pembroke Dock and Pembroke Gazette
Pembrokeshire Herald
Pembrokeshire Times
Penarth Observer
Police Gazette
Pontypool Free Press
Pontypridd Observer
Porth Gazette
Porthcawl News

Primrose League Gazette
Radnor Express
Radnorshire Standard
Y Rhedegydd
Rhondda Leader
Rhondda Socialist
Rhyl Journal
Rhyl Record and Advertiser
Saturday Review
School Board Chronicle
Schoolmaster
Y Seren
Shafts
South Wales Argus
South Wales Daily News
South Wales Daily Post
South Wales Echo
South Wales Gazette
South Wales News
South Wales Press
South Wales Sentinel
South Wales Weekly Argus
South Wales Weekly Post
South Wales Worker
Southern Guardian
Star of Gwent
Suffragette News Sheet
Sunday Chronicle
Swansea and Glamorgan Herald
Swansea Journal
Tenby Observer
The Common Cause
The Graphic
The Observer
The Queen
The Suffragette
The Times
The Tribunal
The Vote
Time and Tide
Votes for Women
Weekly Mail
Weekly Star

Welsh Catholic Herald
Welsh Catholic Times
Welsh Coast Pioneer
Welsh Gazette
Welsh Outlook
Welsh Review
Welshman
Western Daily Press
Western Mail
Woman Teacher
Woman's Dreadnought
Woman's Herald
Woman's Leader
Woman's Signal
Woman's Signal Budget

Women and Progress
Women's Bulletin
Women's Franchise
Women's Freedom League Bulletin
Women's Gazette
Women's Liberal Federation News
Women's Liberal Federation Summary
Women's Penny Paper
Women's Suffrage Journal
Women's Suffrage Record
Women's Tribune
Workers' Dreadnought
Wrexham Advertiser
Young Wales

4. Contemporary pamphlets

Abadam, Alice, *The Feminist Vote, Enfranchised or Emancipated* (London, 1918) [Museum of London].

Beddoe, A. M., *The Early Years of the Women's Suffrage Movement* (Bradford-on-Avon, 1911).

Brailsford, H. N. and Murray, J., *Treatment of the Women's Deputations by the Police* (London, 1911).

Calendar for 1898, with Women's Suffrage Directory (Bristol and London, 1897).

The Election Fighting Fund: What it has Achieved (NUWSS, 1914) [Bodleian].

Equal Franchise, 1918–1928 (1927).

Gladstone, William Ewart, *Female Suffrage: A Letter from the Right Hon. W. E. Gladstone, M.P., to Samuel Smith, M.P.* (London, 1892).

Hardie, J. Keir, *The Citizenship of Women* (London, 1905).

Hoggan, Frances, *The Position of the Mother in the Family in its Legal and Scientific Aspects* (London, 1885).

Leeds, Hester, *Origin and Growth of the Union* (Union of Practical Suffragists, leaflet XII, 1898).

Letter from Samuel Smith, M.P., 7 Delahay Street, Westminster (London, 1891).

List of Woman Poor Law Guardians and Rural District Councillors in England and Wales (London, 1904).

Memorial of Head Mistresses of Girls' Public Secondary Schools (NUWSS, 1909) [BLPES].

McLaren, Eva, *The Duties and Opportunities of Women with Reference to Parish and District Councils* (London, 1894).

McLaren, Eva, *The History of the Women's Suffrage Movement in the Women's Liberal Federation* (London, 1903).

Mitchell, Mrs, *Women's Place in Politics* (London, 1903) [Museum of London].

Morgan, Gwenllian E. F., *The Duties of Citizenship: The Proper Understanding and Use of the Municipal and Other Franchises for Women* (Manchester, 1896).

Nevinson, Margaret Wynne, *Five Years Struggle for Freedom: A History of the Suffrage Movement from 1908–12* (London, 1912).

Opinions on Women's Suffrage (London, 1879) [British Library].

Pallister, Minnie, *The Orange-Box: Thoughts of a Socialist Propagandist* (London, 1924).

Pallister, Minnie, *Socialism for Women* (London, 1925).

Parkes, Margaret Kineton, *The Tax Resistance Movement in Great Britain* (London, n.d.).

Philipps, Nora, *An Appeal to Welsh Women* (London, 1893).

Philipps, Nora, *The Aim and Object of the Welsh Union* (London, 1893).

Proceedings at the Inaugural Meeting of the Women's Franchise League (1889) [Bodleian and WL].

Rees, Sir J. D., *Current Political Problems, with Pros and Cons* (London, 1912).

A Reply to the Letter of Mr. Samuel Smith, M.P., on Women's Suffrage by Mrs. Fawcett (London, 1892).

Smith, Samuel, *Mr Samuel Smith, MP, and Women's Suffrage* (London, 1891).

Some Supporters of the Women's Suffrage Movement (1897) [British Library].

Union of Practical Suffragists (Leaflets) [BLPES].

Woman's Influence: Being Letters Reprinted from the Cambrian News (Aberystwyth, 1894) [NLW].

Women's Suffrage Calendars (Bristol, 1885–99) [Bodleian].

5. ANNUAL REPORTS

Located in the Women's Library, London Metropolitan University, unless otherwise stated.

Actresses' Franchise League.

Artists' Franchise League.

Bristol and West of England Society for Women's Suffrage.

Cardiff and District Women's Suffrage Society [NLW and Cardiff Central Library].

Catholic Women's Suffrage Society / St Joan's Social and Political Alliance.

Central and East of England Society for Women's Suffrage.

Central and Western Society for Women's Suffrage.

Central Committee of the National Society for Women's Suffrage.

Central National Society for Women's Suffrage.

Church League for Women's Suffrage.

Consultative Committee of Women's Organisations.

Ladies' National Association for the Repeal of the Contagious Diseases Acts.

League of the Church Militant.
Llangollen Women's Suffrage Society.
London Society for Women's Suffrage.
Manchester National Society for Women's Suffrage [Manchester Central Library].
Men's League for Women's Suffrage.
Men's Political Union for Women's Enfranchisement.
National Society for Women's Suffrage.
National Union of Societies for Equal Citizenship.
National Union of Women's Suffrage Societies.
National Union of Women Teachers [Institute of Education].
People's Suffrage Federation [BLPES].
Six Point Group [and Institute of Education].
Welsh Union of Women's Liberal Associations [NLW and Cardiff Central Library].
West Lancashire, West Cheshire and North Wales Federation.
Women's Co-operative Guild [BLPES].
Women's Emancipation Union [British Library].
Women's Franchise League [and BLPES].
Women's Freedom League [and Museum of London].
Women's International League for Peace and Freedom [BLPES].
Women's Liberal Federation [BLPES and Bristol University].
Women's Social and Political Union [and Museum of London].
Women's Tax Resistance League.

6. WORKS OF REFERENCE

Banks, Olive, *The Biographical Dictionary of British Feminists, Vol. One: 1800–1930* (Brighton, 1985).
Barrow, M., *Women, 1870–1928: A Select Guide to Printed and Archival Sources in the United Kingdom* (London, 1981).
Crawford, Anne, et al., *The Europa Dictionary of British Women* (London, 1983).
Crawford, Elizabeth, *The Women's Suffrage Movement: A Reference Guide, 1866–1928* (London, 1999).
——, *The Women's Suffrage Movement in Britain and Ireland: A Regional Survey* (London, 2006).
Dictionary of Twentieth-Century British Philosophers, vol. 2 (Bristol, 2005).
Dictionary of Welsh Biography down to 1940 (London, 1959).
Doughan, David and Sanchez, Denise, *Feminist Periodicals 1855–1984: An Annotated Critical Bibliography of British, Irish, Commonwealth and International Titles* (Brighton, 1987).
Gildart, Keith, Howell, David and Kirk, Neville (eds), *Dictionary of Labour Biography, XI* (Basingstoke, 2003).

——, and Howell, David (eds), *Dictionary of Labour Biography, XII* (Basingstoke, 2005).

Gordon, Peter and Doughan, David, *Dictionary of British Women's Organisations, 1825–1960* (London, 2001).

Hannam, June, Auchterlonie, Mitzi and Holden, Katherine, *International Encyclopedia of Women's Suffrage* (Santa Barbara, California, 2000).

Holt, Constance Wall, *Welsh Women: An Annotated Bibliography of Women in Wales and Women of Welsh Descent in America* (Metuchen, New Jersey, 1993).

James, A. J. and Thomas, J. E., *Wales at Westminster: A History of the Parliamentary Representation of Wales, 1800–1979* (Llandysul, 1981).

Jones, Beti, *Etholiadau'r Ganrif / Welsh Elections, 1885–1997* (Talybont, 1999).

Jones, Philip Henry, *A Bibliography of the History of Wales* (3rd edn, Cardiff, 1989).

Matthew, H. C. G. and Harrison, Brian (eds), *Oxford Dictionary of National Biography* (*ODNB*) (Oxford, 2004).

Pugh, Martin, 'Sources on the suffrage question in the National Archives', *Women in the National Archives Online* (Adam Matthew, Marlborough, 2005).

R., A. J. (ed.), *The Suffrage Annual and Who's Who* (London, 1913).

Rees, Ivor Thomas, *Welsh Hustings, 1885–2004* (Llandybïe, 2005).

Smith, Harold, 'Archival report: British women's history, the Fawcett Library's archival collections', *Twentieth Century British History*, 2, no. 2 (London, 1991).

Women, Politics and Welfare: the papers of Nancy Astor, 1879–1964: a listing and guide to parts 1 and 2 of the microfilm collection (Marlborough, 1995).

Women, Suffrage and Politics: the papers of Sylvia Pankhurst, 1882–1960: a printed guide (Reading, 1991).

Women's Suffrage and Government Control, 1906–1922: papers from the Cabinet, Home Office and Metropolitan Police files in the Public Record Office: a listing and guide to the microfilm collection (Marlborough, 2000).

Women's Suffrage Collection from Manchester Central Library: a listing and guide to the microfilm collection (Marlborough, 1995).

7. SECONDARY WORKS

Aaron, Jane, *Pur fel y Dur: Y Gymraes yn Llên Menywod y Bedwaredd Ganrif ar Bymtheg* (Cardiff, 1998).

——, *A View across the Valley: Short Stories by Women from Wales, c. 1850–1950* (Dinas Powys, 1999).

——, *Nineteenth-Century Women's Writing in Wales: Nation, Gender and Identity* (Cardiff, 2007).

——, and Masson, Ursula (eds), *The Very Salt of Life: Welsh Women's Political Writings from Chartism to Suffrage* (Dinas Powys, 2007).

Abrams, Fran, *Freedom's Cause: Lives of the Suffragettes* (London, 2003).

Adam, Ruth, *A Woman's Place, 1910–1975* (London, 1975).

Alberti, Johanna, *Beyond Suffrage: Feminists in War and Peace, 1914–28* (Basingstoke, 1989).

——, *Eleanor Rathbone* (London, 1996).

Andrews, Elizabeth, *A Woman's Work Is Never Done* (Ystrad Rhondda, 1948; repr. edited by Ursula Masson, Dinas Powys, 2006).

Atkinson, Diane, *Suffragettes* (London, 1988).

——, *Suffragettes in the Purple, White and Green: London, 1906–14* (London, 1992).

——, *The Suffragettes in Pictures* (Stroud, 1996).

Banks, Olive, *Becoming a Feminist: The Social Origins of 'First Wave' Feminism* (Brighton, 1986).

Barlow, Robin, *Wales and the First World War* (Cardiff, 2006).

Barnsby, George, *Votes for Women: The Struggle for the Vote in the Black Country, 1900–1918* (Wolverhampton, 1995).

Bartley, Paula, *Emmeline Pankhurst* (London, 2002).

Beddoe, Deirdre, *Discovering Women's History* (London, 1983).

——, 'Women between the wars', in Herbert, Trevor and Jones, Gareth Elwyn (eds), *Wales between the Wars* (Cardiff, 1988), 129–60.

——, *Back to Home and Duty: Women between the Wars, 1918–1939* (London, 1989).

——, 'What about the women?', *Planet*, 117 (1996), 55–61.

——, 'Waiting for no man: Lady Rhondda and *Time and Tide*', *New Welsh Review*, 45 (1999), 35–8.

——, *Out of the Shadows: A History of Women in Twentieth Century Wales* (Cardiff, 2000).

Benn, Caroline, *Keir Hardie* (London, 1992).

Biggs, Caroline Ashurst, 'Great Britain', in Stanton, Elizabeth Cody, Anthony, Susan B. and Gage, Matilda Jocelyn (eds), *History of Woman Suffrage*, 3 (New York, 1886), 834–94.

Billington, Rosamund, 'Women, politics and local Liberalism: from "female suffrage" to "votes for women"', *Journal of Regional and Local Studies*, 5, 1 (1985), 1–14.

Billington-Greig, Teresa, *The Militant Suffrage Movement* (London, 1911).

Bingham, Adrian, '"Stop the flapper vote folly": Lord Rothmere, the *Daily Mail*, and the equalization of the franchise 1927–28', *Twentieth Century British History*, 13, 1 (2002), 17–37.

Bishop, Alan (ed.), *Chronicle of Youth: Vera Brittain's War Diary, 1913–1917* (London, 1981).

Blackburn, Helen, *Women's Suffrage: A Record of the Women's Movement in the British Isles* (London, 1902).

Bland, Lucy, *Banishing the Beast: English Feminism and Sexual Morality, 1885–1914* (London, 1995).

Bohata, Kirsti, '"For Wales, see England?" Suffrage and the new woman in Wales', *Women's History Review*, 11, 4 (2002), 643–56.

Bostick, Theodora, 'The press and the launching of the women's suffrage movement, 1866–1867', *Victorian Periodicals Review*, XIII (1980), 125–31.

——, 'Women's suffrage, the press, and the Reform Bill of 1867', *International Journal of Women's Studies*, 3 (1980), 373–90.

Boussahba-Bravard, Myriam (ed.), *Suffrage Outside Suffragism: Women's Vote in Britain, 1880–1914* (Basingstoke, 2007).

Bradley, Katherine, *Friends and Visitors: A History of the Women's Suffrage Movement in Cornwall, 1870–1914* (Penzance, 2000).

Branson, Noreen, *Britain in the Nineteen Twenties* (London, 1975).

Braybon, Gail, 'Women and the war', in Constantine, Stephen, Kirby, Maurice W. and Rose, Mary B. (eds), *The First World War in British History* (London, 1995), 141–67.

Brittain, Vera, *Testament of Youth* (London, 1933).

Bush, Julia, 'British women's anti-suffragism and the forward policy', *Women's History Review*, 11, 3 (2002), 431–54.

——, *Women Against the Vote: Female Anti-Suffragism in Britain* (Oxford, 2007).

Bussey, Gertrude and Tims, Margaret, *Pioneers for Peace* (London, 1980).

Caine, Barbara, *English Feminism* (Oxford, 1997).

Carr, Catherine, *The Spinning Wheel: City of Cardiff High School for Girls, 1895–1955* (Cardiff, 1955).

Chew, Doris Nield, *Ada Nield Chew: The Life and Writings of a Working Woman* (London, 1982).

Close, David H., 'The collapse of resistance to democracy: Conservatives, adult suffrage and second chamber reform, 1911–1928', *Historical Journal*, 20, 4 (1977), 893–918.

Cobbe, Frances Power, *Life of Frances Power Cobbe by Herself, Vol. 2* (London, 1894).

Codd, Clara, *So Rich a Life* (London, 1951).

Coleman, Verna, *Adela Pankhurst: The Wayward Suffragette, 1886–1961* (Melbourne, 1996).

Collette, Christine, *For Labour and for Women: The Women's Labour League, 1906–1918* (Manchester, 1989).

Cook, Blanche Wiesen, *Crystal Eastman: On Women and Revolution* (Oxford, 1978).

Copelman, Diana, *London's Women Teachers: Gender, Class and Feminism, 1870–1930* (London, 1996).

Cowman, Krista, '"Minutes of the last meeting passed": The Huddersfield Women's Social and Political Union Minute Book, January 1907–1909, a new source for suffrage history', *Twentieth-Century British History*, 13, 3 (2002), 298–315.

——, *'Mrs Brown is a Man and a Brother!' Women in Merseyside's Political Organisations, 1890–1920* (Liverpool, 2004).

Cragoe, Matthew and Williams, Chris (eds), *Wales and War: Society, Politics and Religion in the Nineteenth and Twentieth Centuries* (Cardiff, 2007).

Crawford, Elizabeth, *'From Frederick Street to Winson Green': The Women's Suffrage Movement in Birmingham* (London, 2000).

Dangerfield, George, *The Strange Death of Liberal England* (London, 1936).

Davies, J. Ifor, *The Caernarvon County School: A History* (Caernarfon, 1989).

DiCenzo, Maria, 'Gutter politics: women newsies and the suffrage press', *Women's History Review*, 12, 1 (2003), 15–33.

Dobbie, B. M. Wilmot, *A Nest of Suffragettes in Somerset: Eagle House, Batheaston* (Bath, 1979).

Doughan, David, *Lobbying for Liberation: British Feminism, 1918–68* (London, 1980).

Du Parcq, Herbert, *The Life of David Lloyd George*, vol. 1 (London, 1912).

Edwards, Wil Jon, *From the Valley I Came* (London, 1956).

Egan, David, 'The Swansea Conference of the British Council of Soldiers' and Workers' Delegates, July 1917: reactions to the Russian revolution of February 1917, and the anti-war movement in south Wales', *Llafur: Journal of Welsh Labour History*, 1, 4 (1975), 12–37.

Eoff, Shirley M., *Viscountess Rhondda: Egalitarian Feminist* (Columbus, Ohio, 1991).

Eurig, Aled, 'Agweddau ar y gwrthwynebiad i'r Rhyfel Byd Cyntaf yng Nghymru' (Aspects of the opposition to the First World War in Wales), *Llafur*, 4, 4 (1987), 58–68.

Eustance, Claire, Ryan, Joan and Ugolini, Laura (eds), *A Suffrage Reader: Charting Directions in British Suffrage History* (London, 2000).

Evans, Neil and Jones, Dot, '"To help forward the great work of humanity": women in the Labour Party in Wales', in Tanner, Duncan, Williams, Chris and Hopkin, Deian (eds), *The Labour Party in Wales, 1900–2000* (Cardiff, 2000), 215–40.

Evans, W. Gareth, 'The Welsh Intermediate and Technical Education Act 1889 and the Education of Girls: Gender Stereotyping or Curricular Assimilation?', *Llafur: Journal of Welsh Labour History*, 5, 2 (1989), 84–92.

——, *Education and Female Emancipation: The Welsh Experience, 1847–1914* (Cardiff, 1990).

——, *The Role and Changing Status of Women in the Twentieth Century* (Aberystwyth, 1998).

Fauret, Martine, 'Women resisting the vote: a case of anti-feminism?', *Women's History Review*, 12, 4 (2003), 605–21.

Fawcett, Millicent Garrett, *Women's Suffrage: A Short History of a Great Movement* (London, 1912).

——, *The Women's Victory and After: Personal Reminiscences, 1911–1918* (London, 1920).

——, *What I Remember* (London, 1924).

Fletcher, Sheila, *Maude Royden* (Oxford, 1989).

Fulford, Roger, *Votes for Women* (London, 1957).

Gaffin, Jean and Thoms, David, *Caring and Sharing: The Centenary History of the Women's Co-operative Guild* (Manchester, 1983).

Gaffney, Angela, *Aftermath: Remembering the Great War in Wales* (Cardiff, 1998).

Gallagher, Ann-Marie, Lubelska, Cathy and Ryan, Louise (eds), *Re-presenting the Past: Women and History* (London, 2001).

Garner, Les, *Stepping Stones to Women's Liberty: Feminist Ideas in the Women's Suffrage Movement, 1900–1918* (London, 1984).

Gawthorpe, Mary, *Up Hill to Holloway* (Penobscot, Maine, 1962).

Gibson, John, *The Emancipation of Women* (Aberystwyth, 1891, 1894; repr. with introduction by W. Gareth Evans, Llandysul, 1992).

Gleadle, Kathryn, *Early Feminists: Radical Unitarians and the Emergence of the Women's Equal Rights Movement, 1831–51* (Basingstoke, 1995).

—— and Richardson, Sarah (eds), *Women in British Politics, 1760–1860: The Power of the Petticoat* (Basingstoke, 2000).

Green, Barbara, *Spectacular Confessions: Autobiography, Performative Activism, and the Sites of Suffrage, 1905–1938* (Basingstoke, 1997).

Griffiths, James, *Pages From Memory* (1969).

Griffiths, Winifred, *One Woman's Story* (Ferndale, 1979 edn).

Grigg, John, *Lloyd George: The People's Champion, 1902–11* (London, 1978).

——, *Lloyd George: From Peace to War, 1912–16* (London, 1985).

Hamilton, Margaret, 'Opposition to woman suffrage in England: 1865–1884', *Victorians Institute Journal*, 4 (1975), 59–73.

Hannam, June, *Isabella Ford* (Oxford, 1989).

——, 'Women and the ILP, 1890–1914', in James, David, Jowitt, Tony and Laybourn, Keith (eds), *The Centennial History of the Independent Labour Party: A Collection of Essays* (London, 1992), 206–28.

——, '"An enlarged sphere of usefulness": the Bristol women's movement, *c.*1860–1914', in Dresser, Madge and Ollerenshaw, Philip (eds), *The Making of Modern Bristol* (Midsomer Norton, 1996), 184–209.

——, '"I had not been to London": Women's suffrage – a view from the regions', in Purvis, June and Holton, Sandra Stanley (eds), *Votes for Women* (London, 2000), 226–45.

—— and Hunt, Karen, *Socialist Women: Britain 1880s to 1930s* (London, 2001)

Harrison, Brian, *Separate Spheres: The Opposition to Women's Suffrage in Britain* (London, 1978).

——, 'Women's health and the women's movement in Britain', in Webster, Charles (ed.), *Biology, Medicine and Society, 1840–1940* (Cambridge, 1981), 15–72.

——, *Peaceable Kingdom: Stability and Change in Modern Britain* (Oxford, 1982).

——, 'Women's suffrage at Westminster', in Bentley, Michael and Stevenson, John (eds), *High and Low Politics in Modern Britain* (Oxford, 1983), 80–122.

——, 'Women in a men's house: the women MPs, 1919–45', *Historical Journal*, 29, 3 (1986), 623–54.

——, *Prudent Revolutionaries: Portraits of British Feminists between the Wars* (Oxford, 1987).

——, 'A different world for women: nineteenth century women campaigners', *Twentieth Century British History*, 3, 1 (1992), 76–83.

Heeney, Brian, *The Women's Movement in the Church of England, 1850–1930* (Oxford, 1988).

Hesketh, Phoebe, *My Aunt Edith: The Story of a Preston Suffragette* (Preston, 1992).

Hill, Ethel and Shafer, Olga Fenton (eds), *Great Suffragists – and Why: Modern Makers of Future History* (London, 1909).

Hirshfield, Claire, 'The Actresses' Franchise League and the campaign for women's suffrage, 1908–1914', *Theatre Research International*, 10, 2 (1985), 129–53.

——, 'Fractured faith: Liberal Party women and the suffrage issue in Britain, 1892–1914', *Gender and History*, 2, 2 (1990), 173–97.

Hockey, Primrose, 'Elizabeth Harcourt Mitchell', *Gwent Local History*, 49 (1980), 2–5.

Holcombe, Lee, *Wives and Property* (Oxford, 1983).

Holledge, Julie, *Innocent Flowers: Women in the Edwardian Theatre* (London, 1981).

Hollis, Patricia (ed.), *Women in Public, 1850–1900: Documents of the Women's Movement* (London, 1979).

——, *Ladies Elect: Women in English Local Government, 1865–1814* (Oxford, 1987).

Holt, Ann, 'The battle of Llanystumdwy', *New Society*, 18 September 1987, 19–21.

Holton, Sandra Stanley, *Feminism and Democracy: Women's Suffrage and Reform Politics in Britain, 1900–1918* (Cambridge, 1986).

——, 'The suffragist and the "average woman"', *Women's History Review*, 1, 1 (1992), 9–24.

——, *Suffrage Days: Stories from the Women's Suffrage Movement* (London, 1996).

——, 'Silk dresses and lavender kid gloves: the wayward career of Jessie Craigen', *Women's History Review*, 5, 1 (1996), 129–50.

Hopkin, Deian, 'Patriots and pacifists in Wales, 1914–1918: the case of Capt. Lionel Lindsay and the Rev. T. E. Nicholas', *Llafur: Journal of Welsh Labour History*, 1, 3 (1974), 27–41.

Hopkinson, Diana, *Family Inheritance: A Life of Eva Hubback* (London, 1954).

Hughes, Katherine Price, *The Story of My Life* (London, 1945).

Hughes, Oliver Wynne, *Every Day was Summer: Childhood Memories of Edwardian Days in a Small Welsh Town* (Llandysul, 1989).

Hume, Leslie Parker, *The National Union of Women's Suffrage Societies, 1897–1914* (New York, 1982).

Jalland, Pat, *Women, Marriage and Politics, 1860–1914* (Oxford, 1986).

Jarvis, David, 'Mrs Maggs and Betty: The Conservative appeal to women voters in the 1920s', *Twentieth Century British History*, 5, 2 (1994), 129–52.

Joannou, Maroula, 'Mary Augusta Ward (Mrs Humphry) and the opposition to women's suffrage', *Women's History Review*, 14, 3/4 (2005), 561–80.

—— and Purvis, June (eds), *The Women's Suffrage Movement: New Feminist Perspectives* (Manchester, 1998).

John, Angela V. (ed.), *Our Mothers' Land: Chapters in Welsh Women's History, 1830–1939* (Cardiff, 1991).

——, '"Run like blazes": the suffragettes and Welshness', *Llafur: Journal of Welsh Labour History*, 6, 3 (1994), 29–43.

——, '"A draft of fresh air": women's suffrage, the Welsh and London', *Transactions of the Honourable Society of Cymmrodorion*, new ser., I (1994), 81–93.

——, *Elizabeth Robins: Staging a Life* (London, 1995).

——, '*Chwarae Teg*': Welsh Men's Support for Women's Suffrage* (Aberystwyth, 1998).

——, 'Margaret Wynne Nevinson: gender and national identity in the early twentieth century', in Davies, R. R. and Jenkins, Geraint H. (eds), *From Medieval to Modern Wales: Historical Essays in Honour of Kenneth O. Morgan and Ralph A. Griffiths* (Cardiff, 2004), 230–45.

——, *War, Journalism and the Shaping of the Twentieth Century: The Life and Times of the Henry W. Nevinson* (London, 2006).

—— and Eustance, Claire (eds), *The Men's Share? Masculinities, Male Support and Women's Suffrage in Britain, 1890–1920* (London, 1997).

Jones, Aled, *Politics and Society: A History of Journalism in Wales* (Cardiff, 1993).

——, 'Sir John Gibson and the Cambrian News', *Ceredigion*, XII, 2 (1994), 57–83.

Jones, David, 'Women and Chartism', *History*, 68, (1983), 1–21.

Jones, Ieuan Gwynedd, *Explorations and Explanations: Essays in the Social History of Victorian Wales* (Llandysul, 1981).

Jones, J. Graham, 'Lady Megan's first parliamentary contest: the Anglesey election of 1929', *Transactions of the Anglesey Antiquarian Society and Field Club* (1992), 107–22.

——, 'Crawshay-Williams, Churchill and the suffragettes: a note', *National Library of Wales Journal*, XXX, 4 (1998), 447–55.

——, 'Lloyd George and the suffragettes at Llanystumdwy', *Journal of Liberal Democrat History*, 34/35 (2002), 3–10.

——, 'Lloyd George and the suffragettes', *National Library of Wales Journal*, XXXIII, 1 (2003), 1–33.

Jones, Peter Ellis, *Bangor, 1883–1983: A Study in Local Government* (Cardiff, 1986).

——, 'The women's suffrage movement in Caernarfonshire', *Transactions of the Caernarfonshire Historical Society*, 48 (1987), 75–112.

Jones, Vernon, 'A champion of women's rights', *Carmarthenshire Historian*, XX (1985), 5–21.

Jordan, Jane, *Josephine Butler* (London, 2001).

Kean, Hilda, *Deeds Not Words: The Lives of Suffragette Teachers* (London, 1990).

——, 'Searching for the past in present defeat: the construction of historical and political identity in British feminism in the 1920s and 1930s', *Women's History Review*, 3, 1 (1994), 57–80.

Keating, Joseph, *My Struggle for Life* (London, 1916).

Kenney, Annie, *Memories of a Militant* (London, 1924).

Kent, Susan Kingsley, *Sex and Suffrage in Britain, 1860–1914* (Princeton, 1987).

King, Sarah, 'Feminists in teaching: the National Union of Women Teachers, 1920–1945', in Lawn, Martin and Grace, Gerald (eds), *Teachers: The Culture and Politics of Work* (London, 1987), 31–49.

King, Steven, *Women, Welfare and Politics, 1880–1920: 'We might be trusted'* (Brighton, 2006).

Law, Cheryl, *Suffrage and Power: The Women's Movement, 1918–28* (London: 1997).

Leneman, Leah, *A Guid Cause: The Women's Suffrage Movement in Scotland* (Aberdeen, 1991).

——, *The Scottish Suffragettes* (Edinburgh, 2000).

Lenox, L. Gordon, *A Political Text Book and Glossary, and the Great European War, 1914–15* (Pontypridd, 1915).

Levine, Philippa, *Victorian Feminism, 1850–1900* (London, 1987).

Lewis, Jane (ed.), *Before the Vote was Won: Arguments for and against Women's Suffrage, 1864–1896* (London, 1987).

Lewis, W. J., *Born on a Perilous Rock: Aberystwyth Past and Present* (Aberystwyth, 1980).

Liddington, Jill, *The Life and Times of a Respectable Radical: Selina Cooper, 1864–1946* (London, 1984).

——, *The Long Road to Greenham: Feminsim and Anti-Militarism in Britain since 1820* (London, 1989).

——, *Rebel Girls: Their Fight for the Vote* (London, 2006).

—— and Norris, Jill, *One Hand Tied Behind Us: The Rise of the Women's Suffrage Movement* (London, 1978).

Linklater, Andro, *An Unhusbanded Life: Charlotte Despard – Suffragette, Socialist and Sinn Feiner* (London, 1980).

Lytton, Constance, *Prisons and Prisoners: Some Personal Experiences* (London, 1914).

Mackenzie, H. M. (ed.), *John Stuart Mackenzie* (London, 1936).

Mackenzie, Midge, *Shoulder to Shoulder: A Documentary* (London, 1975).

Maguire, G. E., *Conservative Women: A History of Women and the Conservative Party, 1874–1997* (Basingstoke, 1998).

Malmgreen, Gail (ed.), *Religion in the Lives of English Women, 1760–1930* (London, 1986).

Marlow, Joyce, *Votes for Women: The Virago Book of Suffragettes* (London, 2000).

Martin, Graham, 'The culture of the women's suffrage movement: the evidence of the McKenzie letters', *Llafur: Journal of Welsh Labour History*, 7, 3/4 (1998–9), 101–12.

Martin, Theodore, *Queen Victoria as I Knew Her* (London, 1908).

Marwick, Arthur, *Women At War, 1914–1918* (London, 1977).

Mason, F. M., 'The newer Eve: The Catholic Women's Suffrage Society in England, 1911–23', *Catholic Historical Review*, LXXII, 4 (1986), 620–38.

Masson, Ursula, 'The Swansea suffragettes', in Dee, Luana and Keineg, Katell (eds), *Women in Wales: A Documentary Reader*, vol. 1 (Cardiff, 1987), 67–76.

——, 'Votes for women – the campaign in Swansea', *Minerva: Transactions of the Royal Institution of South Wales*, 1 (1993), 34–8.

——, 'Divided loyalties: women's suffrage and party politics in south Wales, 1912–15', *Llafur: Journal of Welsh Labour History*, 7, 3/4 (1998–9), 113–26.

——, '"Political conditions in Wales are quite different . . .": party politics and votes for women in Wales, 1912–15', *Women's History Review*, 9, 2 (2000), 369–88.

——, '"Hand in hand with the women, forward we will go": Welsh nationalism and feminism in the 1890s', *Women's History Review*, 12, 3 (2003), 357–86.

—— (ed.), *'Women's Rights and Womanly Duties': The Aberdare Women's Liberal Association, 1891–1910* (Cardiff, 2005).

——, 'Women versus "the people": language, nation and citizenship, 1906–11', in Chapman, T. Robin (ed.), *The Idiom of Dissent: Protest and Propaganda in Wales* (Llandysul, 2006), 1–23.

Matthews, Ioan, 'Liberals, Socialists and Labour: politics in east Carmarthenshire, 1906–1912', *Carmarthenshire Antiquary*, XXXIV (1998), 80–95.

Mayhall, Laura E. Nym, 'Creating the "suffragette spirit": British feminism and the historical imagination', *Women's History Review*, 4, 3 (1995), 319–44.

——, 'Domesticating Emmeline: representing the suffragette, 1930–1993', *National Women's Studies Association Journal*, 11, 2 (1999), 1–24.

——, *The Militant Suffrage Movement: Citizenship and Resistance in Britain, 1860–1930* (Oxford, 2003).

McHugh, Paul, *Prostitution and Victorian Social Reform* (London, 1980).

McKenna, Stephen, *Reginald McKenna, 1863–1943: A Memoir* (London, 1948).

Mellown, Muriel, 'Lady Rhondda and the changing faces of British feminism', *Frontiers: A Journal of Women's Studies*, 9, 2 (1987), 7–13.

Melman, Billie, *Women and the Popular Imagination in the Twenties: Flappers and Nymphs* (London, 1988).

Mercer, John, 'Media and militancy: propaganda in the Women's Social and Political Union's campaign', *Women's History Review*, 14, 3/4 (2005), 471–85.

Metcalfe, Agnes Edith, *Woman's Effort: A Chronicle of British Women's Fifty Years' Struggle for Citizenship, 1865–1914* (Oxford, 1917).

Michael, Pamela, Williams, Annie and Evans, Neil, *Project Grace* (Bangor, 1994).

Middleton, Lucy (ed.), *Women in the Labour Movement: The British Experience* (London, 1977).

Mitchell, David, *Women on the Warpath: The Story of the Women of the First World War* (London, 1966).

——, *The Fighting Pankhursts: A Study in Tenacity* (London, 1967).

——, *Queen Christabel: A Biography of Christabel Pankhurst* (London, 1977).

Mitchell, Geoffrey (ed.), *The Hard Way Up: The Autobiography of Hannah Mitchell, Suffragette and Rebel* (London, 1968).

Montefiore, Dora, *From a Victorian to a Modern* (London, 1927).

Moore, Linda, 'Feminists and femininity: a case study of WSPU propaganda and local response at a Scottish by-election', *Women's Studies International Forum*, 5, 6 (1982), 675–84.

——, 'The women's suffrage campaign in the 1907 Aberdeen by-election', *Northern Scotland*, 5, 2 (1983), 155–78.

Mór-O'Brien, A., 'The Merthyr boroughs election, November 1915', *Welsh History Review*, 12, 4 (1985), 538–66.

Morgan, David, *Suffragists and Liberals: The Politics of Women's Suffrage in England* (Oxford, 1975).

Morgan, Kenneth O. (ed.), *Lloyd George Family Letters, 1885–1936* (Oxford and Cardiff, 1973).

——, *Wales in British Politics, 1868–1922* (3rd edn, Cardiff, 1980).

——, 'Peace movements in Wales, 1899–1945', *Welsh History Review*, 10, 3 (1981), 398–430.

——, *Modern Wales: Politics, Places and People* (Cardiff, 1995).

——, *Rebirth of a Nation: Wales, 1880–1980* (new edn, Oxford, 1998).

Morley, Ann, with Stanley, Liz, *The Life and Death of Emily Wilding Davison* (London, 1989).

Morrell, Caroline, *'Black Friday' and Violence against Women in the Suffragette Movement* (London, 1981).

Morris, Dylan, '"Merched y screch a'r twrw": Yr WSPU yn Llanystumdwy, 1912', *Transactions of the Caernarfonshire Historical Society*, 46 (1975), 115–32.

Moyes, Helen, *A Woman in a Man's World* (Sydney, 1971).

Mulvihill, Margaret, *Charlotte Despard: A Biography* (London, 1989).

Murphy, Cliona, *The Women's Suffrage Movement and Irish Society in the Early Twentieth Century* (Hemel Hempstead, 1989).

Murphy, Molly, *Molly Murphy: Suffragette and Socialist* (Salford, 1998).

Neville, David, *To Make Their Mark: The Women's Suffrage Movement in the North East of England* (Newcastle, 1997).

Nevinson, Henry Woodd, *More Changes, More Chances* (London, 1925).

Nevinson, Margaret Wynne, *Life's Fitful Fever: A Volume of Memories* (London, 1926).

Newberry, Jo Vellacott, 'Anti-war suffragists', *History*, 62 (1977), 411–25.

Newsome, Stella, *The Women's Freedom League, 1907–1957* (London, 1958).

Norquay, Glenda (ed.), *Voices and Votes: A Literary Anthology of the Women's Suffrage Campaign* (Manchester, 1995).

Oldfield, Sybil, *Spinsters of this Parish: The Life and Times of F. M. Mayor and Mary Sheepshanks* (London, 1984).

Olstone-Moore, Christopher, *Hugh Price Hughes: Founder of a New Methodism, Conscience of a New Nonconformity* (Cardiff, 1999).

Oram, Alison, *Women Teachers and Feminist Politics, 1900–1939* (Manchester, 1996).

Owens, Rosemary Cullen, *Smashing Times: A History of the Irish Women's Suffrage Movement, 1889–1922* (Dublin, 1984).

Oxford and Asquith, Countess of, *Myself When Young* (London, 1938).

Pankhurst, Christabel, *Unshackled: The Story of How We Won the Vote* (London, 1959).

Pankhurst, E. Sylvia, *The Suffragette: The History of the Women's Militant Suffrage Movement, 1905–10* (London, 1911).

——, *The Suffragette Movement: An Intimate Account of Persons and Ideals* (London, 1931).

——, *The Home Front: A Mirror of Life in England during the First World War* (London, 1932).

——, *The Life of Emmeline Pankhurst: The Suffragette Struggle for Women's Citizenship* (1935).

Pankhurst, Emmeline, *My Own Story* (London, 1914).

Park, Jihing, 'The British suffrage activists of 1913: an analysis', *Past and Present*, 120 (1988), 147–62.

Parnell, Nancy Stewart, *A Venture in Faith: A History of St Joan's Social and Political Alliance, formerly The Catholic Women's Suffrage Society, 1911–1961* (London, 1961).

Parry, Thomas, 'Gwyneth Vaughan', *Cylchgrawn Hanes a Chofnodion Sir Feirionnydd/ Journal of the Merioneth Historical and Record Society*, VIII, 3 (1979), 225–36.

Peacock, Sarah, *Votes for Women: The Women's Fight in Portsmouth* (Portsmouth, 1983).

Pederson, Susan, *Eleanor Rathbone and the Politics of Conscience* (London, 2004).

Pethick-Lawrence, Emmeline, *My Part in a Changing World* (London, 1938).

Pethick-Lawrence, Frederick, *Fate has been Kind* (London, 1942).

Philipps, Melanie, *The Ascent of Woman: A History of the Suffragette Movement and the Ideas Behind It* (London, 2003).

Phillips, Mary, *The Militant Suffrage Campaign in Perspective* (London, 1956).

Phipps, Emily, *A History of the National Union of Women Teachers* (London, 1928).

Picton-Turbervill, Edith, *Life is Good: An Autobiography* (London, 1939).

Pierotti, A. Muriel, *The Story of the National Union of Women Teachers* (London, 1963).

Powell, Violet, *Flora Annie Steel: Novelist of India* (London, 1981).

Prochaska, Frank K., *Women and Philanthropy in Nineteenth-Century England* (Oxford, 1980).

Proctor, Zoë, *Life and Yesterday* (London, 1960).

Pugh, David, 'The suffragette campaign in Newtown during the general elections of 1910', *The Newtonian*, 7 (2001), 10–17.

Pugh, Martin, 'Politicians and the woman's vote, 1914–1918', *History*, 59, (1974), 358–74.

——, *Electoral Reform in War and Peace, 1906–18* (London, 1978).

——, *Women's Suffrage in Britain, 1867–1928* (London, 1980).

——, 'Labour and women's suffrage', in Brown, K. D. (ed.), *The First Labour Party, 1906–14* (London, 1985), 233–53.

——, *The Tories and the People, 1880–1935* (Oxford, 1985).

——, *Women and the Women's Movement in Britain, 1914–59* (Basingstoke, 1992).

——, 'The limits of Liberalism: Liberals and women's suffrage, 1867–1914', in Biagini, Eugenio F. (ed.), *Citizenship and Community: Liberals, Radicals and Collective Identities in the British Isles, 1865–1931* (Cambridge, 1996), 45–65.

——, *The March of the Women: A Revisionist Analysis of the Campaign for Women's Suffrage, 1866–1914* (Oxford, 2000).

——, *The Pankhursts* (London, 2001).

Purvis, June, '"Deeds not words": The daily lives of militant suffragettes in Edwardian Britain', *Women's Studies International Forum*, 18, 2 (1995), 91–111.

——, 'The prison experiences of the suffragettes in Edwardian Britain', *Women's History Review*, 4, 1 (1995), 103–33.

——, *Emmeline Pankhurst: A Biography* (London, 2002).

——, 'Emmeline Pankhurst: a biographical interpretation', *Women's History Review*, 12, 1 (2003), 73–102.

—— and Holton, Sandra Stanley (eds), *Votes for Women* (London, 2000).

Raeburn, Antonia, *The Militant Suffragettes* (London, 1973).

——, *The Suffragette View* (Newton Abbot, 1976).

Ramelson, Marian, *The Petticoat Rebellion: A Century of Struggle for Women's Rights* (London, 1967).

Rendall, Jane, *Equal or Different: Women's Politics, 1880–1914* (Oxford, 1987).

——, 'The citizenship of women and the Reform Act of 1867', in Hall, Catherine, McClelland, Keith and Rendall, Jane (eds), *Defining the*

Victorian Nation: Class, Race, Gender and the British Reform Act of 1867 (Cambridge, 2007), 119–53.

Rhondda, Viscountess, 'The political awakening of women', in *These Eventful Years: The Twentieth Century in the Making, II* (Encyclopaedia Britannica, 1924), 557–90.

——, *This Was My World* (London, 1933).

——, *Notes on the Way* (London, 1937).

Richardson, Mary, *Laugh a Defiance* (London, 1953).

Robbins, Keith, *The Abolition of War: The Peace Movement in Britain, 1914–1919* (Cardiff, 1976).

Roberts, Charles, *The Radical Countess: The History of the Life of Rosalind, Countess of Carlisle* (London, 1962).

Robson, A. P. W., 'The founding of the National Society for Women's Suffrage, 1866–1867', *Canadian Journal of History*, VIII, 1 (1973), 1–22.

Robson, Ann, 'No laughing matter: John Stuart Mill's establishment of women's suffrage as a parliamentary question', *Utilitas*, 2, 1 (1990), 88–101.

Rosen, Andrew, *Rise Up, Women! The Militant Campaign of the Women's Social and Political Union, 1903–1914* (London, 1978).

——, 'Emily Davies and the women's movement, 1862–1867', *Journal of British Studies*, XIX, 1 (1979), 101–21.

Rover, Constance, *The Punch Book of Women's Rights* (London, 1966).

——, *Women's Suffrage and Party Politics in Britain, 1866–1914* (London, 1967).

Rowan, Caroline, 'Women in the Labour Party, 1906–20', *Feminist Review*, 12 (1982), 74–91.

Rowbotham, Sheila, *Hidden from History* (London, 1973).

Rubinstein, David, *Before the Suffragettes: Women's Emancipation in the 1890s* (Brighton, 1986).

——, *A Different World For Women: The Life of Millicent Garrett Fawcett* (Columbus, Ohio, 1991).

Russell, Bertrand and Patricia (eds), *The Amberley Papers: Bertrand Russell's Family Background*, vol. 2 (2nd edn, London, 1966).

Scott, Gill, *Feminism and the Politics of Working Women: The Women's Co-operative Guild, 1880s to the Second World War* (London, 1998).

Shanley, Mary L., *Feminism, Marriage and the Law in Victorian England* (Princeton, New Jersey, 1989).

Sharp, Evelyn, *Unfinished Adventure: Selected Reminiscences from an English-woman's Life* (London, 1933).

Shiman, Lilian Lewis, 'Changes are dangerous: women and temperance in Victorian England', in Malmgreen, Gail (ed.), *Religion in the Lives of English Women, 1760–1930* (1986), 193–215.

Smith, Angela K., 'The Pankhursts and the war: suffrage magazines and First World War propaganda', *Women's History Review*, 12, 1 (2003), 103–18.

——, *Suffrage Discourse in Britain during the First World War* (Aldershot, 2005).

Smith, Harold, 'Sex vs class: British feminists and the Labour movement, 1919–1929', *The Historian* [US], 47 (1984), 19–37.

Smith, Harold L. (ed.), *British Feminism in the Twentieth Century* (Cheltenham, 1990).

——, *The British Women's Suffrage Campaign, 1866–1928* (London, 1998).

Smith, Samuel, *My Life-Work* (London, 1903).

Smyth, Ethel, *Female Pipings in Eden* (London, 1933).

Snook, Lisa, 'Out of the Cage?' Women and the First World War in Pontypridd', *Llafur: Journal of Welsh Labour History*, 8, 2 (2001), 75–88.

Spender, Dale, *There's Always Been a Women's Movement This Century* (London, 1983).

Steel, Flora Annie, *The Garden of Fidelity, being the Autobiography of Flora Annie Steel, 1847–1929* (London, 1929).

Stocks, Mary, *My Commonplace Book* (London, 1970).

Stowell, Sheila, *A Stage of Their Own: Feminist Playwrights of the Suffrage Era* (Manchester, 1992).

Strachey, Ray, *The Cause: A Short History of the Women's Movement in Great Britain* (London, 1928).

Strauss, Sylvia, '*Traitors to the Masculine Cause': The Men's Campaign for Women's Rights* (Westport, Connecticut, 1982).

Swanwick, Helen Maria, *I Have Been Young* (London, 1935).

Taylor, A. J. P. (ed.), *Lloyd George: A Diary by Frances Stevenson* (London, 1971).

Taylor, Margaret Stuart, *The Crawshays of Cyfarthfa Castle* (London, 1967).

Thomas, Catherine, 'Suffragettes in Llanelli', in *Amrywiaeth Llanelli Miscellany*, 4 (Llanelli, 1989), 45–50.

Thomas, Onfel, *Frances Elizabeth Hoggan, 1843–1927* (Brecon, 1970).

Thompson, Dorothy (ed.), *Over Our Dead Bodies: Women against the Bomb* (London, 1983).

——, *British Women in the Nineteenth Century* (London, 1989).

Thompson, Mary and Margaret, *They Couldn't Stop Us! Experiences of Two (Usually Law-Abiding) Women in the Years 1909–13* (Ipswich, 1957).

Tickner, Lisa, *The Spectacle of Women: Imagery of the Suffrage Campaign* (London, 1987).

van Wingerden, Sophia A., *The Women's Suffrage Movement in Britain, 1866–1928* (Basingstoke, 1999).

Vellacott, Jo, 'Feminist consciousness and the First World War', *History Workshop Journal*, 23 (1987), 81–101.

——, *From Liberal to Labour: The Story of Catherine Marshall* (Montreal and Kingston, 1993).

——, *Pacifists, Patriots and the Vote: The Erosion of Democratic Suffragism in Britain during the First World War* (Basingstoke, 2007).

Vincent, J. E., *Letters from Wales* (London, 1889).

Walkowitz, Judith., *Prostitution and Victorian Society: Women, Class and the State* (Cambridge, 1980).

Wallace, Ryland, *'Organise! Organise! Organise!' A Study of Reform Agitations in Wales, 1840–1886* (Cardiff, 1991).

Webb, Catherine, *The Woman with the Basket: A History of the Women's Co-operative Guild, 1883–1927* (Manchester, 1927).

Wilkins, Charles, *The History of Merthyr Tydfil* (Merthyr Tydfil, 1908).

Wiltsher, Anne, *Most Dangerous Women: Feminist Peace Campaigners of the Great War* (London, 1985).

Winslow, Barbara, *Sylvia Pankhurst: Sexual Politics and Political Activism* (London, 1996).

Williams, Sydna Ann, '"Law not war – hedd nid cledd": women and the peace movement in north Wales, 1926–1945', *Welsh History Review*, 18, 1 (1996), 63–83.

8. UNPUBLISHED THESES

Billington, Rosamund H. C., 'The women's education and suffrage movements, 1850–1914: innovation and institutionalisation' (Ph.D., University of Hull, 1976).

Bloxome, Marion, 'The campaign for women's suffrage in Wales, 1912–1914' (BA, Polytechnic of Wales, *c.* 1984).

Collins, Claire, 'Women and labour politics in Britain, 1893–1932' (Ph.D., London School of Economics and Political Science, University of London, 1991).

Dingsdale, Ann, '"Generous and lofty sympathies": the Kensington Society, the 1866 Women's Suffrage Petition and the development of mid-Victorian feminism' (Ph.D., University of Greenwich, 1995).

Eustance, Claire, '"Daring to be free": the evolution of women's political identities in the Women's Freedom League, 1907–30' (Ph.D., University of York, 1993).

Frances, Hilary, '"Our job is to free women": the sexual politics of four Edwardian feminists from *c.*1910. to *c.*1935' (Ph.D., University of York, 1996).

Hall, Frances Joan, 'Cardiff parliamentary elections, 1918–35' (MA, University of Wales, 1991).

Jones, John Graham, 'Wales and the general election of 1929' (MA, University of Wales, 1980).

Law, Vivien Cheryl, 'The women's cause: feminist campaigns, 1918–1928' (Ph.D., University of London Institute of Education, 1993).

McIntyre, Glynis, 'An investigation into the development of women's suffrage in Monmouth town, 1871–1913: with particular reference to the identity and influence of the leading women activists' (BA, University of Wales College Newport, 1993).

Newman, Lowri, 'A distinctive brand of politics: women in the south Wales Labour Party, 1918–1939' (M.Phil., University of Glamorgan, 2003),

Parker, Joan Elizabeth, 'Lydia Becker: her work for women (Ph.D., University of Manchester, 1990).

Pugh, Lowri Catrin, '"The frenzied sisterhood" – astudiaeth o weithgareddau cangen Caerdydd a'r rhanbarth dros bleidleisiau i fenywod, 1908–16' (MA, University of Wales, 2000).

Riley, Linda, 'The opposition to women's suffrage, 1867–1918' (B.Litt., University of Oxford, 1977).

Seltorp, Kirsten, 'The women's suffrage movement in Bristol, 1868–1906' (Copenhagen University, 1982). [Copy in WL]

Thomas, Helen, '"A democracy of working women": the Women's Co-operative Guild in south Wales, 1891–1939' (MA, University of Glamorgan, 2006).

Timms, Marilyn, 'Alice Abadam and inter-war feminism: recovering the history of a forgotten suffragist' (MA, Ruskin College, University of Oxford, 2003).

Woodhouse, M. G., 'Rank and file movements among the miners of south Wales, 1910–1926' (Ph.D., University of Oxford, 1969).

INDEX

Abadam, Alice 42, 101, 134n., 233,
     241n.
   argues for women's suffrage 42
   family background 177
   reaction to partial
      enfranchisement (1918) 10,
      252
   as suffrage activist 177–8, 178n.
Aberbargoed 82, 89
Abercarn 88
Aberconway, Baron 155, 156n.
Aberconway, Lady *see* McLaren,
     Laura
Aberdare 34n., 57, 107, 111, 112n.,
     120n., 125, 127, 147, 157, 180,
     220n., 222, 225, 263, 293
Aberdare, Merthyr and Dowlais
     District Miners' Association 22
Aberdare Leader 94
Aberdovey 107, 111, 119, 128, 157,
     238, 258
Abergavenny 45, 82, 84, 85, 89, 91,
     93, 154n., 172, 175, 221, 243n.
Abergavenny Chronicle 221
Abergele 163, 199, 203
Abertillery 39n., 175, 228, 249n.,
     293, 294
Aberystwyth 24, 28, 29, 30, 34, 36,
     43, 44n., 48, 69, 79, 94, 102,
     107, 111, 112, 119, 157, 160,
     201, 207, 237, 238, 244, 258n.,
     259, 260
Acland, F. D. 162
Actresses' Franchise League 99,
     114, 177–8, 292n.
Aldersley, Margaret 168

Amalgamated Society of Railway
     Servants 75
Amberley, Viscount 18
Amberley, Viscountess Kate 13, 14,
     15, 16, 18, 20n., 21
Ammanford 124, 235
Andrews, Elizabeth 252, 262–3,
     263n.
Anglesey 89, 193
   parliamentary representation of
      1, 147n., 254, 293–4
Anti-Corn Law League 51
Anti-Suffrage Review 200, 201, 202,
     204, 208, 247
anti-suffragists 113, 119, 134, 143,
     165, 169, 183, 209, 216, 218,
     246
   among Wales's MPs 1, 21, 184–6
   arguments of 41, 116, 186–97,
      248, 274–8
   organized anti-suffragism
      197–209, *passim*
   see also National League for
      Opposing Woman Suffrage
Appeal against Female Suffrage, An
     (1889) 197, 198n.
'Appeal from Women of all Parties
     and all Classes' 26
Arscott, Jessie 77
Artists' Franchise League 116,
     178n.
Ashworth, Lilian 16
Asquith, Herbert 64, 65, 79, 82, 86,
     96n., 103, 129, 139, 141, 143,
     147, 151, 180, 205, 215, 242,
     245, 249

Association for Promoting the
    Education of Girls in Wales 43
Astor, Lady Nancy 253, 255, 265,
    267
Australia 196
Ayrton, Phyllis 227

Bach, Miss 88
Baker, Revd Stephen 191
Bala 32, 62, 114
Baldwin, Stanley 220, 265, 267, 274,
    277, 279, 280, 290
Bargoed 157, 158, 160, 235
Baner ac Amserau Cymru 15, 48, 62,
    278
Bangor 26 n., 36, 43, 45, 85, 103,
    136, 144, 147 n., 150, 155, 156,
    158, 160, 161, 162 n., 163, 166,
    173, 175, 201, 202, 207, 232,
    243, 245 n., 257, 265, 271, 272,
    294
Barker, George 75
Barmouth 111, 141, 201
Barrett, Rachel 49, 70 n., 84 n., 125,
    293 n.
    arrest and imprisonment 70, 91,
        94
    as assistant editor of *The
        Suffragette* 83–4
    attitude to the First World War
        229
    becomes suffrage activist 69–70
    family background and
        education 69
    and Pankhurst Memorial 291
    as women's suffrage organizer 57,
        60, 66, 67, 78
Barry 54, 67, 69, 79, 80, 99 n., 106,
    107, 125, 127, 160, 164, 230
Barry Dock News 214
Bath 57, 150, 217
Beaufort, duke of 15, 37 n.
Beaumaris 105

Becker, Lydia 12, 25, 47, 217, 218 n.
Beddoe, Deidre 6
Begg, Ferdinand Faithfull 24, 49,
    133
Bethesda 105, 106, 148, 157
Billington-Greig, Teresa 101, 108
Birkenhead, Lord 274
Birmingham 121
'Black Friday' 95, 145
Blackwood 90 n.
Blaenafon 79, 82 n., 164, 175, 188
Blaenau Ffestiniog 201
Blaina 228
'Blue Books' 48
Boyd, Janet 72, 81, 95
Boyle, Nina 124
Brailsford, H. N. 150
Brecon 46
Brecon County Times 11, 190
Brecon Reporter 11
Breconshire 46
    parliamentary representation of
        11 n.
Bridgend 82, 158, 160
Bright, Jacob 37 n., 156, 217
Bristol 7, 12, 17, 21, 32, 47, 57, 72,
    164, 175
Bristol and West of England Society
    for Women's Suffrage (BSWS)
    14, 16, 20, 22, 132, 133
Britannia 58, 220
British Women's Temperance
    Association (BWTA) 37
Brittain, Vera 219, 270
Brock, Emma 45
Brockway, Fenner 173
Bruce, Henry Austen (1st Baron
    Aberdare) 192, 193
Brynamman 106, 124
Brynmawr 89 n., 107, 112, 120 n.,
    230, 233 n., 235, 236, 237
Buckley 159
Burry Port 168

Butler, Clara 74
Butler, Isaac 74
Butler, Josephine 19, 177, 186 n.,
  238
Butler, Mary 74, 229 n.
by-elections
  Carmarthen Boroughs (1912)
    66–7
  East Carmarthenshire (1912)
    123–4
  Flint Boroughs (1913) 159 n.,
    169–70
  Merthyr Boroughs (1915) 226
  Mid Glamorgan (1906) 55–6, 64,
    66, 77, 134–5
  Mid Glamorgan (1910) 123,
    144 n.
  Pembrokeshire (1908) 65–6, 121,
    137–8
  Swansea District (1915) 170 n.

Caergwrle 158
Caerleon 31, 71 n.
Caerleon Training College 79, 85
Caernarfon 28, 58, 67, 85, 88, 90 n.,
    91, 96, 99 n., 105, 123, 136, 146,
    148, 153, 156, 159, 181 n., 202
Caernarfon Boroughs 122, 144,
    159 n., 272
Caernarfon Gaol 92–3
Caernarfonshire 5, 28, 57, 88, 90,
    146, 148, 157, 159 n., 183, 201,
    271
Caerphilly 157
Caldicot 104, 107, 125, 127, 136,
    175
Calling All Women 291
Cambrian 40
Cambrian News 24, 29, 30, 40, 43, 48,
    132, 209, 213
Campbell-Bannerman, Sir Henry
    139
Canterbury Prison 91

Cardiff 16–17, 18, 19, 20, 21–2, 26,
    28 n., 34, 36 n., 39 n., 41, 42, 43,
    44, 45 n., 54, 55 n., 56, 57, 59,
    60, 67, 69, 74, 75, 76, 77, 79,
    80, 81, 82, 83, 84, 85, 86, 87–8,
    89, 94, 99, 100, 102, 103 n.,
    104, 106, 107, 111, 112, 113,
    115, 125, 127, 136, 137, 140,
    142, 143, 144, 146, 147, 148,
    158, 161, 162, 164, 166, 167,
    175, 176, 177, 179, 180, 192,
    199, 200, 201, 202, 203, 210,
    230, 231, 232, 233, 238, 239,
    242, 243 n., 248, 251, 252 n.,
    253, 257 n., 258, 262, 265, 269,
    271, 272, 276, 284, 292, 293
Cardiff Boroughs 1, 54, 81, 123,
    139, 149, 186, 199, 200 n., 215
Cardiff and District Women's
    Suffrage Society (CDWSS)
    125 n., 140, 157, 158, 160, 162,
    166–7, 170, 171, 182, 230, 232,
    238, 244, 251, 253, 257
Cardiff and Merthyr Guardian 191
Cardiff Progressive Liberal
    Women's Union 61, 148, 179
Cardiff Times 11, 20, 190, 279
Cardiff Women Citizens'
    Association (WCA) 258, 271,
    293, 294, 295
Cardigan 65
Cardiganshire 201
Carmarthen 5, 44, 66, 67, 90, 99 n.,
    106, 107, 157, 160
Carmarthen Boroughs 26, 66, 147,
    208, 294
Carmarthen Journal 11–12, 179–80
Carmarthen Prison 177
Carmarthenshire 10, 69, 124, 177,
    227
Carmarthenshire (East),
    parliamentary representation
    of 123–4, 157, 168–9

Carnarvon and Denbigh Herald 276
Carpenter, E. A. 44n.
'Cat and Mouse Act' (1913) 72, 94,
    97, 147n., 211
Catholic Women's Suffrage Society
    (CWSS) 174n., 177, 255
Ceiniogwerth 48
census boycott 80, 127–8, 129
Central Committee of the National
    Society for Women's Suffrage
    (CCNSWS) 25, 132
Central and East of England Society
    132
Central National Society for
    Women's Suffrage (CNSWS)
    25, 132
Central and Western Society 131–2
Chamberlain, Joseph 193
Chant, Laura Ormiston 27
Chelsea 71, 121, 253–4
Cheltenham 164
Chepstow 13, 27, 157, 204, 243n.
Chester 140, 159n., 163
Chester, Revd Henry 18
Chew, Ada Nield 173
Church League for Women's
    Suffrage (CLWS) 99, 108, 116,
    162, 174n., 175–6, 175n.
*Church League for Women's Suffrage
    Monthly* 175
Churchill, Winston 150n., 274
Clark, Alix Minnie 109, 113,
    118–19, 120, 129, 176, 238,
    259, 260
Clarry, Reginald 263, 282, 284
Cleeves, Mary McCleod 108–9, 118,
    123, 127, 128
Cleeves, Sylvia 118
Cobbe, Frances Power 23
Coedpoeth 89
Colliery Workers' Magazine 263
Collin, Mary 44, 166, 251, 195
Colorado 196

Colwyn Bay 86, 90, 105, 136, 144,
    146, 156, 158, 183, 233, 243n.,
    257, 284
Common Cause, The 2, 143, 152,
    156n., 158, 183, 233, 243, 289,
    295
Conciliation Bills 80, 125, 145–6,
    147, 148–50, 150n., 151, 154,
    155, 165, 167, 178n., 226n.,
    228
Conciliation Committee 80, 128,
    145, 146, 147, 149, 178n., 179
Conservative and Unionist
    Women's Franchise
    Association (CUWFA) 155, 178
Contagious Diseases Acts ix, 10, 19,
    20n., 41, 185, 192, 238
Consultative Committee of
    Women's Organisations 255
Conway, Revd Moncure 13
Conwy 28, 40, 70, 105, 162, 163
Cook, Arthur 227
Cook, Kay 4–5, 7
Cooper, Selina 134, 154n., 168, 173
Corben, Louisa 108, 175
Cornwallis-West, Mary 202
Cornwallis-West, Colonel William C.
    187n., 202
Corris 201
Corrupt Practices Act (1883) 30
Corwen 62, 81, 141
Cory, John 18
Cory, Richard 18, 19
Courtney, Kathleen 167
Cowbridge 78, 106
Craigen, Jessie 19, 22
Crawshay, Rose Mary 13–14, 16,
    20n., 21, 42, 45, 191
Cricieth 82, 91, 153, 161n., 163,
    207, 243n., 257
Cromer, Lord 193, 202
Cross Keys 39n.
Curzon, Lord 193, 202, 215, 247, 249

Cwmbrân 37 n., 82
Cwmtillery 235
Cymric Suffrage Union 62, 72, 74–5
Cymro, Y 278
Cymru Fydd 36

Daily Express 97, 211 n.
Daily Mail 8, 274–5, 282
Darby, C. E. 18
Darby, W. H. 18
Davies, Bessie 163
Davies, Catherine 44
Davies, David 186, 202 n.
Davies, Dilys 43
Davies, Elizabeth 81
Davies, Helen 175
Davies, Hilda 118
Davies, Revd Ivan 61, 62, 163
Davies, Margaret Llewellyn 39
Davies, Mary 63, 237
Davies, Minnie 163, 169
Davies, Rose 263
Davison, Emily Wilding 63, 66, 75,
    84, 210–11
Defence of the Realm Act (1914)
    238, 242
Denbigh 11 n., 12, 32, 67
Denbigh Boroughs 67, 140, 178 n.,
    216, 217, 250 n.
Denbighshire 27 n., 28, 187 n., 200,
    203
  parliamentary representation of
    21, 35, 57, 185
Denbighshire (East)
  parliamentary representation of
    152, 198 n.
Denbighshire (West)
  parliamentary representation of
    202
Despard, Charlotte 101, 102, 104–5,
    107, 110, 114, 136, 233, 253, 268
Dickenson, W. H. 139, 155
Dilke, Sir Charles 135

Disraeli, Benjamin 279
Dobell, Annie Mary 42, 44, 177 n.
Dolgellau 23, 141, 158
Drummond, 'General' Flora 77–8,
    220, 223, 225, 226, 227, 289
Dublin 12, 253
Dundee 150

East, Colonel 239
East London Federation of
    Suffragettes (ELFS) 64, 72,
    221, 233, 243, 236, 237
Ebbw Vale 157, 175, 228, 257 n.,
    293
Edinburgh 12, 72, 228, 257 n., 293
Edmunds, Ella 74
education of women 43
Edwards, Clement 140, 167 n., 217
Edwards, John Hugh 282
Edwards, Mrs (London) 245
Electoral Fighting Fund (EFF)
    165–73, 179, 182, 183
Ellis, Thomas Edward 28
Elmy, Elizabeth Wolstenholme 28 n.
Elveden, Lady 273
employment of women 43–4, 223–4
Englishwoman's Review 12, 47
equal pay 120–1, 121 n., 162, 238,
    253, 254, 281, 293, 295
Equal Political Rights Campaign
    Committee (EPRCC) 255, 268,
    270, 274, 283, 285, 288, 292
Eskrigge, Edith 157
Evans, Dr Erie 182 n.
Evans, Marie Winton 77, 101
Evans, Neil 4–5, 7
Evans, Samuel Thomas 55–6, 64–5,
    77, 122, 134, 135, 186, 199
Evans, Lady (Mrs Samuel) 199
Evening Express 276

Fabian Women's Group 181 n.
Fawcett, Henry 132

Fawcett, Millicent 25, 104–5, 132,
    134, 136, 137, 142–3, 154, 221,
    232, 244–5, 251, 268
Felix-Jones, Ada 118
Fellowship of Reconciliation 225
Ferndale 157
Ffarmers 157, 160
Fielder, Ellen 45
Finland 196
'flappers' 275, 277, 278–9
Flint 26 n., 159
Flint Boroughs 159 n., 169–70, 253
Flintshire 159, 203
    parliamentary representation of
        24, 29 n., 186, 253
Floyd, Lettice 99–100
Folland, Leah (Lily) 260
Fontaine, Olive 81
Ford, Isabella 173
Forestier-Walker, Leolin 282
Forward Cymric Suffrage Union
    (FCSU) 63–4, 72, 99, 154, 219,
    221, 230, 236, 237, 242–3
Forward Suffrage Union 178
Foxley, Barbara 44, 265
Franchise and Registration Bill
    (1913) 154, 181
Free Church League for Women's
    Suffrage 116, 174 n., 176–7
Fussell, Emily see 'Lloyd, Georgina'
Frythones, Y 48, 101

Garrett, Elizabeth 44
Garw valley 120 n., 154 n.
Gatty, Katherine 81, 91, 92, 93
Gawthorpe, Mary 55–6
general elections
    of 1892 28, 49
    of 1895 49
    of 1900 49
    of 1906 54, 64, 67, 134
    of January 1910 67, 108, 109, 110,
        122–3, 144

of December 1910 57, 67, 108,
    109, 110, 123, 144
of 1918 253, 262, 264, 293
of 1922 254
of 1923 254, 260, 264
of 1924 254, 265
of 1929 254, 264, 286 n., 295
George V, King 61, 79
Gibbins, Frederick W. 66, 123
Gibson, John 6, 24, 28, 29–30, 34,
    40, 41, 50, 132, 209, 213–14
Gill, Helga 140–1
Gillett, Ethel 77
Gillett, Lilian 77
Girls' Anti-Suffrage League 203
Gladstone, Helen 159
Gladstone, Herbert 78
Gladstone, William 15 n., 22–3, 33,
    185, 186, 189, 198
Glasgow 160
Glamorgan 99, 107, 130, 227
Glamorgan
    parliamentary representation of
        11
Glamorgan (East)
    parliamentary representation of
        168 n.
Glamorgan (Mid)
    parliamentary representation of
        55–6, 64–5, 66, 77, 122, 123,
        134, 144 n., 186, 199
Glamorgan (South)
    parliamentary representation of
        132
Glamorgan Free Press 89
Glyndyfrdwy 141
Gorseinon 106, 235
Goward, Henry 18
Gower 106, 127
    parliamentary representation of
        260
Grant, James 75
Griffith, Ellis Jones (later Sir Ellis

Jones Ellis-Griffith) 1, 147 n., 148, 150 n.
Griffith, John (*Y Gohebydd*) 15
Griffiths, James 124, 169 n.
Griffiths, Winifred 264
Griffithstown 204
Guest, Lady Charlotte 200 n.
Guest, Ivor Bertie 198 n.
Guest, Ivor Churchill (1st Baron Ashby St Ledgers, 2nd Baron Wimborne, 1st Viscount Wimborne) 155, 186, 194, 199, 200 n., 202 n.
Gwyther, Mary 103 n.
Gymraes, Y 48

Haig, Cecilia 72, 95
Haig, Charlotte 72, 95
Haig, Evelyn 72
Haig, Florence 71, 92 n., 229 n., 234 n.
Haig, George Augustus 72
Haig, Katherine 72 n.
Haldane, Viscount 120
Halifax 57
Hamilton, Cicely 113
Hannam, June 4
Harcourt, Lewis 79
Harcourt, Sir William 24, 29, 186, 194, 195 n., 199
Hardie, Keir 2, 54, 55, 67, 78, 80, 135, 136, 145, 149, 154 n., 166, 168, 225–6
Harlech 90 n.
Harrogate 81
Hartshorn, Vernon 66, 75, 134
Haslam, Lewis 168 n.
Haverfordwest 20, 21, 185 n.
Hawarden 159
Hay-on-Wye 70 n.
Hayward, S. J. 236
Henderson, Arthur 245 n., 246 n., 249

Hereford Times 12
Higginson, Revd Edward 18, 19
Higginson, Emily 18, 19, 45
Hill, Mary Keating 76–7, 115
Hill, Octavia 188
Hilston, Mary 171
Hindshaw, Winifred 118
Hoare, Sir Samuel 254
Hoggan, Frances 28 n., 41, 44
Holloway Gaol 76, 77, 92, 93
Holme, Beatrice 44
Holyhead 90, 105, 148, 158, 201, 204
Holyhead Chronicle 49
Howard, Rosalind (countess of Carlisle) 37
Howell, Mabel 166, 167, 171
Huddersfield 57
Hughes, Annie Harriet *see* 'Gwyneth Vaughan'
Hughes, Revd Daniel 74
Hughes, Ellen 48 n.
Hughes, Hugh Price 33 n.
Hughes, Katherine Price 33 n.
Hughes, Morrie 81
Hughes, Miss (Bangor) 201
Hughes, Revd Owen 81
Hutton, Emilie 118
Hutton, Muriel 118
Hyde, Lady Charlotte 202
Hyde, Sir Clarendon Hyde 123, 179

Independent Labour Party (ILP) 52, 54, 55, 64, 75, 102, 120 n., 134, 166, 167 n., 173, 174, 177, 181, 182 n., 233 n., 263, 264
Independent Suffragette 241
Independent WSPU (IWSPU) 241–2, 249 n.
Ireland 4, 108, 144, 152, 155, 253

James, C. H. 18, 19, 34
James, Elizabeth 28, 34

James, J. W. 18
James, Sarah 19, 20 n.
Jeffrey, Gabrielle 57
Jenkins, Amelia 77
Jenner, Gertrude 16, 17–18, 19, 21, 22, 45 n.
Jevons, Professor H. Stanley 75
John, Angela V. 5–6
John, Edward Thomas 151, 152, 155
Jones, Sir David Brynmor 132, 144 n.
Jones, Edith Lester 74, 87–8, 292
Jones, Dr Helena 60, 70–1, 125, 219 n., 230, 233, 239 n., 240–1
Jones, Ieuan Gwynedd 2–3
Jones, J. Graham 6
Jones, Kate 44 n.
Jones, Peter Ellis 5
Jones, Revd Towyn 124, 169
Jones-Parry, Thomas Love 217
Joynson-Hicks, Sir William 277, 286
Judd, M. A. 120 n.

Keating, Joseph 76 n.
Keating, Matthew 76 n.
Kenney, Annie 53, 54, 57, 66, 70, 76, 94–5, 220, 227, 229 n.
Kensington Society 10
Kirkland, Jenny 118
Kirkland, Margaret 118
Knight, Dorothy 118
Knight, Gwendoline 118
Knight, Lilian 118

Labour Leader 169, 173
Labour Woman 263
Ladies' Petition 10, 13, 20 n., 73, 286
Lampeter 116, 157, 163, 169
Lansbury, George 166
Lewey, Miss (Brynmawr) 120 n.
Lewis, Frances 119
Lewis, Sir John Herbert 253

Liberal Women's Suffrage Union 178
Liberation Society 51
Liverpool 93, 105, 132 n., 186
Llandeilo 106
Llandrillo 61, 62, 163
Llandrindod Wells 58, 106, 224, 273
Llandudno 90, 105, 136, 137, 144, 146, 148, 156, 158, 160, 161, 257 n., 259, 271, 272
Llandulais 163
Llanelli 5, 20, 44, 66, 89 n., 106, 107, 124, 169, 208, 235, 264
Llanfairfechan 105, 148, 201, 204, 272
Llanfyllin 111, 112, 114, 118, 122
Llangattock, Baron *see* Rolls, John Allan
Llangattock, Lady 31, 73
Llangybi 203
Llanidloes 106, 112
Llangollen 141, 152 n., 156–7, 159, 161, 170 n., 176, 231, 232, 243, 256
Llanrug 89
Llantarnam 74
Llanuwchllyn 141
Llanwern 72, 73, 95, 117, 176, 234 n.
Llanwrst 105, 106
Llanwrtyd Wells 68
Llanymynech 175
Llanystumdwy 1, 5, 63, 97, 153, 159, 201
Llewhellin, Margaret 63
Lleyn 148
Lloyd George, David 1, 6, 57, 78, 79, 82, 83, 85, 91 n., 122, 154, 157, 214, 224, 232 n., 244, 249, 272
  attitude to women's suffrage 70, 143, 145, 146, 147, 184, 217–18
  and Conciliation Bills 147–51
  heckled 5, 63, 78, 79, 88, 95–7, 110, 152, 153, 201, 210

and Representation of the
    People Bill (1918) 245, 246 n.
and WSPU during the First
    World War 223, 227 n.
Lloyd George, Megan 254, 303–4
'Lloyd Georgina' 91, 102–3
Lloyd-Morgan, Ceridwen 5
local government 3, 8, 31, 42, 44–6,
    47, 48, 49, 50 n., 145, 149, 182,
    195, 205, 207, 232 n., 237 n.,
    244, 250
    see also poor law guardians;
    school boards
London National Society for
    Women's Suffrage 13
London Society for Women's
    Suffrage 72 n., 73, 144 n.
Lort-Williams, J. 138
Lucas, Margaret Bright 37

MacDonald, James Ramsay 80, 225
McKenna, Reginald 1, 67, 79, 85,
    90, 122, 171–2, 186, 219, 249
McKenzie, Elsie 57, 69, 79 n.
Mackenzie, H. Millicent 44, 253
Mackworth, Humphrey 71 n.
Mackworth, Margaret (2nd
    Viscountess Rhondda) 59,
    71 n., 229 n., 250 n., 270, 283,
    287, 291, 292, 293 n., 294
    autobiography 71, 291–2
    arrest and imprisonment 87,
    91–2, 164, 211–12
    becomes a suffragist 68–9, 71
    and campaign for equal franchise
    255–6, 266–7, 268, 283
    and First World War 223, 228–9,
    232
    on late nineteenth-century
    campaign 49
    as WSPU activist 53, 71, 79, 94–5,
    98
    see also Equal Political Rights

Campaign Committee; Six
    Point Group
McLaren, Sir Charles 133
McLaren, Eva 27, 33, 34
McLaren, Laura (Baroness
    Aberconway) 27 n., 177 n.
McLaren, Priscilla Bright 156 n.
McLaren, Walter 27 n.
Maclaverty, Mary 25, 28, 40, 133–4,
    142
Maesteg 55, 56, 66, 67, 77, 99 n.,
    107, 113
male support 74–5, 85, 94, 118, 136,
    144, 161
Manchester 8, 12, 20, 21, 28 n., 52,
    53, 76, 105
Manchester Guardian 269
Manchester National Society for
    Women's Suffrage 12, 15, 25,
    37 n., 132
Manning, J. W. 18, 42
Manning, Mary 110
Mansell, Mildred 81
Mar, countess of 21
Marion, Kitty 93 n.
Markham, Violet 188, 205
Markiewicz, Constance 253
Marsh, Margaret Elizabeth 45
Martyn, Edith How 101
Masson, Ursula 5, 180
Masterman, Charles 170 n.
Matters, Muriel 108
Menai Bridge 105, 106
Men's Committee for Opposing
    Female Suffrage 200
Men's League for Women's
    Suffrage 65, 147 n., 161
Men's Political Union for Women's
    Enfranchisement 75
Merioneth 28, 38, 62, 119, 139,
    154 n., 157, 201
Merthyr Tydfil 2, 11 n., 12, 13–14,
    18, 19, 22, 23 n., 26 n., 27, 36 n.,

45, 54, 67, 77, 95 n., 141, 149, 157, 160, 163, 166, 167 n., 173, 192, 223, 225–6, 226 n., 233, 257

Merthyr Express 275, 277, 285

Milford Haven 26

Mill, John Stuart 11, 14, 39, 50, 73, 295

Miller, Florence Fenwick 47 n.

Mitchell, Elizabeth Harcourt 16, 31, 41, 73, 74

Mold 159, 169

Mond, Sir Alfred (1st Baron Melchett) 2, 75 n., 145, 146, 152 n., 155, 161, 247, 248

Monmouth 13, 20, 21, 25, 26 n., 28, 31, 40, 73, 133–4, 134 n., 136, 142, 144, 157, 175, 190, 198

Monmouth Boroughs 31 n., 168 n., 282

Monmouthshire 12, 14, 15, 16, 26, 31, 32, 44, 82 n., 144, 164, 175, 200, 203, 204, 227, 228, 230, 243, 251, 253, 265, 268, 273, 284

Monmouthshire (North)
parliamentary representation of 1, 67, 79, 122, 171–2, 183, 186

Monmouthshire (South)
parliamentary representation of 177 n.

Monmouthshire (West)
parliamentary representation of 24, 186

Monmouthshire Beacon 137, 275, 277

Montgomery 68, 122

Montgomery Boroughs
parliamentary representation of 2, 122, 123, 137, 155, 186
WFL branch 107, 108, 110, 111, 112–13, 118–19, 122, 238, 258, 259, 298 n.

Montgomeryshire 109, 114, 175, 176, 198, 201, 237, 238, 244, 259

parliamentary representation of 186, 202

Morgan, Emily 35, 198, 199 n.

Morgan, George Osborne 21, 35, 185, 186 n., 187, 194, 217 n.

Morgan, Gwenllian Elizabeth 46

Morgan, Magdalene 141, 163

Morning Post 86–7, 208

Moullin, Charles Mansell 75

Moullin, Edith Mansell 60–2, 63, 64, 81, 219, 233, 236, 241, 242

Munro, Anna 108

Nantyglo 235, 236

Narbeth 26 n.

National Council for Women 256

National Eisteddfod
in Abergavenny (1913) 84
in London (1909) 79, 96 n., 136, 141, 213
in Wrexham (1912) 1, 63, 79, 94 n., 96, 153, 201, 210

National Federation of Women Teachers (NFWT) 117, 119–20, 120 n., 121, 253, 256

National League for Opposing Woman Suffrage (NLOWS) 2, 9, 184
branches 200–2, 204, 206, 246 n.
and First World War 221, 230
formation 184, 200
organizational problems 201, 204, 205–6
propaganda 201, 206, 208–9
tactics 204–5, 207–8, 246–7

National Society for Women's Suffrage (NSWS) 12, 20, 25, 31, 51, 132

National Union of Conservative and Constitutional Associations 31

National Union of Conservative and Unionist Associations 198

National Union of Societies for
Equal Citizenship (NUSEC)
255, 256, 257–8, 261, 266, 267,
270, 271, 272, 274, 283, 284,
288, 289, 294
National Union of Teachers (NUT)
119, 120, 121, 206
National Union of Women
Teachers (NUWT) 110, 120 n.,
256, 260–1, 261 n., 269, 270,
271, 281, 283, 289, 295
National Union of Women's
Suffrage Societies (NUWSS) 8,
9, 26, 27 n., 35 n., 99, 104, 105,
116, 121, 126, 128, 203, 205,
251, 255, 256, 257, 266, 272,
288, 289, 290, 131–83, *passim*
branch activity 140, 146–7,
149–50, 151, 153, 157–9, 161,
163
caravan tours 140–2, 153, 159
during First World War 221,
230–2, 243–4, 245, 246, 249
electoral activity 134–5, 137–8,
144–5, 165–73
formation 7, 50–1, 131–2
Friends of Women's Suffrage
173, 174, 182
'Great Pilgrimage' 163–5
growth 136–7, 140, 143–4, 156–7,
160–1, 182–3
London demonstrations 125,
135–6, 137, 147–8
male support 161
public hostility towards activists
104–5, 140–2, 153, 163–4,
212–13
relations with WSPU 141–3,
153–4, 162, 164, 211–12
summer school 162
working-class support 173–4,
181–2, 183
see also Election Fighting Fund

Neal, Clara 44, 117, 120, 121,
260–1, 269, 281
Neath 20, 21, 106, 190, 224, 243 n.,
244, 282, 293
Newport 20, 26, 32, 35, 36 n., 38,
39 n., 42, 44, 47, 52, 57, 58, 59,
60, 67, 71, 73, 74, 75, 80, 81, 82,
83, 85, 87, 95, 98, 99 n., 106,
147, 148, 153, 160, 164, 173,
175, 176, 182 n., 200, 201, 202,
203, 204, 205, 206, 207, 208,
211, 224, 230, 243 n., 251, 256,
257 n., 258, 263, 269 n., 271,
282, 284, 288, 291, 293, 294
Newport Women Citizens'
Association (WCA) 256–7,
269 n., 271, 293
Newtown 26 n., 34, 35, 109, 111,
112, 114, 120, 122, 129, 201,
238, 259, 260
Nefyn 148
Nevinson, Margaret Wynne 116–17,
178 n.
New Zealand 196
Newcastle 57
Neyland 138
Nineteenth Century 190, 197
No Conscription Fellowship 225
'North, Phyllis' (Olive Wharry) 91,
92
North Wales Chronicle 11, 49, 96, 147,
160, 213, 275, 286
North Wales Liberal Federation 36
North Wales Observer 49, 275, 277
Northop 159
Norway 196
Nottingham 70, 139 n., 142

Ogmore Vale 62, 120 n.
Open Door Council 255
Ormsby-Gore, William (4th Baron
Harlech) 67, 178 n., 216
Owen, Goronwy 282

Pall Mall Gazette 186 n.
Pallister, Minnie 233 n., 254
Pankhurst, Adela 56, 69, 94
Pankhurst, Christabel 53, 70, 76,
      101, 146 n., 151, 220, 222, 224,
      227, 228, 248, 252 n., 253
Pankhurst, Emmeline 1, 8, 28 n., 52,
      58, 220 n., 222, 266, 267, 287,
      290, 292
Pankhurst, Dr Richard 28 n., 52
Pankhurst, Sylvia 64, 220, 225, 233,
      234, 235, 237, 252 n., 290
Parry, Thomas Henry 170
Peacemakers' Pilgrimage 272–3
Pembroke 12, 20, 82
Pembroke County Guardian 138
Pembroke Dock 20, 26 n., 39 n.,
      138
Pembrokeshire 26, 27 n., 138, 185
   parliamentary representation of
      1, 2, 21, 27 n., 65, 66, 121,
      137–8, 145, 177, 185
Penarth 57, 69, 85, 106, 148, 149,
      157, 158, 160, 164, 230
Penmaenmawr 105, 107, 148, 153,
      163, 243 n.
Penygroes 157
People's Suffrage Federation 182
Pethick-Lawrence, Emmeline 71,
      84 n., 225, 253
Pethick-Lawrence, Frederick 71,
      84 n.
Philipps, J. Wynford (1st Viscount
      St David's) 26, 27 n., 137
Phillips, Jenny 120 n.
Philipps, Leonora (1st Viscountess
      St David's) 26, 27 n., 28 n., 33,
      34, 35–6, 132
Phipps, Emily 44, 101, 119
   becomes a suffragist 110
   and census evasion 127
   and equal franchise campaign
      267, 269, 280–1, 283

friendship with Clara Neal 117,
      260–1
   as parliamentary candidate 121,
      253–4
   and teaching unions 117, 120,
      121, 260–1
Picton-Turbervill, Edith 254
Pilliner, Edith 74
Pochin, Agnes 28 n.
Pontardawe 235
Pontycymmer 62, 117, 120
Pontypool 12, 18, 20, 42, 44, 67, 73,
      74, 80, 82, 83, 99, 157, 160,
      161, 164, 172, 177 n., 204, 219,
      222, 224, 229–30, 243 n.
Pontypridd 104–5, 136, 144, 148,
      155, 157, 161, 164, 214, 243 n.
poor law guardians 45, 195, 260
Port Talbot 243 n.
Porth 75, 211
Porthcawl 82
Porthmadog 82, 90, 218 n.
Potter (Webb), Beatrice 188, 198 n.
Prestatyn 163
Price, Frances 81
Price, Dr William 18
Primrose League 25, 30–1, 31 n., 41,
      46, 73, 74, 148
Prisoners' (Temporary Discharge
      for Ill-Health) Act *see* 'Cat and
      Mouse Act'
Progressive Liberal Women's
      Union 162
Protheroe, Margaret 203
Punch 17, 185 n., 225
Pwllheli 106, 148

Queensferry 224

Radnorshire 45, 72, 81, 95
Rathbone, Eleanor 132, 136, 166,
      170 n., 171, 267, 288
Rathbone, William 132 n.

Reed, Sir Edward 199
Rees, G. Caradoc 67
Rees, Sir J. D. 2, 122, 123, 139, 155, 186, 187, 189, 191, 194, 196, 208, 214
Rees, Sarah Jane (*Cranogwen*) 48 n.
Reform Act, Second (1867) 11–12, 39, 50, 279, 295
Reform Act, Third (1884) 22–4, 24 n., 25
Representation of the People Act (1918) 245–6, 251–2, 280–1
Representation of the People (Equal Franchise) Act (1928) 285–6, 287, 288, 295
Revolution 184
Rhondda 58, 75, 89, 104, 173, 174, 177, 181 n., 211, 227, 235, 236, 241, 263
Rhondda, 1st Viscount *see* Thomas, David Alfred
Rhondda, 1st Viscountess Sybil *see* Thomas, Sybil Margaret
Rhondda, 2nd Viscountess Margaret *see* Mackworth, Margaret
Rhondda Socialist 174
Rhosllannerchrugog 35
Rhydymain 141
Rhyl 26 n., 136, 144, 146, 156, 159, 163–4, 187 n., 201, 202, 243 n., 259
Rice, Charlotte 81
Risca 39 n.
Roberts, Hamlet 170 n.
Roberts, T. Francis 48
Robinson, Annot 181 n.
Roch, Florens 177 n.
Roch, Walter F. 2, 65, 121, 138, 145, 148, 152 n., 161 n., 177 n.
Rollit, Sir Albert 24, 26, 34, 186, 198, 217
Rolls, Major Alexander 21

Rolls, John Allan (1st Baron Llangattock) 31, 73
Ross, Jennie 118
Rowlette, Isabella 134
Ruabon 140
Runciman, Walter 79
Ruthin 67, 202

St Asaph 144, 155
St Joan's Social and Political Alliance 255, 268, 270
St Ledgers, Baron Ashby *see* Guest, Ivor Churchill
Salmon, Dorothy 118, 178 n.
Salmon, Mary 117, 118, 179
Samuels, H. B. 208
Saturday Review 184
school boards 45, 195
Scotland 4, 21, 71, 79, 102, 108, 109, 155
Scott, Mrs Courteney 118
Scourfield, John Henry 1, 21, 185 n., 187, 188, 189, 197
Scratcherd, Alice 29
Selborne, earl of 155
Sennybridge 37 n.
Seren, Y 278
Seren Cymru 62
Service Voting Bill (1915) 242
Seyler, Clarence A. 118
Seyler, Ellen 118
Shafts 48
Shaw, George Bernard 115
Six Point Group (SPG) 255, 256, 261 n., 266, 267–8, 270, 298
Skewen 106
Smith, Catherine 169
Smith, Samuel 24, 29, 186, 187, 189 n., 191, 192, 193, 194, 195, 196, 197, 198, 216
Smollett, P. B. 217 n.
Snowden, Ethel 134, 173
Snowden, Philip 80, 166

Snowdonia 58
Society for Promoting the
    Employment of Women 13
Solomon, Gwladys Solomon 201–2,
    206
Somerset, Lord Henry 15
Somerset, Lady Isabella 37
South Wales Area Group of Women
    Citizens' Associations 293
South Wales Argus 213
South Wales Daily News 23–4, 126, 136
South Wales Daily Post 113, 114 n.,
    279, 287
South Wales Echo 268
South Wales Liberal Federation 36
South Wales Miners' Federation 64,
    75, 134, 226
South Wales and Monmouthshire
    Federation (SWF) (of
    NUWSS) 44, 156, 157, 160, 167,
    168, 170, 171, 231–2, 243, 251
South Wales News 278, 283, 285
South Wales Worker 76
Spencer, Mildred 161
Sproson, Emma 118
Standing Joint Committee of
    Industrial Women's
    Organisations (SJC) 262, 263
Stanger, Henry York 139
Stanton, Charles Butt 226
Star of Gwent 189
Stead, W. T. 196 n.
Steel, Flora Annie 116, 119, 128,
    178 n.
Stevenson, Frances 226, 245 n.
Stewart, Beatrice 161, 176
Strachey, Ray 290
Stuart, Lord Ninian 179 n.
*Suffrage Annual and Women's Who's
    Who* 9
Suffragette, The ix, 2, 58, 59, 67, 70,
    75, 86, 91, 94, 225, 228
Suffragette Fellowship 290–1, 292

Suffragette News Sheet 240, 241
Suffragettes of the WSPU (SWSPU)
    240–1, 241, 245
Summers, J. W. 169
Swansea 2, 5, 11, 18, 19, 20, 21,
    26 n., 31, 36 n., 39 n., 40, 43, 44,
    45, 55 n., 78, 82, 89, 95, 101 n.,
    106, 107, 108–10, 111, 112,
    113, 114, 115, 116, 117, 118,
    120, 123, 125, 127, 128, 129,
    132, 147, 161, 167, 170 n., 175,
    176, 177, 178 n., 179–80, 180 n.,
    207, 222, 224, 230, 237, 238,
    251, 252, 253, 257 n., 258, 260,
    263, 264, 269, 271, 281, 289,
    293, 294 n., 298
Swansea Training College 117, 281
Swanwick, Helena 152, 233
Symons, Margaret 78, 81

Talybont 162
Talysarn 157
Talsarnau 38
Taylor, Ermine 199, 200, 203
Taylor, Helen 14 n., 15 n.
teachers 43–4, 74, 116, 119, 120 n.,
    148, 158, 178, 206, 223, 258,
    260, 261, 271, 281
    see also National Federation of
    Women Teachers; National
    Union of Teachers; National
    Union of Women Teachers
temperance 17, 27, 33, 36–8, 39, 66,
    148, 159, 191 n., 194
Tenby 18, 20, 39, 111, 138
Tennant, Winifred Coombe 244,
    248, 254, 293
Thomas, David Alfred (1st Viscount
    Rhondda) 59, 71, 75 n., 148,
    161, 232 n.
Thomas, Edward ('Cochfarf') 161 n.
Thomas, Fannie Margaret 62, 99,
    117, 120, 121

Thomas, Margaret Haig (2nd Viscountess Rhondda) *see* Mackworth, Margaret
Thomas, Sybil Margaret (1st Viscountess Rhondda) 34, 59, 71–2, 72 n., 73, 81, 98–9, 117, 176, 212, 234 n., 239 n., 278
Thomas, Revd Dr Thomas 18
Thoday, Gwladys 272
Tilly, Revd Alfred 18, 19
Time and Tide 256, 270, 287–8, 292–3, 295
Times, The 11, 23, 142, 189, 198, 199, 208, 284
Ton-du 56, 67, 99 n.
Ton Pentre 39 n.
Tonypandy 58, 235
trade unions 116, 148, 159, 172, 173, 182, 223
Tredegar 175, 228
Tredegar, Lady 153–4
Trefor 140
Trehafod 227
Trelleck 14
Treorchy 75, 157, 177
Turner, Lady 202
Tylorstown 89
Tywyn 141

Undeb Dirwestol Merched Gogledd Cymru (North Wales Women's Temperance Union) 37
Undeb Dirwestol Merched y De (South Wales Women's Temperance Union) 37
Union of Democratic Control 225
Union of Practical Suffragists 32, 38, 178
United Suffragists 221, 236, 239
University College of South Wales and Monmouthshire, Cardiff 44 n., 253

University College of Wales, Aberystwyth 44 n., 48, 69
University of Wales 43
    parliamentary representation of 253, 286 n.
Upholstresses' Union 22
Usk 190, 191, 212
Usk Prison 91, 93, 211
Utah 196

'Vaughan, Gwyneth' (Annie Harriet Hughes) 28, 38
Vaynor 14, 45
Verney, Margaret 43
Victoria, Queen 188
Vivian, Mabel 44
Vote, The 2, 107, 112, 115, 127, 237, 238, 241, 260, 295
Votes for Women 2, 9, 58, 61, 67, 239 n.
Votes for Women Fellowship 71

Wales and Monmouthshire National Conservative and Unionist Council 265, 284
Waite, Revd Joseph 18, 19
Ward, Mary (Mrs Humphry) 188, 197, 198, 247
Waring, L. F. 157, 180
Wells, H. G. 115
Welsh disestablishment 33, 66, 90, 96, 146, 153, 169, 171, 185, 209
Welsh home rule 33, 36, 152, 155
Welsh language 61, 88, 185
    anti-suffrage literature 195, 202 n., 208
    anti-suffrage speakers 201
    periodicals 48
    suffrage literature 20, 59, 67, 84, 141, 158, 160, 163, 174
    suffrage speakers 106, 163
Welsh National Conference of Liberal Women 147
Welsh National Federation 36

Welsh Women's Liberal Union 35
Welsh Women's National Liberal
    Federation 272
Welsh Outlook 229
Welsh Review 26
Welsh Union of Women's Liberal
    Associations (WUWLA) 33, 34,
    36, 37 n., 38, 42, 44 n., 45 n.,
    132 n.
Welshpool 111, 118, 122, 201, 204
Wentworth, Vera 79 n.
West Lancashire, West Cheshire
    and North Wales Federation
    (NWF) (of the NUWSS) 151,
    156, 159, 160, 169, 170 n., 173,
    243
Western Mail 8, 16, 23, 49, 60, 96,
    126, 135–6, 141, 210, 213, 248,
    275, 276, 277, 278, 284, 285,
    287, 293
Wharry, Olive *see* 'North, Phyllis'
Wheeler, Olive 254
Whitchurch 36 n.
White, Charlotte Price 158, 159,
    161, 166, 265, 272
Wilkinson, Jeanette 22
Williams, Annie 57, 58, 75, 100 n.,
    219
Williams, Elizabeth 263, 264 n.
Williams, Dr J. H. 124, 168, 169
Williams, Revd Jamieson 177
Williams, Llewellyn 66, 148
Williams, Margaret 193, 194–5
Williams, Ormond 139
Williams, Tom 75
Wilton, Lilian 74
Wimborne, Lady 192, 197, 198
Winstone, James 226
Woman Teacher 120 n., 260, 261,
    269
Woman's Dreadnought 234, 237
Woman's Leader 2, 289, 295
Woman's Own 295

Woman's Signal 48
Women Citizens' Associations
    (WCA) 257, 269 n., 271, 293,
    294
Women Teachers' Franchise Union
    116, 119 n.
Women Writers' Suffrage League
    116, 177, 178 n.
Women's Bulletin 112 n.
Women's Co-operative Guild
    (WCG) 38–9, 39 n., 174, 182,
    262, 264
Women's Coronation Procession
    61–2, 125, 147–8
Women's Emancipation Union
    28 n., 50
Women's Franchise 197, 110 n.
Women's Franchise League 27–8,
    28 n., 30, 34, 50, 133
Women's Freedom League (WFL)
    8–9, 72, 77, 80 n., 99, 101–30,
    131, 136, 137, 141, 144, 154,
    156, 158, 160, 169 n., 175, 176,
    177, 180 n., 205, 212, 289, 290,
    294, *passim*
  branch activity 102, 107–12,
    115–19
  census evasion 127–8, 129
  during First World War 221, 230,
    233, 236 n., 237–9, 244
  election activity 121–2, 123–4
  and equal franchise campaign
    253, 255, 256, 258–61, 263,
    268, 270, 271, 284
  formation 56, 101–2
  and London demonstrations
    125–6
  militant identity 102–3, 126–30
  propaganda 103, 105–6, 112–14
  public hostility towards 104–5,
    106–7, 122–3
  tax resistance 102, 127, 128, 129

and teaching profession 119–21, 260–1

Women's Gazette 8 n.

Women's Herald 48

Women's Industrial League 255

Women's International League for Peace and Freedom (WIL) 225, 232–3

Women's Labour League (WLL) 117, 181–2, 262, 264

Women's Liberal Associations (WLA) 25, 26, 28 n., 32–6, 47, 146, 179–81, 192, 272, 292
see also Welsh Union of Women's Liberal Associations

Women's Liberal Federation (WLF) 27, 32–3, 33 n., 34, 35, 36, 46, 132 n., 143, 147, 178, 180, 181

Women's Liberal Unionist Association 47 n.

Women's National Anti-Suffrage League (WNASL) 196, 199–200, 204 n., 207, 208

Women's National Liberal Federation 32

Women's Party 220, 224, 227, 228, 248, 252 n.

Women's Peace Council 272

Women's Peace Crusade 225, 233

Women's Penny Paper 48

Women's Social and Political Union (WSPU) 3, 4, 9, 51, 52–100, 101, 102, 104, 109, 117, 121, 125, 126, 128, 129, 131, 135, 136, 137, 141, 142, 143, 144, 145, 146 n., 147, 151, 152, 153, 154, 156, 158, 159, 162, 165, 169 n., 174, 177, 182, 199, 200 n., 203, 205, 210, 211, 212, 240, 266, *passim*
arrests and imprisonments 53, 70, 71, 72 n., 76–7, 78 n., 81–2, 87, 91–2
attacks on property 80, 81–9
branches 56, 67–8, 99
census protest 80
contribution to campaign 99–100, 287–90
dominates historiography 287–92
early impact in Wales 54–6
electoral activity 54, 55–6, 64–7
and First World War 219–30, 233–4
foundation 8, 52–3
fundraising 59
heckling 54, 78–80
hunger striking 71, 72, 80, 92–4, 97, 210, 211–12
London demonstrations 59–61
male support 74–5
negative effects of militancy 209–15
propaganda 57–9, 62, 68–9, 98–9
public hostility towards activists 94–7
Welsh activists 57, 62–4, 68–74
working-class support 75–6

women's suffrage bills 13, 21, 24, 49, 133, 135, 139–40, 145–6, 147, 148–9, 150–2, 154–5, 181, 186, 197, 198, 217, 245–7, 261–2, 264, 285–6

Women's Suffrage Journal 2, 12, 47

Women's Tax Resistance League 102

Women's Total Abstinence Union 37

Women's Unionist Organisation 265, 273, 284

Woodall, William 22, 23, 24 n., 31 n.

Workers' Dreadnought 234

Workers' Socialist Federation 234

Workers' Suffrage Federation (WSF) 234–6

Working Women's Suffrage Union 182 n.

Wrexham 1, 63, 67, 79, 89, 94 n., 96, 140, 148, 153, 159, 201, 210, 286 n.

Wright, Sir Almoth 188–9

Wright, Florence 161

Wyoming 196

'Young Hotbloods' 203

Young Suffragists 203, 285

Young Wales 26, 48–9

Ystalyfera 106

Ystrad Rhondda 157, 160, 177 n.

Ystradgynlais 264 n.